# Social Learning Theory and the Explanation of Crime

Advances in Criminological Theory
Volume Eleven

A Guide for the New Century

# Social Learning Theory and the Explanation of Crime

## Ronald L. Akers
## Gary F. Jensen

editors

Transaction Publishers
New Brunswick (U.S.A.) and London (U.K.)

First paperback printing 2007

Copyright © 2003 by Transaction Publishers, New Brunswick, New Jersey. Chapter 13 Figures 13.1 and 13.2 are reprinted from *Motivation and Delinquency* (Volume 44 of the Nebraska Symposium on Motivation) by permission of the University of Nebraska Press. © 1997 by the University of Nebraska Press.

Library of Congress Catalog Number: 2002021139
ISBN: 1-4128-0649-6
ISSN: 0894-2366
Printed in the United States of America

Library of Congress Cataloging-in-Publication Data

Social learning theory and the explanation of crime: a guide for the new century / editors, Ronald L. Akers and Gary F. Jensen.
     p. cm.—(Advances in criminological theory; v. 11)
  Includes bibliographical references and index.
  ISBN 1-4128-0649-6 (alk. paper)
    1. Criminology. 2. Social learning. I. Akers, Ronald L. II. Jensen, Gary F. III. Series.

HV6018 .S67 2002
364—dc21

# Contents

# Editor's Introduction

# Social Learning Theory and the Explanation of Crime: A Guide for the New Century

*Ronald L. Akers and Gary F. Jensen*

Over thirty-five years ago, Robert L. Burgess and Ronald L. Akers (1966), the senior editor of this volume, published "A differential association-reinforcement theory of criminal behavior" that integrated the differential association theory of the late sociologist, Edwin H. Sutherland, (1947) with reinforcement (operant conditioning) theory from behavioral psychology (Skinner 1959 ). Nearly thirty years have passed since the theory was elaborated and renamed a "social learning" theory in Akers' *Deviant Behavior: A Social Learning Approach* (1973). It has been twenty years since the first major empirical test of full models of the theory was published (Akers et al. 1979). Over that span of time the theory has become standard fare in most textbooks and is among the most discussed and tested of contemporary theories of crime and deviance. Akers and others have continued to develop, elaborate, and test social learning theory on a variety of types of criminal, delinquent, and deviant behavior. The most recent theoretical development has been the attempt to link the processual variables in the theory to macro-level and meso-level social structural variables (see Akers 1998; 2000) in a "Social Structure Social Learning" (SSSL) explanation of crime and delinquency.

As guest editors of Volume 11 of Advances in Criminological Theory, we solicited papers that would continue both the theoretical and empirical elaboration of social learning theory in directions that would serve as a "guide" for the twenty-first century. The chapters were compiled both through direct invitation to authors and through submission in response to our general call for papers. By whatever avenue they reached this point, the chapters were produced independently and autonomously by the authors. They were not

1

restricted to any one central theme or focus in social learning theory. Some of the authors inquired about different topics and the direction to be taken with their respective chapters, but most did not. None of the chapters was specifically commissioned to cover a given topic. As editors, we did not ask for a common format, set of issues, or topics. Rather, our aim was to allow the authors leeway to expose the theory to new empirical data and tests, explore different conceptual, theoretical, or applied issues, to relate it to other theoretical perspectives, or to examine any other aspects of social learning theory of crime and deviance that the authors wanted. The chapters afford many insights into, and raise many questions about, the social learning explanation of crime that we could not have devised or foreseen. This approach has produced variety, and each chapter can be read with profit separately and on its own. Nevertheless, certain themes and continuities have emerged as we have assembled the chapters for the volume.

We did only light editing of the manuscripts and did not attempt to reconcile or ask for rewriting to address disagreement we had with the authors, or disagreements and differences we may have found among the chapters. We do not respond to the critical comments on the theory, or address the questions that are contained in many of the chapters. Thus, our inclusion of a chapter in this volume does not mean that we necessarily concur with all aspects of its analyses or conclusions. The inclusion of a chapter does mean that we believe the contributor adds significantly to our knowledge about the value, problems, and prospects for social learning theory in criminology. The different chapters reflect the historical development of the theory, but move us beyond that. We believe they provide a guide for directions that social learning theory and research in criminology may take as we move into the new century.

In the resurgence of criminological interest in macro-level theory and ecological analysis, including social disorganization and anomie theories of crime and delinquency, it has been recognized that such explanations will ultimately be linked to micro-level processes. However, the major proponents of such approaches have either ignored social learning theory or mistakenly classified it under the label of "cultural deviance" theory (see Akers 1996). A long-term theme in the development of social learning theory has been the relevance of learning theory to macro-level explanations (see Akers 1973, 1998). In chapter 1, we attempt to take additional steps towards a macro-level version of social learning theory by extending it to account for cross-national variations in homicide rates. We argue that there are continuities across levels of explanations and the variables that best fit national variations in homicide are those derived from social learning theory. Indeed, although a recent revival of ecological theory and research has been couched in terms of "social disorganization" theory, the actual variables encompassed in reformulated theories are those that can be inferred from a social learning perspective.

In addition to efforts to apply the theory to inter-national variations, the theory can be "taken global" through cross-cultural applications. Chapters 2 and 3 report direct tests of the theory on individual differences in delinquent behavior within non-Western societies. The clear conclusion from both is that social learning theory (as well other theories) developed by American social scientists is not culture-bound. Rather, the theory identifies common social processes in the etiology of crime and deviance that are operative within any socio-cultural context.

Hwang and Akers test full models of the theory, as well as models of social bonding and self-control theories, on self-reported variations in alcohol and tobacco use among high school students in South Korea. The findings are remarkably similar to those from studies of American adolescent substance use. There is some support for all three theories, but social learning clearly receives the strongest empirical support, explaining very high proportions of the variance and overshadowing the effects of variables derived from the other two theories. The same conclusions are reached by Wang and Jensen in their study of self-reported delinquency (ranging from substance use to property offenses, to fighting) among junior high school students in Taiwan. Again, their findings (as well as those from other research in Asia) are quite similar to findings in North American research. Social learning mechanisms are applicable to the explanation of crime and delinquency across societies and cultures.

Another new direction for social learning theory on both macro and micro levels is the explanation of the "direction" of violence. Batton and Ogle in chapter 4 present a theory of homicide/suicide based on learned differences in dimensions and styles of attribution (e.g., internal or external, stable or unstable, optimistic or pessimistic). The theory can be applied to aggregate level differences in rates of lethal violence, particularly the suicide-homicide ratio (SHR) across groups. They use social learning theory (particularly differential reinforcement of attribution of blame/responsibility and differential exposure to normative orientations toward violence and aggression) to illuminate the process by which individuals develop different attribution styles. These learned styles can help explain gender, racial, and regional differences in lethal violence (calculated from national data on suicide, arrests for homicide, and homicide victimization). Although not intended as a direct test of their integrated theory of lethal violence, the findings are generally consistent with theoretical expectations. Differences among groups in SHR reflect cultural and structural factors that structure social learning.

Social learning mediation of gender variations in violence (in this case violence in dating or courtship relationships) is also explored in the next chapter by Sellers, Cochran, and Winfree. In chapter 5, these authors provide an empirical test of a social learning theory of courtship violence and test the proposition that the difference in commission of intimate violence by men and women is mediated by the social learning process. The models include measures of the principal social learning concepts of imitation, definitions, differential reinforcement, and differential peer association. They find support for the model overall, with substantial amounts of explained variance in courtship violence, although not all of the measures have significant net effects. Further, the social learning variables substantially (but not completely) mediate the gender differences in violence, and the model has the same level of explained variance in separate male and female models (although net effects of the different social learning variables are not the same within the separate models). For both male and females in their sample, differential peer association had strong effects even on intimate violence that is typically done in private outside of a group context.

While Batton and Ogle relate social learning to attribution processes, De Coster relates it to processes of role-taking and proposes a theoretical perspective relevant to both delinquent behavior and depression. And, similar to the preceding chapters, De Coster's analysis in chapter 6 is centered on gender differences. She proposes that role-taking and social learning processes explain why males and females respond differently to the same set of structural and social-psychological factors in deviance with males disproportionately responding with law violating behavior and with females more likely to develop depression. De Coster builds on her previous work with Karen Heimer on gender differences, delinquency, and depression and the work of Heimer and Ross Matsueda on differential social control and symbolic interactionist theory (Heimer and Matsueda 1994; Matsueda and Heimer 1997.). She specifies role-taking (reflected appraisals of self) intertwined with the social learning mechanisms as the common process in both law violation and depression. Differential association in the family, school, peer group, and the community leading to differential exposure to behavioral models of law breaking and emotional depression, definitions favorable to law violation and emotional displays, and actual/anticipated social reactions for delinquency or depression differ by gender and promote the development of reflected appraisals of self as law violators by males or as emotionally depressed by females.

In the next chapter, Jensen also accounts for gender differences in deviance (in this case delinquency) with social learning concepts (differential peer association and definitions/beliefs about law and authority) along with concepts of masculine and feminine self-images. These variables mediate all of the gender effects on measures of the most serious self-reported offenses as well as measures of common forms of delinquency and adolescent deviance. Other combinations of variables such as maternal supervision and perceived impunity do not mediate the effects, and Jensen argues that the findings on gender differences in delinquency are more consistent with social learning than with alternative theories.

Although not specifically the stated intent of the authors in these foregoing chapters, their findings on social learning processes in gender, race, and
other group differences in crime and deviance support the proposition in the
SSSL model that social learning variables mediate the effects of social structure (in the SSSL model gender and other sociodemographic factors indicate
"differential location in the social structure"). The two chapters following,
however, specifically assess the SSSL model against empirical data. In chapter 8, Lanza-Kaduce and Capece incorporate dimensions of social structure in
the SSSL model to account for gender and racial variations, cross-university
variations, and group variations on campus in levels of binge drinking at
eight American universities. While recognizing that there are limitations in
the data for measuring social structure and that the measures of social learning variables in the data set are fairly weak, they argue that the data are
sufficient to provide a reasonable, if tentative, test of the model on this form
of deviant drinking. The findings on the patterns of relationships between
binge drinking and social structural and social learning variables are consistent with theoretical predictions and provide general, but mixed, support for
the SSSL model.

In chapter 9, Bellair, Roscigno, and Velez provide multilevel analyses of
the relationship of adolescent violence to local occupational structure. Their
findings that the effects of community context (occupational structure, economic and racial inequality, and urbanization) on levels of adolescent fighting are largely mediated by social learning processes are supportive of the
SSSL model for both males and females. The patterns of imitation and presence of role models in learning attitudes favorable or unfavorable to violence
by adolescents are shaped by the levels of adults employed in economically
and socially advantaged or disadvantaged occupations.

Steffensmeier and Ulmer take a different, qualitative, approach to differential social organization and the processes of social learning. Their chapter is
in the tradition of Sutherland's (1937) classic case study of a professional
thief. They report additional insights from the life history of a professional
fence, who was the subject of Steffensmeier's *The Fence: In the Shadow of
Two Worlds* (1983). At the time of the interviews on which this chapter is
based, "Manny" was dying of lung cancer. His fifty-year criminal career illustrates differential association/social learning processes with shifts and oscillations in his involvement in criminal activities reflecting the changes and
vagaries of criminal opportunities and interaction with other criminals. The
case study and narrative data were central to the original development of
differential social organization/differential association theory and the discipline is badly in need of contemporary illustrative examples of the link between life (and death) experiences and abstract concepts.

Brezina and Piquero in the next chapter and Horan and Phillips in chapter
12 take an entirely different approach from any of the preceding chapters and

conduct conceptual and empirical analyses of the internal logic of the theory. Brezina and Piquero note that while social learning theory has always specifically included nonsocial reinforcement under the general concept of differential reinforcement, most of the focus of social learning theorists has been on social reinforcement. They argue that the theory may profit from greater attention to the relationship between the concepts of social reinforcement and nonsocial reinforcement in the form of "intrinsic" rewards of engaging in deviant behavior. In particular, they examine the role of social and nonsocial reinforcement processes in delinquency and drug use. They find that the two are very closely related. They propose that social learning theory would predict that social reinforcement, peer norm qualities, and moral beliefs have significant effects on individual differences in adolescents' experiencing intrinsic pleasure or highs from substance use. Both their cross-sectional and longitudinal analyses produce findings consistent with these theoretical expectations.

Horan and Phillips apply a "theory-mapping" strategy to analyze the logic of social learning theory. Theory and research by social learning theorists serves this purpose well because they provide "a compact and theoretically coherent body of work," but the authors argue that the strategy can be fruitfully applied to other areas of theory-driven social research. When applied to social learning the authors propose that the theory as mapped implies a measurement model where concepts such as definitions, differential association, and differential reinforcement are empirically, as well as conceptually, distict from one another. However, their empirical analysis of measurement models using the Boys Town study of adolescent substance abuse and the Iowa study of teenage smoking (see Akers 1998) suggests that the measured concepts are highly correlated and may be "empirically indistinguishable from one another." In short, conceptually distict dimensions of the dynamic social learning process are not revealed in their data. Rather, social learning appears to be a singular phenomenon.

The original statement of the theory by Burgess and Akers (1966) integrated principles of operant conditioning with principles of differential association, and Akers (1973, 1977, 1985, 1998, 2000) has from the beginning recognized and drawn upon the parallel work of psychologists who have applied social learning principles to delinquent, deviant, and antisocial behavior (see Bandura 1977; Patterson et al. 1975; Andrews and Bonta 1998). We are fortunate to be able to include in this volume high quality contributions from this theoretical stream in social learning. Chapter 13 by Wiesner, Capaldi, and Patterson comes from the longstanding and outstanding program of theory and research at the Oregon Social Learning Center founded and directed by Gerald Patterson. In spite of the clear social learning label of the Center, and the close affinity of Patterson's and Akers' approaches, the work of Patterson and his associates at the OSLC has often been mistakenly identified in the criminological literature as a type of control or social bonding theory. This tendency may have partially resulted from some theorists equating the focus on social learning processes in the family and family disciplinary practices in Patterson's early work with the stress on parental attachment and supervision and the rejection of peer influence in Hirschi's (1969) control theory. If so, it is a misinterpretation of the theoretical core of the Center's program which has always included attention to social learning processes in peer groups and in the community as well as in the family. Wiesner et al. portray the basic social learning processes in Patterson's Coercion Model of delinquent and criminal behavior and relate that model to the progression of deviant behavior throughout the life span. In this model, childhood antisocial behavior and subsequent delinquent and criminal behavior are outcomes of reinforcing exchanges in the immediate social environment of the family and then later of peers and others. In this model there is a special emphasis on the functions of negative reinforcement in shaping antisocial and deviant behavior. Coercive or aversive responses to others' attempts to control one's overt deviant behavior may succeed in warding off and perhaps terminating negative sanctions for the undesirable behavior. The outcome of the social interaction, then, is to maximize relative payoff and reinforce the deviant behavior (with a concomitant failure to learn prosocial and accommodative behavior). The model is developed for both early-onset and late-onset offenders and cessation/persistence of offending in adulthood.

The behavioral and social learning approaches in psychology, and the links to social learning in criminology, are also reflected in the final chapter by Cullen, Wright, Gendreau, and Andrews. One of the authors, D. A. Andrews, is a psychologist who has long made use of principles of differential association and behavioral psychology in theory-driven correctional treatment programs and made his work known in sociology and criminology (Andrews 1980). The senior author of this chapter, Francis T. Cullen, is a chief sociological proponent of rehabilitation and treatment policies. Akers has long contended that applied and practical implications of a theory is one of the principal criteria by which theories should be judged (see Akers, 2000), and we are pleased to have this chapter in the volume on the applications of social learning principles in correctional or criminal justice practice. The authors argue persuasively against the anti-treatment, nothing-works orientation in criminology and examine the research record on correctional treatment for its implications for criminological theory. They find that the record is most consistently supportive of the effectiveness of cognitive-behavioral programs based on social learning principles both on their own and in comparison to other treatment approaches.

A common refrain in all of these chapters is the call for continued efforts to test and refine social learning theory and the relationships between social structure and social learning with better measures and better data. They provide a sound basis on which to answer that call. Hopefully, the first half of the new century will be as fruitful for social learning theory in criminology as has been the last half of the old century.

## References

Akers, Ronald L. 1973. *Deviant Behavior: A Social Learning Approach.* Belmont, CA: Wadsworth.
___. 1977. *Deviant Behavior: A Social Learning Approach.* Second Edition. Belmont, CA: Wadsworth.
___. 1985. *Deviant Behavior: A Social Learning Approach.* Third Edition Belmont, CA: Wadsworth. Reprinted 1992. Fairfax, VA: Techbooks.
___. 1996. "Is differential association/social learning cultural deviance theory? *Criminology* 34:229-248.
___. 1998. *Social Learning and Social Structure: A General Theory of Crime and Deviance.* Boston: Northeastern University Press.
___. 2000. *Criminological Theories: Introduction, Evaluation, and Application.* Third Edition. Los Angeles: Roxbury Publishing
Akers, Ronald L., Marvin D. Krohn, Lonn Lanza-Kaduce, and Marcia Radosevich. 1979. "Social learning and deviant behavior: a specific test of a general theory," *American Sociological Review* 44: 635-55.
Andrews, D. A. 1980. "Some experimental investigations of the principles of differential association through deliberate manipulations of the structure of service systems," *American Sociological Review* 45:448-462.
Andrews, D. A. and James Bonta. 1998. *Psychology of Criminal Conduct.* Second Edition. Cincinnati, OH: Anderson.
Bandura, Albert. 1977. *Social Learning Theory.* Englewood Cliffs, NJ: Prentice Hall.
Burgess, Robert L., and Ronald L. Akers. 1966. "A differential association-reinforcement theory of criminal behavior," *Social Problems* 14:128-47.
Heimer, Karen, and Ross Matsueda. 1994. "Role-taking, role-commitment, and delinquency: a theory of differential social control," *American Sociological Review* 59:365-390.
Matsueda, Ross and Karen Heimer. 1997. "A symbolic interactionist theory of role-transitions, role-commitments, and delinquency." In Thornberry, Terence P., ed., *Developmental Theories of Crime and Delinquency.* New Brunswick, NJ: Transaction Publishers.
Patterson, G. R., J. B. Reid, R. Q. Jones, and R. E. Conger. 1975. *A Social Learning Approach to Family Intervention.* Vol. 1. Eugene, OR: Castalia Publishing Co.
Sutherland, Edwin H. 1937. *The Professional Thief.* Chicago: University of Chicago Press.
___. 1947. *Principles of Criminology.* Fourth Edition. Philadelphia: J. B. Lippincott.
Skinner, B. F. 1959. *Cumulative Record.* New York: Appleton-Century-Crofts.
Steffensmeier, Darrell. 1986. *The Fence: In the Shadow of Two Worlds.* Totowa, NJ: Rowman and Littlefield.

# 1

# "Taking Social Learning Global": Micro-Macro Transitions in Criminological Theory

*Gary F. Jensen and Ronald L. Akers*

A major development in criminology over the last ten to fifteen years has been the revival of research testing theories relevant to variation in crime among ecological units, ranging from neighborhoods to societies (e.g., Sampson and Groves 1989; Gartner 1990; Patterson 1991; Bursik and Grasmick 1993; Bellair 1997; Markowitz et al. 2001). This resurgence of macro-level theory and ecological analysis contrasts with the dominant method for testing criminological theories during much of the 1970s and 1980s, the analysis of correlates of self-reported offense behavior based on questionnaire or interview data collected from individuals. That type of research allowed an assessment of the comparative importance of variables central to several distinct theories about motivational and constraining forces affecting the odds of delinquent behavior and, overall, provided substantial support for theories emphasizing the causal primacy of peer and family relationships, school experiences, personal commitments and conventional values. Theories emphasizing economic disadvantage and frustrations in the pursuit of conventional goals (so-called "strain" theories) did not fare as well as theories focusing on social constraints or social learning processes (see Akers 2000; Jensen and Rojek 1998). Such conclusions have generated considerable controversy and one of the lines of argument behind a resurgence of macro-level research flows from a critique of the self-report survey and analyses of survey data collected from individuals.

## Conflicting Themes in the Ecological Revival

In 1987, Thomas Bernard challenged the adequacy of any analyses based on survey data from individuals for testing strain theory, arguing that a proper assessment of Merton's (1938, 1957) version of the theory required analysis of variations at a macro level (referred to as anomie theory at the macro level). Steven Messner and Richard Rosenfeld have endorsed Bernard's position and reiterate the argument that tests at the individual level have no necessary bearing on the adequacy of the theory at the macro level. Indeed, they present examples where variations at the individual level within nations do not apply across nations (2001: 38-46) and propose an "institutional anomie theory" that is supposed to explain variations in "serious" crime among nations.[1] The fact that tests of competing theories using data collected from individuals have provided strong support for social learning theory as opposed to strain theory is considered irrelevant to a global analysis.

Messner and Rosenfeld are very critical of the self-report survey data as measures of "serious" crime and theories supported by such data are depicted as relevant only to minor offenses.[2] In their opinion, the dominance of the self-report method and analyses of data at the individual level constitute an "individualistic bias in contemporary criminology" (Rosenfeld and Messner 1995: 161-164; Messner and Rosenfeld 2001: 38-42). In contrast, their "institutional anomie" theory is supposed to overcome these limitations and explain macro-level variations in serious crimes.

They qualify their critique of individual explanations by stating that "Any macro-level explanation of crime will inevitably be predicated on underlying premises about individual behavior" (2001: 42), and "it is possible ... to link these individual-level theories with macro-level explanations that share a causal logic." However, these statements are countered by (1) the dismissal of the very type of research that has challenged the validity of strain theory at the individual level while supporting social learning theory, (2) the use of examples of discontinuities at different levels of analysis with no discussion of continuities, and (3) the rejection of the analysis of survey data as an appropriate technique for testing macro-level theories or studying truly "serious" crime.

This critique can be contrasted with the approach taken by other theorists and researchers involved in the resurgence of ecological analysis. Much of the central research in a revival of Shaw and McKay's "social disorganization" theory in recent years measures crime using survey data, including data on self-reported offending collected from individuals as well as victimization data (e.g., Sampson and Groves 1989; Sampson, Raudenbusch and Earls 1997; Markowitz, Bellair, Liska and Liu 2001). The survey data is aggregated to create measures appropriate for ecological analysis and used to measure rates of serious crime. Cautions about generalizing from one level of analysis to another are expressed, but survey data are accepted as an appropriate foundation for macro-level analysis.

Moreover, theoretical extensions and elaborations of social disorganization theory convey an impression of continuity between levels of analysis. It is common to acknowledge links between the logic of Hirschi's social control theory (1969) and social disorganization theory. Weak bonds between youth and conventional adults, institutions and values increases the probability of delinquency among individuals in Hirschi's control theory and weak communal institutions or networks increase crime rates at the ecological level. While there has not been a thorough elaboration of the possible transitions and problems in making those transitions, the discussion of links suggests continuity as opposed to discontinuity. In fact, while stressing discontinuities between macro-micro levels in research, Messner and Rosenfeld categorize social disorganization with social control theory, cultural deviance with social learning theory, and anomie with strain theories. As will be discussed below, while there are links between cultural deviance and social learning theory, this coupling is problematic for some depictions of cultural deviance theory.

## The Neglect of Social Learning Theory

The one theory that has received very little attention in this ecological revival is social learning theory. It is included together with cultural deviance theory in Messner and Rosenfeld's classification of theories, but their subsequent discussion focuses entirely on cultural deviance theory. None of the characteristics of contemporary social learning theory are discussed, and the major social learning theorists are relegated to a footnote. Most of their discussion is devoted to Ruth Kornhauser's (1978) controversial interpretation of cultural deviance theory. Moreover, while the links between social disorganization theory and social control theory are mentioned by most of the parties to the ecological revival, virtually nothing is said about links between social learning theory and the ecological perspectives proposed. This neglect is quite surprising when the fact that social learning theory has fared better than any other theory in the explanation of variation in criminal and delinquent behavior using self-report data collected from individuals.

Several possible reasons for this neglect can be proposed. For one, its development was overshadowed by Hirschi's *Causes of Delinquency* (1969). While Hirschi's theory is classified together with social learning theory as an "individualistic" theory of crime, one of the reasons *Causes of Delinquency* became the most quoted work in criminology in the twentieth century was the fact that it proposed differences among social control, cultural deviance and strain theories in macro-level assumptions about American society and conducted analysis relevant to those assumptions and correlates distinctively important to each of those theories. For example, Hirschi reasoned that were America characterized by the class-linked cultural or normative variations emphasized by Walter Miller (1957), then attitudes towards the law and moral beliefs should vary by social class. Variation in such attitudes were found to be correlated with delinquency, but, in contrast to Miller's version of cultural deviance theory, they were not found to be significant correlates of social class. Moreover, if such sizeable subcultures linked to class or race existed, measures of interaction and attachment to adults in such categories should be positive correlates of delinquency for the young. In contrast, Hirschi found that such variables inhibited delinquency in all categories. In short, Hirschi addressed arguments about the subcultural organization of American society by exploring variations across groups and examining correlates within socially differentiated groups. He took the same approach when testing strain theory. If acceptance of widely shared, culturally approved goals facilitated delinquency among disadvantaged youth, then such aspirations should be positive correlates of delinquency among youth in categories where chances of realizing such goals were slight. He did not find that pattern when examining such categories of youth. In short, Hirschi's work was attended to carefully by sociologists because it dealt with criminogenic properties of American social structure and culture.

When Hirschi's work was published, a nascent "social learning theory" was under construction by Ronald Akers, elaborating on Burgess and Akers' (1966) operant reformulation of Sutherland's "differential association" theory. Initially presented as an operant restatement of Sutherland's basic propositions, Akers' specification of a more general social learning theory (1973) elaborated new ideas that distinguished the theory from its predecessors, including cultural deviance theory, and some interpretations of differential association theory. However, since social learning theory did not emerge as a repudiation of alternatives, issues that distinguished it from prior theories were not initially addressed and no specific macro-level counterpart was identified.

Another source of neglect stems from the tendency to link social learning theory to the most extreme versions of cultural deviance theory. For example, Messner and Rosenfeld state that "the idea that criminal behavior is learned (at the individual level) and that crime is entirely a product of culture (at the macro level) quickly runs into several inter-related problems." However, the inter-related problems they address are all problems with a "pure" cultural explanation of crime. They criticize cultural theories for assuming that "all behavior is consistent with underlying values (2001: 47)." But, social learning theory makes no such assumption! Indeed, one of the empirically substantiated features of social learning theory is its delineation of several distinct learning mechanisms, only one of which involves cultural or normative phenomenon. Social learning theory proposes that delinquent behavior is learned and sustained through a variety of non-normative learning processes (direct and vicarious differential reinforcement, imitation and differential association) as well as through normative mechanisms. Normative socialization, or definitional learning processes, involve values and norms, but the separable effects of non-normative processes means that criminal and delinquent activities can be engaged in despite "underlying values."[3] In short, social learning theory posits the very mechanisms that explain why behavior is not always consistent "with underlying values."

Social learning theory is explicitly contrary to both the version of cultural deviance theory that Messner and Rosenfeld cite as its macro-level partner and to Matsueda's initial interpretation of cultural deviance-differential association theory as well. In Matsueda's first test of differential association theory, the effects of all other variables are viewed as channeled through "definitions" (see Matsueda 1982). Indeed, quite recently, Costello and Vowell (1999) reanalyzed Hirschi's data and found Matsueda's interpretation to be wrong. Contrary to Matsueda's initial cultural interpretation of differential association theory, definitions did not fully mediate the effect of variables such as delinquent peer associations. Costello and Vowell interpret such findings as "more supportive of control theory than differential association theory" (1999: 815). Yet, despite the fact that the best fitting model included peer variables (an effect specifically excluded in Hirschi's presentation of control theory), they totally ignore social learning theory. The best fitting model is a social learning model.

## Micro-Macro Issues

In this chapter, we advocate several positions relevant to micro-macro transitions in the development of social learning theory. However, before we can attempt to specify micro-macro links for social learning theory, we need to address some misconceptions about "individual level" versus "macro-level" explanations. There is a tendency in critiques of certain theories as "individualistic" to confuse sources of data and levels of aggregation with levels of explanation. The delineation of "individual" versus "macro-level" explanations and the inclusion of some theories as "individualistic" by Messner and Rosenfeld misrepresent those theories. Not only do we need to address such misconceptions, but the links between the "causal logics" of theories at different levels need to be addressed. Development of any integrated macro-micro theory will require a more precise delineation of the nature of macro-micro issues than has been presented in the criminological literature thus far. The causal logics of theories depicted as applicable at the individual level have implications for their transformation into macro-level theories and/or their compatibility with existing macro-level theories.

When explicit attention is paid to such transitions, the popular classification of social learning theory with cultural deviance theory can be questioned, and the theory can be shown to be quite compatible with a modified version of Sampson's and Wilson's (1995) social-cultural disorganization theory of crime. A criminological theory that successfully addresses micro-macro transitions is to be preferred over theories that can be defended at only one level, or where the research at "micro" or "meso" levels is dismissed as irrelevant to the merits of a theory. James Coleman (1990: 21) expressed such an epistemological rule in his *Foundations of Social Theory*, although he presents it as a standard for evaluating "good" social history: "...[G]ood social history makes transitions between micro and macro levels successfully." Rather than attempt to integrate research at different levels of analysis or explanation, Bernard and Messner and Rosenfeld dismiss research based on data collected from individuals as irrelevant to macro-level versions of criminological theory. In contrast, we argue that the most empirically accurate macro-level theories are likely to be compatible with the causal logic of the best substantiated "micro-level" theories.

## Level of Explanation, Data Sources, and Aggregation

Messner and Rosenfeld argue that "one of the sources of miscommunication in debates about crime is confusion over levels of explanation (2001: 38)." They argue that "The basic question underlying the individualistic approach...is why one person rather than another commits a criminal act." They contrast the individual level of explanation with the macro-level which "focuses on questions about groups and populations" such as "Why do levels of crime vary across social systems?" and "Why is crime patterned in systematic ways across social categories?" Macro-level analysis is depicted as "framed in terms of crime rates" which "unlike questions about individual acts of crime" are to be "explained with reference to other properties of collective units." The theories depicted as "formulated in individualistic terms" are social learning theory, social control theory and strain theory. The dominance of research on these types of theories using the self-report method constitutes the "individualistic bias" they depict as characteristic of contemporary criminology.

Few criminologists would challenge the observation that relationships based on data collected from individuals may have no bearing on variations among states and nations (or vice versa), and few would challenge the value of testing theories about macro-level variation at the macro level. However, their depiction of research testing these social learning, social control and strain theories using self-report data collected from individuals as "individualistic" confuses issues involving levels of explanation and units of analysis with sources of data. Contrary to Messner and Rosenfeld's depiction, none of the self-report research gathered from samples of individuals is used to make statements about individuals in the manner they propose. Rather, the individuals who provide the data are aggregated into categories or groups (e.g., cases from single-parent versus two-parent households, cases with different numbers of delinquent friends, cases with deviant parents and straight parents, males and females, etc.) and rates of delinquency are created using their responses (e.g., an average or percentage). The statements made on the basis of such analysis are statements about odds, percentages, or central tendencies across social categories. Just as a "crime rate" is not a characteristic of individuals, the variance explained, the differences in means, and the differences in percentages or odds are not properties of individuals. The conclusions pertain to social aggregates and the analysis is relevant to answering the question listed by Messner and Rosenfeld under macro-level issues, "Why is crime patterned in systematic ways across social categories?" The data are collected from individuals, but all empirical analysis by criminologists testing these "individualistic" theories aggregates cases into social categories and seeks to answer questions about variation across social categories. A depiction of social control, social learning, and some versions of strain theory as "individualistic" misrepresents the theories because they all conduct analyses that answer questions depicted as "macro" by Messner and Rosenfeld.

The data used in most of the research on these theories is misrepresented as well. While "crime rates" for ecological units can be related to other collective properties of those same units, the rates can be based on self-reports of offending by individuals. Such data are no more "individualistic" than reports of victimization by individuals, or data on individual criminal events as reported to police and aggregated by type of jurisdiction, county, state or society. Were a worldwide self-report survey carried out, such data could be aggregated into a "crime rate" and treated as a property of societies. The analysis could answer questions about variation among societies as well as variation across social categories within those societies. Of course, the results might not be the same for the ecological correlation across societies as for the correlation when categorizing people from all societies, or within individual societies. However, the problem is not generated by collecting data from individuals. Individual data can be aggregated to provide tests about variations in rates among categories for the whole sample, but they can also be aggregated to provide measures across ecological territories such as counties, states and nations. Indeed, the argument that crime rates are a collective social fact that should be related to other collective social facts is most often made when there is no way to "disaggregate" the data to assess the stability of relationships across levels of aggregation. That barrier is a limitation of available data for cross-national analysis, not a sociological virtue.

We can acknowledge that an analysis of variations among societies is "more macro" than an analysis of variations across social categories (which might be called a "meso-level" analysis), but the depiction of survey research testing theories about such variation as "individualistic" and incapable of addressing the truly sociological questions is misleading. Moreover, dismissal of tests of anomie theory at a more micro level (strain theory) as irrelevant precludes an integrated anomie-strain theory. A theory that can make transitions across levels as well as explain discontinuities by level of aggregation or "explanation" should be the ultimate goal of criminology. That goal is more likely to be achieved by a theory that can address issues along a full micro-macro scale.

## Micro-Macro Transitions

Akers has addressed the relation of social learning theory to other theories in recent works (2000) and has been elaborating the relevance of the theory to "macro" issues in criminology as well (1998). Yet, while the basic model is well-elaborated at the micro-level, the transition to a more macro-level version has not been completed. This chapter takes additional steps in that direction by addressing the implications of micro characteristics of the theory for macro-level conceptions of the role of structure and culture in the generation of crime.

In his recent monograph elaborating the links between social structure and social learning, Ronald Akers (1998: 322) attributes variations in crime rates by structural location and culture to differences in the form or outcome of social learning mechanisms. While specification of such linkages should help clarify the fact that social learning theory was intended to be both a sociological and social psychological theory, no specific macro-level version of the theory characterized by specific propositions about key macro-level issues has been posited. However, the conception of processes operating at a micro level or a meso level are more compatible with some macro-level positions than others.

Most major causal theories include cultural or ideational phenomena (values, norms, beliefs and knowledge shared by members of a social system) in one form or another in their explanations of crime and delinquency. However, they also differ in the importance accorded cultural variables, the type of cultural categories emphasized, the causal interrelationships among cultural phenomena in their theory, and in their characterizations of particular "cultures." For example, in his test of differential association theory in 1982, Matsueda argued that, in Sutherland's theory, "definitions" were the key mediating mechanism linking all other variables to delinquency. He challenged Jensen's analysis (1972) in which it was proposed that both parents and peers had direct effects on delinquency, effects that were not fully mediated by normative or ideational variables. Both social control and social learning theory include cultural variables as important to the explanation of crime, but both also allow for direct effects of other "non-cultural" constraining forces (attachment, commitment, and involvement for social control theory), or other types of learning processes (imitation, differential reinforcement and differential association for social learning theory). Research since that 1982 work (including much of Matsueda's own research) has supported the independent relevance of non-cultural mechanisms in the explanation of crime and delinquency (see Matsueda and Heimer 1987; Matsueda 1989; Bartusch and Matsueda 1996).

Acceptance of normative and non-normative learning mechanisms at the micro-level is consistent with the position that both structural and cultural variables have independent consequences for crime rates at the macro level. This implication of social learning theory stands in marked contrast to Messner and Rosenfeld's interpretations of cultural deviance theory in which all variables operate through culture, and is contrary to their depiction of social disorganization theories that have, allegedly, attempted to "expunge" cultural variables. The emphasis on normative and non-normative mechanisms fits best with macro-level models in which cultural variables can be related to structured social relationships/organization/disorganization, but where culture phenomena are differentiated from social relationships and structure.

As Akers states (2001: 195), his theory includes "both behavioral interactional and normative dimensions" with the interactional dimension referring to "the direct association and interaction with others...as well as the indirect association and identification with more distant reference groups." The normative dimension of social learning encompasses "the different patterns of norms, values and attitudes to which an individual is exposed through this association." The interactional dimension can be transformed quite readily into "structure" at a more macro level (e.g., patterned interaction organized around specific functions such as institutional structure) and patterns of norms, values and attitudes are encompassed by the concept of culture. The processes are conceptually distinct and can be linked to distinct macro-level characteristics of social units.

Messner and Rosenfeld's depiction of cultural deviance theory and social disorganization-control theory as "conceptual opposites," with the former channeling all social influences through culture, and the later expunging culture (2001: 49), would seem to preclude linking social learning theory to either of these perspectives. However, just as their depiction of social learning as nothing more than the individualistic version of an extreme cultural deviance theory is misleading, so is their depiction of social disorganization-control theory as an attempt to "expunge" culture from the explanation of crime. Hirschi argued that the sizeable subcultures proposed by Miller did not exist, but he did not exclude cultural variables from his theory. In fact, he proposed that there was consensus on the moral impropriety of law-breaking, shared across structurally differentiated groups, but that there was variation in the degree to which people in these categories accepted such moral beliefs. He dismissed the need for any neutralizing definitions (Sykes and Matza 1957) to explain why people break rules they appear to accept by proposing variation in degrees of internalization of dominant cultural norms. Ironically, institutional anomie theory is a consensus theory as well in that materialistic cultural goals or ambitions are depicted as widely shared across such groups. Limits on opportunity or success in the pursuit of such goals leads to anomie, or the erosion of norms. Hirschi proposed that there was consensus across groups, but that there was variable learning of such norms among members of a social system. Hirschi did not find any evidence of greater normative erosion among disadvantaged than advantaged categories of youth, but he did find variation in moral beliefs (a cultural phenomenon) to have separable effects when explaining variation in law-breaking. In short, control theory, like social learning theory, allows for separable effects of cultural and organizational or relational variables. Indeed, both social control and social learning theory imply that it is failures of agents and institutions of "conventional" socialization that leads to the weak "internalization" of cultural norms and values ( rather than successful socialization into shared goals) that captures the most salient manner in which cultural concepts are relevant to the explanation of crime.

There is a fundamental difference between Hirschi's version of control theory and social learning theory that has implications for linking social learning to some forms of social disorganization theory. Hirschi argued that attachment to peers and parents acted as a barrier to delinquency regardless of the behavior of the objects of attachment (see Jensen and Brownfield 1983). Not only has it been shown that the behavior of parents affects the constraining relevance of attachment, but associations with delinquent peers have a direct, nonspurious effect on involvement in delinquency. Hence, social learning theory would fit best with a macro-level theory that included variations in peer group relationships, and allowed the patterns of behavior exhibited by parents to be reproduced (imitated), at least partially, in the behavior of youth.

"Routine activities theory" is a macro-level theory of rates of victimization that has received substantial support in research on the social ecology of crime (see Cohen and Felson 1979; Felson 2001). That theory attempts to explain ecological variations in crime (as well as some patterns of variation over time) in terms of the availability and vulnerability of unguarded targets and proximity to motivated offenders. Variations in everyday "routine activities" shape the social ecology of crime. Moving the analysis toward a micro level, Osgood, Wilson, O'Malley, Bachman and Johnston (1996) examine the impact of variations in routine activities on deviant behavior based on data collected from individuals, arguing that "unstructured socializing with peers in the absence of authority figures presents opportunities for deviance: In the presence of peers, deviant acts will be easier and more rewarding, the absence of authority figures reduces the potential for social control responses to deviance; and the lack of structure leaves time available for deviant behavior" (1996: 635). Not only did the analysis support these claims, but such variables accounted for "a substantial portion" of the associations between deviance and social background variables such as age, sex, and socioeconomic status.

Although Osgood and his colleagues interpret their results as support for routine activities theory at a more micro level than had been attempted in prior research (with the exception of Jensen and Brownfield 1986), anyone familiar with social learning theory will recognize their statements as direct parallels and confirmation of a social learning model. *Yet, there is not a single citation to social learning theory!* Contemporary social control and self-control theories are cited, but there is not a hint that a theory elaborated for over three decades has any relevance to their conclusions. Ignoring this oversight, it might be proposed that routine activities-opportunity theory is a macro-level partner for social learning theory. If the findings taken as support for routine activities theory could have been predicted by social learning theory, then these two theories might be "integrated." Jensen and Brownfield (1986) note that "exposure and proximity to offenders" are central to differential association and social learning theories of criminality and that the "'victimogenic' variables in routine activities theory have been introduced in earlier theories as 'criminogenic.'"

However, there are several problems in making a transition from social learning theory at the micro level to routine activities theory at the macro level. First, despite parallels, routine activities theory is a theory of criminal victimization. Proximity to motivated offenders is introduced to explain risks of victimization, but there are no statements relevant to motivation or "criminogenic" pressures. Second, routine activities theory does not address the relevance of normative or cultural forces and constraints, while social learning theory posits distinct, separable effects for normative and non-normative learning processes. As stated by Osgood and his colleagues, deviance is more probable when youth spend time in unsupervised activities where they have the opportunity to be reinforced for deviance. There is no specification of the distinct processes that lead to involvement in such situations nor determinants of deviant choices when opportunity is present.

While "opportunity" is central to routine activities theory, some critics of social learning theory argue that it fails to incorporate intervening contingencies such as opportunity. Tittle and Paternoster (2000: 423) criticize social learning theory on the grounds that it does not "take into account things in the social environment that intervene between learned characteristics and their manifestation in actual deviance" (422). The example given to illustrate this shortcoming is as follows: "[A] young man may believe the law is corrupt, have no moral compunctions against theft, and know how to hot-wire an automobile (all learned), yet not steal any automobiles because none is available in his environment, because the cops are so prevalent that the person fears getting caught, or because he hangs with companions who occupy his time doing other things" (2000: 423).

There are serious problems with this criticism. First, the choice not to commit an act because of fear of getting caught is, in fact, encompassed by processes of differential reinforcement and vicarious punishment. Social learning theory specifically incorporates anticipated rewards and punishments, including fear of legal sanctions. Second, the inhibiting effect of "hanging out" with companions who occupy time doing other things is exactly what is encompassed by the concept of differential association. The more time spent with companions who regularly break laws, the greater the probability of law-breaking. The more time spent with companions who "do other things," the lower the probability of law-breaking. Moreover, both routine activities theory and social learning theory imply that the more time spent "hanging out" away from home with companions, relative to "hanging out" at home, the greater the probability of delinquency. The notion that individual choices reflect past experiences and assessments of probable outcomes in specific situations is central to social learning theory.

The statement that opportunity (no car available) is an intervening contingency ignored by social learning theory is simply wrong. Akers specifically incorporates "availability" as the first of his "crucial variables" throughout his presentation of social learning theory. The first variable identified in the list of "crucial variables" for the explanation of drug use is "availability of the drug" (1973: 81). Availability is introduced to explain patterns of addiction by occupation (87-88). It is addressed when dealing with marijuana, hallucinogenic drugs (89, 103) and alcohol (111, 122). For some crimes, opportunity is incorporated into the very phenomenon to be explained, and it would be superficial to introduce a qualifying contingency (e.g., the opportunity for white-collar crime is built into the concept itself). Shoplifting requires that there are shops. Automobile theft cannot occur if there are no automobiles. In short, opportunity to commit an offense as measured by available targets is central to routine activities theory as an ecological theory and is completely compatible with "availability" as a crucial variable incorporated into social learning theory.

The variables introduced to predict the probability of crime from a social learning perspective imply that a promising candidate as a macro or ecological partner for social learning theory should incorporate (1) both social and cultural variables, (2) some form of relative involvement in unstructured peer group activities, (3) cross-generational reproduction of law-breaking, and (4) variations in opportunity relevant to the specific crime or crimes to be explained. There may be unique structured learning processes relevant to different types of crime as well as countervailing learning processes (see Jensen and Brownfield 1983), but this set of variables constitutes a theoretically founded starting point for empirical research.

Robert Sampson and William Julius Wilson outline a theory with three of these characteristics in their proposal of a theory of "race, crime, and urban inequality" (1995: 37-54). Sampson's prior work with Grove, using the British Crime Survey, "showed that the prevalence of unsupervised teenage peer groups in a community had the largest effects on rates of robbery and violence by strangers." The density of local friendship networks and level of organizational participation by residents also had significant inhibiting effects. They concluded that "...communities characterized by sparse friendship networks, unsupervised teenage peer groups, and low organizational participation fostered increased crime rates."

Such findings are presented as support for a "social disorganization" theory of crime. Such theories attribute variation in crime and delinquency over time and among territories to the absence or breakdown of communal institutions (e.g., family, school, church and local government). The concept is defined in terms of the absence of or breakdown of certain types of relationships among people and is intimately tied to conceptions of those properties of relationships among people that are indicative of social or communal "organization." Relationships among people in a given territory are presumed to be especially "organized" when there are high levels of involvement across age-levels in activities coordinated by representatives of communal institutions (e.g., family-heads, pastors, school organizations and local officials). Such organized interaction is presumed to be closely and reciprocally associated with the development of communal bonds.

In the early editions of his classic textbook, *Principles of Criminology* (1934, 1939), Edwin Sutherland invoked the concept of social disorganization to explain increases in crime that accompanied the transformation of preliterate and peasant societies where "influences surrounding a person were steady, uniform, harmonious and consistent" to modern Western civilization which he believed was characterized by inconsistency, conflict and "unorganization" (1934: 64). He believed that the mobility, economic competition and individualistic ideology that accompanied capitalist and industrial development had "disintegrated" both the large family and homogeneous neighborhoods as agents of social control, expanded the realm of relationships that were not governed by family and neighborhood, and undermined governmental controls.

This disorganization of conventional institutions that had traditionally reinforced the law facilitated the development and persistence of "systematic" crime and delinquency. He also believed that such disorganization fostered cultural traditions and cultural conflicts that support such activity. He depicted the "law-abiding culture" as "dominant and more extensive" than alternative criminogenic cultural views and capable of "overcoming systematic crime *if* organized for that purpose" (1939: 8). However, because society was "organized around individual and small group interests," society "permits" crime to persist. Sutherland concluded that "if the society is organized with reference to the values expressed in the law, the crime is eliminated; if it is not organized, crime persists and develops" (1939:8). In later works, he switched from the concept of social disorganization to differential social organization to convey the complexity of overlapping and conflicting levels of organization in a society.

Sampson and Wilson propose a similar theory in which social disorganization generates cultural disorganization. They argue that "poverty, heterogeneity, anonymity, mutual distrust, institutional instability, and other structural features of urban communities impede communication and obstruct the quest for common values, thereby fostering cultural diversity with respect to nondelinquent values." Their position on cultural variables is similar to Hirschi's. In contrast to perspectives where sizeable categories of disadvantaged people embrace "focal concerns" that encourage crime, or where "the dominant component of motivation of 'delinquent' behavior engaged in by members of lower class corner groups involves a positive effort to achieve status, conditions, or qualities valued within the actor's most significant milieu" (1958: 19), Sampson and Wilson argue that "... a system of values emerges in which crime, disorder, and drug use are less than fervently condemned and hence expected as part of everyday life." They argue that "the social isolation fostered by the ecological concentration of urban poverty deprives residents not only of resources and conventional role models, but also of cultural learning from mainstream social networks that facilitate social and economic advancement in industrial society. Social isolation is specifically distinguished from the culture of poverty by virtue of its focus on adaptations to constraints and opportunities rather than internalization of norms.... Unlike the concept of a culture of violence, then, social isolation does not mean that ghetto specific practices become internalized, take on a life of their own, and therefore continue to influence behavior no matter what the contextual environment. Rather it suggests that reducing structural inequality would not only decrease the frequency of these practices; it would also make their transmission by precept less efficient."

Social learning theory mandates the inclusion of cultural variables in the explanation of crime through its emphasis on "definitional" learning, but that feature of the theory can be linked to a variety of different conceptions at a macro level. Discussions of the different ways in which the concept of culture has been introduced into the explanation of crime (see Yinger 1960; Empey 1967) suggest several distinct ways in which the system of values, norms and beliefs characterizing a society can be "disorganized." A cultural system can be disorganized in the sense that there are conflicts among values, norms and beliefs within a widely shared, dominant culture. Matza and Gresham Sykes (1961) propose that in addition to cultural prescriptions stressing the importance of obeying laws, there are widely shared "subterranean" cultural perspectives that encourage crime. While condemning crime in general, law-abiding citizens accord respect and admiration to the person who "pulls off the big con," takes risks and successfully engages in exciting, dangerous activities. Sykes and Matza (1957) also note that despite conventional admonitions prescribing conformity to the law, other cultural norms and beliefs convey the message that breaking the law is not so bad when the victim "had it coming," when those supporting the law are not morally pure themselves; when the offender believes he or she "had no choice"; when "no one was hurt"; or when the offense was motivated by social purposes more important than the law. Such beliefs, or "techniques of neutralization," are learned in quite conventional contexts and are reflected in legal codes as "extenuating circumstances." Thus, the culture shared by people in a society or locale can be "disorganized" in the sense that conflicting moral messages are built into the cultural system itself.

The depiction of a society as a collection of socially differentiated groups with distinct subcultural perspectives that lead some of these groups into conflict with the law is another form of cultural disorganization, typically called cultural conflict. There may be perfectly consistent messages conveyed within a given subculture, but they may conflict with the views of other subcultures. Thorsten Sellin (1938) outlined three ways in which such conflict could occur involving distinct cultural groups. Cultural conflict could occur when (1) groups with different standards overlap or interact in border regions, (2) laws of one group are extended to encompass others and (3) distinct groups migrate into new territories. While Sellin's conflicts involve culturally distinct groups, Walter Miller and others extend the conflict to distinct socially differentiated subcultures within a society as well.

We have already noted that Hirschi rejected versions of cultural conflict theory that presumed sizeable, socially differentiated categories, or communities of people with "conflicting" definitions of the impropriety of lawbreaking (i.e., subcultures). Youth who break the law were engaged in behavior that was disapproved by most adults as well as most youth in their communities, and those residents with the most limited social bonds were most likely to be delinquent. Delinquent youth might exhibit distinct attitudes, but these were not the standards of the larger communities, social classes, regional settings or racial groups to which they belong.

Sampson and Wilson also reject the view that there are distinct subcultures of poverty where the norms espoused and internalized are in conflict with those embodied in law. Rather, they invoke a concept, cultural adaptations to social isolation, that is nearly identical to Kornhauser's "structural values (1978)." Variations in values, norms and beliefs that are "adaptations to constraints and opportunities" are considered distinct from the enduring traditions emphasized by Miller.

Messner and Rosenfeld are critical of Kornhauser's concept because it "undermines the essential distinction" between structure and culture. However, the maintenance of conceptual distinctions does not preclude empirical relationships between structural and cultural variables. Some variations in "definitions" may be adaptations to structured social experiences recurring over significant spans of time—differences that would quickly disappear were those experiences not sustained.

To summarize, "culture" can be introduced into the explanation of crime in quite distinct ways: There can be variations in internalization of a widely shared cultural system, conflicts or inconsistencies in the content of a widely shared culture, conflicts between the culture embodied in law and in the culture taught and internalized in distinct groups or settings, and variations that are adaptations to structured social experiences. Institutional anomie theory introduces the concept of culture in the most novel fashion. From that perspective the internalization of dominant widely shared cultural values stressing pecuniary success provides a cultural pressure towards serious crime and plays a role in undermining non-economic institutions and sources of social control.

Although novel, such an approach raises a paradox that does not have to be addressed by the other theories. How can such a pervasive consensus on cultural goals be maintained when such a value system undermines the very institutions that teach that culture? Successful cultural socialization requires reasonably healthy noneconomic institutions. Yet, such values are depicted as responsible for the weakening of such institutions in Messner and Rosenfeld's theory. No other perspective introduces this dilemma. From a control perspective, weak institutions are unlikely to effectively teach shared values or norms. From a cultural deviance perspective, strong local institutions can generate crime when their values and norms are in conflict with the culture reflected in legal codes. Indeed, a low crime rate could reflect the failure of local institutions to maintain subcultural traditions.

Neither institutional anomie theory nor cultural deviance theory are anchored in evidence to support either conception of the role of culture, at least in relation to the explanation of delinquent behavior. Widely shared cultural consensus cannot be maintained, if that consensus hinders the operation of conventional institutions. All measures relevant to socialization in alleged "subcultural" settings suggest that rather conventional cultural values and norms are emphasized and that those youth who are least integrated into the wider community are most likely to be delinquent.

Both social disorganization-control theory and social learning theory assume that strong adult institutions inhibit crime and are likely to encourage law-abiding conduct. However, social learning theory introduces the possibility of conflicts among learning mechanisms that can explain the perpetuation of crime even when parents are depicted as endorsing law-abiding decisions among their children. Parents may attempt to teach their children not to smoke, but their own smoking behavior affects their children through processes of imitation and perceived vicarious reinforcement. Strong ties to such parents do not have the same inhibiting effect as strong ties to non-smoking parents. The same contingent impacts can be detected for other forms of drug use. In short, the inhibiting impact of attempts to teach norms prohibiting youthful deviance is weakened by contrary learning processes. Yet, there is little evidence that strong bonds to deviant parents is criminogenic. The impact of such inconsistencies is to undermine the inhibiting influence of attachments to others.

Some of the experiences that various groups have with official agents of control, especially police, may generate complexities comparable to those emphasized by concepts such as techniques of neutralization. Youth may be taught that they ought to respect the law and that law enforcement is an honorable and important career. At the same time, a history of bias or discrimination can undermine that authority when police are perceived as unfair or bigoted. A basic cultural respect for the rule of law as a foundation for social order can coexist with perceptions of inequitable, discriminatory or corrupt law enforcement. A perception of injustice in enforcement can generate resentment that appears to outsiders as a subcultural disrespect for law, but that is more akin to the types of adaptation emphasized by Sampson and Wilson and the "structural values" proposed by Kornhauser. If these types of conflicting situations were called "cultural disorganization," then social learning theory would appear to be a micro-partner for a social-cultural disorganization perspective.

## Explaining Global Variations in Crime

There have been numerous attempts to explain variations among nations in homicide rates over the last several decades with Messner and Rosenfeld's study of the effect of political constraints on market forces (i.e., decommodification) one of the most recent. Yet, despite its empirical success in the explanation of a variety of forms of deviance based on data collected from individuals, social learning theory has played no direct role in that line of research. Social learning theory is rarely mentioned as a potentially relevant theory, and when it is mentioned it is typically misrepresented as a subsidiary of cultural deviance theory. Moreover, no social learning theorist has entered the fray.

Yet, when the causal logic of social learning theory is extended to the macro level and applied to violence, the resulting perspective would focus on characteristics of societies that impede or undermine (1) cultural and political consensus and (2) conventional institutional relationships, but enhance (3) unregulated interaction in peer groups, (4) situational opportunities to engage in, or be a victim of, crime, and (5) the development of sustained tendencies for people to resolve interpersonal conflicts through violent action. The emphasis on "heterogeneity," "weak social support networks" and "collective inefficacy" in contemporary versions of social disorganization theory is quite compatible with the first two characteristics, while the third is compatible with claims by Sampson and Groves, Osgood and colleagues about the impact of unsupervised youth groups as a central mediating variable at the neighborhood level. The fourth characteristic reflects either "availability" of a behavioral choice in social learning theory, or "opportunity" as specified by routine activities theory. Social learning theory differs from routine activities theory through its specification that involvement in certain types of routines are both more "criminogenic" and more "victimogenic" than others (Jensen and Brownfield 1986). Finally, the fifth characteristic allows for variations that are generated and sustained by cultural or subcultural tolerance or ambivalence concerning appropriate means of resolving interpersonal disputes (see Luckenbill and Doyle 1989). Such tolerance is especially likely when agents of formal control are not accorded authority to intervene (Sampson and Wilson 1995).

Just as the best fitting model in recent ecological analyses of neighborhoods appears more compatible with social learning theory than alternatives, one of the models proposed to explain societal level variations in homicide appears to correspond better with social learning theory than any alternative theory. In her analysis of global variations in homicide, Rosemary Gartner (1990: 95-96) found that (1) cultural heterogeneity, (2) exposure to violence, (3) unstable family relationships, (4) lack of state support of social welfare, and (5) availability of unguarded targets each explained a significant proportion of variation in homicide rates among eighteen nations.

In her justification for the first two concepts, Gartner hypothesizes that "cultural heterogeneity taps the potential for conflict and an absence of control among groups" and that "exposure to violence (whether direct or indirect) generates violence either through modeling, habituation. or desensitization." Cultural heterogeneity has been central to contemporary social-cultural disorganization theories and conflict theories. Moreover, the notion that "exposure to violence" in one context can carry over to other contexts is a rather straightforward societal level expression of social learning theory.

Gartner uses female employment in the labor force as a measure of a routine activities variable—availability of targets. Of course, the same variable might be treated as a measure of the potential for male-female competition and conflict, or as a measure of variation in supervision of children. Similarly, divorce rates are used as a measure of unstable family relationships, or as a measure of low parental supervision. Yet, divorce is a nonviolent, formal procedure for resolving interpersonal differences and disputes. If it facilitates exiting bad relationships, then it could be argued to lower homicide rates. The exact mechanisms that could generate such distinct consequences of divorce rates for homicide rates have not been directly measured.

Recognizing the huge gap between the measured variables that have been introduced into studies of global variation and the actual, unmeasured processes generating such relationships, we will end this attempt to take social learning "global" by examining the relationships between variables similar to those introduced by Gartner and homicide rates. We expand the set of nations for which homicide rates are available by using data from a variety of sources to fill in missing values. For most societies the homicide rates are based on the average homicide rate derived from reports posted on the Internet by the World Health Organization in their compilation of causes of death (World Health Statistics Annual 1997-1999, Online Edition, 2000). The homicide rate is a three-year average when possible, based on the three most recent reports between 1992 and 1998. To maximize the number of cases other sources of data (Lester 1996; Fox and Levine 2001; Microcase Corporation) were used to fill in missing values. These procedures yielded homicide rates for eighty-two nations as compared to 39-45 for Messner and Rosenfeld and eighteen nations in Gartner's study.

As noted above, since social learning theory includes both normative and non-normative learning processes, it is quite compatible with macro theories that incorporate variations in "culture" into the explanation of crime. However, social learning theory does not imply any specific version of the nature of those cultural influences, nor the exact way in which "culture" influences crime. The meaning of a "culture" or "subculture of violence" can range from normative expectations or approval of violence sustained through a sufficient span of time to be considered a "tradition" to Gartner's "desensitization, habituation, or modeling."

A variety of "cultural" characteristics of societies have been argued to explain high and low rates of crime. For example, in her "cross-cultural" comparison of delinquency among youth in Argentina and the United States, Lois DeFleur (1967) found rates of assault to be several times greater for youth in Argentina. She reports that lower-class youth accept physical aggression as a "socially approved means of settling interpersonal disputes." She also posits that "it is tempting to add an Argentine cultural factor of 'machismo,'" although the fact that both boys and girls had higher rates complicates that interpretation. Stevens (1973: 90) calls machismo "the cult of virility," adding that "[t]he chief characteristics of this cult are exaggerated aggressiveness and intransigence in male-to-male interpersonal relationships and arrogance and sexual aggression in male-to-female relationships." While the exact process has not been specified, there appears to be common agreement that high homicide rates for Latin nations reflects some unmeasured property of "culture."

Both Gartner and Messner and Rosenfeld report that social welfare or "decommodification" policies and investments lower homicide rates, although Messner and Rosenfeld propose a specific causal model in which such policies have both a direct inhibiting effect by alleviating economic pressures as well as an indirect effect by strengthening institutions of informal social control. In our analysis, societal investments in welfare and economic security programs (relative to gross domestic product) were used to measure the decommodification variable. The data are derived from the most recent report by the International Labour Organization on "The Cost of Social Security, 1900-1996" (available on the Internet at www.ilo.org). A measure of inequality is based on the GINI index with the sample mean substituted for missing cases.

As a proxy for other forms of societal violence that can affect homicide rates, we include a classification of each nation in terms of war based on *The State of War and Peace Atlas* (Smith 1997). Nations are coded separately for war involving external enemies as opposed to internal civil war because the later should have greater "exposure to violence" effects without the inhibiting effects that external war can have through increased solidarity. Moreover, several of the Latin American nations are involved in internal conflicts involving the drug trade. Based on James Inciardi's description of the origins of the "cocaine highway" (1986: 73), Columbia, Peru, Equador, and Bolivia were coded as prone to drug or cocaine wars.

Gartner included "cultural heterogeneity" as a correlate of homicide because it was thought to tap "the potential for conflict and an absence of control among groups." This study uses a measure of cultural heterogeneity created by Stark (MicroCase 2000). The multicultural variable is based on a formula calculating the odds that any two persons in a society will differ in their race, religion, ethnicity (tribe), or language group. Some nations such as Japan (less than 1 in 100), Iceland (3 in 100) and Norway (4 in 100) are virtually "homogeneous" while other societies are extremely diverse (e.g., South Africa at 87, Bolivia at 90, and India at 91). Although Gartner presumes such variables affect the potential for conflict and absence of control, they may have their effect in the same manner as proposed by Sampson and Wilson, inhibiting the development of shared respect for agents of control and governmental authority.

Other variables relevant to contemporary versions of social disorganization theory are the "stability" of the government and family relationships. Nations with recently established governments should have higher homicide rates than nations with well-established, relatively stable governments. Nations were coded into these two categories based on Kidron and Segal's, *State of the World Atlas* (1995). Gartner used divorce rates as a measure of unstable family relationships and the same measure is used in this analysis.

Finally, Gartner used the percent of women in the labor force as a measure of "availability." Employment outside the home increases female travel as well as interaction in "unguarded" and recreational activities. Recognizing that it could measure a variety of processes that could either increase or decrease homicide, the same measure is used here (see International Labour Organization 2001). Over two-thirds of women work outside of the home in nations such as Sweden, Iceland and China, compared to less than 20 percent in predominantly Muslim nations such as Iran, Egypt, Pakistan and Syria.

Table 1.1 summarizes the results of a multiple regression analysis for the natural log of homicide rates for eighty-two nations. Percent of females in the labor force, inequality, civil war, Latin American nation, cultural heterogeneity and the government variable are significant correlates of homicide. Neither divorce rates, social welfare, interstate war nor drug wars were significantly related to homicide rates. When insignificant variables are removed from the model, the six significant correlates yielded an $R^2$ of .65.

The results raise serious questions about institutional anomie theory since that theory of global variation in homicide emphasizes the inhibiting impact of social welfare, or "decommodification," on homicide rates. In this multivariate analysis, decommodification does not have a significant effect on homicide rates. This finding may reflect the fact that investments in social welfare require sufficient stability in the government and homogeneity of the population for consensus on such policies to be established. Thus, the same characteristics of nations that facilitate national welfare investments inhibit homicide.

Because these findings are contrary to published findings in support of institutional anomie theory, we examined the intervening links that were proposed to be the mechanisms through which decommodification was supposed to reduce homicide. Decommodification is argued to reduce homicide

**Table 1.1**
**Regression of Homicide Rates (Natural Log) on Key Variables**

N: 82
Multiple R-Square = 0.665
LISTWISE deletion (1-tailed test)  Significance Levels: **=.01, *=.05

|  | Unstand.b | Stand.Beta | Std.Err.b | t |
|---|---|---|---|---|
| FEMEMPLOY | +0.047 | +0.349 | 0.011 | +4.277 ** |
| DIVORCE | -0.088 | -0.062 | 0.122 | - 0.718 |
| GINI | +0.040 | +0.273 | 0.014 | +2.910 ** |
| SOCWELFARE | +0.013 | +0.073 | 0.015 | +0.873 |
| CIVILWAR | +0.799 | +0.233 | 0.259 | +3.083 ** |
| INTERWAR | -0.376 | -0.089 | 0.311 | - 1.207 |
| DRUGWAR | +0.532 | +0.075 | 0.544 | +0.978 |
| LATIN | +032 | +0.329 | 0.295 | +3.502 ** |
| MULTICULT | +0.009 | +0.169 | 0.004 | +2.162 * |
| NEWGOV | +1.022 | +0.369 | 0.207 | +4.948 ** |

by encouraging the creation and stability of familial relationships (i.e., increase birth rates and decrease divorce rates) and to strengthen other institutions that function as sources of informal control (e.g., religious institutions). However, when birth rates and divorce rates are correlated with decommodification, *both relationships are contrary to institutional anomie theory*. Decommodification is negatively correlated with birth rates (r= -.55, p<.01, n=101) and positively related to divorce rates (r= +.34, p<.05, n=89)! Since divorce rates and marriage rates are positively correlated with one another, the relation of decommodification to marriage rates, controlling for divorce rates, was examined. Decommodification is negatively related to marriage rates (r= -.32, p<.05, n=58).

In short, the greater the investment in government programs intended to act as political constraints on the market, the less likely people are to get married and have children, and the freer they are to divorce one another. While contrary to propositions in institutional anomie theory, such findings are not particularly problematic for social learning theory. Any theory that allows people to consider the rewards and costs of alternative choices and institutional commitments can make sense of such findings. Rather than strengthening noneconomic institutions, decommodification lessens dependence on noneconomic institutions for financial support.

The fact that the mediating institutional variables are related in the opposite direction to institutional anomie theory does not mean that decommodification should be a positive correlate of homicide rates. First, it should be noted that these mediating variables do not turn out to be significant correlates of homicide. Second, decommodification is negatively related to inequality and may have an indirect effect, reducing homicide rates through inequality as an intervening variable. To untangle this mystery, we attempted to identify which variables reduced the effect of decommodification to insignificance. The effect of decommodification was reduced to insignificance by any one of three variables—cultural heterogeneity, Latin American nation, or civil war. In contrast, the relation remained significant when either inequality, new government or females in the labor force were introduced individually. Thus, it would be reasonable to propose that the zero-order effect of social welfare disappears because such welfare is negatively correlated with variables that measure conflict, exposure to violence, and cultural heterogeneity. In short, the characteristics of societies that inhibit development of strong social welfare programs are the same characteristics that generate high homicide rates.

In contrast to anomie theory, the data support several observations consistent with social learning theory. First, Latin American societies have higher homicide rates than other societies, despite controls for other variables that could account for such an effect. Without direct measures of "cultural" variables, such findings provide only indirect support for a "tradition" or "culture of violence" argument. The persistence of high homicide rates in the American South despite controls for structural or demographic correlates has encouraged a "cultural" interpretation of regional variations in America, and the results are similar for the Latin nation variable in this global analysis. More research will be necessary before the source of this persistent effect can be identified.

Second, the findings for civil war are consistent with social learning theory and Gartner's notion that "exposure to violence" in one context increases the odds of violence in other contexts. However, it is primarily civil war that has such an effect. Involvement in interstate wars and drug wars does not increase homicide rate. The impact of civil war on homicide rates may reflect (1) the inclusion of civil war deaths in homicide statistics, (2) the social and cultural disorganization associated with civil war, (3) the fact that both forms of violence involve internal conflicts among members of the same social system and/or (4) the effect of civil war on the availability of lethal weapons which can be used in other contexts.

Third, results for heterogeneity and governmental change are quite consistent with those versions of social and cultural disorganization theory which we have argued are most compatible with social learning theory. From a cultural disorganization perspective, social systems characterized by religious, ethnic and racial diversity are especially likely to harbor suspicions and uncertainties about legitimate authority, although there may be strong embracement of the normative worth of law-abiding conduct, and the rule of law in general. In addition, law enforcement policy is likely to stress coercive and punitive means of control, rather than re-integrative forms of control. Re-integrative forms of control are likely to develop in systems with relatively homogeneous populations where the populace can readily identify with offenders (see Braithwaite 1989). In contrast, in heterogeneous societies, the same diversity that precludes strong national policies of decommodification, precludes empathy towards people who are likely to be defined as outsiders.

Finally, if the percent of females in the labor force is accepted as a measure of availability, then the data are consistent with both routine activities theory and social learning theory. Unfortunately, there are no available measures of "routines" that encourage unsupervised peer group interaction that would allow social learning theory to be contrasted with routine activities theory. Social learning theory specifies that certain routines are more victimogenic and criminogenic than others, a specification that is not built into routine activities theory. Moreover, it is not clear whether social learning theory implies comparable relationships between a peer-oriented culture and all forms of crime Since a considerable proportion of homicides involve domestic violence, variations in peer interaction may have little relevance to homicide rates. In contrast, variations in peer interaction and culture may be quite consequential for property crimes that peak in the teenage years.

## Summary and Final Observations

This chapter addressed several issues that have impeded the development and application of social learning theory on a macro level. Social learning theory has fared the best and strain theory has fared the worst in research using self-report survey data. One response to this state of affairs by critics has been to caution us about an "individualistic" bias in criminology, dismissing the relevance of survey data to macro-level issues and reminding us of the hazards of generalizing across levels of analysis or explanation. However, we argue that such critics confuse sources of data with levels of aggregation and levels of explanation. The fact that survey data is collected from individuals does not preclude aggregating it to deal with macro-level topics, as has been done in recent ecological research. Moreover, survey research depicted by critics as addressing "the acts of individuals" does no such thing. All research testing social learning theory has focused on forms of Messner and Rosenfeld's macro-level question, "Why is crime patterned in systematic ways across social categories?" When social learning researchers examine whether youths categorized on the basis of their peer group associations have a higher prevalence and incidence of delinquency, they are proposing one partial answer to exactly that question. The focus is not on acts of individuals. Rather, the focus is on comparing averages or proportions across social categories, or explaining variation among people categorized into more intricate groups.

The fact that social learning theory was presented initially as a reformulation of differential association theory has led some critics to link it to "cultural deviance" theory as its macro-level partner. Once that link is proposed, critics concentrate on the problems with an extreme cultural deviance theory, as if those criticisms applied to social learning theory. Social learning theory does include normative learning mechanisms and does imply that values, norms and beliefs are relevant to the explanation of crime. However, it also differs distinctively from cultural deviance theory in that it allows patterns of crime to be sustained through processes of imitation, modeling and desensitization, differential reinforcement and other processes that are conceptually and empirically distinct from normative, definitional or cultural learning.

Our examination of research reported as part of the ecological revival yielded two observations. First, social learning theory is virtually ignored in attempts to generate hypotheses or explain results. That neglect would not be a source of concern were it not for the fact that much of that research focuses on variables that are more central to social learning theory than the theories that are cited. Osgood and colleagues attempt to elaborate on routine activities by including activities that free youths from adult supervision and increase their involvement with peers. Yet, had routine activities theory never existed, their prediction is a direct derivative of differential association or social learning theory. Indeed, social control theory is cited as a precedent despite the fact that it challenges the criminogenic influence of peers.

Our second observation is that the theories proposed in the explanation of ecological variations in crime include variables uniquely relevant to social learning theory (e.g., Sampson and Groves). Moreover, the same claim can be made about explanations of global variations in homicide. Social learning theory "fits" with routine activities theory in that it includes "availability" as a precondition. Hence, when routine activities theory is supported the results also support social learning theory. However, when theorists start differentiating peer group activities as unusually victimogenic, they are not "elaborating" routine activities theory. The activities differentiated go well "beyond routine activities" (Jensen and Brownfield 1986) to encompass the types of criminogenic routines emphasized in social learning theory. When theorists propose variations in specific types of "definitions" or impediments to the embracement of mainstream cultural values or norms (Sampson and Wilson), they are including variables that cannot be derived from routine activities theory nor institutional anomie theory, but can be derived from social learning and social control theory.

To conclude, we propose that the order of theories in terms of their ability to explain ecological and global variations is actually the same as their order in terms of ability to explain the prevalence and incidence of crime and delinquency based on self-reports collected from individuals. Those analyses that have explained the most variance at the ecological level incorporate variables that cannot be derived from the theories typically cited (e.g., routine activities and social disorganization-control theories), but fit very well with social learning theory. Moreover, macro-level versions of social learning or social control theory explain global variations in homicide better than macro-level versions of strain theory. Rather than dismiss prior research as fatally flawed based on a mythical individualistic bias, we propose that a macro-elaboration of the causal logic embodied in social learning theory promises to reveal continuities across levels of aggregation and levels of explanation.

## Notes

1.  The types of offenses that are deemed to be "serious" and, therefore, within the theoretical domain of institutional anomie have been quite elusive. As a derivative of Merton's theory, it should have applied to those instrumental crimes that were depicted as forms of "innovation" in the pursuit of economic goals. Yet, in the most recent edition of *Crime and the American Dream*, Messner and Rosenfeld dismiss international data on offenses as serious as burglary and propose that the theory applies primarily to homicide. Such elusiveness is disturbing in that our own

analysis of United Nation's data on global variations in burglary rates shows them to be *positively* related to expenditures on decommodification, a central variable in institutional anomie theory, while homicide rates are negatively related (as claimed in their work in *Social Forces*, 1997 ). Of course, if there is only one offense that qualifies as sufficiently "serious" or reliably measured to test the theory, then the theory cannot compete as a general theory of crime. Moreover, analyses presented later in this chapter suggest that other theories are more promising candidates for explaining homicide rates as well.

2.    The dismissal of self-report data as dealing with "minor" offenses is blatantly misleading in several ways. For one, the Uniform Crime Reports "serious" crime index includes the same trivial offenses as self-report surveys. Over one-half of the "Part I" offenses are larcenies, including shoplifting. Second, much, if not most, of the self-report research has differentiated among types of offenses and focused on serious violent offenses, as well as more common property crimes (see Jensen and Rojek 1998: chap. 4).

3.    Ironically, institutional anomie theory can be criticized for according too much influence to cultural values. As presented by Messner and Rosenfeld, cultural pressures for economic success are so strong that they are internalized despite their debilitating effect on families and other institutional sources of informal social. Not only is no explanation given for how such consensus is maintained when it undermines the basic institutions most involved in socialization, but no actual empirical evidence of such consensus is presented. Since economic values provide the motivational pressure for deviance when alternative routes to success are limited, it can be argued that from an institutional anomie perspective "all behavior is consistent with underlying values (2001: 47)." Social learning theory does not require such consensus on values and posits an explanation for why people violate norms and ignore values that they appear to accept.

## References

Akers, R. L. 1977. *Deviant Behavior*. Belmont, CA: Wadsworth.

Akers, R. L., M. D. Krohn, L. Lanza-Kaduce, and M. Radosevich. 1978. "Social Learning and Deviant Behavior." *American Sociological Review* 44 (August): 636-55.

_____. 1998. *Social Learning and Social Structure: A General Theory of Crime and Deviance*. Boston: Northeastern University Publishing Company.

_____. 2000. *Criminological Theories: Introduction, Evaluation, and Application*. Third Edition. Los Angeles, CA: Roxbury Publishing Company.

Bartusch, Dawn Jeglum, and Ross Matsueda. 1996. "Gender, Reflected Appraisals, and Labeling: A Cross-Group Test of an Interactionist Theory of Delinquency." *American Sociological Review* 75: 145-176.

Bellair, P. E. 1997. "Social Interaction and Community Crime: Examining the Importance of Neighborhood Networks." *Criminology* 35: 677-701.

Bernard, T. 1987. "Testing Structural Strain Theories." *Journal of Research in Crime and Delinquency* 24: 262-290.

Braithwaite, J. 1989. *Crime, Shame, and Reintegration*. Cambridge: Cambridge University Press.

Burgess, R. L., and R. L. Akers. 1966. "A Differential Association-Reinforcement Theory of Criminal Behavior." *Social Problems* 14 (Fall):128-47.

Bursik, R. J., Jr., and H. G. Grasmick. 1993. *Neighborhoods and Crime: The Dimensions of Effective Social Control*. New York: Lexington Books.

Cohen, L., and M. Felson. 1979. "Social Changes and Crime Rate Trends: A Routine Activity Approach." *American Sociological Review* 46 (October): 505-24.

Coleman, J. 1990. *Foundations of Social Theory*. Cambridge, MA: Belnap Press.

Costello, B., and P. R. Vowell. 1999. "Testing Control Theory and Differential Association: A Reanalysis of the Richmond Youth Project Data." *Criminology* 37: 815-842.

DeFleur, Lois. 1967. "Cross-cultural comparison of juvenile offenders." *Social Problems* 14: 483-492.

Empey L. T. 1967. "Delinquency Theory and Recent Research." *Journal of Research in Crime and Delinquency* 4: 32-42.

Felson, M. 2001. "The Routine Activity Approach: A Very Versatile Theory of Crime." In R. Paternoster and R. Bachman, *Explaining Criminals and Crime*. Los Angeles, CA: Roxbury Press.

Fox, James Allen, and Jack Levine. 2001. *The Will to Kill: Making Sense of Senseless Murder*. Boston: Allyn and Bacon.

Gartner, R. 1990. "The Victims of Homicide: A Temporal and Cross-national Comparison." *American Sociological Review* 55: 92-106.

Gibbs, Jack P. 1981. *Norms, Deviance, and Social Control*. New York: Elsevier.

———. 1989. *Control: Sociology's Central Notion*. Urbana: University of Illinois Press.

———. 1994. *A Theory About Control*. Boulder, CO: Westview Press.

Hirschi, T. 1969. *Causes of Delinquency*. Berkeley, CA: University of California Press

Inciardi, James A. 1986. *The War on Drugs*. Palo Alto, CA: Mayfield Publishing Company.

International Labour Organization. 2001. *World Employment Report 2001*. Geneva: International Labour Office.

International Labour Organization. 2000. *The Cost of Social Security, 1900-1996*. Geneva: International Labour Office.

Jensen, G. F. 1972. "Parents, Peers and Delinquent Action: A Test of the Differential Association Hypothesis." *American Journal of Sociology* 78 (November): 562-75.

Jensen, G. F., and D. Brownfield. 1983. "Parents and Drugs: Specifying the Consequences of Attachment." *Criminology* 21 (November): 543-54.

———. 1986. "Gender, Lifestyles and Victimization: Beyond Routine Activity." *Violence and Victims* 1: 85-99.

Jensen, G. F., and D. G. Rojek. 1998. *Delinquency and Youth Crime*. Third Edition. Prospect Heights, IL: Waveland Press, Inc.

Kidron, M., and R. Segal. 1995. *State of the World Atlas*. New York: Simon and Schuster.

Kornhauser, R. 1978. *Social Sources of Delinquency: An Appraisal of Analytic Models*. Chicago: University of Chicago Press.

Lester, D. 1996. *Patterns of Suicide and Homicide in the World*. Commack, NY: Nova Science Publishers, Inc.

Luckenbill, D. F., and D. P. Doyle. 1989. "Structural Position and Violence: Developing a Cultural Explanation." *Criminology* 27: 419-436.

Markowitz, F. E., P. E. Bellair, A. E. Liska and J. Liu. 2001. "Extending Social Disorganization Theory: Modeling the Relationship between Cohesion, Disorder, and Fear." *Criminology* 39: 293-321.

Matsueda, R. 1982. "Testing Control Theory and Differential Association." *American Sociological Review* 47: 489-504.

———. 1989. "Moral Beliefs and Deviance." *Social Forces* 2: 428-457.

Matsueda, R., and K. Heimer. 1987. "Race, Family Structure, and Delinquency: A Test of Differential Association and Social Control Theories." *American Sociological Review* 52 826-40.

Matza, D. 1964. *Delinquency and Drift*. New York: John Wiley, 1964.

Matza, D., and G. M. Sykes..1961. "Juvenile Delinquency and Subterranean Values." *American Sociological Review* 26: 712-17.

Merton, R. 1938 "Social Structure and Anomie." *American Sociological Review* 3: 672-682.
_____. 1957. *Social Theory and Social Structure*. New York: Free Press.

Messner, S. F., and R. Rosenfeld. 1997. "Political Restraint of the Market and Levels of Criminal Homicide: A Cross-national Application of Institutional Anomie Theory." *Social Forces* 75: 1393-1416.
_____. 2000. "An Institutional Anomie Theory of Crime." In R. Paternoster and R. Bachman, *Explaining Criminals and Crime*. Los Angeles, CA: Roxbury Press.
_____. 2001. *Crime and the American Dream*. Third Edition. Belmont, CA: Wadsworth.

MicroCase Corporation. 1999-2000. *MicroCase Data Archive*, Bellevue, WA: MicoCase Corporation.

Miller, W. 1958. "Lower Class Culture as a Generating Milieu of Gang Delinquency." *Journal of Social Issues* 14: 5-19.

Oquist, Paul. 1980. *Violence, Conflict, and Politics in Columbia*. New York: Academic Press.

Osgood, D. W., J. K. Wilson, P. M. O'Malley, J. G. Bachman, and L. D. Johnston. 1996. "Routine Activities and Individual Deviant Behavior." *American Sociological Review* 61: 635-655.

Patterson, E. B. 1991. "Poverty, Income Inequality, and Community Crime Rates." *Criminology* 29: 755-776.

Rosenfeld, R., and S. F. Messner. 1995. "Crime and the American Dream: An Institutional Analysis." *Advances in Criminological Theory* 6: 159-181.

Sampson, R. J., and W. J. Wilson. 1995. "Toward a Theory of Race, Crime and Urban Inequality." Pp. 37-54 in *Crime and Inequality*, J. Hagan and R. D. Peterson (Eds.). Stanford, CA: Stanford University Press.

Sampson, R. J., and W.B. Groves. 1989. "Community Structure and Crime: Testing Social Disorganization Theory." *American Journal of Sociology* 94: 774-802.

Sampson, R. J., S. W. Raudenbusch, and F. Earls. 1997. "Neighborhoods and Violent Crime: A Multi-Level Study of Collective Efficacy." *Science* 277: 918-924.

Sellin, T. 1938. *Culture, Conflict and Crime*. New York: Research Council.

Shaw, Clifford, F. Zorbaugh, H. D. McKay, and L. S. Contrell. 1929. *Delinquency Areas*. Chicago: University of Chicago Press.

Smith, D. 1997. *The State of War and Peace Atlas*. Third Edition. New York: Penguin Reference.

Stevens, Evelyn. 1973. "Marianismo: The Other Face of Machismo in Latin America." In Ann Pescatello (ed.), *Male and Female in Latin America*. Pittsburgh PA: University of Pittsburgh Press.

Sutherland, E. H. 1934. *Principles of Criminology*. Second Edition. Philadelphia: J. B. Lippincott
_____.1939. *Principles of Criminology*. Third Edition. Philadelphia: J. B. Lippincott

Sutherland, E. H., D. R. Cressey, and D. F. Luckenbill. 1992. *Principles of Criminology*. Eleventh Edition. Dix Hills, NY: General Hall, Inc.

Sykes, G. M., and D. Matza. 1957. "Techniques of Neutralization: A Theory of Delinquency." *American Journal of Sociology* 22 (December): 664-70.

Taylor, R. B. 2001. "The Ecology of Crime, Fear, and Delinquency: Social Disorganization Versus Social Efficacy." In R. Paternoster and R. Bachman, *Explaining Criminals and Crime*. Los Angeles, CA: Roxbury Press.

Tittle. C. R., and R. Paternoster. 2000. *Social Deviance and Crime: An Organizational and Theoretical Approach*. Los Angeles, CA: Roxbury Press.

Vold, G.B., and T. J. Bernard. 1986. *Theoretical Criminology*. Third Edition. New York: Oxford University Press.

World Health Organization. 2000. *World Health Statistics Annual*, 1997-1999, Online Edition.

Yinger, M. 1960. "Contraculture and Subculture." *American Sociological Review* 25: 625-35.

Zimring, F., and G. Hawkins. 1997. *Crime is Not the Problem: Lethal Violence in America*. New York: Oxford University Press.

# 2

# Substance Use by Korean Adolescents: A Cross-Cultural Test of Social Learning, Social Bonding, and Self-Control Theories

*Sunghyun Hwang and Ronald L. Akers*

The larger question to which the research reported here is addressed is the cross-cultural applicability of criminological theories. Are theories developed and tested in Western societies capable of accounting for crime and deviance not only in North America or in other Western societies but also in non-Western societies with very different traditions, social structure, and culture? Are the theories on which we rely to explain involvement of youth in drug use and on which we base much of our efforts to prevent and control it truly general explanations that identify the causes and processes of adolescent substance use among youth wherever it is found? Are they culture-bound theories that identify variables operative in only one kind of society, or are they generalizable to different kinds of societies?

We approach these questions by testing the empirical validity of social learning (Akers 1973, 1998), social bonding (Hirschi 1969), and self-control (Gottfredson and Hirschi 1990) theories as explanations of adolescent substance use in a sample of urban adolescents in South Korea. These three theories are among the most frequently applied and tested and endorsed by American criminologists as explanations of both serious and minor offending (Ellis and Walsh 1999a, 1999b; Stitt and Giacopassi 1992;). The research literature is extensive and some of it compares social learning with other theories, usually social bonding and strain theories ( Agnew 1991b; Akers 1998, 2000; Akers and Cochran 1985; Akers et al. 1979; Akers and Lee 1999; Benda 1994; Benda and DiBlasio 1991; Costello 2000; Costello and Vowell 1999; Kandel and Davies 1991; Krohn et al. 1984; Longshore 1998; Matsueda and Heimer 1987; McGee 1992; White et al. 1987; Wright et al. 1999). A few studies have been done outside North America (Bruinsma 1992; Kandel and Adler 1982; Lee 1989; Junger-Tas 1992; Yang 1999; Zhang and Messner 1995). There has been some research on adolescent substance use in Korea, but this has been largely descriptive. Korea has been experiencing increases in consumption of alcohol, tobacco, and other substances by both adults and adolescents (Kim and Park 1995; Supreme Public Prosecutors Office 1995; Korean Youth Association 1996). None of this research tests theories of adolescent drug use in Korea.

## Social Learning Theory

Akers' social learning theory focuses on four major explanatory concepts (Akers 1985, 1998; Akers et al. 1979). *Differential association* refers to the individuals and groups (primary groups such as friends and family as well as secondary group such as colleagues and work groups) with whom one identifies and interacts. It is in differential association with others that one is exposed to and learns definitions, is exposed to behavioral models, and receives social reinforcement or punishment for taking or refraining from some action. *Definitions*, as used in social learning theory, are attitudes, general and specific beliefs, or verbalizations which define for the actor what is appropriate or inappropriate; that is, what should and should not be done in a social situation. Thus, one may hold definitions conducive to taking or refraining from some action. *Differential reinforcement* is the balance of rewarding or desired outcomes and negative or undesirable consequences of actions. The greater the reinforcement, on balance, contingent on or anticipated for a given action, the more likely it is to be taken and repeated. The most important of these are social reinforcement and punishment through the approval or disapproval of one's peers, parents, and other significant groups and individuals. *Imitation* is the process of observational learning wherein one models his or her own behavior after that of others.

> Whether individuals will abstain from or take drugs (and whether they will continue or desist) depends on the past, present, and anticipated future rewards and punishments perceived to be attached to abstinence and use (*differential reinforcement*). The physiological effects of drugs and alcohol on the nervous system can function as direct non-social reinforcers and punishers. These effects also acquire secondary or conditioned reinforcing effects (even though they may be initially aversive) by being experienced in the context of group approval and other sources of social reinforcement for use. Individual variations in the probability of social reinforcement, exposure to definitions favorable or unfavorable to drug use, and observation of using and abstinent behavioral models (*imitation*) comes from *differential association* with primary groups of family and friends, other reference groups and significant others, including to some extent distal groups and models portrayed in the mass media. Through these processes the person learns attitudes, orientations, or evaluative knowledge which are favorable or unfavorable to using drugs (*definitions*) as well as the

behavior needed to acquire and ingest drugs in a way that produces effects. The more individuals define use as good, permissible, or excusable rather than holding to general or specific negative attitudes toward drugs, the more likely they are to use them. (Akers 1998: 171)

There is a large body of evidence that provides consistent and strong support of social learning theory as an explanation of adolescent substance use and delinquency. (See Agnew 1991a, 1993, 1994; Akers et al. 1979; Akers and Lee 1996, 1998; Conger and Simons 1995; Dabney 1995; Dembo et al. 1986; Elliott et al. 1985; Inciardi et al. 1993; Kandel and Davies 1991; Kandel and Andrews 1987; Lauritsen 1993; Massey and Krohn. 1986; Matsueda 1982; Matsueda and Heimer 1987; McGee 1992; Patterson and Dishion 1985; Rowe and Gulley 1992; Warr 1993a, 1993b, 1996; Warr and Stafford 1991; Winfree et al. 1989; Winfree et al. 1993; Winfree et al. 1994; Wood et al. 1995).

## Social Bonding Theory

Social bonding theory (Hirschi 1969) hypothesizes that the more strongly individuals are bonded to society (especially through the family, peers, and school) the more likely they are to conform to the norms of conventional society and avoid deviant behavior. This theory relies on four elements of this bonding as its main explanatory concepts.

*Attachment* refers to the affective relationships that one has with other people. The more strongly the youth is attached (the closer the relationships) to others, the less likely he or she is to engage in disapproved substance use or other forms of delinquent behavior. It is the strength of attachment to others, rather than the character of the persons to whom one is attached, that is important. Therefore, social bonding theory proposes that adolescents using the substance will have weak attachment to both conforming and deviant peers. *Commitment* refers to an adolescent's stakes or investments in conformity. The greater this commitment the more the investment is threatened by commission of deviant behavior, and therefore, the greater the likelihood of refraining from disapproved substance use. *Involvement* refers to the notion that individuals who are heavily participating in conventional activities simply do not have much time to engage in deviant behavior. Therefore, the more highly the adolescent scores on conventional involvement, the lower the probabilities of his or her using alcohol, tobacco, or other substances. *Belief* is acceptance of the moral validity of general conventional values, norms, and rules. Adolescents who adopt the general values of their parents, the law, and conventional society are unlikely candidates for substance use or other social deviance. There is a large body of research in the United States that provides support (in the weak to moderate range) for the social bonding theory of adolescent substance use and delinquency (see Hindelang 1973;

Johnson 1979; Stark et al. 1980; Wiatrowski et al. 1981; Krohn and Massey 1980; Krohn, et al. 1983; Agnew 1985, 1991a, 1991b; Cernkovich and Giordano 1992; Rankin and Kern 1994; Bahr et al. 1995).

## Self-Control Theory

Self-control theory (Gottfredson and Hirschi 1990) contends that the propensity to engage in any and all criminal behavior and "analogous" behavior such as alcohol, tobacco, and drug use is caused by low self-control in the presence of opportunity. Low self-control is the outcome of ineffective childhood socialization wherein parents do not closely monitor the child's behavior, do not recognize misbehavior when it occurs, and neglect to punish the child for it. While self-control is posed as an unobservable or latent construct, Gottfredson and Hirschi enumerate a number of elements of low self-control, empirical indicators of which have been widely used as measures of self-control (Arneklev et al. 1993; Grasmick et al. 1993).

*Impulsivity* refers to inability to defer gratification and tendency to act on impulse without attention to longer-term consequences. *Preference for simple tasks* refers to the tendency of the person with low self-control to avoid complex tasks and prefer easily accomplished tasks. People with low self-control also tend to be adventuresome rather than cautious and to be *risk-seeking*. Those who have low self-control have a *preference for physical activities* that require little skill or planning rather than cognitive activity. Those with low self-control also tend to *self-centered* and insensitive to the feelings of others. Finally, not surprisingly, Gottfredson and Hirschi view low self-control as characterized by quick temper, *low tolerance* for frustration and physical rather than verbal response to conflict.

Research using attitudinal indicators of these various dimensions as well as other less direct measures has shown mixed and moderate support for self-control theory among adolescents and adults (Arneklev et al. 1993; Brownfield and Sorenson 1993; Burton et al. 1994; Evans et al. 1997; Gibbs and Giever 1995; Gibbs et al. 1994; Grasmick et al. 1993; Keane et al. 1993; Nagin and Paternoster 1993; Paternoster and Brame 1998; Piquero and Tibbetts 1996; Polakowski 1994; Tremblay et al. 1995; Pratt and Cullen 2000).

Hirschi and Gottfredson (1993, 1994) argue that measuring the various dimensions of self-control by attitudinal measures as is commonly done in the literature, following Grasmick et al. (1993), is not the preferred methodology. Rather they prefer "behavioral" measures of self-control as the independent variables, i.e., measuring analogous behavior such as drinking, smoking, and drug use as independent variables, with measures of crime or delinquency as the dependent variables. And, some researchers do attempt to test the theory in this way (LaGrange and Silverman 1999). The problem with this approach is that it does not measure self-control independently of the very behavior it is supposed to cause:

> ...using such behavioral measures of self-control only perpetuates the tautology problem. In the theory, crime, delinquency, and analogous behavior are *all* explained by the same underlying propensity, called low self-control. Therefore, all of these are measures of the dependent variable (criminal propensity) and none can be used as the measure of the independent variable (self-control). To do so tautologically equates criminal propensity and self-control; it assumes the very causal relationship that one is testing. The same tautology problem is encountered when prior delinquent behavior is taken as a measure of self-control as the independent variable and then correlated with current or future delinquent behavior as the dependent variable. (Akers 2000:113)

The tendency for one form of deviant behavior to be related to another form is well known (e.g., the drugs/crime or drugs/delinquency nexus or the multi-drug use pattern). All general theories claim all forms of deviance and crime are produced by the independent variables, process, or factors proposed by that theory. Proponents of any theory then could nominate some of those forms (say drug use, burglary, and lying) as indicators of the theoretical variables, factors, or process and nominate others (say cheating, robbery, and sexual deviance) as indicators of the dependent variables. It would come as no surprise that such a procedure would greatly enhance the chance that support would be found for the theory. There is no theoretical justification to single out self-control theory as the only theory for which this is allowed.

This becomes an especially acute problem when the dependent variables are measures of substance use that are themselves instances of analogous behaviors. We cannot use frequency of drinking as the indicator of self-control and smoking as the dependent variable and hold that as a valid test of the theory. One cannot use measures of substance use as both the independent (self-control) and dependent (substance use) variables. Therefore, the preferred non-tautological technique for testing self-control theory anytime is to use attitudinal measures rather than analogous behavior measures of self-control. It is the only acceptable technique when testing the theory's propositions that differences in self-control account for differences in the analogous behavior of smoking and drinking.

## Sampling and Procedures

The data in this study were gathered by administering a self-report questionnaire to a sample of adolescents in Pusan, South Korea, in 1999. The target population for the study consisted of high school students attending the tenth and eleventh grades in each of the sixteen districts (Gu) of Pusan. The student population was stratified by district, gender, and high school system (liberal and industrial),[1] and students were selected from those strata at random. A classroom in each randomly selected boys and girls high school was randomly sampled from the required or general enrollment classes and all students (40 to 45) in that class were included in the sample. The questionnaire was administered to all students in attendance in the selected class who had obtained written permission from the school principal prior to the day,[2] a total of 1,035 students. All of them completed the instrument (100 percent response rate). However, twenty-three of the respondents were excluded because their questionnaires were too incomplete. Therefore, the sample size in this study is 1,012. With each class, the teacher was not present during the test. Instead, the researcher introduced himself as a graduate student of sociology, engaged in a study of adolescent substance use. The questionnaire instruments were distributed by the researcher, and the informed consent statement read to the subjects. They were informed as to the complete anonymity of their responses, and were shown the ballot-box style receptacle for the questionnaire instrument. The respondents then completed the instrument and placed it in the box. Administration of the instrument was accomplished within one class period (approximately forty minutes).

## Measurement

### Dependent Variables

The dependent variables in this study are self-reports of use of alcohol and tobacco on two different items, frequency of lifetime use and frequency use in the past year. Response options were: never, once or twice, several times, less than once a month, once or twice a month, at least once a week but not everyday, and every day or nearly everyday.

### Sociodemographic Variables

Although sociodemographic variables can be used to index theoretically relevant structural variables (Akers 1998), they are included here only as control variables in the regression models. These are gender, grade level, school type (liberal or industrial), family structure (living with biological parents, father and stepmother, mother and stepfather, father only, mother only or others), annual family income (six categories from below 500,000 Won[3] to above 3,000,000 Won), parents' occupational level (eight categories from (1) "unemployed" to (8) "professional workers"), parents' educational level (number of years of schooling completed), and religious affiliation (Buddhist, Protestant, Catholic, others, or none).

*Social Learning Variables*

*Definitions.* Following previous research , the concept of definitions was operationalized by four indicators each for alcohol and tobacco use. *Balance of positive-negative definitions* was a single-item Likert measure of the degree to which the respondent's own attitudes, on balance, were approving or disapproving of using alcohol or tobacco (asked separately). *Proscriptive definitions* was a single item Likert measure, asking "is it wrong to use drugs?" *Law abiding/violation definitions* was a single item, asking the respondent's obedient or violating attitudes toward law in general. "Neutralizing definitions" was a scale of three Likert items. For instance, "it is all right for people to use drugs as long as they control it." (The alpha =.52 for this scale is low but it is still retained as a scale in the analysis.)

*Differential Association.* Differential association has both a behavioral dimension (what others with whom one is in primary group interaction are doing) and a normative dimension (what values, norms, and attitudes that others hold). The measures of these dimensions here relate to both the peer and family group. The behavioral dimension is measured by differential peer association, respondents' report of "how often" and what proportion "how many" of one's close friends use alcohol and tobacco, producing a two-item scale for alcohol (alpha =.76) and for tobacco (alpha =.77), and respondents' reports of use of alcohol and tobacco by their fathers and mothers. The normative dimension is measured by the relatively approving or disapproving attitudes regarding teenage consumption of alcohol and tobacco that respondents perceive are held by close friends (peer norm qualities) and parents (parents' norm qualities).

*Differential Reinforcement.* Differential reinforcement is indexed by several measures. There are "parents' rewarding or punishing reaction" (respondents' report of actual or anticipated positive or negative sanctions of parents for respondents' use of drugs, ranging from encouraging their use to turning them into the authorities) and "friends' rewarding or punishing reactions" (respondents' reports of positive or negative sanctions by their friends to respondents' use of drugs, ranging from becoming closer friends to turning them into the authorities). There are three other measures of differential reinforcement: Overall reinforcement balance is the respondents' perception of positive and negative consequences of drinking or smoking, ranging from "mainly good" to "mainly bad." Caught by teachers is the respondents' perception of the probability that school teachers would catch "someone like yourself" using alcohol and tobacco. Rewards-costs of using is the difference when the sum of seven items (each for alcohol and tobacco) measuring perceived detrimental outcomes is subtracted from the sum of seven items measuring perceived benefits of drinking and smoking.

*Imitation* was measured by four single items asking about "observing others using alcohol, tobacco, or other substances has influenced me to use."

This was asked separately for peers, parents or other admired adults, person in the media, and advertisements for alcohol or tobacco. All of the social learning variables were coded so that a positive correlation with frequency of alcohol and tobacco use showed that the relationship was in the theoretically expected direction.

*Social Bonding Variables*

*Attachment.* Attachment was operationalized by five Likert scales measuring school attachment, parental attachment, peer attachment, parental supervision, and religious attachment. "School attachment" included two items on positive feelings toward school and the importance of good grades in school. (Alpha =.34 is low but the scale was still retained in the analysis.) "Parental attachment" was measured by a single item asking about how close the respondent feels to his or her parents. "Peer attachment" was also measured by a single item asking the same question about friends. "Parental supervision" was measured by a single item asking respondents whether their parents usually know where they are when they are away from home. "Religious attachment" was measured by a single item asking how often respondents attend church or temple.

*Commitment.* Commitment had three measures, educational aspiration, occupational aspiration, and grade-point average. "Educational aspiration" was measured by two items (Alpha =.40 is low but the scale is retained in the analysis) asking how far they plan to go in school and how important it is to them that they achieve their scholastic goals. "Occupational aspiration" was measured by a single item, asking how important it is to obtain a well-paid, secure job following completion of their education. The final measure of commitment was reported ranking in class (equivalent to grade-point average in American schools).

*Involvement.* Involvement was measured by a single item, asking how much daily time the student spends on school homework.

*Belief.* Belief was measured by three items asking the extent to which respondents endorsed or held positive attitudes toward values and rules of parents (parental norms), obeying and respecting the law (legal norms), and importance of religion. Akers (1989, 2000) has argued that there is considerable conceptual overlap between the concept of definitions favorable and unfavorable in social learning theory and the concept of belief in social bonding theory. We resolve this here by assigning these indicators of belief in general conventional norms and values as measures of the bonding concept, but recognize that there is still some overlap between the bonding measure of respect for the law and the social learning measure of law abiding/violating definitions.

All social bonding variables were coded so that a negative correlation with frequency of alcohol and tobacco use showed that the relationship was in the theoretically expected direction.

*Self-Control Variables*

As noted earlier, six attitudinal components of what Gottfredson and Hirschi call low self-control, rather than behavioral indicators, were identified: *impulsivity, preference for simple rather than complex tasks, risk seeking, preference for physical rather than cerebral activities, self-centered orientation, and volatile temper linked to a low tolerance for frustration.* Each of these were measured by a single item asking respondents the extent to which they agreed that (on a 4-point Likert scale from "strongly agree" to "strongly disagree") that the characteristic described them personally. Agreement indicated low self-control and a negative correlation the measures with alcohol and tobacco use showed the relationship was in the theoretically expected direction.

## Statistical Analysis

A series of multiple regression analyses are conduced, in which sets of variables (i.e., sociodemographic variables, social learning variables, social bonding variables, and self-control variables) are entered into equations for alcohol and tobacco use. First, to examine the explanatory power of each of the theories of social learning, social bonding, and self-control, separate regression models (one for alcohol use and one for tobacco use) were run that contained only variables derived from that theory (see Tables 2.1 and 2.2). Second, to examine the relative explanatory power of variables derived from the three theories, a full regression model with all theoretical variables and sociodemographic variables and four regression models with different sets of variables omitted were run (see Tables 2.3 and 2.4). Frequency of lifetime use and frequency use in the past year were nearly perfectly correlated for both alcohol and tobacco only frequency use in the past year was retained as the dependent variables in the regression models.

## Results

Table 2.1 indicates that social learning theory is strongly supported as an explanation of both drinking and smoking among Korean adolescents in this sample. The social learning model explains 58 percent of the variance in alcohol use and 67 percent of the variance in tobacco use. The differential peer association variable has the strongest net effect on alcohol (B=.508) and tobacco (B=.541). In addition, measures of differential reinforcement have significant net effects on both alcohol and tobacco consumption, and definitions and imitation variables have significant net effects on tobacco use. At least one of the measures of each of the principal social learning concepts of definitions, differential association, differential reinforcement, and imitation

Table 2.1
Social Learning Models of Adolescent substance Use in Korea

| Variables | Alcohol | Tobacco |
|---|---|---|
| **Definition** | | |
| positive/negative definitions | .032 | .055* |
| proscriptive definitions | .003 | .044* |
| law abiding/violating definitions | -.024 | -.022 |
| neutralizing definitions | -.009 | -.029 |
| **Differential Association** | | |
| differential peer association | .508*** | .541*** |
| father's use | .058* | .018 |
| mother's use | .007 | .006 |
| peers' norm qualities | .047 | .054* |
| parents' norm qualities | -.045 | -.026 |
| **Differential Reinforcement** | | |
| parents' reaction | .042 | .132*** |
| friends' reaction | .065** | -.010 |
| caught by teachers | -.021 | -.024 |
| rewards-costs of use | .056* | .058* |
| overall reinforcement balance | .075** | .109*** |
| **Imitation** | | |
| peers | .024 | .012 |
| parents or other admired adults | .076 | .086* |
| persons in media | .069 | -.016 |
| advertisements | .050 | .057 |
| $R^2$ | .576 | .669 |
| N | 904 | 889 |

\* p< .05
\*\* p< .01
\*\*\* p< .001

have significant independent effects on adolescent smoking in this Korean sample. The levels of explained variance are as high as or higher than the levels found in tests of social learning models on adolescent substance use in the United States, and the relative ranking of the four main sets of social learning variables in their net effects on substance use in this Korean sample are quite similar to what has been found in American studies. Thus, all of these findings on the explanatory power of social learning theory, with the noteworthy exception that definitions favorable and unfavorable have no significant net effect on drinking in this sample, comport well with what is most often found in American studies (see Akers et al. 1979; Spear and Akers 1988, and other studies cited above).

Table 2.2 presents the results of OLS models of alcohol and tobacco use regressed on the social bonding and self-control variables separately. In Table 2.2, the social bonding models appear to have moderate explanatory power for both alcohol use (15 percent of variance explained) and tobacco use (20 percent of explained variance). Although the belief variables do not have significant net effects on either drinking or smoking, most of the variables listed under each of the other social bonding concepts have significant net effects on both alcohol and tobacco use by adolescents. Parental attachment, peer attachment, parental supervision, educational aspirations, grade-point average, and time spent on homework, all have significant net effects on both alcohol and tobacco use, and occupational aspirations has a significant net effect on smoking in this Korean sample .

However, the effects of peer attachment and occupational aspirations on alcohol and tobacco use are positive; the greater the peer attachment and the higher the occupational aspirations, the great the likelihood of using. This is, of course, opposite from the direction theoretically expected by social bonding. But, that is what is typically found in studies among American adolescents as well. Moreover, the social bonding model in general fits the data on these Korean adolescents about as well as it fits data on substance use among American adolescents. (See Akers and Cochran 1985; Krohn and Massey 1980 and other studies cited above.)

The self-control measures in Table 2.2 explain about 12 percent of the variance in alcohol use and tobacco use with significant net effects from impulsivity, risk-seeking, preference for physical activities, and low tolerance. Again, this level of support for the theory in this Korean study is comparable to that found in American studies of self-control theory cited above.

The results of the OLS regression analyses in Table 2.1 and 2.2 show that for both alcohol and tobacco use there is strong support for the social learning theory and moderate support for social bonding and self-control theories when considered in separate models.

**Relative Explanatory Power of the Theoretical Models**

We turn now to an examination of the relative explanatory power of the independent variables from each of the theories when all are placed in the same regression models. To accomplish this purpose, all independent variables, including sociodemographic variables, are placed in a single full re-

Table 2.2
Social Bonding and Self-Control Models of Adolescent substance Use in Korea

| Variables | Alcohol | Tobacco |
|---|---|---|
| **SOCIAL BONDING** | | |
| **Attachment** | | |
| school attachment | -.058 | -.059 |
| parental attachment | -.077* | -.099** |
| peer attachment | .160*** | .122*** |
| parental supervision | -.114*** | -.096** |
| religious attachment | -.017 | -.010 |
| **Commitment** | | |
| educational aspirations | -.135*** | -.193*** |
| occupational aspirations | .047 | .092** |
| grade point average | -.099*** | -.159*** |
| **Involvement** | | |
| time spent on homework | -.156*** | -.166*** |
| **Belief** | | |
| parental norms | -.035 | .027 |
| legal norms | -.031 | .024 |
| importance of religion | .021 | .015 |
| $R^2$ | .154 | .196 |
| N | 1,010 | 1,010 |
| **SELF-CONTROL** | | |
| impulsivity | .103** | .077* |
| preference for simple tasks | -.010 | .019 |
| risk seeking | .187*** | .147*** |
| preference for physical activity | .137*** | .131*** |
| self-centered | -.018 | -.009 |
| low tolerance | .089** | .170*** |
| $R^2$ | .121 | .125 |
| N | 1,010 | 1,010 |

gression equation separately for alcohol use and tobacco use. Then regression models are run successively eliminating a different set of variables from the full equation. As shown in Tables 2.3 and 2.4, Model (1) is the full model, Model (2) eliminates the sociodemographic variables, Model (3) eliminates the social learning variables, Model (4) eliminates the social bonding variables, and Model (5) eliminates the self-control variables.

*Alcohol Use*

Table 2.3 summarizes the result of OLS models of alcohol use regressed on all of the independent variables. The full equation Model (1) explains 61.6 percent of the variance in alcohol use, indicating that the full model does not dramatically improve the level of explained variance beyond that of the social learning model alone ($R^2$=.576 in Table 2.1). As has been found in American studies, the differential peer association variable has the strongest net effect on teenage drinking in all of the models, but several other social learning variables (measures of parent use and differential reinforcement). In Model (1) and all of the models with social learning variables included, only one or two social bonding or self-control variables show significant net effects. Iimpulsivity from self-control theory has significant net effects in the model. Among sociodemographic variables, school type (with industrial school having the higher levels of use) appears to be have substantial effects independently of the theoretical variables, but family income and gender also have significant net effects.

Model (2) shows, however, excluding all of the sociodemographic factors from the equation, trivial effects on the amount of variance explained. The same can be said for Model (4), without the social bonding variables, and Model (5), without the self-control variables; there is very little loss of explained variance when these variables are removed from the full equation. Only Model (3), which excludes the social learning variables, shows any substantial difference from the full equation in Model (1). From Model (3) we see that when the social learning factors are eliminated from the equation, the change in $R^2$ is dramatic ($R^2$ change = .338); the amount of variance explained in the full Model (1) is reduced by more than half. At the same time, the nearly 28 percent of the variance accounted for in Model (3) is substantial. We saw from Table 2.2 that social bonding and self-control theories are able separately to account for at least some of the differences in adolescent drinking in Korea, and at about the same level as they do in American studies. Table 2.3 shows that when the two are combined, they do an even better job.

Nevertheless, the results clearly demonstrate that social learning theory provides the most powerful explanation in this sample just as it does in American samples. Any regression model with social learning variables (regardless of what other variables are present or absent from it) explains a high

Table 2.3
**Comparison of Social Learning, Social Bonding, and Self-control Models of Adolescenet Alcohol Use in Korea**

|  | Models | | | | |
|---|---|---|---|---|---|
|  | (1) | (2) | (3) | (4) | (5) |
| Socio-Demographic Variables | | | | | |
| gender | .051* | | .138*** | .044 | .054 |
| grade level | .008 | | .021 | .011 | .007 |
| school type | .130*** | | .203*** | .132*** | .141*** |
| family structure | .024 | | .005 | .024 | .021 |
| family income | .078*** | | .145*** | .078*** | .083*** |
| parent's SES | .003 | | -.007 | .017 | -.001 |
| Social Learning Variables | | | | | |
| positive/negative definitions | | | | | |
| proscriptive definitions | .042 | .035 | | .045 | .040 |
| law abiding/violating definitions | .010 | .016 | | .000 | .008 |
| neutralizing definitions | --- | --- | | -.020 | --- |
| differential peer association | -.005 | -.012 | | -.003 | .001 |
| father's use | .459*** | .483*** | | .472*** | .458*** |
| mother's use | .060** | .059* | | .058* | .060** |
| peer norm qualities | .021 | .020 | | .013 | .020 |
| parents norm qualities | .048 | .046 | | .043 | .050 |
| parents' reaction | -.044 | -.040 | | -.048 | -.043 |
| friends' reaction | .039 | .040 | | .036 | .042 |
| caught by teachers | .049* | .054* | | .054* | .050* |
| rewards-costs of use | -.008 | -.011 | | -.013 | -.009 |
| overall reinforcement balance | .053* | .053 | | .049 | .058* |
| peers | .061* | .065* | | .064* | .064* |
| parents or other admired adults | -.005 | .013 | | -.012 | .003 |
| persons in media | .059 | .051 | | .067 | .065 |
| advertisements | .069 | .056 | | .070 | .063 |
|  | .044 | .056 | | .048 | .052 |

**Table 2.3 (cont.)**

| | | | Models | | |
|---|---|---|---|---|---|
| | (1) | (2) | (3) | (4) | (5) |
| Social Bonding Variables. | | | | | |
| school attachment | -.016 | -.020 | -.064 | | -.006 |
| parental attachment | -.002 | .005 | -.073* | | .002 |
| peer attachment | .019 | .033 | .104*** | | .019 |
| parental supervision | -.016 | -.022 | -.064* | | -.015 |
| religious attachment | -.019 | -.016 | -.031 | | -.015 |
| educational aspirations | .029 | -.025 | -.018 | | .032 |
| occupational aspirations | -.020 | -.009 | .020 | | -.023 |
| grade point average | -.091*** | -.068** | -.095** | | -.097*** |
| time spent on homework | -.049 | -.072** | -.118*** | | -.049 |
| parental norms | -.029 | -.019 | -.064* | | -.030 |
| legal norms | -.019 | -.022 | -.031 | | -.019 |
| importance of religion | .037 | .035 | .025 | | .036 |
| Self-Control Variables. | | | | | |
| impulsivity | .050* | .060* | .074* | .061* | |
| preference for simple tasks | -.044 | -.048* | -.063* | -.025 | |
| risk seeking | .018 | .025 | .126*** | .026 | |
| preference for physical activity | .016 | .023 | .093** | .019 | |
| self-centered | .008 | .008 | .001 | .001 | |
| low tolerance | .000 | .008 | .047 | .004 | |
| $R^2$ | .616 | .602 | .278 | .603 | .611 |
| $R^2$ Change | | -.014 | -.338 | -.013 | -.005 |
| N | 903 | 903 | 994 | 904 | 903 |

\*    p< .05
\*\*   p< .01
\*\*\* p< .001

(1) = Full model
(2) = Model without sociodemographic variables
(3) = Model without social learning variables
(4) = Model without social bonding variables
(5) = Model without self-control variables

level of variance; any model without them explains moderate levels. By comparison, removal of sociodemographic, bonding, or self-control variables has no significant impact on the predictive power of the remaining model; addition of all of these variables only marginally increases the predictive power over the stand-alone social learning model.

Moreover, all of the social learning variables that show significant effects on alcohol use in Table 2.1 (where only social learning variables are entered), retain significant effects (and at about the same magnitude) in the presence of all of the other variables in Model (1) in Table 2.3. On the other hand, most of the measures of social bonding and self-control theory that show significant effects on drinking among these Korean adolescents when tested in separate regression equations (Table 2.2), show no significant effect when placed in the same regression equation with social learning variables. A reasonable inference to draw from this is that the social bonding and self-control variables have an effect mainly because they are correlated with, and probably mediated by, social learning variables. Again, these findings are quite similar to studies comparing social learning, social bonding, and other theories done with America sample (see Akers and Cocrhan 1985; Benda 1994; Akers and Lee 1999).

*Tobacco Use*

These findings on teenage drinking in the Korean study are essentially replicated, but with somewhat higher levels of explained variance, for teenage smoking. Table 2.4 presents the results of the OLS multiple regression equations for tobacco use. Model (1) of Table 2.4 explains 69.5 percent of the variance in tobacco use, again with differential peer association variable having the strongest net effect on tobacco use, but with several other social learning variables having significant beta weights, including at least one measure of each of the four major explanatory concepts in the theory, and only one bonding and one self-control variable having significant effects. As was found with drinking behavior, removal of any set of variables other than social learning variables, Models (2) through (5), makes essentially zero difference in the predictive power of the model. Only in Model (3), which has no social learning variables, is there a large reduction in explained variance compared to the full Model (1). When social learning variables are excluded, the model still produces a sizeable $R^2$, but it is only about half of that produced by the full model with social learning variables included. Measures of bonding and self-control elements bear about the same relationship with social learning variables in their effects on smoking behavior as was found for drinking behavior, Models (1), (2), (4), and (5). That is, in these models with measures of the social learning process most of the bonding and self-control effects on tobacco use disappear, suggesting that the relationships are largely spurious, mostly mediated through social learning variables.

## Conclusions, Limitations, and Implications

The purpose of this study was to examine how well social learning, social bonding, and self-control theories, proposed and developed by Western sociologists but tested mainly with samples of American youth, explain adolescent substance use (in this case consumption of alcohol and tobacco) in a non-Western Asian society. The conclusion of the study is that the theories do apply in Korean society and in about the same way that they apply in American society. Multivariate analyses indicated that social learning models explained 58 percent of the variance in alcohol use and 67 percent of the variance in tobacco use. Social bonding variables explained 15 percent of the variance in alcohol use and 20 percent in tobacco use, while 12 percent of the variance in alcohol use and 13 percent in tobacco use was explained by the self-control variables. Social learning theory most clearly applies cross-culturally (especially that part of the associational process affected by peers).

The other two theories are also cross-culturally applicable. The caveat is that the support for social bonding and self-control theories hold only when the effects of social learning variables are not considered. When elements of social bonding or self-control variables were placed in the same regression equations with the social learning variables, most of their effects disappeared. Again, these results are in general accord with the previous studies conducted in the United States (Akers and Cochran 1985; White et al. 1986; McGee 1992; and Benda 1994). Social learning theory has been consistently and substantially supported by research in this country, and this study shows that it can be taken globally.

The present research has some obvious limitations. First, the analysis is based only on Korean adolescents in Pusan, an urban metropolitan area. There may be considerable differences in adolescent drug use in urban compared to rural areas. The Pusan metropolitan area might be among the most affected by American influence in Korea, and it is possible that the similarity of findings from studies in the United States reflects a greater Westernization of this urban region than would be found in other, more rural, regions of Korea. Therefore, additional research is needed to assess the extent to which these findings would apply to adolescents in non-metropolitan areas in Korea. It is also important for future research to test the theories in many other societies, not only in Asia, but in Latin America, African, Eastern Europe, Russia, the Middle East, and elsewhere. The findings here would predict that the theories, especially social learning, will withstand empirical scrutiny in most if not all of these other societies, but that remains to be confirmed by future research.

Comparing the findings in another society with findings in American research as was done here is revealing, but it is not the ideal way to make direct comparisons of variations in predictive power of various theoretical models

Table 2.4

**Comparison of Social Learning, Social Bonding, and Self-Control Models of Adolescent Tobacco Use in Korea**

| | Models | | | | |
|---|---|---|---|---|---|
| | (1) | (2) | (3) | (4) | (5) |
| Socio-Demographic Variables | | | | | |
| gender | -.014 | | .215*** | -.018 | -.011 |
| grade level | .001 | | .011 | .009 | .002 |
| school type | .082** | | .238*** | .091*** | .083** |
| family structure | .004 | | .035 | -.002 | .002 |
| family income | .070*** | | .121*** | .070*** | .071*** |
| parents' SES | .006 | | .022 | .021 | .005 |
| Social Learning Variables | | | | | |
| positive/negative definitions | | | | | |
| proscriptive definitions | .055* | .057* | | .056* | .055* |
| law abiding/violating definitions | .039 | .039 | | .041 | .042 |
| neutralizing definitions | --- | --- | | -.012 | --- |
| differential peer association | -.023 | -.026 | | -.018 | -.025 |
| father's use | .504*** | .511*** | | .524*** | .504*** |
| mother's use | .007 | .005 | | .012 | .011 |
| peer norm qualities | .000 | .004 | | .001 | -.011 |
| parents norm qualities | .055* | .054* | | .052* | .057* |
| parents' reaction | -.030 | -.030 | | -.026 | -.031 |
| friends' reaction | .125*** | .130*** | | .125*** | .125*** |
| caught by teachers | -.007 | -.014 | | -.003 | -.012 |
| rewards-costs of use | -.013 | -.019 | | -.013 | -.016 |
| overall reinforcement balance | .046 | .053* | | .049* | .043 |
| peers | .103*** | .103*** | | .107*** | .106*** |
| parents | -.006 | .008 | | -.009 | -.002 |
| other adults | .084* | .079* | | .085* | .085 |
| advertisements | -.005 | -.020 | | -.009 | -.011 |
| | .056 | .063 | | .063 | .059 |

Table 2.4 (cont.)

| | Models | | | | |
|---|---|---|---|---|---|
| | (1) | (2) | (3) | (4) | (5) |
| Social Bonding Variables | | | | | |
| school attachment | -.032 | -.037 | -.054 | | -.034 |
| parental attachment | -.016 | -.011 | -.101** | | .014 |
| peer attachment | .041 | .051* | .070* | | .035 |
| parental supervision | -.025 | -.025 | -.028 | | -.027 |
| religious attachment | -.037 | -.038 | -.028 | | -.032 |
| educational aspirations | .012 | -.013 | -.034 | | .010 |
| occupational aspirations | -.002 | .001 | .047 | | .000 |
| grade point average | -.069*** | -.053* | -.161*** | | -.070*** |
| time spent on homework | -.043 | -.063** | -.121*** | | .009 |
| parental norms | .004 | .005 | -.019 | | .010 |
| legal norms | .011 | .005 | .020 | | .010 |
| importance of religion | .012 | .013 | .022 | | .007 |
| Self-Control Variables | | | | | |
| impulsivity | | | | | |
| preference for simple tasks | -.002 | .009 | .037 | .003 | |
| risk seeking | -.018 | -.019 | -.038 | .001 | |
| preference for physical activity | -.023 | -.021 | .104*** | -.019 | |
| self-centered | -.013 | -.015 | .062* | -.011 | |
| low tolerance | -.017 | -.020 | .003 | -.027 | |
| | .063** | .066** | .115*** | .065** | |
| $R^2$ | .695 | .689 | .340 | .684 | .691 |
| $R^2$ Change | | -.006 | -.355 | -.011 | -.004 |
| N | 888[4] | 888 | 994 | 889 | 888 |

* p< .05
** p< .01
*** p< .001

(1) = Full model
(2) = Model without sociodemographic variables
(3) = Model without social learning variables
(4) = Model without social bonding variables
(5) = Model without self-control variables

in different societies. The better way to make the comparison, assuming resources allow it, would be to collect primary data with exactly the same instrument (properly translated, of course) and exactly the same measures on samples drawn in the same way and within the same time period(s) in different societies. Thus, instead of referring to how the findings do or do not conform to those found in previous research in the United States, the data analysis could directly compare the findings from the cross-cultural samples. Future research should also do a better job of identifying and measuring macro-level dimensions of the sociocultural context. That is, future research should directly construct and test models postulating the interface of macro- and micro-level variables and processes such as the Social Structure Social Learning model (Akers 1998).

It is also important to consider the implications of restricting these analyses to only those adolescents enrolled in schools, and not those adolescents who have dropped out or been kicked out of school. It is fair to assume that adolescents who are kicked out of schools or incarcerated will have different substance use experience than those still enrolled. This assumption is most likely to be true when future comparisons are expanded, as they should be, beyond smoking and drinking to use and abuse of opiates, cocaine, amphetamines, and other drugs and to other forms of criminal, delinquent, and deviant behavior. For this reason, there remains a need for further research on this topic to include adolescents not enrolled in schools. However, it should be noted for purposes of cross-cultural comparisons this sampling of population of in-school adolescents only is also typical of studies in the United States. Further, the kind of multi-society research suggested above could still make valid comparisons as long as the same type of sampling (in-school, out-of-school, or both) was done for all research sites.

The data in this study are cross-sectional. Potential limitation of cross-sectional data concerns the inability to specify the changes in measures as a youth moves through adolescence. A study which collects its dependent and independent variables at the same time has an inherent difficulty in assessing a causal direction when explaining relationships. The temporal ordering is not clearly ascertainable in cross-sectional studies. Therefore, future research should collect longitudinal data using a panel study format, with data collection beginning preferably early in the middle school, if not elementary school, years. It should be remembered, of course, that longitudinal research has its own limitations (Gottfredson and Hirschi 1987), and does not often produce findings that run counter to conclusions about adequacy of various theories based on cross-sectional research. Moreover, if data collection is carried out the same way at all sites, it will still allow for unbiased comparison of theories cross-culturally whether the data are cross-sectional or longitudinal. Nonetheless, firmer conclusions about causal ordering, sequencing, reciprocal effects, and other issues are better handled with panel data, and future research should include, to the extent feasible, such longitudinal data collection.

The policy implications for the present research and future research of the kind just outlined are significant. The same kind of cognitive/behavioral treatment and prevention programs based on social learning principles (see Andrews and Bonta 1998; Akers 2000) or on some combination of social learning, bonding, and perhaps self-control principles (see Hawkins and Weis 1985) identifying school, family, and peer interventions that have been applied in the United States, with at least a modicum of success, should be among the first programs implemented in other societies. Programs introduced in Korea should be cognizant of the differences between the liberal and industrial high school contexts, which remain even when social learning, bonding, and self-control measures are taken into account. If the findings elsewhere confirm the findings here about the importance of the educational system, so that differences in drug use can be expected in different types of schools, the programs should be differentially implemented to target those schools with the greater likelihood of adolescent substance use problems.

## Notes

1.  In Korea, all students spend six years in elementary school then go up to three years of middle school. Middle school graduation is mandatory. Upon graduation from middle school level, students have to take a national test. Those who score well on the test can enter into a "liberal" high school that is preparatory to university entry. Those who do not do well normally will select one of the "industrial" high schools such as the technical, commercial, and informational high schools according to their preferences. Most high school seniors in the liberal school are able to enter into four years of university after taking another national test which is similar to the SAT test in the United States. On the other hand, industrial high school students try to get a manual job after graduation and have essentially no opportunity for a college or university education. There are separate high school for boys and girls.
2.  However, there is an attrition in the sample: students who have been kicked out of school or have moved to a different school district.
3.  One U.S. dollar is equal to 1,300 Korean Won.
4.  Number of cases for equation (1) to (5) in tables 3 and 4 range between 888 and 994, reflecting listwise deletion of missing data. Listwise deletion is for the cases that have missing values for any of the variables named and are omitted from the analysis.

## References

Agnew, Robert. 1985. "Social Control Theory and Delinquency: A Longitudinal Test." *Criminology* 23: 47-62.
___. 1991a. "The Interactive Effects of Peer Variables on Delinquency." *Criminology* 29: 47-72.
___. 1991b. "A Longitudinal Test of Social Control Theory and Delinquency." *Journal of Research in Crime and Delinquency* 28:126-156.

\_\_\_. 1993. "Why Do They Do? An Examination of the Intervening Mechanisms between Social Control Variables and Delinquency." *Journal of Research in Crime and Delinquency* 30: 245-266.

\_\_\_. 1994. "The Techniques of Neutralization and Violence." *Criminology* 32: 555-580.

Akers, Ronald L. 1973. *Deviant Behavior: A Social Learning Approach*. Belmont, CA: Wadsworth.

\_\_\_. 1985. *Deviant Behavior: A Social Learning Approach*. Third Edition. Belmont, CA: Wadsworth. Reprinted 1992. Fairfax, VA: Techbooks.

\_\_\_. 1998. *Social Learning and Social Structure: A General Theory of Crime and Deviance*. Boston: Northeastern University Press.

\_\_\_. 2000. *Criminological Theories: Introduction, Evaluation, and Application*. Third Edition. Los Angeles, CA: Roxbury Publishing Company.

Akers, Ronald L., and Gang, Lee. 1996. "A Longitudinal Test of Social Learning Theory: Adolescent Smoking." *Journal of Drug Issues* 26: 317-343.

\_\_\_. 1999. "Age, Social Learning, and Social Bonding in Adolescent Substance Use." *Deviant Behavior* 20: 1-25.

Akers, Ronald L., and John Cochran. 1985. "Adolescent Marijuana Use: A Test of Three Theories of Deviant Behavior." *Deviant Behavior* 6: 323-346.

Akers, Ronald L., Marvin. D. Krohn, Lonn Lanza-Kaduce, and Marcia Radosevich. 1979. "Social Learning and Deviant Behavior: A Specific Test of a General Theory." *American Sociological Review* 44: 636-655.

Andrews, D. A. and James Bonta. 1998. *Psychology of Criminal Conduct*. Second Edition. Cincinnati, OH: Anderson.

Arneklev, Bruce J., Harold G. Grasmick, Charles R. Tittle, and Robert J. Bursik, Jr. 1993. "Low Self-Control and Imprudent Behavior." *Journal of Quantitative Criminology* 9: 225-247.

Bahr, Stephen J., Anastasios C. Marcos, and Suzanne L. Maughan. 1995. "Family, Educational and Peer Influences on the Alcohol Use of Female and Male Adolescents." *Journal of Studies on Alcohol* 56: 457-469.

Benda, Brent B. 1994. "Testing Competing Theoretical Concepts: Adolescent Alcohol Consumption." *Deviant Behavior* 15: 375-396.

Benda, Brent B., and Frederick A. DiBlasio. 1991. "Comparison of Four Theories of Adolescent Sexual Exploration." *Deviant Behavior* 12: 235-257.

Brownfield, David, and Ann Marie Sorenson. 1993. "Self-Control and Juvenile Delinquency: Theoretical Issues and an Empirical Assessment of Selected Elements of a General Theory of Crime." *Deviant Behavior* 14: 243-264.

Bruinsma, Gerben J. N. 1992. "Differential Association Theory Reconsidered: An Extension and Its Empirical Test." *Journal of Quantitative Criminology* 8: 29-49.

Burton, Velmer S., T. Francis, T. Cullen, David Evans, and R. Gregory Dunaway. 1994. "Reconsidering Strain Theory: Operationalization, Rival Theories, and Adult Criminality." *Journal of Quantitative Criminology* 10: 213-239.

Cernkovich, Stephen, and Peggy Giordano. 1992. "School Bonding, Race, and Delinquency." *Criminology* 30: 261-291.

Conger, Rand D., and Ronald L. Simons. 1995. "Life-Course Contingencies in the Development of Adolescent Antisocial Behavior: A Matching Law Approach." In Terence P. Thornberry (ed.), *Developmental Theories of Crime and Delinquency*. New Brunswick, NJ: Transaction Publishers.

Costello, Barbara J. 2000. "Techniques of Neutralization and Self-Esteem: A Critical Test of Social Control and Neutralization Theory." *Deviant Behavior* 21: 207-330.

Costello, Barbara J,. and Paul R. Vowell. 1999. "Testing Control Theory and Differential Association: A Reanalysis of the Richmond Youth Project Data." *Criminology* 37: 815-842.

Dabney, Dean. 1995. "Neutralization and Deviance in the Workplace: Theft of Supplies and Medicines by Hospital Nurses." *Deviant Behavior* 16: 313-331.

Dembo, Richard, Gary Grandon, Lawrence La Voie, James Schmeidler, and William Burgos. 1986. "Parents and Drugs Rvisited: Some Further Evidence in Support of Social Learning Theory." *Criminology* 24: 85-103.

Ellis, Lee, and Anthony Walsh. 1999a. "Gene-Based Evolutionary Theories in Criminology." *Criminology* 35:229-275.

_____. 1999b. "Criminologists' Opinions about Causes and Theories of Crime and Delinquency." *The Criminologist* 24: 1, 4-6.

Elliott, Delbert S., David Huizinga, and Suzanne S. Ageton. 1985. *Explaining Delinquency and Drug Use*. Beverly Hills, CA: Sage.

Evans, T. David, Francis T. Cullen, Velmer S. Burton, Jr., R. Gregory Dunaway, and Michael L. Benson. 1997. "The Social Consequences of Self-Control: Testing the General Theory of Crime." *Criminology* 35: 475-504.

Gibbs, John J, and Dennis Giever. 1995. "Self-Control and Its Manifestations among University Students: An Empirical Test of Gottfredson and Hirschi's General Theory." *Justice Quarterly* 12: 231-255.

Gibbs, John J., Dennis Giever, and Jamie S. Kerr. 1994. Parental Management and Self-Control: An Empirical Test of Gottfredson and Hirschi's General Theory. Paper presented at the 46th Annual Meeting of the American Society of Criminology, Miami, FL.

Gottfredson, Michael R.. and Travis Hirschi. 1987. "The Methodological Adequacy of Longitudinal Research on Crime." *Criminology* 25: 581-614.

___. 1990. *A General Theory of Crime*. Stanford, CA: Stanford University Press.

Grasmick, Harold G., Charles R. Tittle, Robert J. Bursik, Jr., and Bruce J. Arneklev. 1993. "Testing the Core Empirical Implications of Gottfredson and Hirschi's General Theory of Crime." *Journal of Research in Crime and Delinquency* 30: 5-29.

Hawkins, J. David, and Joseph G. Weis. 1985. "The Social Development Model: an Integrated Approach to Delinquency Prevention." *Journal of Primary Prevention* 6: 73-97.

Hindelang, Michael J. 1973. "Causes of Delinquency: A Partial Replication and Extension." *Social Problems* 20: 471-487.

Hirschi, Travis. 1969. *Causes of Delinquency*. Berkeley: University of California Press.

Hirschi, Travis, and Michael Gottfredson. 1993. "Commentary: Testing the General Theory of Crime." *Journal of Research in Crime and Delinquency* 30: 47-54.

Hirschi, Travis, and Michael R. Gottfredson, eds. 1994. *The Generality of Deviance*. New Brunswick, NJ: Transaction Publishers.

Inciardi, James A., Ruth Horowitz, and Anne E. Pottiger. 1993. *Street Kids, Street Drugs, Street Crime: An Examination of Drug Use and Serious Delinquency in Miami*. Belmont, CA: Wadsworth.

Johnson, Richard E. 1979. *Juvenile Delinquency and Its Origins: An Integrated Theoretical Approach*. New York: Cambridge University Press.

Junger-Tas, Josine. 1992. "An Empirical Test of Social Control Theory." *Journal of Quantitative Criminology* 8: 9-28.

Kandel, Denise B,. and Israel Adler. 1982. "Socialization into Marijuana Use among French Adolescents: A Cross-Cultural Comparison with the United States." *Journal of Health and Social Behavior* 23: 295-309.

Kandel, Denise B., and Kenneth Andrews. 1987. "Processes of Adolescent Socialization by Parents and Peers." *International Journal of the Addictions* 22: 319-342.

Kandel, Denise B., and Mark Davies. 1991. "Friendship Networks, Intimacy, and Illicit Drug Use in Young Adulthood: A Comparison of Two Competing Theories." *Criminology* 29: 441-469.

Keane, Carl, Paul S. Maxim, and James J. Teevan. 1993. "Drinking and Driving, Self-Control, and Gender: Testing a General Theory of Crime." *Journal of Research in Crime and Delinquency* 30: 30-45.

Kim, Joon-Ho, and Cheong-Sun Park. 1995. *A Research on Juvenile Drug Abuse: In Terms of Smoking and Drinking*. Seoul, Korea: Korean Institute of Criminology.

Korean Youth Association. 1996. *A Research on Present Conditions and Preventive Strategies of Adolescent Drug Abuse*. Seoul, Korea: Ministry of Culture and Sports, Korean.

Krohn, Marvin D., Lonn Lanza-Kaduce, and Ronald L. Akers. 1984. "Community Context and Theories of Deviant Behavior: An Examination of Social Learning and Social Bonding Theories." *Sociological Quarterly* 25: 353-372.

Krohn, Marvin D., and James L. Massey. 1980. "Social Control and Delinquent Behavior: An Examination of the Elements of the Social Bond." *Sociological Quarterly* 21: 529-544.

Krohn, Marvin D., James L. Massey, William F. Skinner, and Ronald M. Lauer. 1983. "Social Bonding Theory and Adolescent Cigarette Smoking: A Longitudinal Analysis." *Journal of Health and Social Behavior* 24: 337-349.

LaGrange, Teresa C., and Robert A. Silverman. 1999. "Low Self-Control and Opportunity: Testing the General Theory of Crime as an Explanation for Gender Differences in Delinquency." *Criminology* 37: 41-72.

Lauritsen, Janet L. 1993. "Sibling Resemblance in Juvenile Delinquency: Findings from the National Youth Survey." *Criminology* 31: 387-410.

Lee, Ching-Mei. 1989. "The Study of Social Learning and Social Bonding Variables as Predictors of Cigarette Smoking Behavior among Ninth-Grade Male Students in Taipei, Taiwan, The Republic of China." Ph. D. Dissertation. Department of School and Community Health, University of Oregon, Eugene.

Longshore, Douglas. 1998. "Self-Control and Criminal Opportunity: A Prospective Test of the General Theory of Crime." *Social Problems* 45: 102-113.

Massey, James L., and Marvin D. Krohn. 1986. "A Longitudinal Examination of an Integrated Social Process Model of Deviant Behavior." *Social Forces* 65: 106-134.

Matsueda, Ross L. 1982. "Testing Control Theory and Differential Association: A Causal Modeling Approach." *American Sociological Review* 47: 489-504.

Matsueda, Ross L., and Karen Heimer. 1987. "Race, Family Structure, and Delinquency: A Test of Differential Association and Social Control Theories." *American Sociological Review* 52: 826-840.

McGee, Zina T. 1992. "Social Class Differences in Parental and Peer Influence on Adolescent Drug Use." *Deviant Behavior* 13: 349-372.

Nagin, Daniel S., and Raymond Paternoster. 1993. "Enduring Individual Differences and Rational Choice Theories of Crime." *Law & Society Review* 27: 467-496.

Paternoster, Raymond, and Robert Brame. 1998. "The Structural Similarity of Processes of Generation Criminal and Analogous Behaviors. *Criminology* 36: 633-669.

Patterson, Gerald R,. and Thomas J. Dishion. 1985. "Contributions of Families and Peers to Delinquency." *Criminology* 23: 63-79.

Piquero, Alex, and Stephen Tibbetts. 1996. "Specifying the Direct and Indirect Effects of Low Self-Control and Situational Factors in Offenders Decision Making: Toward a More Complete Model of Rational Offending." *Justice Quarterly* 13: 481-510.

Polakowski, Michael. 1994. "Linking Self- and Social Control with Deviance: Illuminating the Structure Underlying a General Theory of Crime and Its Relation to Deviant Activity." *Journal of Quantitative Criminology* 10: 41-78.

Pratt, Tavis C., and Francis T. Cullen. 2000. "The Empirical Status of Gottfredson and Hirschi's General Theory of Crime: a Meta-Analysis." *Criminology* 38: 931-964

Rankin, Joseph H., and Roger Kern. 1994. "Parental Attachments and Delinquency." *Criminology* 32: 495-516.

Rowe, David C., and Bill L. Gulley. 1992. "Sibling Effects on Substance Use and Delinquency." *Criminology* 30: 217-234.

Spear, Sherilyn, and Ronald L. Akers. 1988. "Social Learning Variables and the Risk of Habitual Smoking among Adolescents: The Muscatine Study. *American Journal of Preventive Medicine* 4: 336-348.

Stark, Rodney, Lori Kent, and Daniel P. Doyle. 1980. "Religion and Delinquency: The Ecology of a 'Lost' Relationship." *Journal of Research in Crime and Delinquency* 19: 4-24.

Stitt, B. Grant, and David J. Giacopassi. 1992. "Trends in the Connectivity of Theory and Research in Criminology." *The Criminologist* 17: 1, 3-6.

Supreme Public Prosecutors Office. 1995. *A White Paper on Crime*. Seoul, Korea: Ministry of Justice.

Tremblay, Richard E., Bernard Boulerice, Louise Arseneault, and Marianne Junger Niscale. 1995. "Does Low Self-Control during Childhood Explain the Association between Delinquency and Accidents in Early Adolescence?" *Criminal Behavior and Mental Health* 5: 439-451.

Warr, Mark. 1993a. "Age, Peers, and Selinquency." *Criminology* 31: 17-40.

___. 1993b. "Parents, Peers, and Delinquency." *Social Forces* 72: 247-264.

___. 1996. "Organization and Instigation in Delinquent Groups." *Criminology* 34: 11-38.

Warr, Mark, and Mark Stafford. 1991. "The Influence of Delinquent Peers: What They Think or What They Do?" *Criminology* 29: 851-866.

White, Helene Raskin, Valerie Johnson, and A. Horowitz. 1986. "An Application of Three Deviance Theories to Adolescent Substance Use." *International Journal of the Addictions* 21: 347-366.

White, Helene Raskin, Robert J. Pandina, and Randy L. LaGrange. 1987. "Longitudinal Predictors of Serious Substance Use and Delinquency." *Criminology* 25: 715-740.

Wiatrowski, Michael D., David B. Griswold, and Mary K. Roberts. 1981. "Social Control Theory and Delinquency." *American Sociological Review* 46: 525-41.

Winfree, L. Thomas, Curt T. Griffiths, and Christine S. Sellers. 1989. "Social Learning Theory, Drug Use, and American Indian Youths: A Cross-Cultural Test." *Justice Quarterly* 6: 395-417.

Winfree, L Thomas, Christine S. Sellers, and Dennis L. Clason. 1993. "Social Learning and Adolescent Deviance Abstention: Toward Understanding the Reasons for Initiating, Quitting, and Avoiding Drugs." Journal of Quantitative *Criminology* 9: 101-125.

Winfree, L. Thomas, G. Larry Mays, and Teresa Vigil-Backstrom. 1994. "Social Learning Theory, Self-Reported Delinquency, and Youth Gangs: A New Twist on a General Theory of Crime and Delinquency." *Youth & Society* 26: 147-177.

Wood, Peter B., John K. Cochran, Betty Pfefferbaum, and Bruce J. Arneklev. 1995. "Sensation-Seeking and Delinquent Substance Use: An Extension of Learning Theory." *Journal of Drug Issues* 25: 173-193.

Wright, Bradley R. Entner, Avshalom Caspi, Terrie E. Moffitt, and Phil A. Silva. 1999. "Low Self-Control, Social Bonds, and Crime: Social Causation, Social Selection, or Both?" *Criminology* 37: 479-514.

Yang, Shu-Lung. 1999. The Girl's Delinquency: An Empirical Test of a General Theory of Crime and Social Learning Theory in Taiwan. Paper presented at the annual meeting of American Society of Criminology, Toronto, Ontario, Canada.

Zhang, Lening, and Steven F. Messner. 1995. "Family Deviance and Delinquency in China." *Criminology* 33: 359-388.

# 3

# Explaining Delinquency in Taiwan:
# A Test of Social Learning Theory

*Shu-Neu Wang and Gary F. Jensen*

The amount of criminological research testing theories of delinquency has grown rapidly over the last several decades, generating a considerable body of knowledge about the correlates of delinquency. However, any review of that body of work will reveal that such research is based on data from samples in Western industrial nations, especially the United States. Very little is known about the generalizability of research findings based on such samples to non-Western nations or cultures. Low crime rates in Asian societies are used routinely to highlight high rates of violence in the United States, but there is a paucity of research assessing either variations by social background or testing criminological theories using data from such societies.

Although there has been too little research in Asian settings for any defini-tive conclusions about causes and correlates of crime and delinquency, a review of existing studies reveals several patterns that are quite consistent with those found for American youth. In a study of Korean youth, Axenroth (1983) compared delinquent and non-delinquent youth and found a measure of social class to be a significant correlate. In a more recent study of youth in Tianjin, China, Zhang and Messner (1995) also found a significant negative relationship using official delinquent designation as the dependent variable. Such findings are quite compatible with research in North America where at least two-thirds of those studies examining class differences in "official" delinquency report a significant negative relationship (Tittle, Villemez and Smith 1978).

Zhang and Messner (1995) drew on a variety of theories and conclude that family deviance, harsh discipline, parental spoiling and friends' deviance are positive independent correlates of official delinquency while conventional moral commitments and crowding are significant negative correlates. Age and gender were significant correlates as well with older juveniles and females exhibiting lower odds of official delinquency. Such findings are quite compatible with the body of delinquency research for North America, although no American studies have focused on spoiling as a variable.

Shao Daosheng conducted a *Preliminary Study of China's Juvenile Delinquency* (1992) focusing on officially labeled delinquent youth. The age range encompassed by that category in China ranges from 14 through 25 years of age and, thus, includes young adults. Drawing on a variety of unpublished studies, Daosheng reports that, when compared to control groups, labeled delinquent youth in China are more likely to come from broken or disrupted homes, to be school dropouts, to be unemployed when out of school, to come from lower or working-class families, and to be experienced with pornographic materials. Although the crime rate for people in this age range is much lower in China than in the United States, cross-sectional differences between labeled youth and comparison groups are quite comparable.

The most common method for testing theories of delinquency in North America has been through the collection of survey data on offensive behavior and studies using this technique have been conducted in Japan, India and the Philippines. A study in Japan (Tanioka and Glaser 1991) compared youth who wore school uniforms with youth who did not and found significantly more serious delinquency among those who did not wear uniforms. In 1978 Hartjen and Priyardarsini (1984) surveyed youth in Tamil Nadu and in 1991 Hartjen and Kethenini (1993) conducted similar surveys in Madras and New Delhi. Hartjen and Kethineni found that arrest rates for juveniles in India dramatically underestimated the true volume of offenses and that common forms of delinquent misconduct appear as widespread among male Indian youth as is found for males in surveys in Western societies. Youths in India do appear to have lower rates of drug use and serious delinquency. Moreover, while the male-to-female ratio of arrest was about 10:1, the gender ratio using self-reports was about 2:1. Thus, the gender ratio using self-reports is similar to that observed for American youths while the gender ratio in police statistics is much greater for youth in India than in the United States. They also conclude that the patterns and correlates found suggest that the same theoretical approaches substantiated in North American research are likely to apply in India.

Shoemaker (1994) used the self-report technique to explore delinquency among youth in the Philippines and found that the strength of social bonds, delinquent peers and attitudes favorable to lawbreaking explained male delinquency but not female delinquency. In contrast to Axenroth's (1983) study, the sons of high status fathers were more delinquent than the sons of low status fathers. Such a finding has some precedent in North American research in that Hagan, Gillis and Simpson (1985, 1987) report that when self-report measures of common forms of delinquency are used, some measures of class advantage are slight positive correlates of delinquency. Regarding gender, the difference observed was very close to that noted in self-report data from India with the male rate about twice the female rate.

Some criminologists speculate that some variables introduced to explain delinquency in America should be more important correlates of delinquency in Asian societies than in Western societies. For example, Axenroth (1983) proposed that class position is more likely to be a significant correlate of delinquency in research in developing than developed societies because people are more likely to be classified at birth into classes with distinctive life styles and opportunities. He did find a negative relationship between official delinquency and social class standing as did Zhang and Messner (1995) among Chinese youth. However, this finding is quite compatible with research using arrest or referral data in North America.

In contrast, when self-reports are used to measure delinquency, the results for Asian settings are quite similar to findings using the self-report method in North America. Shoemaker (1994) reports a positive relationship between fathers' status and self-reports among youth in the Philippines, and Hartjen and Priyadarsini (1984) report a nonlinear relationship. Among youth in India the highest rates of self-reported delinquency were found at the bottom of the SES scale with an upturn for the most advantaged categories. Such inconsistencies using official versus self-report measures are not surprising in view of North American research where similar inconsistencies have been widely noted, discussed and interpreted. Self-report research has generally yielded small and insignificant relationships which can tip positive or negative, depending on the measures of class, class categories and/or delinquency used.

Zhang and Messner (1995) suggest that the pervasive salience of the family in Chinese life should make family relations a more important predictor of official delinquency than peer group relationships among the Chinese in contrast to North American research where peers are a key influence. While their analysis does show family relations and family deviance to be important correlates, peer group relationships were more salient than expected for explaining delinquency among Chinese youth. In fact, the same basic model reported in literature on American youth was supported by their findings on Chinese youth.

### The Current Investigation

This study builds on that small body of research on crime in Asian societies through the use of the self-report method to study patterns of juvenile offending and to test contemporary theories of delinquency among junior high students in Taipei, Taiwan. In their study of a city in mainland China using official designations as delinquent to measure offense behavior, Zhang and Messner (1995: 370) note that "self-report methodology has not been developed or applied in China, and the validity and even the feasibility of such procedures is uncertain." Since the validity and feasibility of any method is uncertain when applied to new populations the only way to begin addressing such issues is to begin such research. Hence, a set of generalizations derived from American research can provide an initial foundation for self-report research on delinquency in this new setting.

## Hypotheses Involving Social Background

There is considerable precedent for a number of expectations about correlates of delinquency in Taiwan were patterns found for American youth applicable to that setting. Research on American samples (See Agnew 2001; Jensen and Rojek 1998; and Shoemaker 1996 for reviews) has generated several observations about the effect of gender, economic well-being and family structure on self-reports of delinquency:

1.  *Among basic background correlates of delinquency, gender is the strongest correlate with measures of economic well-being entering into weak negative relationships with self-reported delinquency.*
2.  *Measures of a youth's own status (e.g., standing in school) are stronger correlates of delinquency than measures of parental status.*
3.  *Presence of both natural parents in the household slightly lowers involvement in delinquency.*
4.  *Mother's employment outside the household is not a significant correlate of self-reported delinquency.*
5.  *Measures of the quality of family relationships are more strongly related to delinquency than measures of family structure.*

Since there is variation in research findings within American society, it would be surprising were there not some variations between the general findings based on American research and analysis of similar issues in an Asian setting. However, as noted in the review of prior research, there have been few surprises to this point in time.

## Hypotheses Involving Generic Mechanisms

If prior research were used to select generic mechanisms encouraging and inhibiting delinquency, then variables that should be included in an explanation of delinquent behavior include (1) the *opportunity* to commit offenses, (2) personal *investments* in the pursuit of goals that would be jeopardized by a delinquent or criminal record, (3) *bonds* to conventional people and institutions such as family, school and religion, (4) acceptance of certain *conventional values, norms, and beliefs*, especially those involving the law and authority, and (5) *relationships with delinquent or criminal people*, especially peers. "Structural" variables that are included in discussions of delinquency such as gender, age, social standing and race are expected to affect delinquency to the degree that they affect these generic mechanisms.

Criminologists familiar with variation in theoretical models will recognize this basic model as an expression of a "social learning" theory of delinquency. Although some of these variables have been central to the a social-disorganization-social control tradition in criminology (Hirschi 1969) and to a normatively oriented differential association-cultural deviance tradition (Miller 1958), the only theory encompassing all of these variables is contemporary social learning theory as developed by Ronald Akers. Social learning theory incorporates both normative and non-normative learning processes as well as vicarious and imitative learning mechanisms that can function to sustain law-abiding or delinquent conduct (Akers 1973, 1979). In contrast to social control theory, social learning theory emphasizes the independent influence of social learning processes involving delinquent peers. In contrast to extreme versions of cultural deviance theory (e.g., Miller 1958), social learning theory identifies socialization into distinct cultural norms that facilitate delinquency as only one of several ways in which learning processes can result in delinquency. In contrast to strain and frustration theories (see Agnew 1985, 1992, and Messner and Rosenfeld) which stress disjunction between learned conventional goals and reality as the central motivating force leading to delinquency, social learning theory allows delinquency to be learned through imitation, differential reinforcement by significant others and normal interaction with peers.

Social learning theory allows delinquency to be encouraged as a product of weak internalization of norms embodied in law, internalization of conflicting norms and beliefs characterizing the conventional culture, and/or distinct sub-cultural normative traditions. Finally, structural and relational variables can have an impact independent of any normative or cultural influences through other learning processes (imitation, differential reinforcement and differential association).

Robert Agnew (1985, 1992) has proposed a "revised strain theory," in which he proposes that anger, stress and other negative emotional states should be significantly related to delinquency. Such negative affect is viewed as the mediating mechanism that might connect family violence, school failure and a variety of negative experiences to delinquent behavior. Although this type of motivational force is cited as an extension of a structural strain-status frustration tradition (Merton 1938, 1957; Cohen, 1955; Cloward and Ohlin 1959, 1961), the same argument can be derived from social learning theory. Many forms of delinquent behavior can be viewed as cathartic activities, temporarily alleviating anger and stress by striking at direct and proxy targets. However, the view that social conditions or circumstances that violate legitimate expectations lead to anger, and that delinquency is one means of coping with or expressing anger, was not specifically proposed in the development of social learning theory and can be considered as compatible with a strain-theory logic as well.

The following hypotheses should withstand empirical scrutiny, if prior criminological research on self-reports of delinquency are generalizable to Taiwanese youth:

6. *Involvement in delinquency is positively correlated with interaction with delinquent peers (Differential association/social learning theories).*
7. *Involvement in delinquency is negatively correlated with degree of acceptance of conventional moral beliefs (Differential association/social learning, social bond theories).*
8. *Involvement in delinquency is a positive correlate of feelings of stress and anger (Negative-affect version of strain theory).*
9. *Involvement in delinquency is positively correlated with the parental violence towards youth (Differential association/social learning theories, negative-affect theory) .*
10. *Delinquent peers and degree of acceptance of conventional moral beliefs are the key mediating mechanisms through which family and school variables indirectly affect delinquency (Differential association/social learning theory).*
11. *Anger and stress enter into direct positive correlations with delinquency, independent of other motivational or constraining influences (Negative-affect version of strain theory).*

Examination of such a wide range of variables and relationships, including hypotheses about comparative explanatory power and direct and indirect relationships, constitutes a rather rigorous test of the generalizability of American theories and models in a new setting.

## Hypotheses Involving "Unique" Correlates

While prior research is a relevant starting point for research in new settings, we can also posit hypotheses that reflect potentially unique features of this new research setting. We have already noted Zhang and Messner's (1995) hypothesis that the pervasive salience of the family in Chinese life should make family relations a more important predictor of official delinquency than peer group relationships. Although the hypothesis was not supported, we address it using self-report data. However, we can address a more specific question involving the "extended" family in Taiwan: Does the presence of grandparents in the household enhance the control capacities of Taiwanese families? About 12 percent of youth included in the sample analyzed in this research report having both a grandmother and grandfather living in the household and an additional 11 percent report having a grandmother living in the household. A very small percentage (1.4 percent) report having a grandfather but no grandmother. Thus, fully one-quarter of the sample of Taiwanese youth have one or more grandparents in their household.

One critic of research on the family in America notes that "Grandparents have been the forgotten subjects in family research" (Flaherty et al. 1987; see Scott and Black 1989 as well). Indeed, one recent study of correlates of incarceration among American youth (Harper and McLanahan 1998) reports that a grandparent in the household reduced the probability of incarceration among black youth, but only in father-absent households. This finding suggests that, rather than serving as an additional, cumulative source of social control, grandparents function as "backup" sources of social control. Although this finding may apply more to judges' decisions to incarcerate than to the explanation of offense behavior (i.e., they are more likely to release youth, the more sources of familial supervision available), it suggests that the role of grandparents needs to be examined in both American and Asian settings. We can propose the following hypothesis about the impact of grandparents of delinquency among Taiwanese youth:

12. *Involvement in delinquency will be inhibited by the presence of grandparents in the home for father-absent households, but not for intact households (i.e., "backup" control).*

While the impact of grandparents may not be unique to the Taiwanese setting, the fact that such backup control is available in one-fourth of Taiwanese households suggests that the extended family may function as one source of low rates of delinquency in Asian societies relative to America.

## Sample and Method

The data to be used in this analysis were collected from 935 students in nine junior high schools in December 1992, using an eight-page questionnaire patterned after surveys in the United States but written in Chinese. The nine schools were randomly selected from Taipei junior high schools and the students included were a random sample from within those schools. The students were all from grade-level 2, encompassing youth between twelve and thirteen years old. The questionnaires required no names or identification to assure anonymity and were completed by the students by checking the appropriate boxes or entering the appropriate information themselves. The study was introduced as a study of children and their families being conducted by university personnel.

Fifty-two percent of the respondents in the survey were male and approximately 11 percent reported living in households without the father present (cf. 27 percent of American children). Over three-fourths of respondents indicated that they lived in a family-owned home. About 38 percent of fathers were reported to have less than a high school education and only 30 percent were reported to have some post-high school education. About 50 percent of mothers had less than a high school education with only 20 percent reported to have had some education beyond high school. About 40 percent of mothers were homemakers and about 2 percent of fathers were reported to be unemployed. The most common occupational classification for fathers or mothers was as a white-collar worker for a private firm (23 percent of mothers and 33 percent of fathers).

When asked to rate their family's economic well-being compared to classmates, 68 percent rated their families as falling in "the middle." Two percent rated their families as "upper" and 23 percent as "upper middle." Only 6 percent chose "lower middle" or "lower" as indicative of their economic well-being. About 15 percent indicated that their family had financial problems. When presented a list of eight appliances and electronics items (T.V., refrigerator, VCR, air conditioner, car, radio, piano, satellite dish and CD player) the average family had 5.4 such possessions.

Students were asked to indicate how commonly they engaged in a variety of activities, including smoking, drinking, using illegal drugs, running away from home, threatening other people, fighting, vandalism, theft, robbery and gambling. They could respond never, rarely, sometimes or all the time. The percentages of males and females reporting involvement in such activities are summarized in Table 3.1. Getting into fights is the most commonly reported activity among boys with over one-half reporting that they have been in a fight at some time.

In contrast, only 11.5 percent of females have been involved in fights, yielding a male-female ratio of 4.5:1. The male to female ratios range from 1.7:1 for running away from home to 18.5:1 for reports of police arrest. All of the differences by gender are statistically significant with the exception of running away from home.

Only 18 of 486 males report having been arrested as compared to one of 444 females. Nine boys and one girl report having been referred to juvenile court. As was the case for research in India, arrest and referral data (in this case self-reports of agency contact) imply much larger gender ratios than do survey data. These data add to the building suspicion that references to huge disparities by gender in Asian settings, as well as low overall rates of juvenile misbehavior, may be a product of differences in reactions to delinquent behavior rather than actual behavior. Drug use is exceptionally low but forms of juvenile delinquency such as fighting and theft are quite common in comparison to the impressions that would be generated by reports of contact with justice officials.

Table 3.1
Self-Reported Delinquency among Taiwanese Students

| OFFENSE | MALES | FEMALES | RATIO |
|---|---|---|---|
| FIGHTING | 52.1 | 11.5 | 4.5 |
| VANDALISM | 39.6 | 24.3 | 1.7 |
| DRINK | 31.0 | 16.6 | 1.9 |
| SCHOOL | 25.8 | 8.8 | 2.9 |
| GAMBLE | 25.5 | 7.4 | 3.3 |
| SMOKE | 24.1 | 11.0 | 2.2 |
| THEFT | 21.4 | 7.2 | 2.9 |
| ROBBERY | 13.6 | 5.2 | 2.6 |
| THREATEN | 12.6 | 5.6 | 2.2 |
| RUNAWAY | 6.4 | 3.8 | 1.7 |
| DRUGS | 2.3 | 0.5 | 4.6 |
| **AGENCY DATA** | | | |
| ARREST | 3.7 | 0.2 | 18.5 |
| JUVENILE COURT | 1.8 | 0.2 | 9.0 |

**Tests of Hypotheses 1-5**

The first set of hypotheses about basic background correlates was tested by generating bivariate correlation coefficients for a delinquency scale based on the same types of offenses that enter into typical delinquency indices used in American research (theft, fights, robbery and vandalism). In order to assure variation in the intensity of delinquent involvement, the answers to the self-report questions were coded as follows: 0 = Never, 1 = Rarely, 2 = Sometimes, 3 = All the time. The delinquency index is the score generated by adding responses to the questions "How often have you" (a) " robbed someone," (b) "got into fights," (c) "vandalized property," and (d) "stolen something." The mean score was 1.14 with 52 percent of respondents choosing never for all four items. The mean for girls was .62 and the mean for boys was 1.62. Only 13 students had missing scores based on this procedure.

The correlation between the delinquency score and gender is -.31 which exceeds the correlations for any other measure of social differentiation or stratification. Mother's and father's education, perceived family financial problems, father's unemployment and mother's occupation were significant correlates and were related in the direction expected. However, the coefficients were all very weak and within the range typically found in American

## Table 3.2
## Tests of Hypotheses 1-5

| *Hypothesis 1: Supported 6/6* | *r=* |
|---|---|
| Gender | - .311** |
| Dad's Unemployment | +.077* |
| Mom's Education | - .078** |
| Dad's Education | - .058* |
| Financial problems | +.057 |
| Luxury Possessions | +.027 |
| Economic rank | - .020 |
| *Hypothesis 2: Supported 12/12* | |
| Rank Grades | - .243** |
| School Grades | - .185** |
| Dad's Unemployment | +.077* |
| Mom's Education | - .078** |
| Dad's Education | - .058* |
| Financial problems | +.057 |
| Luxury Possessions | +.027 |
| Economic rank | - .020 |
| *Hypothesis 3, 4, 5: Supported 32/32* | |
| Family Supervision | - .243** |
| Family Discussion | - .149** |
| Parental Quarreling | - .135** |
| Parental Understanding | - .112** |
| Intact | - .089** |
| Mom Works | +.055 |
| Dad's Unemployment | +.077* |
| Mom's Education | - .078** |
| Dad's Education | - .058* |
| Financial problems | +.057 |
| Luxury Possessions | +.027 |
| Economic rank | - .020 |

*Significant at .05;  ** Significant at .01

research. Moreover, several of the measures (possessions, relative economic rank, father's occupation and home ownership) were not significantly related to the delinquency score. Consistent with American research and the first hypothesis about background correlates, *the most impressive correlation is found for gender with measures of economic well-being entering into weak negative relationships with self-reported delinquency.*

The students were asked to report their absolute scores in the previous semester and their assessment of their rank relative to their classmates. The correlations for those two measures of a youth's own academic status are significantly related to the delinquency score with coefficients of -.183 and -.126 respectively. Consistent with American research and the second hypothesis, *measures of a youth's achievement in school are stronger correlates of self-reported delinquency than measures of parental status.* The higher the academic scores, the lesser the involvement in delinquency. In fact, when the delinquency index was regressed on average scores together with mother's and father's education only the youth's academic scores persisted as a significantly correlate of delinquency.

Correlations relevant to the hypotheses about family structure and relationships are summarized in Table 3.2 as well. Children in households with both natural parents present report less delinquency than children in homes without the natural father present (-.089). Consistent with American research and the third hypothesis, *presence of both natural parents in the household slightly lowers involvement in delinquency.* Moreover, consistent with American research and the fourth and fifth hypotheses, *mother's employment in the labor force does not correlate significantly with delinquency* and *measures of parental quarreling, understanding and family supervision enter into stronger relationships than does the intact status of the household.*

Contrary to prior research, presence of a stepfather does not significantly increase delinquency scores. This relationship is very weak in American research and is even weaker in these data. However, it should be noted that only eight youth reported having a stepfather living in the household. Of those eight, four reported that the mother was remarried. Reconstructed families may be too rare in Taiwan to generate a reliable difference in a sample this size. It may also be the case that the extended family buffers the impact of stepfathers relative to their small impact in American research.

### Tests of Hypotheses 6-11

To this point, the survey data on delinquency among Taiwanese youth have behaved quite similarly to survey data on American youth. With one minor exception, variations by gender, economic well-being, academic performance and home structure are comparable to those found among American youth. Such findings not only suggest potential universal features to delinquency but suggest that survey data may show similar generic processes at work in its explanation. While "structural" variables have been found to explain only a small proportion of variation in delinquency multivariate analyses using more proximate variables such as delinquent peers, attitudes towards law and authority, bonds to parents and school, family deviance, anger, and parental supervision have been found to explain between one-fourth and one-third of the variance in delinquency in American research.

The most strongly related proximate variable in American research has been interaction with delinquent peers. This variable has been central to differential association and social learning theories of delinquency. The Taiwanese data included one measure relevant to association with delinquent peers, running around with a "gang." In American research (a) between five and six percent of males identify themselves as members of gangs, (b) gang identifiers are significantly more delinquent than non-identifiers and (c) males are about twice as likely to so identify as are females (see Esbensen and Huisinga 1993; Esbensen, Huisinga and Weither 1993; Thornberry et al. 1993). Among Taiwanese youth 5.3 percent of males and 2.0 percent of females have, at some time, defined themselves as "running around with a gang." Consistent with American research and the sixth hypothesis, those who indicate such activity are significantly more involved in serious delinquency than those who do not (r = +.41).

Attitudes towards law-breaking and authority have been consistent correlates of delinquency in American research as well. The Taiwanese data included three items tapping attitudes towards violence: (1) "Fighting is the best solution for a conflict," (2) "Fierce and tough people are superior to others" and (3) "If someone harasses you, you should strike him or her." A factor score based on these items was generated (Cronbach's alpha = .70) and entered into a multiple regression together with delinquent peers predicting the delinquency index. Both pro-violent attitudes and gang membership were found to be significant independent correlates of serious delinquency (See Table 3.3). The data are consistent with the seventh hypothesis.

As noted in the review of recent research in America measures of "anger" or "stress" have been found to be correlated with delinquency independent of other variables. The Taiwanese students were given the statements, "You always feel anxious and want to beat somebody and throw things" and " You are always upset and want to cry." They were also asked how often they were "anxious," how often they were "upset" and how often they were "restless." Response options for all of these items were "always," "sometimes," "rarely" or "never." Since feelings of anger did not differ by gender and feelings of anxiety and being upset are more commonly acknowledged as psychological states for girls than boys, such states are not good candidates for explaining gender differences. However, they may be relevant to explaining delinquency.

Table 3.3
Regression Models Predicting Delinquency among
Junior High Students in Taiwan

| Variable(s) Added | $R^2 = .165$ | $R^2 = .268$ | $R^2 = .289$ | $R^2 = .294$ | $R^2 = .308$ | $R^2 = .362$ |
|---|---|---|---|---|---|---|
| Gang Friends | +.407** | +.345** | +.344** | +.332** | +.323** | +.317** |
| Violent Attitudes | | +.326** | +.315** | +.310** | +.287** | +.220** |
| Anger/Stress | | | +.146** | +.136** | +.122** | +.174** |
| Parental Violence | | | | +.072* | +.065* | +.062* |
| Family Supervision | | | | | -.125** | -.095** |
| Gender | | | | | | -.249** |

* Significant at the .05 level. ** Significant at the .01 level.

Cronbach's alpha for this set of items was .79 and they all appear to measure one underlying factor. When entered into a multiple regression analysis together with the gang item and attitudes towards violence, the anger-anxiety score entered into an independent positive association with delinquency as did gang membership and attitudes. Consistent with research in America and hypotheses eight and eleven, measures of anger are significant positive correlates of self-reported delinquency and make a contribution to explained variance in self-reported delinquency independent of attitudes towards law-breaking and association with delinquent peers.

The main focus of the Taiwanese survey was on family violence, and students were asked, "What do your parents do when you disagree with them?" Parental responses involving violence or threats of violence included "slapped your face," "pushed, grabbed or shoved you," "threatened to hit you," "threw something at you," "kicked and beat you," "threatened you with a knife or weapon," and "hurt you with a knife or weapon." Students could respond never, rarely, sometimes or always. A score weighing the responses by seriousness was created for the father and the mother and summed to measure parental violence towards the respondent. When entered into a multiple regression analysis with the gang, attitudes and anger-stress score, parental violence is also a significant independent correlate of self-reported delinquency. The $R^2$ for the four variables is .29 with each variable entering into a separable relationship with delinquency (beta = +.332 for gang, +.310 for attitudes and +.136 for anger stress). These results are consistent with the ninth hypothesis.

We also examined the more intricate claims about delinquent peers and attitudes favorable to lawbreaking as mediating mechanisms explaining the impact of other variables (Hypothesis 10). The findings of independent effects for the delinquent peer variable, attitudes, anger-stress and parental violence suggests that peers and attitudes do not mediate fully the impact of anger and parental violence. However, most other variables that were related in bivariate analyses failed to enter into significant relationships when introduced together with the basic set of four. For example, parental quarreling, parental understanding and average academic scores were not significant independent correlates of delinquency despite the fact that they each entered into significant bivariate relationships with delinquency. Neither intact homes nor any of the measures of parental status or family well-being were significant correlates in the multivariate analysis. Thus, contrary to Hypothesis 10, delinquent peers and acceptance of conventional moral beliefs do not mediate the effect of other generic variables although they do play a role together with other variables attenuating or eliminating direct effects for several variables that were related in bivariate analysis.

We did find one traditional variable central to prior research that did retain a separate independent correlation with delinquency—family supervision. Youth who indicate that their family knows where they are and who they are with when they go out report less delinquency than those who are relatively free from family supervision and this form of indirect control appears to lower the odds of delinquency independent of delinquent peers, attitudes towards violence, parental violence and feelings of anger or stress. Together these five variables generate an $R^2$ of .31.

Since these variables are related to gender we also added respondent's gender to the analysis. Together with the five basic variables the addition of gender increased $R^2$ to .36. The bivariate correlation for gender was -.31 and the separable effect in the multivariate analysis is -.25. Hence, unlike other background variables, gender has a separate independent relationship with delinquency. Controls for gender do not eliminate the independent effects of basic proximate variables but neither do they fully explain the impact of gender. In contrast, several studies using American samples have reported eliminating the direct relationship between gender and delinquency by controlling for similar variables (see Heimer 1995; Bartusch and Matsueda 1996; Jensen Chap. 7 this volume).

Shoemaker (1994) reported that he could not explain a significant proportion of variance in delinquency among Philippine girls. We conducted analyses within each gender category to assess whether the explained variance attributed to these variables was limited to males. In contrast to Shoemaker, there was no such limitation. All five variables are related to delinquency among boys with an $R^2$ of .29 and all five are related among girls with an $R^2$ of .44. The fact that explained variance was actually greater for girls than for boys prompted further exploration of interaction effects between gender and each of the variables. Using analysis of covariance we found striking interaction effects for the delinquent peer variable with a slope of 5.38 for girls ($r = .604$) and 2.78 for boys ($r = .342$). The difference in slopes was significant at beyond the .000 level. While only eight girls identify themselves as "running around with a gang" their score on the delinquency index is 5.9 as compared to 0.51 among nongang girls. Among boys the 23 males who so identify have a mean of 4.26 as compared to 1.48 among nongang boys. The gang variable appears to be the key source of the variation in $R^2$ in that attitudes towards violence, stress and family supervision are comparably related among girls and boys with no significant interaction.

Since few studies have found any evidence of unique relationships by gender this interaction was unanticipated and our attempts to explain it are post hoc interpretations. With only eight girls reporting running around with a gang, it is not possible to test complex hypotheses about the relationship. However, we can suggest possible explanations. For one, it may be the case that in a highly patriarchal society girls are more constrained by parents and gender-specific cultural norms than boys. Differentials in constraints by gender would have two consequences. First, there may be more numerous routes for boys to become involved in delinquency without peer group support than is the case for girls. Some form of peer group support may be more crucial for female delinquency in a system where such behavior is strongly contra-normative than in systems where girls have more freedom from adult control. Second, while fewer girls than boys are likely to escape parental and adult control, when girls do escape they may have fewer individualistic options for survival outside of the family. Both boys and girls may be vulnerable to exploitation and victimization when they escape the home, but young females may be especially vulnerable in a system where their roles are strictly limited.

### The Extended Family

While the analysis suggests that the correlates of self-reports of delinquency are remarkably similar across societies, the presence of grandparents in "extended" households may provide additional control beyond that exerted by parents and/or back-up control when parental control is jeopardized. We examined the relationship within households having both natural parents present and in father absent homes (see Table 3.4). The presence of grandparents is associated with significantly reduced delinquency scores in broken homes, but not among youth who report they are living with both natural parents. In broken homes the delinquency score with no grandparents present was 1.85 as compared to 1.03 with a grandparent (r= -.217). Thus, the mere presence of additional adults does not lower the odds of delinquency. Rather, it appears that grandparents may be available to help control and socialize children when home circumstances necessitate it. When grandparents are living in the household the average delinquency score is comparable to that found for youth in intact homes (1.09).

Although the impact of grandparents was examined because of the possibility that extended families might inhibit delinquency in Asian societies, the findings do not necessarily point to a unique correlate of delinquency in

Table 3.4
Delinquency by Home Type and Grandparent(s)

| Home Type | Intact | | Broken | |
|---|---|---|---|---|
| Grandparent(s) | Yes | No | Yes | No |
| Mean | 1.005 | 1.114 | 1.026 | 1.850 |
| r= | -.029 n.s. | | -.217* | |
| Test of Differential Slopes | F= 4.16 | | Prob= .042 | |

Taiwan. Grandparents or other relatives might play a similar role in attenuating the impact of single parent or broken homes on delinquency in America as well. One study of grandmothers in black families notes that "Grandparents have been the forgotten subjects in family research" (Flaherty et al. 1987) and another notes that "the Black community should be viewed as a complex of family and kin networks" (Scott and Black 1989). The fact that typical measures of family structure are only weakly related to delinquency may reflect more complex relationships than are typically studied in American research. Hence, rather than pointing to a unique feature of Taiwanese society the findings on grandparents should prompt further research on extended family systems in American society.

## Summary and Observations

The correlates of delinquency in Taiwanese society are very similar to those observed in Western settings and the models or theories that have endured empirical test in American research apply quite well to junior high school students in Taiwan. Youth attending school in urban industrial settings in a global world system are likely to be subject to similar pressures, pulls and problems in Asian and Western societies. While there may be variations in the salience of various social institutions and groups across societies, variation in delinquent behavior within a social system is likely to be shaped by variations in experiences within such contexts that are common across settings—the family, school and peer groups. Moreover, it appears that the basic learning mechanisms identified by social learning theorists are applicable across societies and cultures.

There are obvious limitations to this study. (1) It is a cross-sectional survey of junior high school students and we cannot deal with the issues that a longitudinal design would allow. However, given the reservations expressed about the use of the self-report method in any form initial research will be limited to cross-sectional tests. The findings are remarkably similar to those found in cross-sectional data from American youth. (2) Only one question about delinquent peers was included in the survey and future surveys should more thoroughly explore the influence of delinquent peers. However, when American youth have been given similar questions the results have been quite similar and the peer variable in the Taiwanese survey entered into relationships throughout the analysis in the same manner as American research. (3) There were fewer questions about distinct forms of delinquency than would be included in the typical American survey and the response categories were categorical rather than numeric. Future surveys should ask about a wider range of acts but it should be noted that the basic model supported with the Taiwanese data has been found to be applicable across a variety of types of delinquency in American research.

There is sufficient consistency emerging from self-report research in new settings to propose that the common image of delinquency and youth crime as rampant and growing problems in the United States but rare occurrences in Asian settings is partially a product of agency statistics. Youth worldwide may be far more similar than bodies of government statistics lead us to believe. There may be far less societal variation in the common types of juvenile misbehavior than in the odds of such transgressions entering into agency records. Moreover, it appears that reliance on agency statistics would lead to a greatly exaggerated view of the gender gap in delinquency and youth crime in Taiwan relative to youth in the United States. When self-report offense behavior is considered, the gender ratios are much smaller than agency data would imply, just as the contrast with American youth is not nearly as dramatic.

The consistency in findings across settings should encourage further research in Asian settings but such research should attempt to go beyond the generic variables and measures used in American research. For example, while variables such as honor and interpersonal deference are raised as possible explanations for low rates of officially recorded crime in Asian settings, the Taiwanese survey included no questions specifically dealing with such issues. This study suggests that attempts to parallel classic American surveys are likely to yield results comparable to American research. But, ultimately, such research should go beyond prior studies to explore the relevance of social and cultural characteristics that may have quite different meaning and consequences in American and Asian settings.

## References

Agnew, R. 1985. "A Revised Strain Theory of Delinquency." *Social Forces* 64: 151-167.

_____. 1992. "Foundation for a General Strain Theory of Crime and Delinquency." *Criminology* 30: 47-87.

_____. 2001. *Juvenile Delinquency: Causes and Control.* Los Angeles, California: Roxbury Publishing Company.

Akers, R. L. 1973. *Deviant Behavior: A Social Learning Approach*, Belmont, CA: Wadsworth.

_____. 1998. *Social Learning and Social Structure: A General Theory of Crime and Deviance.* Boston: Northeastern University Press.

_____. 2000. *Criminological Theories: Introduction, Evaluation and Application.* Third Edition. Los Angeles, CA: Roxbury Publishing Company.

_____, M. D. Krohn, L. Lanza-Kaduce, and M. Radosevich. 1979. "Social Learning and Deviant Behavior." *American Sociological Review* 44: 636-655.

Axenroth, Joseph B. 1983. "Social Class and Delinquency in Cross-Cultural Perspective." *Journal of Research in Crime and Delinquency* 20 (2): 164-182.

Bartusch, Dawn Jeglum, and Ross Matsueda. 1996. "Gender, Reflected Appraisals, and Labeling: A Cross-Group Test of an Interactionist Theory of Delinquency." *American Sociological Review* 75: 145-176.

Braithwaite, John. 1989. *Crime, Shame and Reintegration.* Cambridge: Cambridge University Press.

Cloward, R. A., and L. E. Ohlin. 1960. *Delinquency and Opportunity.* New York: Free Press.

Cohen, A. K. 1956. *Delinquent Boys.* New York: Free Press.

Daosheng, Shao. 1992. *Preliminary Study of China's Juvenile Delinquency.* Beijing, China: Foreign Language Press.

Esbensen, Finn-Aage, and David Huisinga. 1993. "Gangs, Drugs, and Delinquency in a Survey of Urban Youth." *Criminology* 4: 565-589.

Esbensen, Finn-Aage , David Huisinga, and Anne W. Weither. 1993. "Gang and Non-Gang Youth: Differences in Explanatory Variables." *Journal of Contemporary Criminal Justice* 9: 94-116.

Flaherty, M. J., L. Facteau, and P. Garver. 1987. "Grandmother Functions in Multigenerational Families: An Exploratory Study of Black Adolescent Mothers and Their Infants."*Maternal-Nursing Journal* 16: 61-73.

Gottfredson, Michael R., and Travis Hirschi. 1990. *A General Theory of Crime.* Stanford, CA: Stanford University Press.

Hagan, J., A. R. Gillis, and J. Simpson. 1985. "The Class Structure of Gender and Delinquency: Toward a Power-Control Theory of Common Delinquent Behavior." *American Journal of Sociology* 90: 1151-1178.

Hagan, J., J. Simpson, and A. R. Gillis. 1987. "Class in the Household: A Power-Control Theory of Gender and Delinquency." *American Journal of Sociology* 92: 788-816.

Harper, Cynthia C., and Sara McLanahan. 1998. "Father Absence and Youth Crime." Paper presented at the meeting of the American Sociological Association, San Francisco.

Hartjen, C. A., and S. Priyardarsini. 1984. *Delinquency in India.* New Brunswick, NJ: Rutgers University Press.

Hartjen, C. A., and S. Kethenini. 1993. "Culture, Gender and Delinquency: A Study of Youth in the United States and India." *Women and Criminal Justice* 5 (1): 36-67.

Hirschi, T. 1969. *Causes of Delinquency.* Berkeley: University of California Press.

Jensen, G. F., and D. G. Rojek. 1998. *Delinquency and Youth Crime.* Third Edition. Prospect Heights, IL: Waveland.

Merton, R. K. 1957. *Social Theory and Social Structure.* New York: Free Press.

Nye, F. I. 1958. *Family Relationships and Delinquent Behavior*. New York: John Wiley.

Reckless, W. 1967. *The Crime Problem*. New York: Appleton-Century-Crofts.

Reiss, A. J. 1951. "Delinquency as the Failure of Personal and Social Controls." *American Sociological Review* 16: 196-207.

Scott, J. W., and A. Black. 1989. "Deep Structures of African American Family Life: Female and Male Kin Networks." *Western Journal of Black Studies* 13: 17-24.

Shoemaker, Donald J. 1994. Male-Female Delinquency in the Philippines: A Comparative    Analysis." *Youth and Society* 25 (3): 299-329.

_____. 1996. *Theories of Delinquency: An Examination of Explanations of Delinquent Behavior*. New York: Oxford University Press.

Sutherland, E. H., and D. R. Cressey. 1978. *Criminology*. Tenth Edition. Philadelphia: J. B. Lippincott.

Tanioka, I., and D. Glaser. 1991. "School Uniforms, Routine Activities, and the Social Control of Delinquency in Japan. *Youth and Society* 23: 50-75.

Tittle, C. R. 1983. "Social Class and Criminal Behavior: A Critique of the Theoretical Foundation." *Social Forces* 62: 334-358.

Tittle, C. R., W. J. Villemez, and D. Smith. 1978. "The Myth of Social Class and Criminality." *American Sociological Review* 43: 643-56.

Thornberry, Terence B., Marvin Krohn, Alan J. Lizotte, and Deborah Chard-Wierschem. 1993. "The Role of Juvenile Gangs in Facilitating Delinquent Behavior." *Journal of Research in Crime and Delinquency* 30: 55-87.

Zhang, L., and S. F. Messner. 1995. "Family Deviance and Delinquency in China." *Criminology* 33 (3): 359-388.

# 4

# "Who's It Gonna Be—You or Me?" The Potential of Social Learning for Integrated Homicide-Suicide Theory

*Candice Batton and Robbin S. Ogle*

## Introduction

Most lethal violence research has approached homicide and suicide as separate and independent phenomena. However, at various times over the last 150 years, an "integrated" model focusing on both homicide and suicide model has been the focus of scholarly research. The integrated theory conceptualizes homicide and suicide rates as alternative manifestations of the same underlying causal forces. It is a macro-level theory that focuses primarily on the manner in which broad social and cultural forces impact both the amount and direction of lethal violence in society. The theory does have social psychological underpinnings that revolve around the attribution of blame, and it is this issue that social learning theory is particularly well suited to address. More specifically, it is well established that homicide and suicide rates vary across social groups. The integrated homicide-suicide theory would suggest that group differences in the likelihood of homicide relative to suicide is a function of differential attributions of blame. Social learning theory provides a conceptual framework for thinking more deeply about this issue and considering the extent to which group differences in attributions of blame are likely to occur.

Our goal is to discuss how social learning theory contributes to our understanding of the direction of lethal violence and group differences in homicide and suicide rates. We begin with a brief description of the intellectual foundation and key causal mechanisms of the integrated homicide-suicide theory. We then examine how social learning theory can explain how a process at the individual level (i.e., the attribution of blame) is ultimately manifested in aggregate level, group differences in lethal violence rates. Differences in lethal violence rates based on categories of gender, race, and region are considered as well as the extent to which attribution and violence research supports this theoretical integration. Finally, limitations and directions for future research are proposed.

## Intellectual Foundations for an Integrated Homicide-Suicide Theory

In contemporary U.S. society, homicide and suicide are often regarded as separate and independent phenomena that stem from different root causes. While homicide is typically seen as an act of violence and aggression resulting from extreme feelings of anger, frustration or vengefulness, suicide is more often perceived as a personal act of desperation due to extreme sadness, despair, or a sense of hopelessness. However, in a larger historical sense, a link between homicide and suicide has existed in lay or popular thought for centuries. There is evidence of homicide and suicide being conceptualized as alternative expressions of the same underlying phenomenon in Western cultural traditions dating back to the fifth century (Unnithan, Huff-Corzine, Corzine, and Whitt 1994:10). In fact, at times, homicide and suicide have been defined as equivalent acts, distinguished only by the victim, in terms of legal, moral, and religious rhetoric.

Scholarly interest in the homicide-suicide link is also well established, dating back to the 1800s. With the publication of Durkheim's *Suicide* (1951 [1897]), sociological interest greatly diminished. However, there was a resurgence of interest in the mid-1950s stimulated by Henry and Short's (1954) study of homicide and suicide and Gold's (1958) research on the socialization of aggression. Studies of the homicide-suicide relationship continued into the early 1970s when, as before, interest subsided. Recently, interest has once again been revitalized in Unnithan et al.'s (1994) *The Currents of Lethal Violence.*

## Integrated Homicide-Suicide Theory

The integrated theory argues that homicide and suicide rates are a function of two sets of causal mechanisms. *Forces of production* are cultural and structural factors that affect frustration levels in society and the total amount of lethal violence. In contrast, *forces of direction* are cultural and structural factors that affect the direction of lethal violence (i.e., suicide vs. homicide) through their impact on the manner in which blame for negative outcomes and life events is attributed. Factors that increase internal attributions of blame increase rates of suicide relative to homicide while factors that facilitate the externalization of blame increase homicide relative to suicide. The essence of the integrated model is captured with the "stream analogy," which states homicide and suicide rates can be conceptualized as two distinct channels in a single stream of lethal violence. Forces of production can be thought of as those factors that affect the total volume of water in the stream. Forces of direction are factors that affect whether the water in the stream is directed into one channel or the other.

Violence studies have found differences in the internalization and externalization of lethal aggression across social groups. For example, suicide and homicide offending rates vary across gender and racial/ethnic groups. The integrated theory suggests group differences in lethal violence rates are largely a function of forces of production and direction differentially affecting members of different social groups. In other words, group differences in homicide and suicide rates are likely to stem from differences in the impact of cultural and structural factors that contribute to (1) the development or build up of feelings of frustration and aggression, and (2) the manner in which blame and responsibility for negative outcomes and life events are attributed. We assert that social learning theory can enhance our understanding of the factors that underlie group differences in lethal violence rates by shedding light on the process by which attribution style is developed and by highlighting the importance of social interaction and the broader social and cultural context in which social behavior occurs.

## Attributions of Blame and Social Learning Theory

In an attempt to learn more about attributions of blame and responsibility for negative outcomes, researchers have studied how individuals locate causality for both positive and negative outcomes and events. Joiner and Wagner (1995:778) have proposed three dimensions along which causal attributions vary. *Internal* attributions locate the causes of outcomes or events within the individual (e.g., task failure due to effort or ability, success due to innate intelligence), while *external* attributions locate causes outside of the individual in the environment (e.g., task failure due to distraction, success due to luck). The second dimension refers to temporal stability. While *stable* attributions define causal factors as fairly permanent or constant over time (e.g., ability, intelligence, or lack thereof), *unstable* attributions define causes as variable (e.g., success or failure due to degree of effort). The third dimension refers to similarity across situations. Attributions that are fairly constant across situations (e.g., task failure due to stupidity, success due to intelligence) are *global* while attributions that tend to be situation specific or more limited in their scope of effects are *specific* (e.g., task failure due to absence of instructions, success due to a good teacher).

Attribution style can be conceptualized as existing on a continuum defined at each extreme by an ideal type: *optimistic* and *pessimistic*. An optimistic style of attribution is characterized by the tendency to attribute successes and positive outcomes to factors that are internal, global, and stable (e.g., high exam score due to being smart and a good student). In contrast, negative outcomes and task failures tend to be attributed to external, specific, and unstable factors (e.g., failing exam score result of a bad teacher or poorly constructed exam). A pessimistic style of attribution involves locating causality for positive and negative outcomes in the opposite way. Successes and positive outcomes tend to be attributed to external, unstable, and specific factors (e.g., high exam score due to luck, an easy exam, or easy grading) while failures and negative outcomes are often attributed to internal, stable, and global factors (e.g., failing grade due to lack of ability or low intelligence).

Attribution style is not an innate or inherited trait. Instead, a stable style of attribution tends to emerge during adolescence as a result of socialization experiences (Nolen-Hoeksema and Girgus 1994). The foundation for attribution style begins to develop during childhood as individuals internalize and incorporate the feedback they receive from others regarding causal attributions into self-concept. The feedback children receive about their own positive and negative outcomes from primary group members, such as parents, caretakers, older siblings, and teachers, is particularly important (Dweck and Goetz 1978). In the course of social interaction, feedback is internalized, affecting the development of self-concept and its continual reproduction over time as described by Cooley's (1922) concept of the "looking-glass self." As Schulman (1995:160) notes, "[t]he explanations individuals habitually make for their successes and failures lead to expectations that affect their reactions to future successes and failure. These expectations create self-fulfilling prophecies that either enhance or undermine performance." While a positive self-concept contributes to, and is reproduced by, an optimistic attribution style because of the reciprocal relationship between self-concept and evaluative feedback, a negative self-image tends to contribute to, and be reinforced by, a pessimistic attribution style, especially with negative outcomes (Lochel 1983; Maracek and Mettee 1972).

The relevance of Akers' (1997) social learning theory to the discussion of attribution style is fairly straightforward. According to social learning theory, social interaction provides the context for the learning that occurs in the development of attitudes, beliefs, and norms with respect to violating and upholding the law. This view is quite consistent with research finding that attribution style emerges as a result of learning, and specifically, learning that occurs as a product of social interactions (Dweck and Goetz 1978; Lochel 1983). Akers (1997:64) asserts that primary groups are central to the learning process because the associations and social relationships that exert the greatest influence on the learning process (1) occur earlier rather than later in life (i.e. priority), (2) are more enduring over time rather than fleeting (i.e., duration), (3) involve more frequent interaction and contact (i.e., frequency), and (4) involve persons who are important and emotionally bonded to us. Attribution researchers agree emphasizing feedback from significant others (e.g., parents, teachers) (Dweck and Goetz 1978).

In addition to the evaluative feedback that individuals receive for their performance on specific tasks, the more general cultural messages that exist pertaining to group differences in abilities, characteristics, and social status are also important in the formation of attribution style (Deaux 1976). Akers (1997:64) makes a similar point noting that individuals are exposed to and learn behavioral norms and definitions of law violation through their direct associations with specific groups, but also through indirect associations with more distant reference groups. Members of different social groups are often socialized into different norms, values, and beliefs with respect to a variety of issues, such as the experience of anger, the expression of aggression, and whether or not they have control over outcomes and life events. They also learn ways of understanding the relative position of groups in society as well as rationales for stratification that may be rooted in history (e.g., blacks and the legacy of slavery, Southerners and the Civil War) or in beliefs about innate differences between groups (e.g., men and women).

To the extent that members of social groups receive differential feedback regarding the causes or sources of negative outcomes and life events, group differences in attribution styles are likely. According to the integrated homicide-suicide theory, group differences in attribution styles should be manifested in lethal violence rates; specifically rates of suicide relative to homicide. In addition to group differences in attribution style, both social learning theory and attribution research stress the importance of considering more general cultural messages that distinguish between social groups and the manner in which they might be related to the direction of violence and aggression (DuCette, Wolk, and Friedman 1972; Guimond, Begin, and Palmer 1989; Miller 1984).

## Sex Differences in Lethal Violence

Perhaps the most fundamental group distinction in society is differentiation based on gender. Research on social behavior reveals significant differences in the socialization of males and females. Traditional gender role socialization has emphasized behavioral norms accentuating strength, independence, rationality, and assertiveness for males, and dependence, emotionality, and passivity for females (Deaux 1976; Delphy and Leonard 1992; Kessler and McKenna 1978). While these qualities have historically defined masculinity and femininity in an ideal sense, men and women rarely exemplify these characteristics in their ideal states. Instead, gender can be better understood as existing on a continuum. When we look at these characteristics aside from a discussion of gender, they clearly are not value-free. Those representing femininity are things that are generally devalued by society while those representing masculinity are largely deemed positive. For example, rationality is typically more positively valued than emotionality, which is often linked to lack of control, over-reaction, erratic behavior, and poor judgment.

Gender differences in socialization contribute to the development of differential attribution styles among men and women. Males are more likely to attribute task success and positive outcomes to stable factors (e.g., ability, intelligence) and task failure or negative outcomes to variable factors (e.g., lack of effort, distraction). In contrast, females are more likely to attribute successes and positive outcomes to variable factors (e.g., luck, ease of task) and failures and negative outcomes to stable and internal factors (e.g., lack of ability). Not only are males and females likely to exhibit differential attribution styles in evaluations of their own behavior, but observers (both males and females) are also likely to make differential causal attributions based on the sex of the person being observed (Deaux 1976:338). Gender differences are especially apparent for negative outcomes where females are more likely to exhibit a pessimistic style and males an optimistic style (Dweck and Goetz 1978).

Several researchers emphasize the causal role of gender differences in socialization practices (Barry, Bacon, and Child 1957; Veroff 1969). Nolen-Hoeksema and Girgus (1995:67-69) identify several ways traditional gender role expectations may impact attribution style. First, causal attributions for success and failure often become increasingly sex-biased as children mature. As girls mature and compete in more highly valued and traditionally masculine areas (e.g., science, medicine, skilled labor), they may increasingly receive feedback that their successes stem from external, variable, and specific factors (e.g., luck, affirmative action) and their failures from internal, stable, and global factors (e.g., lack of ability, women's personality). At the same time, boys tend to get opposite messages about the causes of their successes (i.e., internal, stable, global) and failures (i.e., external, variable, specific). Research on attributions surrounding stereotypically masculine tasks supports this idea. Weitz (1982) also reports evidence of a link between gender roles and attribution style finding that women who participated in feminist conscious raising groups developed greater external attributions of blame and a greater sense of control over their lives.

Second, Nolen-Hoeksema and Girgus (1995) suggest that gender differences in attribution may be related to changes in the control over and the number of opportunities that boys and girls have as they mature. During adolescence, girls are more likely to be restricted for safety reasons while boys are often encouraged to try new activities (Gilligan 1982; Simmons and Blyth 1987). Also, females are more likely to experience discrimination and harassment in the occupational and educational realms, which can have a real impact on the future opportunity structure (Nolen-Hoeksema 1990). In and of themselves, these experiences contribute to the development of a stable, global attribution style for negative events because of feelings of uncontrolability. If negative outcomes are linked with being female, they may be seen as due to internal factors as well (Nolen-Hoeksema and Girgus 1995:68).

Third, Nolen-Hoeksema and Girgus (1995) argue that girls and boys often respond differently to changes in physical appearance that occur during adolescence. Girls tend to be less satisfied with their bodies and physical appearance than boys (Dornbusch, Carlsmith, Duncan, Gross, Martin, Ritter, and Siegel-Gorelick 1984), which likely stems from societal pressures on girls to achieve an ideal body shape that is a physical impossibility for most young women. Dissatisfaction with this relatively stable characteristic is likely to contribute to a more negative self-concept and pessimistic outlook for girls than boys as they feel a sense of frustration and helplessness over trying to control their body shape (Allgood-Merten, Lewinsohn, and Hops 1990; Nolen-Hoeksema and Girgus 1995).

In addition to affecting the development of attribution style, socialization experiences are also important because they result in gender differences in attitudes and norms concerning anger and aggression. As Averill (1982) notes, the emotion most closely linked to externalized violence and aggression is anger, but research indicates that men and women are socialized to process anger differently. According to Lerner (1980), the experience and expression of anger is governed by constituative rules (i.e., when it is appropriate to get angry and at what level) and regulative rules (i.e., appropriate means of dissipating anger). While men are socialized into both sets of these rules, women are not taught regulative rules because they have only one constituative rule, which states aggression is not acceptable behavior (Bernardez-Bonesatti 1978; Ogle, Maier-Katkin, and Bernard 1995). Instead, women are taught to "cognitively reinterpret" their anger into feelings of guilt or hurt. In other words, women are socialized to internalize feelings of anger and interpret, or redefine, them as guilt or hurt, which results in self-blame rather than externalized blame.

The concept of cognitive reinterpretation is consistent with violence research finding lower levels of externalized aggression for women than men. The majority of violent acts are perpetrated by males with only a small proportion committed by females (Belknap 2001; Steffensmeier and Allan 2000). Analyses of both victimization and arrest data for recent years have found that females comprise only 14-17 percent of violent offenders and the number is even smaller when only lethal cases are considered (Pastore and Maguire 2000). Historical studies indicate the gender gap in violent offending is not a recent development; instead, it has persisted over time (Gottfredson and Hirschi 1990).

When the aforementioned research is considered within the context of the integrated homicide-suicide theory, it leads to the prediction that females and males should exhibit differential rates of homicide relative to suicide. Because of gender differences in attribution style and norms governing the experience and expression of aggression, females are more likely to internalize aggression while males are more likely to externalize aggression. This is likely to lead to a greater proportion of female perpetrated lethal aggression being self-directed (i.e., suicidal) and a greater proportion of male perpetrated aggression being other-directed (i.e., homicidal). The fact that males engage in higher rates of both suicide and homicide than females is well established. However, of particular interest is gender differences in the *relative* likelihood of suicide and homicide.

The suicide-homicide ratio (SHR) has been used to represent the relationship between homicide and suicide rates. It is calculated by dividing suicide rates by the sum of homicide and suicide rates (i.e., SHR=S/[S+H]) (Gold 1958; Hackney 1969; Unnithan et al. 1994). The SHR ranges between 0 and 1. Higher SHR values indicate that a greater proportion of lethal violence is suicidal as opposed to homicidal. Lower SHR values indicate a greater proportion of lethal violence is comprised of homicide in comparison to suicide.

We calculated male and female SHR values from national level, U.S. suicide rate and homicide offending rate data.[1] Suicide rates were taken from Vital Statistics reports, compiled by the National Center for Health Statistics. Homicide arrest rates were taken from Uniform Crime Report data, compiled by the Federal Bureau of Investigation. Although arrest data have several limitations when used to study the incidence of crime, biases diminish as the crime seriousness increases (O'Brien 1985; Smith 1986; Steffensmeier and Allan 1988). Furthermore, they are useful for estimating relative differences in crime rates by age, sex, and race groups and do not simply reflect differences in ability to avoid arrest (Hindelang 1981; Skogan 1974: Smith 1986; Steffensmeier and Allan 1988). Therefore, we use arrest data to estimate homicide offending.

Figure 4.1 contains male and female SHR values for 1963-1998. Consistent with our theoretical approach, the data indicate that female SHR values were higher than those for males throughout the entire span of time. Thus, over the past 35-40 years, female-perpetrated lethal violence was more likely to be self-directed while a greater proportion of male-perpetrated lethal violence was other-directed.

## Racial Differences in Lethal Violence

Social learning theory sheds light on racial differences in lethal violence rates as well as gender differences. While a significant amount of research has focused on gender differences in causal attributions, there is a paucity of

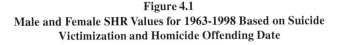

Figure 4.1
Male and Female SHR Values for 1963-1998 Based on Suicide
Victimization and Homicide Offending Date

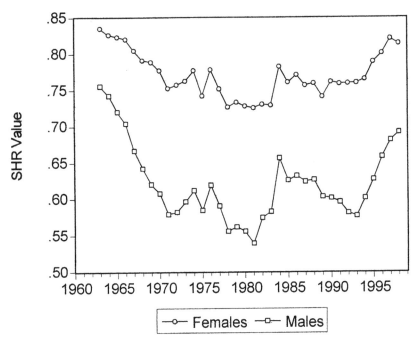

information on this issue with reference to race. However, studies of social, economic, and cultural differences and inequalities between racial groups support the idea that differential styles of attribution are likely to develop along racial lines. In discussing this idea, we focus specifically on the experiences of black Americans in the U.S. because of the abundance of research documenting their historical experiences in this society. However, the applicability of social learning theory is not limited to a comparison between whites and blacks. Instead, this perspective could be used to think more deeply about how differences in social and cultural experiences across racial and ethnic groups impact attribution styles and norms governing anger and aggression.

Significant differences exist between racial groups in terms of access to resources and inequality, with the greatest gap between white and black Americans. The most obvious inequalities can be seen in the economic realm. For example, in 1998, median family income for black families ($25,400) was 62 percent of that for white families ($40,900) (U.S. Census Bureau 2000). Poverty statistics also reflect a gross economic disparity. In 1998, 8 percent of white families had incomes below the poverty line compared to 23 percent of black families. More than one-third (37 percent) of black children are raised below the poverty line compared to only 15 percent of white children (U.S. Census Bureau 2000). Arguably, poverty line data belie the problem since an even greater percentage of people receive some form of public assistance. In 1991, almost 50 percent of black Americans received public assistance, which was three times the percent of whites (Healey 1995).

Racial inequalities are also evidenced by unemployment rates. While white unemployment rates doubled between 1970 and 1992, those for blacks quadrupled (Walker, Spohn, and DeLone 1996). This is the largest proportion of unemployed black Americans since the Great Depression (Hacker 1992) although black rates have been at least twice as high as white rates since the 1940s (Healey 1995). Bureau of Labor Statistics (2001) data indicate unemployment rates have diminished for both whites and blacks since the early 1990s, but those for blacks remain more than twice as high as those for whites. For example, in 2000, white unemployment rates were 3.5 compared to 7.6 for blacks. The problem is exacerbated for black teens whose unemployment rate in 2000 was 24.7 compared to 11.4 for white teens. Focusing on unemployment may actually obscure a larger issue whereby black Americans have increasingly fallen out of the ranks of the unemployed and joined the nonemployed who are no longer actively seeking work. People who feel so discouraged and disenfranchised that they have stopped seeking employment or participating in the mainstream society are included as are persons who make a living within the "underground economy" doing intermittent work, both licit and illicit, for cash off the books.

Discrepancies in income, poverty, and unemployment figures are a manifestation of a larger historical trend occurring in American society since the 1970s involving a steady deterioration of the economic status of blacks relative to whites (Walker et al. 1996). As the U.S. economy increasingly became service-oriented in the latter part of the twentieth century, many of the manual labor jobs in industry and manufacturing disappeared (Healey 1995). Like their white counterparts, upper-middle and upper class black Americans may have been able to capitalize on the increasing white collar economy of the 1980s and 1990s (Wilson 1980). However, this was not the case for the majority of blacks who were (and still are) disproportionately likely to be members of the lower classes and less likely to have the educational credentials and professional experiences required for access to many occupational opportunities (Healey 1995; Wilson 1980). Many of the service sector jobs that were available to persons lacking educational and occupational experience offered low wages, no benefits, no security, and no chance for advancement (Healey 1995). As a result, the economic status of many members of the lower classes, who are disproportionately likely to be racial and ethnic minorities, descended even closer to poverty contributing to the development and expansion of what is known as the urban underclass (Lawson 1992; Wilson

1992). Impoverishment and diminishing job opportunities are not the only problems facing many urban neighborhoods. One result of greater social class differentiation is that the middle classes have increasingly left urban, inner-city neighborhoods for residential communities in the suburbs. This has contributed to the further destabilization of inner-city areas as the middle classes have, in a sense, taken their affluence, articulateness, and leadership skills with them (Healey 1995). As a result, many urban neighborhoods have lost their tax base for schools and community maintenance, informal networks for legitimate job opportunities have diminished, and few middle-class role models remain to encourage socialization to middle-class goals and values. Skogan (1990) asserts that many inner-city neighborhoods are progressing toward community collapse, which involves among other things, diminishing jobs and legitimate businesses and growing illegitimate opportunities. As Walker et al. (1996) note, the drug trade has become a major cultural and economic aspect of many inner-city communities and has fostered the development of gangs and violence. The presence of drugs, gangs, and violence in turn increases criminal socialization and forces community members to make a choice between conformity or victimization.

As inner-city neighborhoods decline, educational systems also deteriorate. In *Savage Inequalities,* Kozol (1991) graphically describes this process, emphasizing the role of property taxes in school funding and the impact on quality of education. A declining tax base often leads to fewer school resources and deteriorating physical plants, both of which make it more difficult to attract and retain good teachers who can often find higher wages in more affluent school districts. As a result of scarce resources, many children in impoverished urban neighborhoods have more negative educational experiences and receive a lower quality education. This affects the risk of dropping out as well as the likelihood of pursuing a college education (and doing so successfully). While these problems are not restricted to minority children, they are disproportionately affected because they are more likely to live in impoverished neighborhoods than whites.

Education statistics provide further evidence. In 1998, nearly 25 percent of blacks did not complete high school compared to 15 percent of whites (U.S. Census Bureau 2000). At the college level, more than 25 percent of whites completed a four-year college degree or more compared to less than 15 percent of black Americans. Educational attainment discrepancies translate into earning differentials that exacerbate the gap that already exists between blacks and whites with the same level of education. In 1998, whites with a bachelor's degree earned on average $44,900 compared to only $36,400 for college-educated black Americans. Over time, trends such as these contribute to the historical maintenance of blacks in the lower echelons of the occupational realm (Georges-Abeyie 1981; Hawkins 1985; Oliver 1989).

In studying racial inequalities, several researchers have noted the existence of a negative outlook toward self and world on the part of many black Americans (Georges-Abeyie 1981; Hacker 1992; Hawkins 1983, 1985, 1995; Oliver 1989; Wilson 1980). West (1993:12-3) refers to this phenomenon as nihilism stating that, "[i]t is primarily a question of speaking to the profound sense of psychological depression, personal worthlessness, and social despair so widespread in black America." In other words, nihilism refers to a negative world and self-view whereby failure to achieve is attributed to external factors beyond the control of the individual. This way of understanding inequity in our society, and the reasons for it, is learned through both formal and informal socialization processes in the family, the school, and the community. Oliver (1989) asserts that young people, and especially young blacks, are socialized to attribute blame and responsibility for negative outcomes to external factors as a result of their exposure to "prowhite socialization." Prowhite socialization adversely impacts black Americans by facilitating what Oliver (1989) refers to as "dysfunctional cultural adaptation" whereby blacks, as a group, adjust to structurally induced social pressures by adopting a negative, or pessimistic, self- and world view. As Oliver (1989:259) notes in his review of the literature on ideology and culture crisis among blacks,

> Ideology gives structure to how group members define themselves and their experiences. A major aspect of the Euro-American cultural ideology is that people of European descent are inherently more intelligent, beautiful, industrious, and just than nonwhite people. All Americans (black, white, Hispanic, Asian, etc.) are exposed to prowhite socialization messages disseminated by the school system, mass media, and religious institutions.... Exposure to prowhite socialization also exerts an adverse impact on black Americans including: (a) the internalization of a Euro-American mode of assessing self, other blacks, American society, and the world; (b) the loss of historical memory of their African cultural heritage; and (c) self-hatred and depreciation of their people and culture.

Arguably, the processes described by West (1993) as "nihilism" and by Oliver (1989) as "dysfunctional cultural adaptation" are conducive to the externalization of blame in the case of failure and negative outcomes among black Americans. As both note, the social conditions in which many blacks live often give rise to negative views including feelings of alienation and a sense of having little or no control over outcomes. In other words, these conditions contribute to the development and maintenance of an external locus of control. This is important because performance, skill acquisition, and achievement motivation are affected by the extent to which a person believes outcomes are due to effort and ability (Atkinson 1958; Crandall 1963; Rotter 1966). This research is consistent with the idea that blacks are more likely than whites to attribute blame and responsibility for negative outcomes to external factors.

Racial disparities in attribution style and views of self and world develop as a result of social learning processes and have implications for the integrated homicide-suicide theory. In comparison to whites, blacks are expected to exhibit higher rates of homicide relative to suicide because of socialization into greater external attributions of blame. Research on racial differences in lethal violence rates support this notion in that black Americans exhibit higher rates of both homicide offending and victimization than whites (Flowers 1988; Hawkins 1985; Messner and Rosenfeld 1999; Walker et al. 1996). Conversely, suicide rates have historically been higher for whites than blacks (Lane 1999; National Center for Health Statistics 2001).

In Figure 4.2 we present SHR values for white and black Americans for 1979-1998.[2] Murder arrest rates were constructed from data on murder arrests contained in the annual *Uniform Crime Report* publications and population data taken from the *Statistical Abstract of the United States*, published annually by the U.S. Census Bureau. Although murder arrest rates are not the most accurate measure of externalized lethal aggression, our primary interest is in relative differences between blacks and whites and, as noted above, arrest rates are useful in studies of relative differences.

**Figure 4.2**
**White and Black American SHR Values for 1979-1998 Based on Suicide Victimization and Homicide Offending Data**

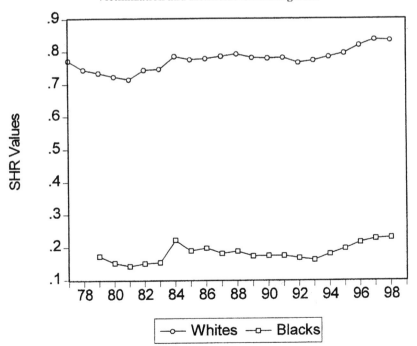

The data in Figure 4.2 indicate SHR values for whites are significantly higher than those for blacks. As expected, in comparison to blacks, a greater proportion of the lethal violence engaged in by whites is self-directed as opposed to other-directed. Conversely, a greater proportion of black lethal violence is other-directed, as indicated by much lower SHR values. In sum, SHR values for black and white Americans are consistent with the expectations about relative differences in self- and other-directed lethal violence rates stemming from a combined social learning theory and integrated homicide-suicide approach.

## Regional Differences in Lethal Violence

Region is another area that may be associated with differences in the likelihood of internalized and externalized violence as a result of variations in cultural norms and values concerning both aggression and attributions of blame and responsibility. The notion that attribution style may be linked to culture is not new (DuCette et al. 1972; Guimond et al 1989; Miller 1984; Oettingen 1995). For example, Oettingen and Morawska (1990) studied the relationship between culture and attribution style in their examination of the religious and secular writings of Russian Jews. In another study, Oettingen and Seligman (1990) found that the more oppressive and controlling political system of communist East Berlin resulted in a greater external attributions of blame for negative outcomes, which were often seen as beyond the control of the individual. In contrast, positive outcomes were rare, unexpected, and unpredictable, and, therefore, tended to be attributed to specific and variable factors when they did occur (Oettingen 1995). Many East Berliners believed better living conditions existed on the other side of "the wall" and, therefore, attributed differences to the different political system.

Given the findings of cross-cultural research, it makes sense to consider the possibility that attribution styles may differ within the U.S. along regional lines. Historians and social scientists have found evidence of cultural differences between the South and other regions of the U.S.. Arguably, regional variations in aspects of culture have deep historical roots that can be traced to the Civil War and the tumultuous political, economic, and social conditions that preceded and followed the war (Nisbett and Cohen 1996; Wyatt-Brown 1982). A large body of research has amassed documenting how this facet of American history has had long lasting effects, reaching into the twentieth and twenty-first centuries, especially in the area of racial inequalities.

Lethal violence researchers have also detected regional differences. Beginning with Redfield (1880), researchers have found for more than a century that the South has higher homicide rates than other regions of the U.S. (Brearley 1932; Huff-Corzine, Corzine, and Moore 1986; Messner 1983; Nelsen,

Corzine, and Huff-Corzine 1994; Nisbett and Cohen 1996). The source of this discrepancy has been the subject of ongoing scholarly debate since the late 1960s with researchers arguing the relative merits of cultural and social structural explanations. A handful of studies have also examined regional variations in both self-directed and other-directed violence. Porterfield (1949) was one of the first to find that, not only did the South have higher homicide rates, it also had relatively low suicide rates. Hackney (1969) reported a similar finding twenty years later finding a relationship for whites, but not blacks. After being neglected for another twenty-five years, the effect of southernness on the direction of violence was recently reexamined by Unnithan et al. (1994) who found that southernness was associated with higher levels of homicide relative to suicide for both whites and blacks.

The integrated homicide-suicide theory combined with social learning theory would suggest regional differences in rates of homicide relative to suicide arise out of both cultural and structural factors that (1) increase the likelihood of external attributions of blame and responsibility, and (2) result in different norms governing violence and the use of aggression. Unnithan et al. (1994) note that there are no studies focusing specifically on regional differences in attribution style in the U.S. However, studies of southern history and culture suggest that southerners are more likely to externalize blame and responsibility for negative outcomes and events than people from other regions of the country. Research also suggests that the South may be distinct in terms of the norms surrounding violence and aggression.

Hackney (1969) asserts that the tendency to externalize blame arose out of the historical experiences of the South, which resulted in the view of the external environment as threatening and hostile. Prior to the Civil War, white supremacist ideology provided the foundation for the economic, political, and social structure in the South (Van Evrie 1993). For example, it justified the institution of slavery, which was necessary for the plantation economy system. By denying blacks access to the political realm (e.g., voting, representation, election to political office), whites maintained power and control throughout the South, including areas where they were a numerical minority, and effectively blocked any challenges to the system that benefited them (Brantley 1987; Dauphine 1989).

During the Civil War, the South attempted to secede from the Union as a means of protecting the status quo of southern culture and society. However, the attempt was unsuccessful and, during the ensuing Radical Reconstruction, the economic, political, and social systems that had been a part of the Old South were dismantled and replaced with northern ideals (Taylor 1974). White southerners responded to this affront with a hostile outlook toward the North and an aggressive attitude geared toward retaining as much of their proud cultural heritage as possible while struggling with an impoverished economy (Taylor 1974). Among other things, the dismantling of the southern social system contributed to the rise of white supremacist organizations that used terror as a means of maintaining the subordinate position of blacks and the dominant position of whites in southern society (Brantley 1987; Dauphine 1989). In consideration of the radical cultural and structural changes that were imposed on the South by the Union, it makes sense to think that southerners would be more likely than non-southerners to attribute blame for negative outcomes to external factors (Hackney 1969).

In addition to impacting attributions of blame, studies suggest that the unique historical experiences of the South also gave rise to distinct cultural views concerning violence and the use of aggression (Abrahamson and Carter 1986; Hurlbert 1989; Reed 1982). Hackney (1969) and Gastil (1971) were among the first to posit a connection between norms and attitudes concerning violence and regional differences in homicide rates. It was argued that the South was characterized by a subculture of violence whereby there are a greater number of social situations in which an aggressive response is defined as acceptable or appropriate (Gastil 1971; Hackney 1969). It is important to note that southerners are not more approving of violence in general (Corzine, Huff-Corzine, and Whitt 1999). Instead, they are more likely to condone the use of violence in specific situations involving insults or affronts to personal honor, reputation, or family name, and situations involving self-defense or the defense of one's family or home (Corzine and Huff-Corzine 1989; Nisbett and Cohen 1996).

Nisbett and Cohen (1996) argue that southern attitudes toward violence and aggression are interwoven with concepts of masculinity. They assert that honor and personal reputation are highly valued in what they call a culture of honor. Men are socialized to protect and defend that honor. Insults or affronts to honor, and especially those involving female family members, are seen as challenges to masculinity that require a response. By punishing the one delivering the insult or making that person rescind the comment, a man retains his own personal honor and proves his masculinity.

Another aspect of southern culture that likely contributes to high rates of other-directed lethal violence is the positive imagery surrounding guns and gun ownership in the South. Numerous studies have found that attitudes toward gun ownership are much more favorable in the South than in other regions of the country. Although favorable views toward guns might be argued to contribute to both homicide and suicide rates, we assert that their impact is greater on homicide rates because of the situational nature of many homicides. A large proportion of homicides are rooted in conflict and involve a high level of stress and emotionality. Under these conditions, the mere presence of a loaded gun may increase the likelihood that an argument or fight might turn lethal if one party uses the gun against the other either in self-defense or as a result of rage (Zimring and Hawkins 1997). While emotionality clearly affects suicide as well, it could be argued that the likelihood of a suicide attempt is not greatly impacted by the presence (or absence) of a gun.

When all of these aspects of southern culture are taken into consideration—norms governing the use of violence and aggression, conceptions of masculinity, as well as the widespread support of gun ownership—it is not surprising that rates of other-directed lethal aggression are higher in the South than in other regions of the U.S. The finding that internalized lethal aggression is also relatively low in the South compared to other regions makes sense as well because of the greater likelihood of external attributions of blame for negative outcomes and events that stem from the unique history of the South.

State level data on homicide and suicide rates provide preliminary support for this view. We calculated SHR values for the South and non-South for two time periods, 1982 and 1997, based on suicide and homicide rates. We use homicide victimization rates because they are a better proxy for homicide offending than murder arrest rates since a portion of homicides are not defined as murders, and therefore, do not have the possibility of culminating in an arrest, and not all criminal homicides result in an arrest. Furthermore, although some homicides involve multiple victims and/or offenders, the majority of homicides involve one victim and one offender. Therefore, data on the number of victimizations can be a proxy for the number of offenders, which is often unknown and more difficult to calculate with any degree of accuracy. Data on suicide and homicide victimization rates were extracted from various editions of the *Statistical Abstract of the United States,* published annually by the U.S. Census Bureau.

In Figure 4.3 we present SHR values for southern and non-southern states for 1982 and 1997. A great deal of scholarly debate has revolved around how to capture the effects of southern culture (Corzine et al. 1999; Huff-Corzine et al. 1986). We defined the South in accordance with two common designations: (1) Confederate South (i.e., AL, AK, FL, GA, LA, MS, NC, SC, TN, TX, and VA), and (2) the South as defined by the Census Bureau (i.e., the 11 Confederate states plus DE, KY, MD, OK, and WV). SHR values were calculated for each state as well as regional averages. Higher SHR values mean a greater proportion of a state's lethal violence is self-directed rather than other-directed. In contrast, lower SHR values mean a greater proportion of other-directed rather than self-directed lethal violence. The average SHR values provide preliminary support for the notion that southern states are likely to be characterized by a greater proportion of externalized violence than northern states as indicated by their relatively low SHR values. Specifically, the average SHR values for the Confederate South were .50 (1982) and .45 (1997) and were similar for the Census South at .53 (1982) and .42 (1997). These figures are lower than those for the non-South, which were .69 for both 1982 and 1997 indicating a greater proportion of suicidal relative to homicidal violence.

Figure 4.3
SHR Values for the South and Non-South for 1982 and 1997

| | SHR Values | | | | |
|---|---|---|---|---|---|
| | **1982** | **1997** | | **1982** | **1987** |
| | | **Non-Southern States** | | | |
| Alaska | .50 | .70 | Nebraska | .80 | .73 |
| Arizona | .66 | .64 | Nevada | .69 | .70 |
| California | .57 | .55 | New Hampshire | .85 | .84 |
| Colorado | .72 | .77 | New Jersey | .52 | .62 |
| Connecticut | .59 | .67 | New Mexico | .67 | .65 |
| Hawaii | .77 | .74 | New York | .39 | .55 |
| Idaho | .82 | .83 | North Dakota | .92 | NA |
| Illinois | .48 | .44 | Ohio | .64 | .70 |
| Indiana | .64 | .63 | Oregon | .73 | .80 |
| Iowa | .82 | .83 | Pennsylvania | .65 | .64 |
| Kansas | .65 | .67 | Rhode Island | .74 | .72 |
| Maine | .88 | .86 | South Dakota | .75 | .85 |
| Massachusetts | .69 | .78 | Utah | .75 | .82 |
| Michigan | .54 | .56 | Vermont | .89 | NA |
| Minnesota | .83 | .78 | Washington | .73 | .73 |
| Missouri | .53 | .62 | Wisconsin | .79 | .73 |
| Montana | .79 | .83 | Wyoming | .74 | .82 |
| **Confederate South** | | | **Census South (+ Confederate States)** | | |
| Alabama | .46 | .50 | Delaware | .70 | .73 |
| Arkansas | .54 | .54 | Kentucky | .61 | .65 |
| Florida | .55 | .65 | Maryland | .51 | .48 |
| Georgia | .48 | .58 | Oklahoma | .56 | .63 |
| Louisiana | .43 | .43 | West Virginia | .63 | .73 |
| Mississippi | .35 | .47 | | | |
| North Carolina | .56 | .57 | | | |
| South Carolina | .49 | .55 | | | |
| Tennessee | .55 | .57 | | | |
| Texas | .42 | .59 | | | |
| Virginia | .63 | .60 | | | |
| Average SHR Values | 1982 | 1997 | | | |
| Non-South | .69 | .69 | | | |
| Confederate South | .50 | .45 | | | |
| Census South | .53 | .42 | | | |

## Summary and Conclusions

In this paper we have attempted to demonstrate how Akers' social learning theory contributes to the understanding of group differences in lethal violence rates posed by the integrated homicide-suicide theory. The integrated homicide-suicide theory is a macro-level approach geared toward explaining variations in rates of lethal violence across social groups. It would suggest that differences between groups in rates of suicide relative to homicide stem from cultural and structural factors that differentially impact attributions of blame and responsibility. Factors that increase internal attributions of blame are argued to increase the likelihood that lethal aggression will be self-directed while those that increase external attributions of blame increase the risk that lethal aggression will be other-directed.

It has been our goal to explore the usefulness of social learning theory for explicating the concept of attribution style as it is used in the integrated homicide-suicide theory of lethal violence. Therefore there are some limitations to the approach we have taken. First, this chapter does not include empirical tests of the theoretical ideas presented. Instead, we have explored potential theoretical connections based upon the guidance provided by previous research. Hopefully, future research will pursue the more detailed specification of variables to expand this theoretical foundation and test its applicability to a variety of social groups. Second, we have not attempted to fully incorporate all of the concepts from social learning theory into our discussion, primarily because of space limitations and the exploratory nature of this project. Third, in our discussion of factors that affect attribution style for each group, we make no claim to have addressed every factor that may lead to group differences in attribution style or in norms governing anger and aggression. Instead, we have attempted to provide a basic overview of theoretical connections and foundations for differences that are rooted in cultural and historical experiences.

Akers' social learning theory enhances our understanding of the direction of lethal violence by explaining how and why social groups are likely to vary in terms of how they attribute blame and responsibility for negative outcomes and life events. First, attribution style is not an innate or inherited characteristic. Instead it is learned, and it is learned specifically through social interaction. As social learning theory points out, interactions with significant others in primary groups are particularly important in the formation of definitions, or attitudes and beliefs, associated with behaviors. Second, social learning theory highlights the significance of secondary groups and reference group identification and the more general cultural messages that individuals receive concerning attributions and ways of assigning causality to negative outcomes. While differential associations with secondary and reference groups may be less influential than those with primary groups, they are still important and provide much of the social and cultural context for behavior and learning. Third, beyond learning styles of attribution, social learning theory draws attention to how differential reinforcement may occur with respect to the learning of other attitudes and norms that are relevant to the direction of aggression. For example, through differential learning experiences and environments, groups acquire differential norms governing both the experience of anger and the expression of aggression. We have attempted to identify some of these social and cultural norms and theorized their link with the direction of lethal aggression. This theoretical integration predicts significant group differences in the direction of lethal violence for sex, race, and region. While our propositions are consistent with the findings of previous research on these groups, hopefully future research will investigate this in more detail.[3]

## Notes

1.  To date, integrated model research has been based on victimization rates even though the theory pertains to forces that affect the risk of engaging in violence rather than the risk of being targeted by violence. Researchers have relied on victimization rates because valid and reliable measures of homicide offending are not available. For example, arrest data do not include those persons who were able to avoid detection by police or for whom there was insufficient evidence linking the person to the crime. They also do not contain persons who committed non-criminal homicides, such as in cases of self-defense or the killing of a felon during the commission of his/her crime. While a significant proportion of homicide offenders may not be captured by official statistics, this is less likely to be a problem with homicide victims since a body is almost always discovered by authorities. Since homicide victimization is more easily discerned and counted more accurately than homicide offending and most homicides involve one victim and one offender, victimization rates have been used as a proxy for homicide offending. Clearly not all homicide victims are killed by a single offender, but multiple offender incidents are relatively rare.

    While it is fairly safe to infer the presence of a homicide offender on the basis of a homicide victim, this inference cannot be made when studying gender differences in victims and offenders. Knowledge of the sex of the victim does not tell us anything about the sex of the offender. Although the majority of homicide victims and offenders are male, it is impossible to infer with any degree of certainty the sex of the offender simply by knowing the sex of the victim. Thus, female homicide victimization rates cannot be equated with female homicide offending rates. Likewise, male homicide victimization is not an accurate measure of male homicide offending. For this reason, victimization rates for males and females are not used as indicators of their respective level of homicide offending. Instead, arrest rates for males and females are relied upon to provide a sense of relative differences between males and females in the perpetration of other-directed lethal violence. Previous research indicates that even though arrest rates may not be the most accurate indicator of homicide offending, they do provide a fairly accurate sense of relative differences in homicide offending between members of different social groups (Hindelang 1981; Smith 1986; Skogan 1974).

2.  Although suicide rates for whites are available for most of the twentieth century, black suicide rates are only available from 1979 to the present. Prior to this time, data in annual *Vital Statistics* publications were categorized in terms of white and non-white.

3.  Akers long ago proposed a social learning explanation of violent and suicidal behavior. He proposed a relationship between the learning process in suicidal/self-injurious behavior and group rates (Akers 1973). His focus was on group variations in the probability of social reinforcement of suicidal behavior and exposure to definitions justifying suicide. While recognizing the relevance of that earlier analysis to our purposes here, we have not attempted to elaborate or develop it along the lines begun by Akers. Rather in this chapter we have proposed a different focus,

not on the direct reinforcement of suicidal behavior, but on group variations in probability of learning attributions of blame/responsibility that can account for group variations in lethal violence (both suicide and homicide).

## References

Abrahamson, M., and V. J. Carter. 1986. "Tolerance, Urbanism and Region." *American Sociological Review* 51: 287-294.

Akers, R. L. 1973. *Deviant Behavior*. Belmont, CA: Wadsworth.

_____.1997. *Criminological Theories: Introduction and Evaluation*. Second Edition. Los Angeles, CA: Roxbury Publishing Company.

Allgood-Merten, B., P. Lewinsohn, and H. Hops. 1990. "Sex Differences in Adolescent Depression." *Journal of Abnormal Psychology* 99: 55–63.

Atkinson, J. 1958. *Motives in Fantasy Action and Society*. Princeton, NJ: VanNostrand.

Averill, J. 1982. *Anger and Aggression*. New York: Springer-Verlag.

Barry, H., M. Bacon ,and I. Child. 1957. "A Cross-Cultural Survey of Some Sex Differences in Socialization." *Journal of Abnormal and Social Psychology* 55: 327-332.

Belknap, J. 2001. *The Invisible Woman: Gender, Crime, and Justice*. Belmont, CA: Wadsworth.

Bernardez-Bonesatti, T. 1978. "Women and Anger: Conflicts with Aggression in Contemporary Women." *Journal of American Medical Women's Association* 33: 215–219.

Brantley, D. 1987. "Blacks and Louisiana Constitutional Development, 1890-Present: A Study in Southern Political Thought and Race Relations." *Phylon* 48: 51-61.

Brearley, H. C. 1932. *Homicide in the United States*. Chapel Hill, NC: University of North Carolina Press.

Bureau of Labor Statistics. 2001. *Labor Force Statistics from the Current Population Survey*. <http://stats.bls.gov/cpsatabs.htm> (Accessed 10/01/01).

Cooley, C. H. .1922. *Human Nature and the Social Order*. New York: Charles Scribner's Sons.

Corzine, J., and L. Huff-Corzine. 1989. "On Cultural Explanations of Southern Homicide: Comment on Dixon and Lizotte." *American Journal of Sociology* 95: 178-182.

Corzine, J., L. Huff-Corzine, and H. P. Whitt. 1999. "Cultural and Subcultural Theories of Homicide." Pp 42-57 in M. D. Smith and M. P. Zahn (Eds.), *Homicide: A Sourcebook of Social Research*. Thousand Oaks, CA: Sage Publications.

Crandall, V. 1963. "Achievement." In H. Stevenson (ed.), *National Society for the Study of Education Yearbook: Part 1, Child Psychology*. Chicago, IL: University of Chicago Press.

Dauphine, J. 1989. "The Knights of the White Camelia and the Election of 1868: Louisiana's White Terrorists: A Benighting Legacy." *Louisiana History* 30 (2): 173-190.

Deaux, K. 1976. "Sex: A Perspective on the Attribution Process." In J. Harvey, W. Ickes, and R. Kidd (eds.), *New Directions in Attribution Research: Volume 1*. Hillsdale, NJ: Lawrence Erlbaum Associates.

Delphy, C., and D. Leonard. 1992. *Familiar Exploitation*. Cambridge, MA: Polity Press.

Dornbusch, S., J. Carlsmith, P. Duncan, R. Gross, J. Martin, P., Ritter, and B. Siegel-Gorelick. 1984. "Sexual Maturation, Social Class, and the Desire To Be Thin among Adolescent females." *Developmental and Behavioral Pediatrics* 5: 308–314.

DuCette, J., S. Wolk, and S. Friedman. 1972. "Locus of Control and Creativity in Black and White Children. *Journal of Social Psychology* 88: 297-298.

Durkheim, E. (1951 [1897]). *Suicide: A Study in Sociology*. New York: Free Press.

Dweck, C., and T. Goetz. 1978. "Attributions and Learned Helplessness." In J. Harvey, W. Ickes, and R. Kidd. (eds.). *New Directions in Attribution Research: Volume 2.* Hillsdale, NJ: Lawrence Erlbaum Associates.

Flowers, R. B. 1988. *Minorities and Criminality.* Westport, CT: Greenwood Press.

Gastil, R. 1971. "Homicide and a Regional Culture of Violence." *American Sociological Review* 36: 412-427.

Georges-Abeyie, D. E. 1981. "Studying Black Crime: A Realistic Approach." In P. Brantingham and P. Brantingham (eds.). *Environmental Criminology.* Beverly Hills, CA: Sage Publications.

Gilligan, C. 1982. *In a Different Voice: Psychological Theory and Women's Development.* Cambridge, MA: Harvard University Press.

Gold, M. 1958. "Suicide, Homicide, and the Socialization of Aggression." *American Journal of Sociology* 63: 651-661.

Gottfredson, M., and T. Hirschi. 1990. *A General Theory of Crime.* Stanford, CA: University of Stanford Press.

Guimond, S., G. Begin, and D. L. Palmer. 1989. "Education and Causal Attributions: The Development of 'Person-Blame' and 'System-Blame' Ideology." *Social Psychology Quarterly* 52: 126-140.

Hacker, A. 1992. *Two Nations: Black and White, Separate, Hostile, Unequal.* New York: Charles Scribner's Sons.

Hackney, S. 1969. "Southern Violence." *American Historical Review* 39: 906-925.

Hawkins, D. F. 1983. "Black and White Homicide Differentials: Alternatives to an Inadequate Theory." *Criminal Justice and Behavior* 10 (Dec): 407-440.

Hawkins, D. F. 1985. "Black Homicide: The Adequacy of Existing Research for Devising Prevention Strategies. *Crime and Delinquency* 31 (1): 85-103.

Hawkins, D. F. 1995. *Ethnicity, Race, and Crime.* Albany: State University of New York Press.

Healey, J. F. 1995. *Race, Ethnicity, Gender, and Class: The Sociology of Group Conflict and Change.* Thousand Oaks, CA: Pine Forge Press.

Henry, A., and J. Short. 1954. *Suicide and Homicide: Some Economic, Sociological and Psychological Aspects of Aggression.* Glencoe, IL: The Free Press.

Hindelang, M. 1981. "Variations in Sex-Race-Age-Specific Incidence Rates of Offending." *American Sociological Review* 46: 461-474.

Huff-Corzine, L., J. Corzine, and D. C. Moore. 1986. "Southern Exposure: Deciphering the South's Influence on Homicide Rates." *Social Forces* 64: 906-924.

Hurlbert, J. S. 1989. "The Southern Region: An Empirical Test of the Hypothesis of Cultural Distinctiveness." *Sociological Quarterly* 30: 245-266.

Joiner, T., and K. Wagner. 1995. "Attributional Style and Depression in Children and Adolescents: A Meta-Analytic Review." *Clinical Psychology Review* 15 (8): 777-798.

Kessler, S., and W. McKenna. 1978. *Gender: An Ethnomethodological Approach.* Chicago: University of Chicago Press.

Kozol, J. 1991. *Savage Inequalities: Children in America's Schools.* New York: Crown Publishers.

Lane, R. 1999. *Violent Death in the City: Suicide, Accident, and Murder in Nineteenth-Century Philadelphia.* Second Edition. Cambridge, MA: Harvard University Press.

Lawson, B. 1992. *The Underclass Question.* Philadelphia, PA: Temple University Press.

Lerner, H. G. 1980. "Internal Prohibitions against Female Anger." *The American Journal of Psychoanalysis* 40: 137-147.

Lochel, E. 1983. "Sex Differences in Achievement Motivation." Pp 193-220 in J. Jaspars, F. Fincham, and M. Hewstone (eds.), *Attribution Theory and Research: Conceptual, Developmental, and Social Dimensions.* London: Academic Press.

Maracek, J., and D. Mettee. 1972. "Avoidance of Continued Success as a Function of Self-Esteem, Level of Esteem Certainty and Responsibility for Success." *Journal of Personality and Social Psychology* 22: 98-107.

Messner, S. 1983. "Regional and Racial Effects on the Urban Homicide Rate." *American Journal of Sociology* 88: 997-1007.

Messner, S., and R. Rosenfeld. 1999. "Social Structure and Homicide: Theory and Research." In D. Smith and M. Zahn (eds.), *Homicide: A Sourcebook of Social Research.* Thousand Oaks, CA: Sage Publications.

Miller, J. 1984. "Culture and the Development of Everyday Social Explanation." *Journal of Personality and Social Psychology* 46: 961-978.

National Center for Health Statistics. 2001. *GMWK290 Death Rates for 72 Selected Causes by 10-Year Age Groups, Race, and Sex: United States, 1979-98.* <http://www.cdc.gov/nchs/datawh/statab/unpubd/mortabs/gmwk290.htm> (Accessed 10/13/01).

Nelsen, C. B., J. Corzine, and L. Huff-Corzine. 1994. "The Violent West Reexamined: A Research Note on Regional Homicide Rates." *Criminology* 149-161.

Nisbett, R. E., and D. Cohen. 1996. *Culture of Honor: The Psychology of Violence in the South.* Boulder, CO: Westview Press.

Nolen-Hoeksema, S. 1990. *Sex Differences in Depression.* Stanford, CA: Stanford University Press.

Nolen-Hoeksema, S., and J. Girgus. 1994. "The Emergence of Gender Differences in Depression during Adolescence." *Psychological Bulletin* 115: 424-443.

———. 1995. "Explanatory Style and Achievement, depression, and Gender Differences in Childhood and Early Adolescence." In G. Buchanan and M. Seligman (eds.), *Explanatory Style.* Hillsdale, NJ: Lawrence Erlbaum Associates.

Oettingen, G. 1995. "Explanatory Style in the Context of Culture." In G. Buchanan and M. Seligman (eds.), *Explanatory Style.* Hillsdale, NJ: Lawrence Erlbaum Associates.

Oettingen, G., and E. Morawska. 1990. "Explanatory Style in Religious vs. Secular Domains in Russian Judaism vs. Orthodox Christianity." Unpublished manuscript, University of Pennsylvania.

Oettingen, G., and M. E. Seligman. 1990. "Pessimism and Behavioural Signs of Depression in East vs. West Berlin." *European Journal of Social Psychology* 20: 207-220.

Ogle, R. S., D. Maier-Katkin, and T. J. Bernard. 1995. "A Theory of Homicidal Behavior among Women." *Criminology* 33 (2): 173-193.

Oliver, W. 1989. Sexual Conquest and Patterns of Black-on-Black Violence: A Structural-Cultural Perspective. *Violence and Victims* 4 (4): 257-272.

O'Brien, R. M. 1985. *Crime and Victimization Data.* Beverly Hills, CA: Sage Publications.

Pastore, A., and K. Maguire. 2000. *Sourcebook of Criminal Justice Statistics 1999.* U.S. Department of Justice, Bureau of Justice Statistics. Washington, DC: U.S. Government Printing Office.

Porterfield, A. L. 1949. "Indices of Suicide and Homicide by States and Cities: Some Southern-Non-Southern Contrasts with Implications for Research." *American Sociological Review* 14: 481-490.

Redfield, H. 1880. *Homicide, North and South.* Philadelphia, PA: J. B. Lippincott.

Reed, J. S. 1982. *One South: An Ethnic Approach to Regional Culture.* Baton Rouge: Louisiana State University Press.

Rotter, J. 1966. "Generalized Expectancies for Internal vs. External Control of Reinforcement." *Psychological Monographs* 81: 1-28.

Schulman, P. 1995. "Explanatory Style and Achievement in School and Work." In G. Buchanan and M. Seligman (eds.), *Explanatory Style.* Hillsdale, NJ: Lawrence Earlbaum Associates.

Simmons, R., and D. Blyth. 1987. *Moving into Adolescence: The Impact of Pubertal Change and School Context.* New York: Aldine DeGruyter.

Skogan, W. G. 1974. "The Validity of Official Crime Statistics: An Empirical Investigation." *Social Science Quarterly* 55: 25-38.

_____. 1990. *Disorder and Decline.* New York: Free Press.

Smith, D. 1986. "The Era of Increased Violence in the United States: Age, Period, or Cohort Effect?" *Sociological Quarterly* 27 (2): 239-251.

Steffensmeier, D., and E. Allan. 2000. "Looking for Patterns: Gender, Age, and Crime." In J. Sheley (ed.), *Criminology: A Contemporary Handbook.* Belmont, CA: Wadsworth,

_____. 1988. "Sex Disparities in Arrests by Residence, Race, and Age: An Assessment of the Gender Convergence/Crime Hypothesis." *Justice Quarterly* 5 (1): 53-80.

Taylor, J. 1974. *Louisiana Reconstructed, 1863-1877.* Baton Rouge: Louisiana State University Press.

U.S. Census Bureau. 2000. *Statistical Abstract of the United States 2000.* Washington, DC: U.S. Government Printing Office.

Unnithan, P., L. Huff-Corzine, J. Corzine, and H. Whitt. 1994. *The Currents of Lethal Violence: An Integrated Model of Suicide and Homicide.* Albany: State University of New York Press.

Van Evrie, J. 1993. *White Supremacy and Negro Subordination.* New York: Garland Publishers.

Veroff, J. 1969. "Social Comparison and the Development of Achievement Motivation." In C. Smith (ed.), *Achievement-Related Motives in Children.* New York: Russell Sage.

Walker, S., C. Spohn, and M. DeLone. 1996. *The Color of Justice: Race, Ethnicity, and Crime in America.* Belmont, CA: Wadsworth.

Weitz, R. 1982. "Feminist Consciousness Raising, Self-Concept, and Depression." *Sex Roles* 8: 231-241.

West, C. 1993. *Race Matters.* Boston, MA: Beacon Press.

Wilson, W. J. 1980. *The Declining Significance of Race: Blacks and Changing American Institutions.* Second Edition. Chicago: University of Chicago Press.

_____. 1992. *The Ghetto Underclass.* Newbury Park, CA: Sage Publications.

Wyatt-Brown, B. 1982. *Southern Honor: Ethics and Behavior in the Old South.* New York: Oxford University Press.

Zahn, M., and P. McCall. 1999. "Trends and Patterns of Homicide in the 20th-century United States." In D. Smith and M. Zahn, (eds.), *Homicide: A Sourcebook of Social Research.* Thousand Oaks, CA: Sage Publications.

Zimring, F., and G. Hawkins. 1997. *Crime is not the Problem: Lethal Violence in America.* New York: Oxford University Press.

# 5

# Social Learning Theory and Courtship Violence: An Empirical Test*

*Christine S. Sellers, John K. Cochran, and L. Thomas Winfree, Jr.*

Over the last thirty-five years, Akers' social learning theory has become one of the most discussed, cited, and researched theoretical explanations of criminal behavior. Many criminologists have acknowledged Akers' theory as the most important revision of Edwin Sutherland's classic differential association theory (Liska and Messner 1999:63; Vold et al. 1998: 195). Some consider it an even more general theory than Sutherland's since it includes wider sources of learning than differential association theory (Paternoster and Bachman 2001:175). Indeed, as Cullen and Agnew (1999:79) observe, micro-level theories, including both differential association and social learning, "have had a major impact on crime research and now constitute the leading theories of crime."

Akers' social learning theory incorporates both sociological and psychological processes into a comprehensive explanation of crime, deviance, and conformity. Akers' social learning theory originated with a restatement of Sutherland's (1947) differential association theory, using behavioral learning principles to delineate the mechanism by which deviant behavior is learned (Burgess and Akers 1966. Initially identified as "differential association-reinforcement theory," the theory began with Sutherland's contention that criminal behavior is learned through interaction with others, especially in intimate, primary groups. By illustrating the compatibility of this notion with the operant conditioning principle that individual behavior is shaped by its consequences in the environment, Burgess and Akers (1966) were able to explain in precise terms exactly how criminal behavior is learned. The theory thus integrates symbolic interaction processes from sociology with principles of reinforcement and punishment from psychology.

In 1973, Akers proposed a more fully explicated version of social learning theory, which he applied to a variety of deviant behaviors, including deviant drug and alcohol use, sexual deviance, suicide, and mental illness. Among the forms of criminal behavior he included were white collar crime, professional crime, organized crime, and violent and "compulsive" crime (Akers 1973. Also within this seminal work, "differential association-reinforcement theory" made the conceptual leap to "social learning theory," as reflected in the title: *Deviant Behavior: A Social Learning Approach*. In subsequent editions of this book, Akers (1977; 1985) provided additional insights into social learning theory and its application to general deviant behavior. Finally, in 1998, Akers further elaborated upon the theory by incorporating the role of social structure into the social learning mechanism, an idea that grew out of his study of drugs, including alcohol (Akers 1992:13-14).

Akers' social learning theory has been subjected to more than 100 empirical tests (Sellers et al. 2000). Much of the empirical research designed to test the explanatory efficacy of social learning theory has focused on general delinquency (Warr and Stafford 1991) and, particularly, substance use (Akers et al. 1979; Akers et al. 1989; Krohn et al. 1985; Sellers and Winfree 1990; Winfree and Bernat 1998; Winfree and Griffiths 1983; Winfree et al. 1989). Principles derived from Akers' theory have also been applied to the study of youth gang membership and activities (Winfree et al. 1994a; 1994b; Winfree et al. 2001). Indeed, Akers (1998: 110-117; see also Akers 2000: 82-90) has reviewed dozens of data-based examples of the successful application of social learning theory to the study of crime and delinquency. Only rarely, however, has the theory been investigated for its ability to explain other forms of deviant behavior, such as computer crime (Skinner and Fream 1997), academic cheating (Lanza-Kaduce and Klug 1986), driving under the influence (DiBlasio 1986), premarital sex (DiBlasio and Benda 1990), and sexual coercion (Boeringer et al. 1991. While more scarce than studies of drug use and delinquency, this body of research tends to verify Akers' earliest assertions about the general nature of his theory.

Despite the relatively large body of research that supports social learning theory, there exist some notable lacunae in the extant empirical literature. One important criticism is that the theory seems to work best only when applied to what are described as "minor forms" of youthful misbehavior, whereas studies of serious offending, especially by adults, are largely absent from the literature (Curran and Renzetti 2001; Rojek and Jensen 1996; Morash 1999). Although several of the empirical works cited above clearly call into question this charge, focusing the theory's constructs on a serious form of misconduct such as violence would help to confirm the truly general nature of the theory.

Another shortcoming of the extant research on social learning theory is that many tests of social learning theory have addressed as their dependent variable only those forms of behavior largely committed by adolescents in a social or group context, such as cigarette smoking, alcohol and marijuana use, and gang behavior. Certainly one would expect that behavior committed in the presence of others engaging in the same behavior is likely to garner more immediate consequences from the environment than acts that are committed outside the view of others. But is it logical that deviant acts committed in private are therefore not learned through the same process as those committed in a group context? Can the learning derived from associations with others still manifest itself outside the group context? Designing a test of social learning theory in which the dependent variable is an act that is normally committed in isolation rather than in a general social context should provide a more demanding test of social learning principles.

Finally, Morash (1999) observes that most of the research on social learning theory has neglected the role of gender and gender structure within the social learning model. Although Akers (1999) rightly counters that he incorporates gender as an important locator within the social structure in his social structure-social learning (SSSL) model (Akers 1998), he acknowledges that little effort has been made yet to test empirically the extent to which gender differences in various deviant behaviors may be mediated by social learning variables. He predicts that social learning should mediate "a *substantial portion* of the relationship between *most* of the structural variables in the model [including gender] and crime" (Akers 1998: 340, emphasis in original) rather than completely account for the entire gender difference in the behavior. Moreover, Akers (1999:485) calls for future research to investigate the extent to which gender differences in more serious crime, such as violence, are mediated by social learning. Interestingly, though, he speculates that a greater portion of the gender effect for serious crime would remain unmediated by social learning variables than would be the case for less serious crime.

The present study explores these critical gaps in the social learning research by focusing on the ability of the social learning model to account for a more serious behavior enacted in relative isolation from the group context. Specifically, we investigate the extent to which social learning variables account for the use of violence against an intimate partner. Moreover, in an effort to further explore the role of gender in the social learning model, we also investigate the extent to which gender differences in the use of violence against a partner are mediated by the social learning process.

## Intimate Violence: A Social Learning Approach

The study of violence against partners in intimate relationships began in the 1970s with the investigation of spouse abuse, particularly the use of physical aggression by husbands against their wives (Martin 1976; Walker 1979). Although wife abuse is a serious problem in its own right, another form of intimate violence that has received comparatively little attention in the literature is violence against partners in non-marital, courtship relationships. Serious scientific attention did not turn toward this phenomenon until the 1980s (Makepeace 1981). Early descriptive studies recorded experiences of aggression in dating relationships among students, with prevalence rates averaging 22 percent in high school samples and 32 percent in college samples (Sugarman and Hotaling 1989). Violence within dating relationships is typically accompanied by alcohol use (Makepeace 1981; Bogal-Albritten and Albritten 1985), attitudes accepting of violence (Cate et al. 1982; Stets and Pirog-Good 1987), and feelings of jealousy (Makepeace 1981; Laner 1983). Dating violence is highly likely to occur in private settings where no third parties are present (Laner 1983; Roscoe and Kelsey 1986). Significantly, while women are slightly more likely than men to report being victimized by a dating partner, they are also more likely than men to report their own use of aggression against a partner (Sugarman and Hotaling 1989; Archer 2000).

Gender differences in the use of violence against a partner has been a matter of controversy in the intimate violence literature (see Archer 2000 for a review and meta-analysis). Family conflict researchers (Straus 1990; Straus and Gelles 1988), who typically find evidence of mutual combat in heterosexual relationships, argue that similar processes can account for the use of aggression by both men and women (see also Moffitt et al. 2000). Feminist researchers (Dobash et al. 1992) argue that evidence of mutual combat is an artifact of faulty measurement generated by the use of Straus' (1979) Conflict Tactics Scale (CTS), which fails to gather information on situational context and extent of injury in violent interactions between partners. In studies where degree of injury is measured, men are more likely to inflict greater injury on women (Archer 2000), a finding which feminist researchers attribute to a patriarchal society characterized by male coercive power over women in an effort to control them (Dobash and Dobash 1980; Pagelow 1984). Johnson (1995) observes, however, that most studies that assess the degree of injury utilize samples of women in shelters or men in offender treatment programs, while most studies that utilize the CTS examine general community samples. Thus variation in the observation of gender differences in intimate violence may be due to sampling biases rather than, or in addition to, measurement error.

Most of the extant research on courtship violence has described the nature and extent of the problem and provided some insight into the situational characteristics of such behavior. However, systematic theories of courtship violence that elucidate why it occurs and the conditions under which it is likely to occur are quite scarce. Two initial efforts, though, have made significant strides toward this end. "Intergenerational transmission theory" proposes that witnessing or experiencing violence during childhood may translate into future use of violence or victimization in adulthood (Straus et al. 1980).

The theory implies that by witnessing violence between parents, or through violent victimization by a parent during childhood, the child learns to imitate this behavior in his or her later intimate relationships. The findings of empirical research testing this contention, however, are rather mixed and inconclusive (Sugarman and Hotaling 1989). Alternatively, in perhaps the most comprehensive theoretical effort to date, DeKeseredy and Schwartz (1993) offer a "male peer support" theory, which proposes that societal patriarchy, as well as the patriarchy that develops within the dating relationship itself, produces stress for the male partner when his authority is challenged. This form of stress may occur when his partner refuses sex, engages him in arguments, or threatens to end the relationship. The experience of stress leads the man to seek support from male peers, typically within all-male social groups (e.g., fraternities, athletic teams, gangs, etc.). Within these groups, values are promulgated that legitimate, justify, and even encourage the abuse of certain types of women. Although the male peer support model offers a fairly well-developed theoretical explanation of courtship aggression, one shortcoming is that its explanatory scope is limited to the specific instance of male abuse of women in heterosexual relationships. Since the causal factor identified in the model is specific to the dynamics of traditional male-female gender roles, the theoretical model cannot be easily extended to female aggression against men.

While extant theories of courtship violence have limitations, a common thread in each of these theories is the notion that violence against intimates is learned, either by imitation across generations or through the transmission of group values. What is lacking in current theories of courtship violence, however, is a systematic, logical explanation that can delineate the specific mechanisms by which violence and aggression are learned and that is sufficiently general in scope to account for all incidents of courtship violence, regardless of the gender of the victim and offender. One theory in the general criminological literature that meets these criteria is Akers' (1973) social learning theory.

Akers' social learning model consists of four elements. First, imitation refers to the extent to which one emulates the behavior of individuals one admires. These models are likely to be significant others with whom one has a personal relationship. In the present case, the theory predicts that individuals who *personally observe* others whom they admire engaging in acts of violence against a partner are more likely to engage in the behavior as well.

Definitions, the second element of the social learning model, refers to the attitudes or level of approval individuals hold regarding morals and laws in general as well as specific deviant behaviors. In Akers' model, deviant behavior does not require positive acceptance of the behavior; instead, morals or conventional values that are weakly held or temporarily neutralized may be sufficient to generate deviance. Clearly, such a proposition has important implications for intimate violence: the more individuals endorse and internalize rules and values against such violence, the less likely they are to resort to such conduct against a partner.

Differential association is the third component of the social learning model, referring to the attitudes and patterns of behavior to which one is exposed in interaction with others. The impact of this exposure may vary according to the frequency, duration, priority, and intensity of the association with others. In terms of courtship violence, the theory predicts that the use of physical violence against a partner is higher among those whose close associates engage in the conduct themselves.

Finally, differential reinforcement refers to the configuration of anticipated costs and rewards associated with a given behavior. An act that is anticipated to reap more rewards than costs is more likely to be enacted or repeated. Persons in dating relationships most likely to engage in violence are said to view the act itself as providing some social and/or nonsocial compensations or benefits. Such rewards may lie in the act itself, as in domination over another or the feeling of control such violence may appear to bring the aggressor, or they may lie in the support the aggressor receives from others for the violence. If rewards are forthcoming, then, according to the theory, the behavior will continue. Conversely, an act that is anticipated to elicit more costs than rewards is likely to be avoided or stopped. In the case of courtship violence, costs are those social and/or nonsocial losses a person suffers—or could suffer—as a direct result of engaging in intimate violence. For example, the fear of arrest or social approbation may be sufficient to extinguish or prevent intimate violence. Guilt, an internal psychological factor, and familial disapproval, a social one, could also function as costs and result in the avoidance or cessation of intimate violence (Grasmick and Bursik 1990; Williams and Hawkins 1989).

In summary, as applied to the explanation of courtship violence, social learning theory proposes that the use of violence is more likely among those who have witnessed others whom they admire using aggression against a partner, who hold definitions less disapproving of violence against a partner, who associate with others who also hold these definitions and use violence themselves, and who anticipate greater rewards than costs for the use of violence against a partner. This social learning model of courtship violence has much in common with earlier efforts to explain this behavior and holds great promise as a comprehensive theoretical explanation of courtship violence.

Boeringer and Akers (see Boeringer er al. 1991; Akers 1998) found support for a social learning model (with measures of all of the major social learning variables) of sexual aggression and rape in dating and acquaintance relationships in two studies of university males. The current study goes beyond that research to test a full social learning model of direct physical assault between parties in dating or courtship relationships among university students and includes both male and female respondents. Such acts are typically committed in a dyad outside the presence of others or in a group context.

Such a test provides further investigation of the explanatory scope of social learning theory beyond minor acts of youthful misconduct typically committed in the company of others. Using a modified version of the measures of social learning concepts recommended by Akers et al. (1979), the model is tested with a sample of young adult university students who have been involved in at least one serious dating relationship. To explore the role of gender in the social learning model, we also examine the extent to which gender differences in the use of aggression in a dating relationship may be accounted for by social learning variables.

## Methods

The data for this study were obtained through a self-administered survey of 1,826 students attending a large urban university in Florida (see Sellers 1999. The students were surveyed in graduate and undergraduate classes randomly selected from the course offerings of five colleges (Arts and Sciences, Business Administration, Education, Engineering, and Fine Arts) during the first four weeks of the spring 1995 semester. Courses were sampled from each college in proportion to the enrollments each contributed to the total semester enrollment for the university. This sampling strategy targeted a total of approximately 2,500 students, but absenteeism on the day of the survey and enrollments of students in more than one of the sampled courses produced an overall response rate of 73 percent. The current study is based upon a subset of the original sample, consisting of those students who report that they are currently or have recently been involved in a serious dating relationship (N = 1,228); these relationships include those who report that they are or recently were dating, going steady, engaged, and/or cohabiting.

*Dependent Variable: Courtship Violence*

The dependent variable for our analyses makes a binary distinction between those who report that they have employed at least one form of physical violence against a current or recent dating partner (coded 1) and those who report no acts of physical aggression (coded 0). Drawing from the physical aggression items in the Conflict Tactics Scale (Straus 1979), our respondents were asked to indicate how many times during a current "committed" dating relationship they had (1) thrown something at their partner; (2) pushed, grabbed, or shoved their partner; (3) slapped their partner; (4) kicked, bit, or hit their partner; (5) hit their partner with something; (6) beat up their partner; (7) threatened their partner with a knife or gun; or (8) used a knife or gun against their partner. While response options were initially fixed along a seven-point ordinal scale (0 = never 1 = once 2 = twice, 3 = three to five times, 4 = six to ten times, 5 = eleven to twenty times, and 6 = more than twenty times), we collapsed these responses into 0 = never and 1 = one or more times to determine simply whether or not the respondent had used violence against a partner in a current relationship. We also asked respondents to indicate how many partners in past serious relationships against whom they had used these eight conflict tactics. Thus, we were able to add together the number of partners in both current and past relationships against whom the respondent had used violence. However, because of the low frequency of dating violence among our respondents (61.3 percent reported no acts of violence against any partner), scores of one or more on this summed index were censored to create a single dichotomous prevalence measure.

*Independent Variables: Social Learning Concepts*

Five variables are employed as measures of the key theoretical components of Akers' social learning theory. *Imitation,* the number of admired models observed using violence against their partner, is a seven-item additive index. Respondents were asked to indicate whether or not they had "actually seen" any of the following "admired" role models use physical actions (hitting, slapping, etc.) against a spouse or partner: (1) father or stepfather, (2) mother or stepmother, (3) siblings, (4) other relatives, (5) friends, (6) actors on TV/movies, (7) others.

*Definitions,* attitudes toward courtship violence and the law, is an additive scale comprised of the following Likert-type statements to which respondents were asked to indicate the degree to which they agreed or disagreed (1= strongly disagree; 4 = strongly agree): (1) It is against the law for a man to use violence against a woman, even if they are in an intimate relationship; (2) It is against the law for a woman to use violence against a man, even if they are in an intimate relationship; (3) Laws against the use of physical violence, even in intimate relationships, should be obeyed; (4) We all have a moral duty to abide by the law; (5) In dating relationships, physical abuse is never justified; (6) Physical violence is a part of a normal dating relationship; (7) I believe victims provoke physical violence; and (8) It's OK to break the law if we do not agree with it. The first five of these items have been reverse coded so that high values on the additive scale are indicative of a system of respondent attitudes supportive of courtship violence.

Differential reinforcement is operationalized by two separate additive indexes. The first, *rewards,* is an eight-item additive index of the number of anticipated social and non-social benefits of dating violence; the second, *costs,* is also an eight-item additive index of the number of anticipated social and non-social costs of dating violence. Respondents were asked to indicate which of the following things have happened/would happen as a result of using physical actions (such as hitting, kicking, slapping, punching, etc.) against their partner during a disagreement: (1) It gave/would give me a satisfying or rewarding feeling; (2) It made/would make me feel more masculine or tough; (3) It ended/would end the argument; (4) It got/would get my partner off my back; (5) I felt/would feel powerful; (6) My friends respected/ would respect me more; (7) I felt/would feel more in control; (8) My partner respected/would respect me more; (9) It made/would make my relationship even more stressful; (10) My friends criticized/would criticize me; (11) I got/ would get arrested; (12) It made/would make me feel out of control; (13) I felt/ would feel ashamed; (14) It made/would make the argument worse; (15) My family criticized/would criticize me; and (16) I felt/would feel guilty. The first eight items are used in the construction of the rewards index and the remaining eight in the construction of the costs index.

Finally, *differential association* is measured by a single four-point, ordinal-scale item; respondents were asked to indicate about how many of their "closest friends" had ever used physical actions (hitting, slapping, etc.) in a disagreement with a spouse or partner: 0 = none or almost none; 1 = less than half; 2 = more than half; and 4 = all or almost all.

*Control Variables*

In addition to these five measures of social learning concepts, our analyses include the following exogenous variables as statistical controls: gender (0 = female; 1 = male), respondents' age (in years), total annual family income from all sources (nine-point ordinal scale), race/ethnicity (0 = non-white; 1 = white), and membership in a fraternity/sorority (0 = non-member; 1 = member).

## Results

Because we employ a dichotomous dependent variable and both continuous and categorical independent variables, the method of analysis used is logistic regression. The reduced model in Table 5.1 presents the results of a logistic regression analysis testing the effects of gender on the prevalence of respondents' self-reported use of violence in their current or recent dating relationships. Results indicate that even after controlling for the effects of other sociodemographic variables, gender is significantly related to the prevalence of courtship violence, with women more likely than men to use physical aggression against a partner (b = -1.054) in a dating relationship. The model, however, explains less than 10 percent of the variation in the prevalence of courtship violence.

The social learning model in Table 5.1 presents the results of a logistic regression analysis testing the effects of the five social learning theory constructs on the prevalence of respondents' self-reported use of violence. This

## Table 5.1
### Logistic Regression Models for the Effects of Gender and Social Learning on the Prevalence of Courtship Violence

| | Reduced Model | | | | | Social Learning Model | | | | |
| --- | --- | --- | --- | --- | --- | --- | --- | --- | --- | --- |
| | b | se(b) | X² | p | Odds Ratio | b | se(b) | X² | p | Odds Ratio |
| Male | -1.054 | .131 | 64.35 | .0001 | 0.348 | -.667 | .161 | 17.24 | .0001 | 0.513 |
| Imitation | | | | | | .259 | .060 | 18.75 | .0001 | 1.296 |
| Definitions | | | | | | -.031 | .027 | 1.27 | .2604 | 0.970 |
| Rewards | | | | | | .127 | .092 | 1.93 | .1653 | 1.136 |
| Costs | | | | | | -.342 | .036 | 92.81 | .0001 | 0.710 |
| Peer Association | | | | | | .499 | .156 | 18.57 | .0001 | 1.646 |
| Age | .021 | .018 | 1.41 | .2344 | 1.022 | .005 | .021 | 0.07 | .7958 | 1.005 |
| Income | .001 | .024 | 0.00 | .9699 | 1.001 | -.005 | .027 | 0.03 | .8635 | 0.995 |
| White | .132 | .141 | 0.88 | .3477 | 1.141 | .402 | .168 | 5.74 | .0166 | 1.495 |
| Greek | .010 | .182 | 0.00 | .9550 | 1.010 | .109 | .207 | 0.29 | .5924 | 1.115 |
| Intercept | -.709 | | | | | .553 | | | | |
| Pseudo R² Corrected R² | .054 .095 | | | | | .189 .331 | | | | |
| -2 Log Likelihood (intercept) (model) | 1625.309 1554.847 | | | | | 1502.33 1238.38 | | | | |
| Model X² | 70.462 (df=5) | | | | | 263.95 (df=10) | | | | |
| N | 1228 | | | | | 1131 | | | | |

model also controls for the influence of several sociodemographic variables, as well as gender. In this test of the social learning model, we observe mixed support for Akers' social learning theory in that the parameter estimates of the effects of these constructs attain statistical significance for most, but not all, of the five variables. Nevertheless, this model explains 33 percent of the variation in the prevalence of courtship violence.

Examining the relative effects of the social learning variables, the imitation, peer association, and anticipated costs variables are significantly associated with self-reported courtship violence (b = .259, .499, and -.342, respectively). Thus, the odds of involvement in courtship violence in this sample increases as the proportion of peers and the number of admired models observed using violence against their partners increases; these odds decrease as the expected/anticipated social and non-social costs of courtship violence increase. However, the parameter estimates for the effects of the definitions and the expected/anticipated social and non-social rewards scales each fail to attain statistical significance.

To determine the extent to which the gender effect on courtship violence is mediated when social learning variables are added to the model, we can compare the odds ratio for gender in the reduced model (0.348) with that for gender in the expanded social learning model (0.513). The results indicate that while the gender effect remains statistically significant in the expanded model, it also decreases substantially. In the reduced model, women are 1.65 times more likely than men to use aggression against a dating partner. When social learning variables are controlled, women are only 1.49 times more likely than men to use aggressive tactics, a reduction of almost 25 percent in the gender effect. These data indicate that social learning at least partially mediates the gender effect on prevalence of courtship violence, and the tendency of women in this sample to use aggression more than men can thus be partially accounted for by gender differences in the social learning context.

To further explore these gender differences in the social learning of courtship violence, we estimate logistic regression models separately for males and females; results are presented in Table 5.2. First, while the effects of social and non-social costs of courtship violence are significant in both the male and female models, its influence is stronger in the female model (b = -.422 versus -.190), and this difference in effect (d = .232) is statistically significant (z = 3.05, p < .0014; see Paternoster et al. 1998). On the other hand, the effect of social and non-social rewards of courtship violence is significant among males but not females (b = .361 versus .015). Similarly, while the influence of peer association on the prevalence of courtship violence is significant for both males and females (b = .624 versus .438), the effect is significantly stronger for males (d = .187; z = 7.75, p < .0001). The influence of imitation is significant in both the male and female models (b = .204 versus .290), but its effects are not significantly different across these models (d = .086; z = 0.55,

## Table 5.2
### Logistic Regression Models for the Effects of Social Learning on Prevalence of Courtship Violence, by Gender

| | Males | | | | | Females | | | | |
|---|---|---|---|---|---|---|---|---|---|---|
| | b | se(b) | X² | p | Odds Ratio | b | se(b) | X² | p | Odds Ratio |
| Imitation | .204 | .102 | 3.98 | .0461 | 1.227 | .290 | .076 | 14.77 | .0001 | 1.337 |
| Definitions | -.015 | .044 | 0.12 | .7338 | 0.985 | -.036 | .035 | 1.06 | .3039 | 0.964 |
| Rewards | .361 | .153 | 5.58 | .0182 | 1.435 | .015 | .116 | 0.02 | .9007 | 1.015 |
| Costs | -.190 | .061 | 9.79 | .0018 | 0.827 | -.422 | .046 | 84.85 | .0001 | 0.656 |
| Peer Association | .624 | .197 | 10.00 | .0016 | 1.866 | .438 | .144 | 9.29 | .0023 | 1.549 |
| Age | .017 | .034 | 0.27 | .6125 | 1.017 | .004 | .027 | 0.02 | .8886 | 1.004 |
| Income | .031 | .046 | 0.45 | .5038 | 1.031 | -.020 | .034 | 0.37 | .5435 | 0.980 |
| White | .369 | .305 | 1.47 | .2258 | 1.446 | .425 | .205 | 4.29 | .0384 | 1.529 |
| Greek | .423 | .369 | 1.32 | .2514 | 1.527 | .026 | .246 | 0.01 | .9160 | 1.026 |
| Intercept | 1.561 | | | | | 1.043 | | | | |
| Pseudo R² | .113 | | | | | .181 | | | | |
| Corrected R² | .217 | | | | | .211 | | | | |
| -2 Log Likelihood (intercept) | 470.93 | | | | | 964.06 | | | | |
| (model) | 415.80 | | | | | 809.74 | | | | |
| Model X² | 55.13 (df=9) | | | | | 154.33 (df=9) | | | | |
| N | 434 | | | | | 697 | | | | |

p = .2912). Interestingly, despite gender differences in the effects of specific social learning variables, each model explains roughly the same amount of variation (21 versus 22 percent) in the prevalence of courtship violence.

## Discussion and Conclusion

The extant research testing Akers' social learning theory has focused primarily on less serious acts of youthful misconduct, committed largely within the context of the peer group. This study explores whether social learning processes are also at work in the commission of acts that take place in relative privacy, away from the presence of peers. In an attempt to expand the already voluminous research on social learning theory, this study tests the ability of social learning concepts to predict the prevalence of violence between partners in intimate, dating relationships. Not only is such violence more serious than most behaviors examined in the extant social learning research, but these acts of aggression typically occur between intimate partners when no other peers are present (Laner 1983; Roscoe and Kelsey 1986).

The social learning model estimated here accounts for about 33 percent of the variation in the probability of using violence against a dating partner. Although effect sizes have exceeded 60 percent explained variance in some tests of the theory for less serious forms of misbehavior (Akers et al. 1979), the amount of explained variance observed here is generally greater than that of other theories attempting to explain courtship violence (for example, see Sellers 1999). However, in the present analysis, only three of the five social learning concepts stand out as predictors of courtship violence. Peer association, consistent with much of the empirical research on social learning, is the strongest predictor of courtship violence. Thus, even when peers are typically absent during the commission of the aggressive act, they maintain a strong influence on the individual's behavior. Perceived costs of violence is also a significant predictor, in that lower perceived costs increase the odds of using violence against a partner. The findings for both peer association and perceived costs are consistent with DeKeseredy and Schwartz' (1993) male peer support theory, which argues that men who abuse women in dating relationships are likely to be encouraged by male peers and to perceive few negative consequences or official responses to their aggressive behavior.

The significance of imitation as a predictor of courtship violence is notable for a couple of reasons. First, it provides evidence consistent with the predictions of intergenerational transmission theory, in that witnessing violence by others directly influences one's own aggressive behavior. Second, it is rare that the imitation variable is even included in tests of social learning theory (Sellers et al. 2000) and rarer still that the variable achieves statistical significance when other social learning variables are included in the model. Akers (1998) argues that the influence of imitation is typically restricted to behavioral onset. We believe that in our data, the indicator of prevalence of courtship violence is a strong proxy measure of onset for two reasons. First, with our binary indicator, those with a score of "0" on this variable report no onset of courtship violence, while those with a score of "1" report at least one physically aggressive act committed at least once; the latter includes, by definition, the initial use or onset of courtship violence. Second, before we dichotomized it, this variable was an index of the frequency of use of several forms of courtship violence. However, its distribution was very highly skewed: nearly the entire sample scored values of either "0" or "1" on the summed frequency of use index. Thus, a score of "1" on the dichotomized variable employed here is highly likely to indicate the first and only use of courtship violence reported by our subjects. Hence, our measure of prevalence is also a likely indicator of onset, and our observation that imitation significantly predicts this variable is thus consistent with theoretical predictions.

It should also be noted that neither perceived rewards nor definitions exert a significant influence on courtship violence in the total sample. The failure of perceived rewards to attain statistical significance may be due to measurement error. As is often the case in measures of differential reinforcement in prior social learning research, consequences of deviant behavior that may be viewed as positive to some may hold little value to others; for example, feeling powerful or tough may appeal to some but not others. Moreover, respondents are presented with only eight possible "rewards" for violence; this list may have omitted other positive consequences salient to some respondents. Thus, some respondents may perceive aggression as highly beneficial to themselves, yet their score on the rewards index fails to reflect this perception.

The failure of the definitions scale to influence use of aggression contradicts much of the early research on attitudinal acceptance of violence and involvement in dating aggression (Cate et al. 1982; Stets and Pirog-Good 1987). Indeed, although the scale carries a possible range of values from 8 to 32, its mean score is only 10.5 (s.d.= 2.8), demonstrating little variation among respondents in their attitudes toward violence. We speculate that university students in 1995 were likely to be more heavily indoctrinated against endorsement of violence than their counterparts attending college fifteen years earlier, when the violent attitude-behavior correlation was first established in the dating violence literature. Thus, the responses of more contemporary students to these attitudinal items may reflect a social desirability phenomenon.

In addition to investigating the application of social learning theory to deviant behavior enacted in isolation from peers, we also explore the role of gender in the social learning model as it applies to violence against dating partners. First, we observe that, like much of the prior research on courtship violence, women are more likely than men to report their own use of physical aggression against an intimate partner. This result is likely due in part to our use of the CTS in a sample that includes both offenders and non-offenders, victims and non-victims of courtship violence (Archer 2000; Johnson 1995). Given the current debate over the meaning and validity of our observation of female predominance in courtship aggression (Archer 2000; Dobash et al. 1992; White et al. 2000), future research may benefit from using alternative measures of violence and different samples to further explore the role of social learning theory in the explanation of courtship violence.

Although the present analysis cannot further inform this debate, it does demonstrate that the gender effect on courtship violence—however controversial—is at least partially mediated by social learning variables. In particular, the predominance of women reporting use of aggression in intimate relationships can be partially explained by gender differences in environments conducive to the learning of courtship violence. Men and women are thus learning different content through different learning mechanisms that seem to discourage courtship violence by men and at least neutralize courtship violence by women.

Our data demonstrate several gender differences in the learning of courtship violence. First, it is not surprising that peer association emerges as a stronger predictor of courtship violence for men than for women, consistent with the predictions of male peer support theory (DeKeseredy and Schwartz 1993). What is unexpected is that peer association still serves as the strongest predictor of courtship violence, among all other social learning variables, for women. This observation appears to contradict male peer support theory, which attributes the emergence of the male peer group to structural patriarchy (DeKeseredy and Schwartz 1993). Evidently, women in this sample also have peers who provide encouragement or justification for using physical aggression against a partner; what our data cannot ascertain—and future research might explore—is whether women's violence-supportive peers are male or female.

Like peer association, perceived costs also significantly predicts courtship violence for both men and women; however, the variable exerts a greater influence on women than men. It is likely that, although men may perceive few negative consequences for their aggression, women perceive even fewer (Miller and Simpson 1991. Thus, women are even more likely than men to believe they can use physical aggression against a partner with impunity. Moreover, Archer (2000) argues that although patriarchy may encourage some men to use violence as a means to control women, an additional set of values persists in American society that demands from men restraint in their use of physical aggression toward women; indeed, such behavior may even be viewed as cowardice or unmanliness. As a result, in cultures that include the norm of disapproval of men's violence against women, "these values will have the greatest impact in a relationship that can be ended by the woman at little cost" (Archer 2000: 668). Thus, especially in dating relationships, which are easily broken, women may be more likely to use violence than men because they perceive little cost to themselves.

Although perception of costs exerts a greater influence on courtship violence for women, perception of rewards is only influential for men. As noted above, this observation may be due to measurement error. In addition to the possibility that several benefits of violence may have been omitted from the measure, the items that are included in the rewards index may be gender-biased, suggesting compensations more appealing to men (e.g., "it would make me feel more masculine or tough") than to women. Additional research providing a more thorough measure of the reinforcements for courtship aggression is thus warranted.

In summary, our study has provided evidence that social learning theory can be applied to violent or aggressive behavior commonly committed outside the presence of the peer group. Additionally, our analysis indicates that gender differences in a learning environment conducive to courtship violence may partially explain the gender differences we find in the use of physical aggression against a dating partner. Nevertheless, we must be careful to point out that, although social learning theory partially mediates the gender effect on courtship violence, much of the gender effect retains an independent influence on the dependent variable. Morash points out that "social structure not only presents differential learning but also produces differences in power, opportunities, and resources" (1999: 457). It is thus important that further research on the role of gender in social learning theory include measures of variation in power, opportunity, and resources. Further theoretical development of the role of gender in social learning theory is also warranted. At present, Akers' analysis of the role of social structure in the social learning model, especially in his more recent social structure-social learning theory (Akers 1998), is at best inchoate. Although he describes in some detail four major structural constructs, he presents dozens of structural-level concepts, including gender, with little elucidation of how each might operate within the social learning process. Morash observes, for example, that "there is considerable variation . . . in the degree to which girls and boys in the U.S. are socialized differently; and it is not clear how these differences affect social learning in ways that explain gender differences in delinquency or crime" (1999: 457). Given the strong and persistent empirical  correlation between gender and crime, additional theoretical development is clearly needed to explain why males and females find themselves in different learning environments and how various learning mechanisms, such as differential association and reinforcement, differentially affect males and females. This expanded theoretical development of social learning theory is likely to open fruitful avenues of empirical research and substantially deepen our understanding of gender, crime, and deviance.

## Note

* The authors wish to acknowledge the contributions made by Becky Wylie Jardine for her assistance in survey administration, coding, and data entry and by Shelly A. Stack and Donna L. Brooks for earlier reviews of the literature on courtship violence

## References

Akers, Ronald L. 1973. *Deviant Behavior: A Social Learning Approach*. Belmont, CA: Wadsworth.

_____. 1977. *Deviant Behavior: A Social Learning Approach*. Second Edition. Belmont, CA: Wadsworth.

_____. 1985. *Deviant Behavior: A Social Learning Approach*. Third Edition. Belmont, CA: Wadsworth.

_____. 1992. *Drugs, Alcohol, and Society: Social Structure, Process and Policy*. Belmont, CA: Wadsworth.

_____. 1998. *Social Learning and Social Structure: A General Theory of Crime and Deviance*. Boston: Northeastern University Press.

_____. 1999. "Social learning and Social Structure: Reply to Sampson, Morash, and Krohn." *Theoretical Criminology* 3 (4): 477-493.

_____. 2000. *Criminological Theories: Introduction, Evaluation, and Application*. Third Edition. Los Angeles: Roxbury Press.

Akers, Ronald L., Marvin D. Krohn, Lonn Lanza-Kaduce, and Marcia Radosevich. 1979. "Social Learning and Deviant Behavior: A Specific Test of a General Theory." *American Sociological Review* 44: 635-655.

Akers, Ronald L., Anthony J. La Greca, John K. Cochran, and Christine S. Sellers. 1989. "Social Learning Theory and Alcohol Behavior among the Elderly." *Sociological Quarterly* 30: 625-638.

Archer, John. 2000. "Sex Differences in Aggression between Heterosexual Partners: A Meta-Analytic Review." *Psychological Bulletin* 126 (5): 651-680.

Boeringer, Scot, Constance L. Shehan, and Ronald L. Akers. 1991. "Social Contexts and Social Learning in Sexual Coercion and Aggression: Assessing the Contribution of Fraternity Membership." *Family Relations* 40: 558-564.

Bogal-Albritten, R., and W.L. Albritten. 1985. "The Hidden Victims: Courtship Violence among College Students." *Journal of College Student Personnel* 19: 201-204.

Burgess, Robert L., and Ronald L. Akers. 1966. "A Differential Association-Reinforcement Theory of Criminal Behavior." *Social Problems* 14: 128-147.

Cate, R.M., J.M. Henton, J. Koval, F.S. Christopher, and S. Lloyd. 1982. "Premarital Abuse: A Social Psychological [erspective." *Journal of Family Issues* 3: 79-90.

Cullen, Francis T., and Robert Agnew. 1999. *Criminological Theory: Past to Present*. Los Angeles, CA: Roxbury Press.

Curran, Daniel, and Claire M. Renzetti. 1994. *Theories of Crime*. Boston, MA: Allyn and Bacon.

DeKeseredy, Walter S., and Martin D. Schwartz. 1993. "Male Peer Support and Woman Abuse: An Expansion of DeKeseredy's Model." *Sociological Spectrum* 13: 393-413.

DiBlasio, F. 1986. "Drinking Adolescents on the Road." *Journal of Youth and Adolescence* 15 (2): 173-188.

DiBlasio, F., and Bruce B. Benda. 1990. "Adolescent Sexual Behavior: A Multivariate Analysis of a Social Learning Model." *Journal of Adolescent Research* 5 (4): 449-466.

Dobash, R.E., and R.P. Dobash. 1980. *Violence Against Wives: A Case Against the Patriarchy*. London: Open Books.

Dobash, R.P., R.E. Dobash, M. Wilson, and M. Daly. 1992. "The Myth of Sexual Symmetry in Marital Violence." *Social Problems* 39: 71-91.

Grasmick Harold G., and Robert J. Bursik. 1990. "Conscience, Significant Others, and Rational Choice: Extending the Deterrence Model." *Law and Society Review* 24: 837-862.

Johnson, M.P. 1995. "Patriarchal Terrorism and Common Couple Violence: Two Forms of Violence against Women." *Journal of Marriage and the Family* 57: 283-294.

Krohn, Marvin D., William F. Skinner, James L. Massey, and Ronald L. Akers. 1985. "Social Learning Theory and Adolescent Cigarette Smoking: A Longitudinal Study." *Social Problems* 32: 455-473.

Laner, Mary Reige. 1983. "Courtship Abuse and Aggression: Contextual Aspects." *Sociological Spectrum* 3: 69-83.

Lanza-Kaduce, Lonn, and Mary Klug. 1986. "Learning to Cheat: The Interaction of Moral Development and Social Learning Theories." *Deviant Behavior* 7: 243-259.

Liska, Allen E., and Steven F. Messner. 1999. *Perspectives on Crime and Deviance*. Third Edition. Upper Saddle River, NJ: Prentice-Hall.

Makepeace, James M. 1981. "Courtship Violence among College Students." *Family Relations* 30: 97-102.

Martin, Del. 1976. *Battered Wives*. San Francisco: Glide Publications.

Miller, Susan L., and Sally S. Simpson. 1991. "Courtship Violence and Social Control: Does Gender Mmatter?" *Law and Society Review* 25: 335-365.

Moffitt, Terrie E., Robert F. Krueger, Avshalom Caspi, and Jeff Fagan. 2000. "Partner Abuse and General Crime: How Are They the Same? How Are They Different?" *Criminology* 38 (1): 199-232.

Morash, Merry. 1999. "A Consideration of Gender in Relation to *Social Learning and Social Structure: A General Theory of Crime and Deviance*." *Theoretical Criminology* 3 (4): 451-462.

Pagelow, Mildred D. 1984. *Family Violence*. New York: Praeger.

Paternoster, Raymond, and Ronet Bachman. 2001. *Explaining Criminals and Crime: Essays in Contemporary Criminological Theory*. Los Angeles, CA: Roxbury Press.

Paternoster, Raymond, Robert Brame, Paul Mazerolle, and Alex Piquero. 1998. "Using the Correct Statistical Test for the Equality of Regression Coefficients." *Criminology* 36 (4): 859-866.

Rojek, Dean G., and Gary F. Jensen. 1996. *Exploring Delinquency: Causes and Control*. Los Angeles: Roxbury Press.

Roscoe, B., and T. Kelsey. 1986. "Dating Violence among High School Students." *Psychology* 23 (1): 53-59.

Sellers, Christine S. 1999. "Self-Control and Intimate Violence: An Examination of the Scope and Specification of the General Theory of Crime." *Criminology* 37 (2): 375-404.

Sellers, Christine S., and L. Thomas Winfree, Jr. 1990. "Differential Associations and Definitions: A Panel Study of Youthful Drinking Behavior." *International Journal of the Addictions* 25: 755-771.

Sellers, Christine S., Travis C. Pratt, L. Thomas Winfree, Jr., and Francis T. Cullen. 2000. "The Empirical Status of Social Learning Theory: A Meta-Analysis." Paper presented at the annual meeting of the American Society of Criminology, San Francisco.

Skinner, William F., and A. M. Fream. 1997. "A Social Learning Theory Analysis of Computer Crime among College Students." *Journal of Research in Crime and Delinquency* 34: 495-518.

Stets, Jan E., and Maureen A. Pirog-Good. 1987. "Violence in Dating Relationships." *Social Psychology Quarterly* 50: 237-246.

Straus, Murray A. 1979. "Measuring Intrafamily Conflict and Violence: The Conflict Tactics (CT) Scales." *Journal of Marriage and the Family* 41: 75-88.

_____. 1990. "The Conflict Tactics Scales and Its Critics: An Evaluation and New Data on Validity and Reliability." Pp. 49-73 in Murray A. Straus and Richard J. Gelles (eds.), *Physical Violence in American Societies.* New Brunswick, NJ: Transaction Publishers.

Straus, Murray A., and Richard J. Gelles. 1988. "Violence in American Families: How Much is There and Why Does It Occur?" Pp. 141-162 in E.W. Nunnally, C.S. Chilman, and F.M. Fox (eds.), *Troubled Relationships.* Newbury Park, CA: Sage Publications.

Straus, Murray A., Richard J. Gelles, and Suzanne Steinmetz. 1980. *Behind Closed Doors: Violence in the American Family.* New York: Anchor/Doubleday.

Sugarman, David B., and Gerald T. Hotaling. 1989. "Dating Violence: Prevalence, Context, and Risk Markers." Pp. 3-32 in Maureen A. Pirog-Good and Jan. E. Stets (eds.), *Violence in Dating Relationships: Emerging Social Issues*, New York: Praeger.

Sutherland, Edwin H. 1947. *Principles of Criminology.* Fourth Edition. Philadelphia: J. B. Lippincott.

Vold, George B., Thomas J. Bernard, and Jeffrey B. Snipes. 1998. *Theoretical Criminology.* Fourth Edition. New York: Oxford University Press.

Walker, Lenore E. 1979. *The Battered Woman.* New York: Harper and Row.

Warr, Mark, and Mark Stafford. 1991. "The Influence of Delinquent Peers: What They Think or What They Do?" *Criminology* 4: 851-866.

White, Jacquelyn W., Paige Hall Smith, Mary P. Koss, and A.J. Figueredo. 2000. "Intimate Partner Aggression—What Have We Learned? Comment on Archer (2000)." *Psychological Bulletin* 126 (5): 690-696.

Williams, Kirk R., and Richard Hawkins. 1989. "The Meaning of Arrest for Wife Assault." *Criminology* 27: 163-181.

Winfree, L. Thomas, Jr., and Frances P. Bernat. 1998. "Social Learning, Self-Control, and Substance Abuse by Eighth Grade Students: A Tale of Two Cities." *Journal of Drug Issues* 28 (2): 539-558.

Winfree, L. Thomas, Jr., and Curt Taylor Griffiths. 1983. "Social Learning and Adolescent Marijuana Use: A Trend Study of Deviant Behavior in a Rural Middle School." *Rural Sociology* 48 (3): 219-239.

Winfree, L. Thomas, Jr., Teresa Vigil Bäckström, and G. Larry Mays. 1994a. "Social Learning Theory, Self-Reported Delinquency, and Youth Gangs: A New Twist on a General Theory of Crime and Delinquency." *Youth & Society* 26 (2): 147-177.

Winfree, L. Thomas, Jr., Frances P. Bernat, and Finn-Aage Esbensen. 2001. "Hispanic and Anglo Gang Membership in Two Southwestern Cities." *The Social Science Journal* 38: 105-117.

Winfree, L. Thomas, Jr., G. Larry Mays, and Teresa Vigil Bäckström. 1994b. "Youth Gangs and Incarcerated Delinquents: Exploring the Ties between Gang Membership, Delinquency, and Social Learning Theory." *Justice Quarterly* 11: 229-256.

Winfree L. Thomas, Jr., Curt T. Griffiths, and Christine S. Sellers. 1989. "Social Learning Theory, Drug Use, and American Indian Youths: A Cross-Cultural Test." *Justice Quarterly* 6: 395-417.

# 6

# Delinquency and Depression: A Gendered Role-Taking and Social Learning Perspective*

*Stacy De Coster*

Much research and theorizing in sociology has focused on the problem of why individuals engage in deviance. Whereas criminologists approach this problem by asking why individuals engage in crime and delinquency, mental health researchers ask why individuals experience negative affect, such as depression. The answers criminologists and mental health researchers provide to these seemingly disparate questions are remarkably similar (compare Agnew 1992 with Pearlin et al. 1981; Matsueda 1992 with Thoits 1985, 1986; Shaw and McKay 1942 with Aneshensel and Sucoff 1996), suggesting that law violation and depression may be the outcomes of similar structural conditions and social psychological processes. Indeed, researchers recently have begun to combine arguments from criminology and the sociology of mental health to propose common causes of law violation and depression (e.g., De Coster and Heimer 2001; Ge et al. 1996; Hagan 1988; Hagan and Wheaton 1993).[1] Cullen (1983), however, notes that the preoccupation with locating the *causes* of deviance has led to much less consideration of the equally important question of what it is that leads individuals or groups to express deviance in one form (law violation) as opposed to another (depression). Thus, he calls for theoretical explanations that seek to understand the shared causes of different forms of deviance, while simultaneously seeking to understand the social factors that channel deviance in one direction rather than another.

This chapter responds to Cullen's (1983) call by developing a theoretical perspective on the common causes of law violation and depression and by discussing also why individuals or groups may respond to these causes with different forms of deviance. In developing this theoretical perspective, I draw upon interactionist and social learning theories of law violation and depression. My explanation of common causes proposes that disadvantaged structural positions, stressful life events, and role-taking are shared antecedents of both law violation and depression. The role-taking process I discuss highlights the relevance of social relationships, self-identities, and social learning for understanding why individuals engage in deviance. Further, I argue that this process provides information pertaining to individual or group differences in deviant responses. Specifically, I propose that role-taking and social learning can help explain why males are more likely to respond to the common causes of deviance with law violation and females are more likely to respond to these causes with depression. I focus attention on gender variation in deviance because gender appears to be among the most important variables that channel individuals into law violation versus depression (e.g., Horwitz and Raskin White 1987; Kandel and Davies 1982).[2]

The theoretical perspective in this chapter proposes the following mechanisms leading to both law violation and depression: (1) Social-structural positions influence the likelihood that youths are exposed to stressful life events, which can lead to law-violating and depressive responses; (2) stressful life events and deviant responses to them, in turn, shape social relationships with conventional and deviant others (i.e., differential associations); (3) these social relationships subsequently shape three elements of role-taking—reflected appraisals, definitions of deviance, and anticipated reactions to deviance--that ultimately influence law violation and depression. I propose that these common causes also provide insight into the gendered channeling of deviance because the content of role-taking and social learning varies across gender.

The chapter proceeds as follows: I begin with a discussion of an interactionist perspective proposed recently to explain the common causes of law violation and depression (De Coster and Heimer 2001). I next discuss how this perspective can be used to understand the channeling of deviance in gendered directions. In the following sections, I extend the interactionist perspective on common causes to include arguments derived from social learning theory (Akers 1977, 1985, 1998; Burgess and Akers 1966). In the discussion of social learning as a precursor to deviance, I also describe the role that it plays in filtering or channeling males into law violation and females into depression.

## An Interactionist Explanation of Law Violation and Depression

Researchers have begun to recognize that law violation and depression share many of the same structural and social-psychological antecedents. Some of these shared antecedents include urban-dwelling, disadvantaged economic status, stressful life events, weak social relationships, and deviant and/or negative self-identities (e.g., De Coster and Heimer 2001; Dornfeld and Kruttschnitt 1992; Hagan and Wheaton 1993; Hoffmann and Su 1998; Lempers and Clark-Lempers 1990).

In a recent paper, Heimer and I developed a theoretical explanation for the common causes of law violation and depression that incorporated these shared antecedents (De Coster and Heimer 2001). In that paper, we synthesized arguments from the differential social control theory of law violation (Heimer and Matsueda 1994; Matsueda 1992) and from Thoits' (1985, 1986) symbolic interactionist theory of mental health problems. In particular, our arguments centered on the role-taking process through which individuals take the perspectives of significant others, view themselves and situations from the perspective of these others, and fit their actions into ongoing social transactions (Mead 1934). Through role-taking, individuals form reflected appraisals of self, or views of the self from the perspective of others (Felson 1985). Consistent with differential social control theory and with interactionist theories of mental health, we showed empirically that reflected appraisals of self were important determinants of both law violation and depression.

In addition, we discussed how reflected appraisals emerge through social interactions and are influenced by exposure to stressful life events and social-structural positions (De Coster and Heimer 2001). Specifically, reflected appraisals of self are determined in part by attachments to conventional groups. Following differential social control theory (Heimer and Matsueda 1994; Matsueda and Heimer 1997), we argued that this is because attachments to groups increase the chances that they serve as significant others in the role-taking process.[3] Attachments to groups, or social relationships, are influenced in turn by stressful life events and short-term deviant responses to stress exposure. Specifically, individuals who respond to stress with law violation and/or depression may select out of social relationships with conventional others, and conventional others may choose not to interact often with these deviant individuals. Finally, we linked social-structural positions to law violation and depression by proposing that individuals in disadvantaged positions have fewer social and economic resources to avoid the stressful experiences that lead to deviant reflected appraisals through role-taking.

Consistent with this interactionist theory, our empirical test of common antecedents supported the following sequence of events: Social structural positions influenced the ability of youths to avoid stressful events, such as parental divorce, criminal victimization, and serious illness (see also Cohen and Felson 1979; Link and Phelan 1995). These stressful events combined with short-term deviant responses to them (i.e., law violation and depression) to threaten attachments with significant others. Weakened emotional attachments, in turn, affected the formation of deviant reflected appraisals (see also Matsueda and Heimer 1997; Thoits 1985), which led ultimately to future law violation and depression. Specifically, reflected appraisals of self as a rule-violator led to law violation, and reflected appraisals of self as psychologically distressed resulted in depression. We argued that this occurred because individuals are motivated to behave in accord with their self-images.

We noted that reflected appraisals of self as distressed did not increase the chances of law violation, and reflected appraisals of self as a rule-violator did not increase the chances of depression (De Coster and Heimer 2001). This implies that although social identities are important antecedents of both law violation *and* depression, the specific aspects of self that are relevant for law violation versus depression differ. Nonetheless, we maintained that role-taking is a *common process* that leads to both forms of deviance. Moreover, the structural positions, stressful events, and weakened social relationships that influenced role-taking and the formation of reflected appraisals as a rule-violator and as a distressed person were the same. In short, disadvantaged structural positions, stressful events, and weak social relationships comprised the common causes of law violation and depression because each of these elements influenced the role-taking process leading to identity formation and, eventually, to both forms of deviance.

In addition to these common causes, gender remained a strong predictor of both law violation and depression, net of the social-structural and social-psychological variables considered in our study. Specifically, females were more likely than males to become depressed, and males were more likely than females to engage in law violation. Moreover, the formation of self-identities varied across gender, with males being more likely to form reflected appraisals as rule-violators and females being more prone to form reflected appraisals as distressed persons. This finding, which may provide important insights into the channeling of deviance across gender, is consistent with prior research and theorizing on labeling, self-identities, and deviance.

*Gender and Reflected Appraisals*

The labeling perspective implies that males are more likely than females to be labeled as rule-violators, in part because males engage in more law-violating behaviors than females and in part because law violation is consistent with stereotypes of law violation as a male phenomenon (Farrell and Swigert 1978). Alternatively, females are more likely to be labeled as distressed because they are more likely than males to become depressed and because depression is consistent with stereotypes of depression and other withdrawing emotions as female phenomena. Indeed, some researchers propose that there are gender-appropriate and gender-inappropriate forms of deviance (see Schur 1984; Harris 1977). On the one hand, law-violating behaviors are considered to be more appropriate for males than females because these behaviors are consistent with characteristics that are considered to be masculine, including aggressiveness, rationality and strength (see Heimer 1996; Heimer and De Coster 1999; Simpson and Elis 1995). Depression, on the other hand, is much more consistent with definitions of femininity, which emphasize passivity, nurturance, and physical and emotional weakness, but is the antithesis of masculinity (see Horwitz and Raskin White 1987).

The labeling of individuals in ways that are consistent with stereotypical depictions of appropriate and inappropriate forms of deviance, in turn, influences reflected appraisals of self. This is consistent with our finding that males were more likely than females to form reflected appraisals as rule-violators, and females were more likely than males to form reflected appraisals as distressed (De Coster and Heimer 2001; see also Bartusch and Matsueda 1996). These gender differences in *levels* of reflected appraisals may play an important part in channeling male and female deviance.

Gender differences in the *effects* of reflected appraisals on law violation and depression also may play a key role in explaining gendered deviance. Research demonstrates that rule-violating self-identities have a greater impact on male law violation than on female law violation. (Bartusch and Matsueda 1996; Koita and Triplett 1998). These studies follow other research on gender and deviance by arguing that this may be because law violation is inconsistent with definitions of femininity. Specifically, the motivation for females to behave in accord with a law-violating identity is at odds with the motivation to achieve gender in social interactions (Schur 1984; see also Heimer 1996). For males, these motivations are compatible and thereby more powerful. The motivation for males to behave in accord with an identity as a distressed person, however, conflicts with the motivation to achieve gender; whereas, these motivations are compatible for females. This suggests that reflected appraisals as a distressed person may have a larger impact on female depression than on male depression.

Within the interactionist model of common causes, then, gender differences in the formation of self-identities and in the effects of self-identities may provide insight into the channeling of deviance in gendered directions. Whereas males may be more likely to form reflected appraisals as rule violators, females may be more likely to form reflected appraisals as distressed persons. In addition, self-identities as a rule-violator may be a more potent predictor of male law violation than of female law violation, whereas self-identities as a distressed person may predict female depression more so than male depression.

## Extending the Interactionist Perspective on Law Violation and Depression

My previous research with Heimer focused only on the reflected appraisals element of the role-taking process as a common cause of law violation and depression. In the remaining sections, I extend these arguments to incorporate additional aspects of role-taking—definitions of law violation and anticipated reactions of others—which are emphasized by social learning theories of crime and delinquency, as well as the differential social control perspective.

### Role-Taking, Social Learning, and Law Violation

Both differential association and social learning theory emphasize definitions favorable and unfavorable to law violation, which include beliefs, attitudes, values, and rationalizations regarding crime and delinquency (Burgess and Akers 1966; Sutherland 1947). Akers (1973) maintains that through direct and observational learning, these definitions of law become associated with positive and negative reinforcements and punishments (see also Akers 1977, 1985, 1998; Akers et al. 1979; Burgess and Akers 1966). The likelihood that an individual will break the law depends on the reinforcement history associated with definitions favorable and unfavorable to crime. From this perspective, crime and delinquency occur when law-violating definitions—attitudes, values, and rationalizations that normalize criminal behaviors—have been reinforced more or punished less than definitions that oppose law violation. Because law-violating others may provide more reinforcements and fewer punishments for illegal behaviors, relationships with criminal others may increase the chances of law violation. These relationships also may provide the individual with models for behavior and thereby increase the chances of law violation when the individual imitates criminal behaviors (see Akers 1977).

These social learning arguments can be embedded within the role-taking process discussed in the earlier explication of common causes by Heimer and myself. According to the logic of both social learning and differential social control theories, individuals can call up the reinforcement histories associated with potential lines of action through role-taking the perspectives of others (Akers 1998; Heimer and Matsueda 1994). Individuals whose reinforcement histories have promoted law-violating definitions may be more prone to contemplate criminal behaviors as viable lines of action through role-taking, and they may also be more likely to conclude that such behaviors constitute acceptable lines of action. In short, it can be said that learned definitions shape behavior in concrete situations because they serve as behavioral cues when individuals contemplate lines of action through role-taking.

Individuals also consider the anticipated reactions of significant and generalized others to law violation through role-taking. This allows the individual to consider the consequences of such reactions for group membership, self-image, and extrinsic rewards (McCall and Simmons 1978). The logic of

both social learning and differential social control theories suggest that behaviors that have received positive rewards for the individual and/or others
(vicarious learning) in the past will be the behaviors imagined to receive
positive rewards, and thereby will be the behaviors likely to be pursued.
Thus, the reinforcement schedules associated with law-violating definitions
and behaviors influence law violation in part because they influence anticipated reactions to behaviors in a given situation.

Consistent with these arguments, research demonstrates that both law-
violating definitions and anticipated reactions to law violation influence
crime and delinquency. Specifically, law-violating definitions increase the
chances of delinquent and criminal behaviors, and anticipated negative reactions to law violation reduce the chances of these behaviors (e.g., Akers et al.
1979; Akers and Lee 1996; Alexander and Langford 1992; Heimer and
Matsueda 1994; Jensen 1972). Moreover, the effects of law-violating definitions and anticipated reactions are invariant across gender (Heimer 1996;
Heimer and De Coster 1999).[4] Thus, gender differences in the *impact* of these
social learning variables on law violation may provide little by way of understanding why males are more likely than females to engage in law violation.

This does not imply, however, that social learning has little to offer for
understanding the gendered channeling of deviance. In fact, research and
theorizing suggest that males are more likely than females to learn law-violating definitions and are less likely than females to anticipate negative reactions to law violation when role-taking the perspective of others (Heimer
1995; Heimer and De Coster 1999; Huessman et al. 1992). Some theoretical
arguments propose that these gender differences in *levels* of learned definitions and anticipated reactions are linked to gender socialization (see Heimer
1996; Heimer and De Coster 1999).

Research on gender socialization consistently demonstrates that youths
are rewarded for enacting gender-appropriate behaviors and punished for
gender-inappropriate behaviors (e.g., Fagot 1978, 1985; Fagot and Hagan
1991; Snow, Jacklin and Maccoby 1983). As discussed earlier, law violation
is more inappropriate for females than it is for males because it is the antithesis of nurturance, passivity, and physical weakness, which characterize definitions of femininity. Indeed, some theorists argue that law-violating females
are treated as though they are "doubly deviant" because their behaviors depart from definitions of appropriate behaviors for people in general, as well as
from definitions of appropriate deviance for members of a particular gender
group (see Schur 1984). Simply stated, females may be punished more harshly
than males when they engage in law-violating behaviors. Thus, it is not
surprising that females anticipate stronger sanctions for law violation than
males when they imagine the reactions of others through role-taking. It also is
not surprising that females are less likely to learn law-violating definitions
that allow them to conclude through role-taking that law violation is an

acceptable line of action. In short, law-violating definitions and anticipated reactions to law violation are likely to be central for understanding not only the causes of crime and delinquency but also the channeling of deviance in gendered directions.

These definitions of behavior and anticipated reactions are influenced in turn by social relationships (e.g., Akers 1977; Heimer and Matsueda 1994). Individuals who share close relationships with law-violating others are likely to hold definitions favorable to law violation and to anticipate positive reactions and/or rewards for law violation because significant others likely have rewarded them in the past for such attitudes and/or behaviors. Moreover, significant others may serve as models for law-violating behaviors, and thereby directly influence such behaviors (Akers 1973, 1998; Burgess and Akers 1966). Alternatively, individuals who share close relationships with conventional others may be more prone to holding definitions unfavorable to law violation and to anticipating negative reactions for law-violating behaviors because their significant others likely have punished them in the past for such attitudes and/or behaviors.

Consistent with these arguments, research shows that law-violating definitions and anticipated reactions to law violation mediate partially or fully the relationship between delinquent peer associations and delinquency (e.g., Akers et al. 1979; Heimer and Matsueda 1994; Jackson, Tittle and Burke 1986; Matsueda 1982). Similarly, these social learning variables play a part in mediating the relationship between associations with conventional others and law violation (e.g., Conger 1976). Research also demonstrates that these findings apply to both male and female youths. However, males are more likely than females to associate with delinquent peers, which contributes to gender differences in law violation (e.g., Heimer and De Coster 1999).

Overall, social relationships may influence law violation directly because significant others serve as models for behavior. These relationships also may influence law violation indirectly by shaping three central elements of role-taking—reflected appraisals, definitions, and anticipated reactions of others—that affect law violation. Although my previous work with Heimer incorporated only reflected appraisals of self into our explanation for the common causes of law violation and depression, definitions and anticipated reactions also may be important aspects of the common process leading to both deviant responses. Each of these factors also may contribute to the channeling of deviance in gendered directions. The research I have discussed in this section suggests that social learning is more likely to lead to male law violation than female law violation because males are more likely to learn definitions favorable to crime and delinquency and are also less likely to anticipate negative reactions for law violation. In the next section, I discuss how these social-learning elements of role-taking may affect depression, as well as gender differences in depression.

*Role-Taking, Social Learning, and Depression*

Research and theorizing in the sociology of mental health proposes that feelings and emotions are governed by sets of expectations, values, and beliefs (Heise and Calhan 1995; Hochschild 1979, 1983; Kemper 1981; Rosenberg 1990; Thoits 1985, 1989). Individuals learn these emotion norms— or definitions of appropriate and inappropriate feelings and emotions— through the same mechanisms that they learn definitions of behavior, including imitation and conditioning through reinforcements and punishments (e.g., Dorr 1985; Lewis and Saarni 1985; Malatesta and Haviland 1982; Pollak and Thoits 1989). Indeed, a large body of literature on the socialization of emotions has emerged centered on this claim. [5]

A central theme in the literature on emotion socialization is that individuals learn cultural standards pertaining both to the experience of emotions as well as the expression of emotions. Norms governing the expression of emotions—"display rules"—are considered to be relevant for understanding the emotions individuals experience because emotions or feelings that are displayed through surface acting eventually may affect actual (or deep) emotion and feeling states (see Buck, Miller and Caul 1974; Ekman, Levenson and Frieson 1983; Hochschild 1979). For instance, smiling or acting happy may induce an actual state of happiness. Thus, the learning process relevant for understanding individual emotions and feelings includes learning about appropriate emotions as well as appropriate displays of emotions.

Existing research and theorizing suggests that the socialization of emotional displays in fact may be the primary mechanism through which individuals learn cultural (or subcultural) standards for emotions and feelings. This is because emotional displays, or expressions of emotions, are more visible and thereby more directly accessible for socialization than are actual feelings and emotions (see Lewis and Saarni 1985; Malatesta and Haviland 1985). One mechanism through which appropriate displays of emotions and feelings are learned is imitation (see Bandura 1986). Indeed, research indicates that children copy the emotional displays or behaviors of people in their social environment, just as they copy other behaviors (see Dorr 1985; Lewis and Saarni 1985; Malatesta and Haviland 1982). Consistent with this, research findings demonstrate that older infants are more like their mothers in facial expressions of emotions and feelings than are younger infants (see Malatesta and Haviland 1982). Presumably this is because children imitate parental emotional expressions.

Individuals also learn about appropriate emotional displays through operant conditioning, wherein socialization agents punish inappropriate emotions and reward appropriate emotions. Although emotions such as sadness, depression, and anger may seem acceptable or even appropriate in the face of unpleasant or stressful experiences, some theorists propose that there is a general cultural norm against these negative emotions (see Sommers 1984; Thoits 1985). Consistent with this cultural norm, Maletesta and Haviland (1985) find that parents are more likely to reward positive emotions in young children and punish (often through nonresponse) negative emotions. Their study demonstrates that by six months, infants display far fewer emotions than displayed earlier in life. Importantly, this reduction in emotional displays is proportionately greater for negative emotions that are not responded to by parents than for positive emotions that receive reinforcement. Moreover, the reduction in negative emotional displays is proportionately greater for males than for females (Malatesta and Haviland 1985). This may be due to differential reinforcement for emotions and emotional displays across gender. In fact, research shows that girls receive more positive attention than boys at early ages when they cry or show other passive, withdrawing emotions (Lewis and Michalson 1983). As discussed above, this is likely because passive, withdrawing emotions are much more consistent with definitions of femininity than with definitions of masculinity (see Schur 1984). Arguably, then, differential reinforcement schedules for negative emotions may play an important part in explaining why females are more likely than males to express deviance in the form of depression.

The socialization of emotions is supplemented in arenas other than the family as well. For instance, research demonstrates that daycare workers and peers play important roles in teaching individuals about appropriate emotions and emotional displays (see Camras 1985; Leavitt and Power 1989). Leavitt and Power's (1989) qualitative study of daycare workers uncovered many instances where young children were taught that they would not be accepted if they displayed negative emotions, such as sadness or anger. Sometimes caregivers taught this message overtly, referring to the children sarcastically as babies and using phrases such as, "only babies cry." Other times, this message was conveyed more subtly. For instance, caregivers often chose to ignore crying children because they believed this would spoil the child and reinforce crying behaviors. In both instances, the child learns that crying is associated with negative reactions and is an unacceptable emotional behavior.

In peer groups, messages concerning the unacceptability of negative emotions are further reiterated. Waas and Graczyk's (1999) study finds that second, fourth and sixth grade youths view negatively their peers who are always unhappy, who cry a lot, who always think something bad will happen, and who worry a lot. This study also reports that negative views of depressed or anxious youths are stronger among males than among females. In other words, boys are more likely than girls to be rejected by their peers for feeling and/or displaying anxiety or depression. Within the social learning framework, peer withdrawal can be viewed as a punishment for negative emotions and inappropriate emotional displays. Thus, through peer rejection, youths learn that depression and displays of depression are unacceptable and often accompanied by negative social sanctions.

Overall, this discussion suggests that conditioning through reinforcements and punishments combines with direct imitation or modeling to influence what individuals learn about appropriate emotions and emotional displays. In other words, individuals learn definitions of emotions and emotional displays through reinforcements, punishments, and modeling. This discussion also suggests that males more so than females learn from parents and peers that negative emotions are unacceptable. Therefore, this learning process may help explain why females are more likely than males to express deviance in the form of depressive affect.

Once learned, definitions of emotions provide cultural standards against which individuals can judge the appropriateness of their feelings and emotions in a given situation. Thoits' (1984, 1985, 1986) symbolic interactionist perspective on mental health proposes that people judge the appropriateness of feelings and emotions in the same way that they judge the appropriateness of behaviors—by casting themselves as objects from the perspectives of significant others and reference groups. In other words, individuals reflect upon the appropriateness of their feelings and emotions through role-taking. Consistent with the arguments discussed above, this can involve consideration of both learned definitions of appropriate/inappropriate emotions and anticipated reactions of others to inappropriate emotions.

The discussion of negative emotions to this point suggests that definitions and feelings of depression are likely to be associated with negative sanctions rather than positive rewards, especially among males. Thus, when contemplating their depressive feelings through role-taking, individuals are likely to imagine disapproval by significant and generalized others, as well as the loss of valued rewards that may accompany this disapproval. Those who imagine negative reactions and loss of rewards for deviant emotions often engage in efforts to bring their emotions back in line with cultural norms (see Hochschild 1979, 1983; Thoits 1985).[6]

Supportive others can facilitate these efforts by providing redefinitions of stressful situations or by providing validation for one's deviant feelings and reactions (Thoits 1985). Although validation of negative emotions typically is not the same as providing definitions that favor such emotions, there may be some conditions under which supportive others indeed do generate new feeling norms for the individual. For instance, Thoits' (1985) theoretical arguments imply that prolonged contact with similarly depressed individuals, contact with several depressed individuals, and ineffective threats of punishment may be important for understanding the situations under which definitions that favor (or neutralize) depression might emerge. This argument is supported by research on adolescent peer groups and depression, which suggests that individual distress levels grow increasingly similar to peer levels of distress over time (e.g., Hogue and Steinberg 1995). It may be the case that through modeling and/or lack of punishment, individuals learn from depressed peers that depressive emotions may be acceptable. Thus, close relationships with emotionally deviant others may influence an individual's emotions because these relationships provide the individual with definitions that neutralize or justify depression and/or because the group does not provide negative sanctions for deviant emotions. In this way, depressive feelings may become increasingly persistent through role-taking over time. Alternatively, close relationships with conforming others are likely to result in role-taking that curbs depressive affect because these relationships provide the individual—especially males—with definitions of depression as inappropriate and/or with negative sanctions for depressive feelings.[7]

In sum, the role-taking process leading to depression may involve the same elements as the process leading to law violation. Specifically, learned definitions and anticipated reactions of others are likely to combine with reflected appraisals to influence depression. These elements of role-taking are influenced, in turn, by relationships with conventional and deviant others. Moreover, these elements of role-taking may help explain why females are more likely than males to become depressed. I discuss in the next section how these arguments can be incorporated into the earlier interactionist explanation of common causes proposed by Heimer and myself. In doing this, I also discuss the channeling of deviance in gendered directions.

## An Extended Theory of Common Causes and Gendered Channeling of Deviance

Based on the above discussions, I extend the original interactionist perspective on common causes proposed by Heimer and myself to incorporate differential association/social learning elements of role-taking. The extended perspective proposes the following: Social-structural positions influence exposure to stressful events because individuals who occupy disadvantaged social positions often lack the social and economic resources that would enable them to avoid stressful circumstances (see Cohen and Felson 1979; Link and Phelan 1995). Individuals who are exposed to stress may respond in turn with law violation (Agnew, 1985, 1992; Brezina, 1996, 2000) and/or depression (Aneshensel 1992; Colten and Gore 1991; Pearlin et al. 1981). Indeed, stress exposure has been one of the central explanatory concepts in previous attempts to specify common causes of law violation and depression (see Chassin et al. 1993; Dornfeld and Kruttschnitt 1992; Hoffmann and Su 1997, 1998).

Stress and its deviant responses subsequently may influence social relationships and role-taking in ways that increase the chances of future deviance. Specifically, individuals who respond to stressful experiences with law

violation and/or depression may select out of conventional social relationships, both by their own choosing and by the choosing of conventional others who do not want to associate with the deviant individual. At the same
time, the deviant may find solace or companionship in relationships with
similarly situated deviant others. These social relationships, or differential
associations, may influence role-taking in three important ways that are relevant to future law violation and depression and to the channeling of deviance in gendered directions.

First, differential associations influence the learning of definitions favorable and unfavorable to deviance. Relationships with deviant others may
provide individuals with definitions that neutralize and/or justify deviance;
whereas relationships with conventional others provide individuals with definitions unfavorable to deviance. Indeed, Thoits' (1985) symbolic interactionist
arguments in the mental health literature imply that prolonged contact with
distressed others may provide individuals with definitions of depressive emotions as acceptable or even appropriate. As a result, role-taking with distressed others is likely to increase the chances of persistent depressive feelings.
Likewise, theories of law violation discuss the importance of role-taking with
law-violating others in the production of definitions favorable to law violation (e.g., Akers 1973, 1998; Heimer and Matsueda 1994). Alternatively, relationships with conventional others reduce the chances that individuals learn
deviant definitions and/or increase the learning of definitions unfavorable to
deviance (see Akers 1998).

The discussion of deviant definitions throughout, however, suggests that
gendered socialization by conventional parents and peers may contribute to
gender differences in *levels* of learned definitions favoring law violation and
depression. Specifically, females may be more likely than males to learn
definitions unfavorable to law violation in conventional groups because law-
violating behaviors are more inappropriate for females than for males. Alternatively, males may learn more definitions unfavorable to depression in
conventional groups because passive, withdrawing emotions are more inappropriate when displayed or experienced by males than females (see Schur
1984).

Additionally, relationships with nonconventional others may play a part
in explaining gender differences in definitions of deviance. Research demonstrates that one reason males are more likely than females to learn law-violating definitions is because they are more likely to associate with law-violating
peers (e.g., Heimer and De Coster 1999). Females, however, associate more
often with peers who are willing to discuss deviant emotions, such as depression. Indeed a consistent finding in the literature on peer groups is that females spend more time than males discussing emotions and personal problems
with one another (e.g., Johnson and Aries 1983; Thorne and Luria 1986).
Through associations with conventional and nonconventional others, then,

males and females may differ in the types of definitions of deviance they are likely to learn. Males more often learn definitions that favor or neutralize law violation, and females more often learn definitions that favor or neutralize depression.

Second, differential associations influence anticipated reactions to deviance. Attachments or close relationships with deviant groups rather than conventional groups may increase the chances that individuals are rewarded and not punished for deviance. Thus, when individuals call up the reinforcement and punishment schedules associated with deviant definitions and behaviors through role-taking, they are unlikely to anticipate loss of valued rewards. Indeed, individuals whose relationships are with nonconventional others may conclude through role-taking that deviance will bring social rewards and positive consequences for self. Criminological theories have discussed previously how this process relates to law violation (e.g., Akers 1973, 1998; Heimer and Matsueda 1994), and Thoits' (1985) arguments about mental health suggest that it applies to depressive affect as well.

Individuals who are close to conventional rather than deviant others, however, are likely to anticipate loss of valued rewards when they contemplate deviant lines of action because significant others likely have punished and not rewarded deviant behaviors in the past. The evidence presented throughout suggests that males and females may differ with respect to the likelihood that they anticipate negative reactions to law violation and depression. Whereas females are reacted to more negatively by conventional others for engaging in law violation, males are reacted to more negatively for experiencing or expressing depressive emotions (e.g., Waas and Graczyk 2000). These differences in the actual reactions to male and female deviance may be relevant for understanding the channeling of deviance in gendered directions because they influence anticipated reactions to deviance. Arguably, males may anticipate more negative reactions to depression than to law violation; whereas females may anticipate more negative reactions to law violation than to depression. These differences have clear implications for why males are more likely than females to engage in law violation and why females are more prone than males to experience depressive affect.

Finally, as argued previously (De Coster and Heimer 2001), differential associations may affect law violation and depression by influencing the formation of reflected appraisals. Whereas relationships with conventional others may provide the individual with nondeviant self-identities, relationships with deviant others likely produce deviant identities. Specifically, attachments to conventional groups may reduce the chances that individuals form reflected appraisals as rule-violators and/or as distressed individuals. Alternatively, attachments to deviant groups may increase the chances that individuals form deviant reflected appraisals of self because these groups do not serve the supportive role of assisting individuals in redefining themselves as nondeviant in the face of stress. In short, attachments to law-violating others may lead to the formation of reflected appraisals of self as a rule-violator, and attachments to depressed others may lead to reflected appraisals of self as a distressed person.

Research indicates that this relationship between reflected appraisals and deviance may be relevant for understanding the gendered channeling of deviance. The labeling arguments discussed earlier suggest that males will be more likely than females to form reflected appraisals as rule-violators; whereas females will be more likely than males to form reflected appraisals as distressed persons. This presumably is because males and females differ with respect to the types of deviance in which they engage and because significant others are likely to label individuals in ways consistent with gendered expectations of appropriate deviance. Thus, gender differences in levels of reflected appraisals as rule-violators and distressed persons may play a part in channeling deviance in gendered directions. These reflected appraisals also may influence males and females differently. Whereas reflected appraisals as a rule violator have a greater impact on male law violation than on female law violation (Bartusch and Matsueda 1996; Koita and Triplett 1998), reflected appraisals as a distressed person may have a greater impact on female depression than on male depression. Thus, reflected appraisals may be central for understanding both the common causes of law violation and depression, as well as the gendered channeling of deviance.

In addition to influencing deviance through these three role-taking mechanisms, differential associations may influence law violation and depression directly, due to imitation or modeling. Moreover, initial deviant responses to stressful events may influence future law violation and depression directly. That is, law violation and depression may occur in the absence of role-taking through habitual or scripted responses over time (Mead 1934). To the extent that males are more likely than females to associate with law-violating others and to respond initially to stress with law violation, these differential associations and initial responses to stress will play a part in channeling male deviance in law-violating directions. Similarly, the channeling of female deviance in depressive directions likely is influenced by the greater propensity of females than males to associate with others who view expressions and displays of negative emotions as acceptable under some conditions and by the greater likelihood of females to respond initially to stress with passive, withdrawing emotions.

Overall, the process leading to law violation and depression can be summarized in the following sequence: Social-structural positions influence exposure to stress and deviant responses to stress. Stress exposure and its deviant responses, including both law violation and depression, subsequently shape social relationships or attachments to conventional and nonconventional groups. Attachments to these groups, in turn, affect role-taking in ways that ultimately increase future law violation and depression. Thus, structural positions, stress exposure, social relationships, and the role-taking process are common causes of law violation and depression. However, the *content* of social relationships, social learning, and role-taking may vary systematically across gender, thereby channeling deviance in dissimilar directions for males and females.

## Conclusions

This chapter responds to Cullen's (1983) call for theoretical explanations that seek to understand the shared causes of different forms of deviance, while simultaneously seeking to understand the social factors that channel deviance in one direction rather than another. In doing this, I have extended a recently proposed interactionist perspective on the common causes of law violation and depression to include arguments from social learning perspectives in the criminological and mental health literatures. This extended perspective on common causes proposes that three elements of role-taking—deviant definitions, anticipated reactions to deviance, and deviant reflected appraisals—are central for understanding the common causes of law violation and depression. The chapter also embedded these role-taking mechanisms within their larger social context by discussing the impact of social-structural positions, stressful life events, and differential associations on role-taking. Thus, the common causes of law violation and depression consist of disadvantaged structural positions, exposure to stress, deviant associations, and role-taking. I further have proposed that the content of social learning and role-taking is central for understanding why it is that males are more likely to express deviance in the form of law violation and females are more likely to express deviance in the form of depression. In particular, I have argued that the specific content of deviant reflected appraisals, anticipated reactions, and definitions may be key to understanding the channeling of deviance in gendered directions because gender socialization and gendered expectations lead to systematic differences across gender in the content of these elements of role-taking.

## Notes

*     Direct all correspondence to Stacy De Coster, University of Massachusetts, Amherst, Department of Sociology, 738 Thompson Hall, 200 Hicks Way, Amherst, MA 01003-9277. I thank Karen Heimer and Rodney Engen for helpful comments on earlier drafts of the paper.
1.     Note that classic theorists, such as Merton (1938) and Shaw and McKay (1942), offered general theories of deviance that focused on a broad array of outcomes, including law-violating and mental health outcomes. Additionally, recent social learning and control theories of deviance have been posited as general theories that

can explain a wide variety of deviant outcomes, ranging from suicide and mental illness to drug use and violent crime (Akers 1973, 1977, 1985; Gottfredson and Hirschi 1990; Tittle 1995). These theories, however, do not provide explicit explanations for why some individuals respond to deviance-producing circumstances with law violation and others with mental health problems, such as depression.

2.  Cullen (1983) proposes that social class, urban dwelling, and race also may be relevant for understanding the channeling of deviance. My discussion of law violation and depression focuses specifically on the role of gender in channeling deviance because research findings consistently demonstrate that males are more likely than females to engage in law violation (Hindelang 1971, 1979; Steffensmeier and Cobb 1981), whereas females are more likely to become depressed (Al-Issa 1982; Avison and McAlpine 1992; Gjerde and Humphrey Block 1988; Gove and Tudor 1973). Research on social class, urban dwelling, and race in criminology and the sociology of mental health demonstrates that these factors influence law violation and depression similarly, with disadvantaged individuals being more likely than their advantaged counterparts to engage in law violation *and* to become depressed (e.g., Aneshensel and Sucoff 1996; Hagan and Peterson 1995; Kessler and Neighbors 1986; Sampson and Groves 1989). Thus, gender is likely to be more important than these other factors for understanding the *channeling* of deviance when focusing on law violation and depression as alternative forms of deviance.

3.  Thoits (1986) proposes that one of the ways in which supportive others—or people to whom one is attached—aid individuals in fighting depression and restoring psychological well being is by allowing them to redefine themselves as psychologically healthy, rather than distressed. Thus, attachments to groups are important for understanding the formation of identity, or reflected appraisals of self as psychologically healthy, in the role-taking process.

4.  Although Heimer (1996) reported that negative anticipated reactions of peers reduced delinquency among females but not males, she also reported that this difference was statistically non-significant across gender.

5.  Although depression is not always considered to be an emotion, I consider the socialization of emotions literature to be relevant for understanding depression. A main distinction that has been made between depression as an emotion versus depression as a mood is based on the argument that emotions have objects (see Crawford et al. 1992). For instance, when someone is angry, they are angry *at* someone or *about* something. Following this logic, depression sometimes is an emotion—e.g., when someone is depressed about something that has happened. However, when depression persists without an object, it becomes a mood (Thoits 1989). It may be the case that individuals experience depression as an emotion (perhaps one or several times) before depression becomes a persistent mood. Indeed, dealing with depression solely as a mood that overcomes an individual is likely to underestimate the social causes of depressive affect. Moreover, psychologists consider depression to be an *affective* disorder, i.e., a disorder of feelings and emotions (see Real 1997). Thus, I draw on arguments from the socialization of emotions literature in my discussion of the social causes of depression.

6.  Resolution of the discrepancy between actual emotions and normative emotions can involve either changing actual emotions to be more normative and/or redefining norms to correspond better with actual emotions. I entertain these possibilities in the discussion of social support.

7.  This suggests that whether or not situated depressive feelings become persistent depressive moods over time is conditioned by role-taking, learned definitions, and anticipated reactions of others.

## References

Agnew, Robert. 1985. "A Revised Strain Theory of Delinquency." *Social Forces* 64:151-167.

_____. 1992. "Foundation for a General Strain Theory of Crime and Delinquency." *Criminology* 30:47-87.

Akers, Ronald L. 1973. *Deviant Behavior: A Social Learning Approach.* Belmont, CA: Wadsworth.

_____. 1977. *Deviant Behavior: A Social Learning Approach.* Second Edition. Belmont, CA: Wadsworth.

_____. 1985. *Deviant Behavior: A Social Learning Approach.* Third Edition. Belmont, CA: Wadsworth.

_____. 1998. *Social Learning and Social Structure: A General Theory of Crime and Deviance.* Boston: Northeastern University Press.

Akers, Ronald L., Marvin D. Krohn, Lonn Lannza-Kaduce, and Marcia Radosevich. 1979. "Social Learning and Deviant Behavior: A Specific Test of a General Theory." *American Sociological Review* 44:635-55.

Akers, Ronald L., and Gang Lee. 1996. "A Longitudinal Test of Social Learning Theory: Adolescent Smoking." *Journal of Drug Issues* 26:317-43.

Al-Issa, Ihsan. 1982. *Gender and Psychopathology.* New York: Academic Press.

Alexander, Rudolph, and Lyndon Langford. 1992. "Throwing Down: A Social Learning Test of Student Fighting." *Social Work in Education* 14:114-125.

Aneshensel, Carol S., and Clea A. Sucoff. 1996. "The Neighborhood Context of Adolescent Mental Health. *Journal of Health and Social Behavior* 37:293-301.

Aneshensel, Carol S. 1992. "Social Stress: Theory and Research." *Annual Review of Sociology* 18:15-38.

Avison, William R., and Donna D. McAlpine. 1992. "Gender Differences in Symptoms of Depression Among Adolescents." *Journal of Health and Social Behavior* 33:77-96.

Bandura, Albert. 1986. *Social Foundations of Thought and Action: A Social Cognitive Theory.* Englewood Cliffs, NJ: Prentice-Hall.

Bartusch, Dawn Jeglum, and Ross L. Matsueda. 1996. "Gender, Reflected Appraisals, and Cross-Gender Labeling: A Cross-Group Test of an Interactionist Theory of Delinquency." *Social Forces* 75:145-172.

Brezina, Timothy. 1996. "Adapting to Strain: An Examination of Delinquency Coping Responses." *Criminology* 34:39-60.

_____. 2000. "Delinquent Problem-Solving: An Interpretive Framework for Criminological Theory and Research." *The Journal of Research in Crime and Delinquency* 37:3-32.

Buck, Ross W., Robert E. Miller, and William F. Caul. 1974. "Sex Personality, and Physiological Variables in the Communication of Affect Via Facial Expression." *Journal of Personality and Social Psychology* 30:587-96.

Burgess, Robert L., and Ronald L. Akers. 1966. "A Differential Association-Reinforcement Theory of Criminal Behavior." *Social Problems* 14:128-147.

Caldwell, Mayta A., and Letitia Anne Peplau. 1982. "Sex Differences in Same-Sex Friendships." *Sex Roles* 8:721-32.

Camras, Linda A. 1985. "Socialization of Affect Communication." In Michael Lewis and Carolyn Saarni (eds.), *The Socialization of Emotions.* New York: Plenum Press.

Chassin, Laurie, David R. Pillow, Patrick J. Curran, Brooke S.G. Molina, and Manuel Barrera, Jr. 1993. "Relation of Parental Alcoholism to Early Adolescent Substance Use: A Test of Three Mediating Mechanisms." *Journal of Abnormal Psychology* 102:13-19.

Cohen, Lawrence E., and Marcus Felson. 1979. "Social Change and Crime Rate Trends: A Routine Activity Approach." *American Sociological Review* 44:588-608.

Colten, Mary Ellen, and Susan Gore. 1991. *Adolescent Stress: Causes and Consequences.* New York: Walter De Gruyter, Inc.

Conger, Rand. 1976. "Social Control and Social Learning Models of Delinquency: A Synthesis." *Criminology* 14:17-40.

Crawford, June, Susan Kippax, Jenny Onyx, Una Gault, and Pam Benton. 1992. *Emotion and Gender: Constructing Meaning from Memory.* Newbury Park, CA: Sage Publications.

Cullen, Frances T. 1983. *Rethinking Crime and Deviance Theory: The Emergence of a Structuring Tradition.* Totowa, NJ: Rowman and Allanheld.

De Coster, Stacy and Karen Heimer. 2001. "The Relationship Between Law Violation and Depression: An Interactionist Analysis." *Criminology* 39: 799-836.

Dornfeld, Maude, and Candace Kruttschnitt. 1992. "Do the Stereotypes Fit? Mapping Gender-Specific Outcomes and Risk Factors." *Criminology* 30:397-419.

Dorr, Aimee. 1985. "Contexts for Experience with Emotion, with Special Attention to Television." In Michael Lewis and Carolyn Saarni (eds.) *The Socialization of Emotions.* New York: Plenum Press.

Ekman, Paul, Robert W. Levenson, and Wallace V. Friesen. 1983. "Autonomic Nervous System Activity Distinguishes among Emotions." *Science* 221:1208-1210.

Fagot, Beverly I. 1978. "The Influence of Sex of Child on Parental Reactions to Toddler Children." *Child Development* 49:449-465.

_____. 1985. "Beyond the Reinforcement Principle: Another Step Toward Understanding Sex Role Development." *Developmental Psychology* 21:1097-1104.

Fagot, Beverly I., and Richard Hagan. 1991. "Observations of Parent Reactions to Sex-Stereotyped Behaviors: Age and Sex Effects." *Child Development* 62:617-628.

Farrell, Ronald A., and Victoria Lynn Swigert. 1978. "Prior Offense Record as a Self-Fulfilling Prophecy." *Law and Society Review* 12:437-53.

Felson, Richard B. 1985. "Reflected Appraisal and the Development of Self." *Social Psychology Quarterly* 48:71-77.

Ge, Xiaojia, Karin M. Best, Rand D. Conger, and Ronald L. Simons. 1996. "Parenting Behaviors and the Occurrence and Co-Occurrence of Adolescent Depressive Symptoms and Conduct Problems." *Developmental Psychology* 32:717-31.

Gjerde, Per F., and Jeanne Humphrey Block. 1988. "Depressive Symptoms and Personality During Late Adolescence: Gender Differences in the Externalization-Internalization of Symptom Expression." *Journal of Abnormal Psychology* 97:475-86.

Gottfredson, Michael R., and Travis Hirschi. 1990. *A General Theory of Crime.* Stanford, CA: Stanford University Press.

Gove, Walter R., and Jeanette F. Tudor. 1973. "Adult Sex Roles and Mental Illness." *American Journal of Sociology* 78:812-35.

Hagan, John. 1988. *Structural Criminology.* Cambridge: Polity Press.

Hagan, John, and Blair Wheaton. 1993. "The Search for Adolescent Role Exists and the Transition to Adulthood." *Social Forces* 71:955-80.

Hagan, John, and Ruth Peterson. 1995. *Crime and Inequality.* Stanford, CA: Stanford University Press.

Harris, Anthony R. 1977. "Sex and Theories of Deviance." *American Sociological Review* 42:3-16.

Heimer, Karen. 1995. "Gender, Race, and the Pathways to Delinquency: An Interactionist Analysis." In John Hagan and Ruth D. Peterson. *Crime and Inequality.* Stanford, CA: Stanford University.

_____. 1996. "Gender, Interaction, and Delinquency: Testing a Theory of Differential Social Control." *Social Psychology Quarterly* 59:39-61.

Heimer, Karen, and Stacy De Coster. 1999. "The Gendering of Violent Delinquency." *Criminology* 37:277-317.

Heimer, Karen, and Ross L. Matsueda. 1994. "Role-Taking, Role-Commitment, and Delinquency: A Theory of Differential Social Control." *American Sociological Review* 59:365-390.

Heise, David R., and Cassandra Calhan. 1995. "Emotion Norms in Interpersonal Events." *Social Psychology Quarterly* 58:223-40.

Hindelang, Michael J. 1971. "Age, Sex, and the Versatility of Delinquent Involvements." *Social Problems* 18:522-35.

_____. 1979. "Sex Differences in Criminal Activity." *Social Problems* 27:143-56.

Hochschild, Arlie Russell. 1979. "Emotion Work, Feeling Rules, and Social Structure." *American Journal of Sociology* 85:551-75.

_____. 1983. *The Managed Heart: The Commercialization of Human Feeling.* Berkeley, CA: University of California Press.

Hoffmann, John P., and Susan S. Su. 1997. "The Conditional Effects of Stress on Delinquency and Drug Use." *Journal of Research in Crime and Delinquency* 34:46-78.

_____. 1998. "Stressful Life Events and Adolescent Substance Use and Depression: Conditional and Gender Differentiated Effects." *Substance Use and Misuse* 33:2219-2262.

Hogue, Aaron, and Laurence Steinberg. 1995. "Homophily of Internalized Distress in Adolescent Peer Groups." *Developmental Psychology* 31:897-906.

Horwitz, Allan V., and Helene Raskin White. 1987. "Gender Role Orientations and Styles of Pathology Among Adolescents." *Journal of Health and Social Behavior* 28:158-70.

Huessman, L. Rowell, Nancy G. Guerra, A. Zelli, and L. Miller. 1992. "Differing Normative Beliefs about Aggression for Boys and Girls." In Karo Bjorkqvist and Pirkko Niemela (eds.), *Of Mice and Women: Aspects of Female Aggression.* San Diego, CA: Academic Press.

Jackson, Elton F., Charles R. Tittle, and Mary Jean Burke. 1986. "Offense-Specific Models of the Differential Association Process." *Social Problems* 33:335-56.

Jensen, Gary F. 1972. "Parents, Peers, and Delinquent Action: A Test of the Differential Association Perspective." *American Journal of Sociology* 56:294-300.

Johnson, Fern L., and Elizabeth J. Aries. 1983. "Conversation Patterns among Same-Sex Pairs of Late-Adolescent Close Friends." *Journal of Genetic Psychology* 142:225-38.

Kandel, Denise, and Mark Davies. 1982. "Epidemiology of Depressive Mood in Adolescents." *Archives of General Psychiatry* 39:1205-1212.

Kessler, Ronald C., and Harold W. Neighbors. 1986. "A New Perspective on the Relationship Among Race, Social Class, and Psychological Distress." *Journal of Health and Social Behavior* 27:107-115.

Kemper, Theodore D. 1981. "Social Constructionist and Positivist Approaches to the Sociology of Emotions." *American Journal of Sociology* 87:336-62.

Koita, Kiyofumi, and Ruth A. Triplett. 1998. "An Examination of Gender and Race Effects on the Parental Appraisals Process: A Reanalysis of Matsueda's Model of the Self." *Criminal Justice and Behavior* 25:382-400.

Lewis, Michael, and Linda Michalson. 1983. *Children's Emotions and Moods: Developmental Theory and Measurement.* New York: Plenum Press.

Lewis, Michael, and Carolyn Saarni, 1985. *The Socialization of Emotions.* New York: Plenum Press.

Leavitt, Robin Lynn, and Martha Bauman Power. 1989. "Emotional Socialization in the Postmodern Era: Children in Day Care." *Social Psychology Quarterly* 52:35-43.

Lempers, Jacques D., and Dania Clark-Lempers. 1990. "Family Economic Stress, Maternal and Paternal Support and Adolescent Distress." *Journal of Adolescence* 13:217-29.

Link, Bruce, and Jo Phelan. 1995. "Social Conditions as Fundamental Causes of Disease." *Journal of Health and Social Behavior* (Extra Issue):80-94.

Malatesta, Carol Zander, and Jeannette M. Haviland. 1982. "Learning Display Rules: The Socialization of Emotion Expression in Infancy." *Child Development* 53:991-1003.

____. 1985. "Signals, Symbols, and Socialization: The Modification of Emotional Expression in Human Development." In Michael Lewis and Carolyn Saarni (eds.), *The Socialization of Emotions*. New York: Plenum Press.

Matsueda, Ross L. 1982. "Testing Control Theory and Differential Association: A Causal Modeling Approach." *American Sociological Review* 47:489-504.

____. 1992. "Reflected Appraisals, Parental Labeling, and Delinquency: Specifying A Symbolic Interactionist Theory." *American Journal of Sociology* 97:1577-1611.

Matsueda, Ross L., and Karen Heimer. 1997. "A Symbolic Interactionist Theory of Role-Transitions, Role-Commitments and Delinquency. In Terence P. Thornberry (ed.), *Developmental Theories of Crime and Delinquency*. New Brunswick, NJ: Transaction Publishers.

McCall, George J., and Jerry L. Simmons. 1978. *Identities and Interactions: An Examination of Human Associations in Everyday Life* . New York: Free Press.

Mead, George H. 1934. *Mind, Self, and Society*. Chicago: University of Chicago Press.

Merton, Robert K. 1938. "Social Structure and Anomie." *American Sociological Review* 3:672-682.

Pearlin, Leonard, Morton A. Lieberman, Elizabeth G. Menaghan, and Joseph T. Mullan. 1981. "The Stress Process." *Journal of Health and Social Behavior* 22:337-56.

Pollak, Lauren Harte, and Peggy Thoits. 1989. "Processes in Emotional Socialization." *Social Psychology Quarterly* 52:22-34.

Real, Terrence. 1997. *I Don't Want to Talk About It: Overcoming the Secret Legacy of Male Depression*. New York: Simon and Schuster.

Rosenberg, Morris. 1990. "Reflexivity and Emotions." *Social Psychology Quarterly* 53:3-12.

Sampson, Robert J., and W. Byron Groves. 1989. "Community Structure and Crime: Testing Social-Disorganization Theory." *American Journal of Sociology* 94:774-802.

Schur, Edwin M. 1984. *Labeling Women Deviant: Gender, Stigma, and Social Control*. New York: Random House.

Shaw, Clifford R., and Henry D. McKay. 1942. *Juvenile Delinquency in Urban Areas*. Chicago: University of Chicago Press.

Simpson, Sally S., and Lori Elis. 1995. "Doing Gender: Sorting out the Caste and Crime Conundrum." *Criminology* 33:47-81.

Snow, Margaret E., Carol N. Jacklin, and Eleanor E. Maccoby. 1983. "Sex Differences in Father-Child Interaction at One Year of Age." *Child Development* 52:227-32.

Sommers, Shula. 1984. "Reported Emotions and Conventions of Emotionality Among College Students." *Journal of Personality and Social Psychology* 46:207-15.

Steffensmeier, Darrell J., and Michael J. Cobb. 1981. "Sex Differences in Urban Arrest Patterns, 1934-79." *Social Problems* 29:37-50.

Sutherland, Edwin H. 1947. *Principles of Criminology*. Fourth Edition. Philadelphia: J. B. Lippincott.

Thoits, Peggy A. 1984. "Coping, Social Support, and Psychological Outcomes: The Central Role of Emotion." In Phillip Shaver (ed.) *Review of Personality and Social Psychology*, Vol. 5. Beverly Hills, CA: Sage Publications.

_____. 1985. "Self-Labeling Processes in Mental Illness: The Role of Emotional Deviance." *American Journal of Sociology* 91:221-249.

_____. 1986. "Social Support as Coping Assistance." *Journal of Consulting and Clinical Psychology* 54:416-423.

_____. 1989. "The Sociology of Emotions." *Annual Review of Sociology* 15:317-342.

Thorne, Barrie, and Zella Luria. 1986. "Sexuality and Gender in Children's Daily Worlds." *Social Problems* 33:176-190.

Tittle, Charles R. 1995. *Control Balance: Toward a General Theory of Deviance.* Boulder, CO: Westview Press.

Waas, Gregory A., and Patricia A. Graczyk. 1999. "Child Behaviors Leading to Peer Rejection: A View from the Peer Group." *Child Study Journal* 29:291-306.

# 7

# Gender Variation in Delinquency: Self-Images, Beliefs and Peers as Mediating Mechanisms

*Gary F. Jensen*

In a review of research on gender differences in delinquency nearly a quarter of a century ago, Jensen and Eve (1976: 429) stated that "[N]umerous investigations carried out at different points in time, in different regions of the nation, in a variety of different cities and sociodemographic groups, using a variety of alternative measures of delinquency (both official and unofficial) and divergent research techniques have consistently discovered a sex differential in delinquency. This may be more than can be said of any other statistical regularity in the study of delinquency...." More recent reviews of research continue to support that same conclusion (e.g., see Jensen and Rojek 1998; Bartusch and Matsueda 1996: 146; Shoemaker 1996). Offense rates are higher for males than females, with the greatest disparities for the most serious and/or destructive offenses. In short, it is safe to conclude that gender remains one of the most robust correlates of crime and delinquency among the sociodemographic background variables studied by criminologists.

While a growing variety of theories have been proposed to explain gender variation, only a small number of studies have conducted tests of hypotheses derived from those theories and most of that research has focused on a very limited number of variables, limited samples and/or limited measures of delinquency. Several studies have focused on "masculinity" or gender-linked self-images as crucial variables for explaining the gender difference, several have focused on delinquent peers and others have focused on variables such as grades in school and internalization of conventional beliefs. This study attempts a comprehensive examination of gender variations, focusing on mediating mechanisms central to social learning and symbolic interactionist perspectives on delinquency.

## Prior Research

Concerted attention to gender variation began in the mid-1970s with Adler's *Sisters in Crime* (1975) and Simon's *Women and Crime* (1975) and since that time it has become common for treatises, textbooks and edited readers to devote special attention to the gender gap and/or female crime and delinquency (e.g., see Shoemaker 1996; Traub and Little 1994; Siegel and Senna 1997). Moreover, it is now incumbent upon any new theoretical approach to crime to address the gender gap (e.g., see Gottfredson and Hirschi 1990: 144-149; Tittle 1995: 228-241). In fact, gender variation has been a central and distinguishing focus of some recent theories such as power-control theory (Hagan, Gillis and Simpson 1985, 1990; Hagan, Simpson and Gillis 1987; Hagan 1989) and differential social control or "reflected appraisals" theory (Heimer 1995, 1996; Bartusch and Matsueda 1996). Research on gang delinquency, long presumed to be limited primarily to males, has shifted to encompass females as well with interesting results (see Bowker and Klein 1983; Campbell 1990; Bjerregaard and Smith 1993; Esbensen and Huisinga 1993).

Although gender has been moving closer to center stage in theoretical criminology, the actual amount of empirical research testing theories of gender variation is quite limited. The first multivariate analysis of survey data on gender differences was reported by Jensen and Eve in 1976. Based on the dominant and emerging sociological theories at that time, they expected that the difference between male and female students would be explained by variations in bonds to conventional others, values and institutions as well as differential involvement in inhibiting and facilitating social activities. Using Hirschi's Richmond Youth Study data, those variables were found to explain much of the difference with gender reduced to explaining between .5 and 2 percent of the variation when introduced together with social bond variables and delinquency friends. In short, variables central to opportunity, social control, social learning and differential association theories appeared to explain a goodly proportion of the gender variation. Since such variables did not explain the gender difference entirely the door was left open for explanations stressing gender variation in the validity of self-report data as well as additional social psychological, sociocultural or bio-social variables.

In 1979 Cullen, Golden and Cullen used self-report data from a nonrandom sample of college students to study the relationship between stereotypical masculine behavior traits and self-reports of past delinquency. They reported that masculinity was a significant correlate of several forms of delinquency, that it partially explained the gender difference, but that the independent effect of gender remained quite strong. Gender-linked self-images were relevant to the gender difference but could not fully explain it.

In 1984 Farnworth used self-report data on 99 black fifteen-year-old youth and reported that sex differences in violence persisted when controls for family and school variables were introduced. Using a much larger sample, Morash (1986) was able to show that girls are less likely to associate with delinquent peers and that such associations partially explained gender differences in offense behavior. However, gender remained a significant correlate of a composite delinquency index and property offenses even when such associations were taken into account.

There have been five quite recent attempts to explain the gender difference in self-reported delinquency: Rowe, Vazsonyi and Flannery (1995), Heimer (1995), Bartusch and Matsueda (1996), LaGrange and Silverman (1999) and Liu and Kaplan (1999). Three of these studies partially explained the gender difference. Rowe and his colleagues analyzed data from 418 sibling pairs (836 cases) and found that a latent trait connecting impulsivity, rebelliousness and deceitfulness as manifest traits was relevant to explaining differences in delinquency by gender. However, that trait failed to explain about one-third of the gender gap. LaGrange and Silverman accomplished a similar reduction using data from 2,000 Canadian high schools students. They examined the role of self-control and opportunity, variables central to Gottfredson and Hirschi's self-control theory of crime (1992), and were able to "substantially reduce, but not eliminate, the impact of gender" (1999: 62). Finally, Liu and Kaplan introduced delinquent peers, conventional values, negative sanctions and achievement frustration in a panel study of 2,753 adolescents and reported that "Much of the gender difference in delinquency is accounted for by these mediating variables" (1999: 211).

In contrast, two studies report reducing the direct contribution of gender to delinquency to statistical insignificance. Using 1988 Monitoring the Future data on high school seniors, Karen Heimer (1995) succeeded in eliminating the direct effect of gender by introducing grades earned at school, self-esteem, tastes for risk and traditional gender beliefs. She also considered variations in the relevance and direction of effects for such variables and attributes the gender difference in delinquency to both differences in means on causal variables and differential slopes by gender. While unique in its success at explaining the gender difference, it has to be noted that the indices used in the study yielded relatively small gender differences. Judging from the observed means reported in the appendix, the gender ratio in violence was about two male offenses for every female offense, which can be contrasted with a ratio of between five and six to one for juvenile arrest rates for assault using F.B.I. statistics (see Jensen and Rojek 1998: 97).

In another study, Bartusch and Matsueda (1996) concluded that when introduced together with parents' appraisals of youth as sociable, successful, distressed or a rule-violator (and the youths' own reflected appraisals on these same variables) the unexplained portion of the gender gap is not statistically significant. However, it should be noted that the measure of delinquency used included status offenses. Since status offenses are either unrelated to gender (Farnworth 1984) or, in some instances, positively related to gender (see Hagan, Gillis and Simpson 1993), the delinquency scale used may minimize the gender difference. Status offenses were reported on separately but no evidence was presented that the gender gap in serious or "criminal" offenses could be explained by the theory.

In sum, most studies have reported significant residual variation by gender in their multivariate analyses and the two that reported the most success explaining the difference had unusually small differences to explain. In addition, each study focused on a limited set of variables. Masculinity, rebelliousness, delinquent peers, grades in school and a variety of other variables have each been studied as potential mediating mechanisms, but the scope of variables included in any one study is quite limited. Neither Heimer nor Bartush and Matsueda included delinquent peers in their analysis and only one study (Cullen, Golden and Cullen 1979) examined gender-linked self-conceptions. Yet, delinquent peers is a key variable in differential association (Sutherland and Cressey 1970) and social learning theories (Akers, Krohn, Lanza-Kaduce and Radosevich 1978, Akers 1985, 1996, 1998) and gender-linked values and self-images are central to recent feminist critiques of extant theory and research.

Feminist critics have raised basic issues about the images and biases they believe are reflected in most theory and research, especially a tendency to view female conformity as a product of limited options or constraints. In a recent review of theory and research on female delinquency and gender differences in delinquency, Chesney-Lind and Shelden (1992: 99) argue that "girls' lower delinquency, particularly serious and violent delinquency, may be the result of the positive attributes that girls accumulate as a consequence of growing up female and identifying with the positive aspects of their gender." For example, control balance theory (Tittle 1996) focuses on constraints limiting female imagination and control deficits to explain gender variation. Power-control theory (Hagan, Gillis and Simpson 1985, 1993) focuses on a combination of constraints coupled with differential encouragement of risk-taking by gender in preparation for entrepreneurial careers. Males are depicted as active agents with a masculine value system operating as an active source of deviant choices while females conform because of constraints or the absence of those positive male traits. A feminine value system is imposed and passive and low rates of female crime are explained by what females lack rather than what they have.[1]

While this chapter does not undertake a thorough examination of the feminist critique, the treatment of certain variables reflects that criticism.

Drawing on Chesney-Lind and Shelden, it is argued that among "the positive attributes that girls accumulate as a consequence of growing up female and identifying with the positive aspects of their gender" is a tendency towards gender-linked self-images in which caring, forgiveness and cooperation take precedence over the pursuit of dominance, competition and autonomy. Carol Gilligan (1982) depicts this contrast in terms of "different voices" with issues of hierarchical dominance and autonomy central to the male voice and issues of care and connection central to the female voice. Consistent with Bartusch and Matsueda's "reflected appraisals" theory it is presumed that gender-linked self-conceptions are formed through social interaction and socialization experiences. Such orientations are presumed to vary among both females and males with females falling, in the aggregate, toward the "feminine" end and males falling towards the "masculine" end of a continuum.

The fact that the attempts to explain the gender difference in terms of "masculinity" partially reduced the gender difference means that other mediating mechanisms must be examined. Delinquent peers have been central to both social learning and differential association theory and four of the studies reviewed above found that variable to be an important mediating mechanism. Although central to the social learning theory, power control theory (Hagan, Gillis and Simpson 1985, 1993) does not include delinquent peers in its model as tested and it is not a central variable in either social control (Hirschi 1969) or self-control (Gottfredson and Hirschi 1990) theories.

Another learning mechanism central to differential association, social learning, social control, self-control and symbolic interactionist theories is the degree to which youths have internalized or been normatively socialized to accept certain conventional normative beliefs or definitions favorable or unfavorable to the violation of law. Indeed, in Matsueda's early research (1981) such beliefs were advocated as "the" mediating mechanism explaining the impact of all other variables, including the impact of delinquent peers and parental controls. While not central to Bartusch and Matsueda's test of reflected appraisals theory, variable learning of values, norms and beliefs in symbolic interaction within primary groups is central to both differential association theory, differential control and social learning theory.

## The Current Research

This study will focus on the three variables that are most promising as key mediating mechanisms explaining gender variation in serious and common forms of violence and property crime from a social learning-interactionist perspective: (1) "feminine" self-images centering on cooperation vs "macho" self-images emphasizing dominance, (2) internalization of conventional moral beliefs, and (3) interaction with delinquent peers. Since power control theory focuses on perceived risk of punishment and parental controls as mediating mechanism, the impact of these two variables will be examined as well. Finally, although prior research suggests that a liberated gender ideology *will not* be a key mediating mechanism (see Chesney-Lind and Shelden 1998: 95-97), such beliefs will be included in the analysis to provide a further test of that argument. The ability to consider such a wide range of relevant variables in a single analysis makes this test far more comprehensive than other studies in the literature.

The mediating impact of such variables will be examined using data gathered by Hindelang, Hirschi and Weiss in 1978-79 in Seattle as part of their major study, *Measuring Delinquency* (1981). The Seattle survey was designed to assess the reliability and validity of the self-report method among sociodemographic categories of youth. Hence, data were collected from a disproportionate stratified random sample of youth, over-representing males and black youth and serious delinquents. Police and court records were used to construct two distinct subsamples—one with police records only and one with court records only. To create an "officially non-delinquent subsample" they gathered data from public high school students as well, excluding any that appeared in the police and court subsamples.

The Seattle sample overcomes many of the criticisms leveled at prior sample surveys. By over-representing youths with official records it should include the "serious offenders" that are thought to be missed in typical samples. Moreover, the sample will allow examination of the role of key mediating mechanisms in the explanation of officially recorded offenses, self-reported offenses and offense behavior of youth who identify themselves as gang members. The common criticism that self-report data yield different results than official data can be addressed directly by examining both types of data. Elliott's (1994) critique of unfounded attacks on self-report methods shows most such arguments to be invalid and this study will directly address similar issues.

The data examined in this study are almost twenty years old and critics might contend that the results are not necessarily generalizable to the end of the twentieth century. All research is subject to such possible constraints but there are several points to be made in defense of using this body of data. First, the basic variables examined in this study are based on theories that are far older than the data. Even theories proposed in the 1980s and 1990s focus on variables that were central to earlier theories and most cite foundations in earlier criminological and sociological perspectives. Second, the major theories cited in this research have been proposed as "general" theories which means that they should be able to explain the gender difference in 1978 as well as in the 1990s. Third, although there may have been some downward movement in gender ratios for arrests and some forms of crime, the Monitoring the Future surveys on self-reported delinquency among high school seniors yield similar male-female gender ratios for theft and violence in 1978 as in 1995 (see Jensen and Rojek 1998). The differences to be explained do not appear to be fundamentally different in these spans of time. Fourth, the one variable examined in separate studies spanning three decades, delinquent peers, was found to be a significant and mediating variable at all points in time and the two most recent studies reported a residual direct effect of gender, a finding comparable to research using survey data from the late 1960s and 1970s. In summary, the Seattle survey provides a unique opportunity to test theories of gender variation using a unique range of variables to examine gender variation in both official and survey measures of delinquency.

Few people would challenge the assumption that a person's self-acknowledged "sex" precedes other variables measured in this study. On the other hand, since these data were gathered at a single point in time we will not be able to demonstrate definitive causal paths between hypothetical intervening mechanisms and delinquent behavior. It has become commonplace to argue that longitudinal, panel data measuring independent, dependent and intervening variables at several points in time is necessary to untangle the mechanisms generating differences among sociodemographic groups. However, in an assessment of the National Survey of Youth, a major source of existing research findings claiming relevance to issues of causal order, Janet Lauritsen (1998: 127) reports that survey measures of delinquency in that data set are of questionable validity for studying change among individuals over time. She found systematic shifts in self-reports over time that had little to do with actual delinquent or criminal behavior. Her assessment constitutes a serious challenge to a large body of panel research and similar issues will have to be examined for other panel studies. In contrast, she reiterates the view that self-report measures are valid and reliable for the very type of analysis reported here.

### The Gender Variations to be Explained

The mean number of offenses, gender ratios and correlations with gender for agency-recorded, self-report offenses and serious offenses by gang members [2] are summarized in Table 7.1. While the correlations may appear small it is important to note that references to the gender difference using F.B.I. arrest statistics have been stated in terms of the "ratio" of the male arrest rate to the female rate. In 1980 the ratio of arrest rates for juvenile males and females ranged from 2.6 for larceny to 13.6 for burglary in the Uniform Crime Reports (Jensen and Rojek 1992: 94). The ratio of male to female juvenile court referral rates was about three to one (Jensen and Rojek 1992: 95). The ratios in Table 7.1 indicate that when gender variations in official and survey measures are assessed in a comparable manner the ratios are comparable to those noted using official data (see Appendix for specific items). The gender contrast is substantial for major property crimes and serious violence and rela-

Table 7.1
Means, Ratios and Correlations, Offense Categories [a] by Gender

| Category | Male Mean | Female Mean | Ratio | r |
|---|---|---|---|---|
| Agency data | | | | |
| Total Official Offenses | .90 | 28 | 3.2/1 | -.16* |
| Self-Reported Offenses | | | | |
| All Robberies | .54 | .14 | 3.9/1 | -.09* |
| (Armed) | .10 | .005 | 20.0/1 | -.07* |
| All Assaults | .69 | .15 | 4.6/1 | -.12* |
| (Aggravated) | .16 | .02 | 8.0/1 | -.08* |
| Major Property | 1.36 | .26 | 5.2/1 | -.14* |
| All Common Property | 2.24 | 1.24 | 2.2/1 | -.12* |
| (Shoplifting) | 1.00 | .45 | 1.1/1 | -.10* |
| Vandalism | 3.22 | .28 | 11.5/1 | -.19* |
| All Status Offenses | 6.11 | 5.72 | 1.1/1 | -.02 |
| (Runaway) | .12 | .15 | 0.8/1 | +.03 |
| Self-Reported UCR Type b | 2.46 | .54 | 4.6/1 | -.16* |
| Total Self-Reported Offenses (Including Status Offenses) c | 13.88 | 7.57 | 1.8/1 | -.17* |
| UCR Offenses by &any Identifiers d | 0.84 | 07 | 13.0/1 | -.10* |

a Self-reported offenses for specific categories described in Appendix

b Based on self-reports of offenses approximating the Uniform Crime Reports, Part I, serious crimes index—armed robbery, aggravated assault and major property crimes

c Based on all self-reported offenses described in the Appendix.

d Self-report,ed UCR Type offenses committed by youth who identify themselves as gang members (description in text)

* Statistically significant

tively small for common property crime. The ratio for vandalism using the survey data is sizeable but comparable to the ratio of juvenile male to female arrest rates in F.B.I. data in 1980 of between 12 and 13 to one. Gender is not a significant correlate of status offenses and girls report more instances of running away from home than boys—another pattern quite consistent with prior studies (see Chesney-Lind and Shelden 1998). The gender ratio for serious offenses by self-identified gang youth is 13 to 1. In short, the gender variations in survey data are no less distinct than those noted using national F.B.I. arrest data or Seattle agency records. The patterns observed are quite similar when the different types of data are approached in the same manner. There are significant gender variations to explain (with the exception of status offenses) and they are especially prominent for offenses involving weapons, destruction and serious loss or harm.

### Mediating Mechanisms

Since this analysis is guided by theories of gender variation, questionnaire items were examined both in terms of face validity as measures of gender-related concepts and their empirical relations to gender. For example, responses to the item *"I'm a little bit tougher and meaner than most kids my age"* can be interpreted as indicative of the extreme end of a masculinity or "macho" self-image continuum for adolescent males. The idea that "real" men are supposed to be tough and mean is stressed in quite conventional contexts where boys are taught proper male attitudes, ranging from organized sports to rough-housing with male relatives. In the juvenile male world being "tough, mean and bad" takes on a "positive" connotation and such words can become a sign of respect and admiration in male peer groups.

There are numerous items in the Seattle survey relevant to other types of attitudes that should differ by gender as well. For example, youth responded to items about their self-perceptions as someone (1) who gets even rather than forgive and forget, (2) who is "nice" to people, (3) who likes to brag about her/himself, (4) who tries to tell the truth, (5) who can't seem to stay out of trouble. Two of these items (bragging and telling the truth) varied only slightly by gender and were dropped from the analysis. In contrast, boys were significantly more likely than girls to define themselves as tough and mean, unforgiving and prone to trouble. They were less likely to accept a description as a "nice" person. A high score based on acceptance of toughness, unforgiveness and impulsivity and rejection of niceness would seem to tap a macho identity at one end of the continuum as distinct from a more feminine identity as nice, forgiving and gentle at the other.[3]

The items used fit Jack Katz's (1988: 80-113) description of the "ways of the bad ass" particularly well. Katz's "bad ass" sustains an aura of toughness, meanness and unpredictability which "transcends rationality." The bad ass falls at the extreme "macho" end of a continuum, negating the attitudes or values reflected at the feminine pole. While extreme versions of this identity may develop in environmental circumstances where there are few alternative sources of respect and power for teenagers (see Jankowski 1991), similar attitudes are reflected in adolescent "machoism" and the power among males of such words as "wussy" and "pussy." At the extreme, being male requires a rejection of feminine virtue and overt demonstrations of volatility, unpredictability and meanness.

It should be noted that these items are distinct from many prior measures of masculinity which tend to focus on qualities such as "leadership," "ambition" and "success" (Norland, Weisel and Shover 1981) or "independence," "objectivity," and "self-confidence" (Cullen, Golden and Cullen 1979). Indeed, some of the traits that capture a macho vs feminine attitude in this study might be negatively related to some of the traits used in other studies. An aura of toughness, meanness and unpredictability which "transcends rationality" does not fit well with some notions of "objectivity" and "leadership." Moreover, on the feminine pole, willingness to forgive, to be nice to people and to avoid trouble does not have to preclude scoring high on ambition, self-confidence and objectivity.

The survey also included two items relevant to a liberated gender ideology ("In general, the women's movement is a good idea" and "There's something wrong with girls asking boys to go out on dates"). If these items tap the same ideology as prior studies, then *they should not be positive correlates of delinquency* since prior research has consistently pointed towards gender identity rather than egalitarian or feminist ideologies as significant correlates. Although both relationships were significant, gender was barely related to the item about girls asking boys out (+.044) as compared to the endorsement of "the women's movement" as a good idea (+.12).

The Seattle survey included items that have been used in past research to measure attitudes and beliefs about the law and authority: "It's all right to get around the law if you can get away with it," "Everybody steals something once in a while," "To get ahead, you have to do some things that are not right" and "I have a lot of respect for the Seattle police." Prior research has consistently shown that opportunistic attitudes towards the law and variations in respect for conventional authority are significant correlates of self-reported delinquency and the major theories of delinquency all incorporate such beliefs in one form or another.[4]

These "definitions" or "beliefs" have been incorporated into numerous theories of delinquency in one form or another and a variety of complex issues would have to be addressed to discern which of these many versions is best measured by the items used in this study.[5] Both attitudes towards authority and a self-image as tough and mean are consistent with the "negativistic" contracultural attitudes stressed in Cohen's theory of gang delinquency (1955).

Many of the items have been used to measure the strength of conventional moral beliefs in Hirschi's social control theory (1969) and most fit Gottfredson and Hirschi's (1990) description of characteristics of people low in "self-control." They can be considered as measures of normative learning stressed in social learning theory (Akers 1985) or "definitions favorable to the violation of the law" in differential association theory (see Matsueda 1982). Similarly, they tap many of the characteristics of the lower-class "focal concerns" stressed by Miller (1958) or the "existential perspective" described by Rainwater (1970: 139). The self-image and belief items are consistent with Heimer and Matsueda's (1994) differential control theory and Bartusch and Matsueda's (1996) theory of "reflected appraisals" as well.

Two items measure perceived risk of punishment for law-breaking: "It's easy to steal something from a store without getting caught," "People who break the law are almost always caught and punished." The risk items are relevant to deterrence, social learning, power-control, social control and rational choice theories of delinquency (see Akers 1996 for a discussion of these theories). Gender was not significantly related to the general item about people but was related to the items about shoplifting (-.17). Boys are more likely than girls to believe it is easy to shoplift and get away with it.

Interaction with law-breaking friends was measured by a question about "How many of your best friends have been picked up by the police?" The number of best friends picked up by police was multiplied by the intensity of interaction with best friends ("Outside of school, how often do you hang around with your best friends?") to generate a measure of intensity of interaction with delinquent friends. This variable has been central to differential association theory and social learning theory and has consistently explained some proportion of gender variation in prior research. The girls in the survey had fewer friends they know to have been picked up by the police (-.26) and spend less time hanging out with friends than do boys (-.06). Agnew's (1991) research on peer variables and delinquency suggests that number of delinquent friends and time spent with such friends interact with time spent most consequential when a youth has lots of delinquent friends. This same interaction was found in the Seattle data and the measure used in the analysis was created by multiplying the number of best friends who have been picked up by police by time spent with best friends.

Parental controls were measured by items asking youth whether their mother (father) knew where they were and who they were with when away from home. Such items have been used to measure parental supervision since Hirschi's (1969) research on social control theory in the 1960s. The notion that variation in delinquency among sociodemographic categories and individuals can be partially explained by variation in parental controls has been advocated since Bonger's (1916) classic work in the early 1900s and has been incorporated into numerous contemporary perspectives, ranging from social control and social learning theory to power control theory. Moreover, one of the claims distinguishing differential association theory from social control theory has been whether such parental controls affect delinquency directly (control theory) or only indirectly (differential association theory) through their effect on delinquent attitudes and relationships (see Matsueda 1982; Heimer and Matsueda 1994). The variation by gender in the Seattle survey was particularly prominent for mothers' supervision (+.26) but was significant for fathers' supervision as well (+.12).

### Findings

Since gender-linked self-images and interaction with delinquent peers have been found to explain, partially, the gender difference in prior research, those two variables were examined first. Consistent with Cullen, Golden and Cullen (1979) and Morash (1986), the relationship between gender and serious UCR-type offenses (see Appendix) is marginally significant when interaction with delinquent friends and gender-linked self-images are introduced. Association with delinquent peers has much the same effect as in Morash's (1986) study. When delinquent friends is introduced by itself the beta relating gender to violence is reduced to -.11 and is statistically significant. However, when delinquent peers and self-images are considered together, gender has a marginally significant effect (Table 7.2, Panel A) which disappears when negative moral beliefs are included in the analysis. Gender has no significant direct effect on the index of the most serious self-reported offenses when all three mediating mechanisms are controlled (see Table 7.2, Panel B).

Of course, a variety of other variables might work just as well in explaining the gender gap and it would be premature to accord unique explanatory status to these two. However, when a liberated gender ideology, risk of apprehension and mother's supervision were added to the analysis, none of these additional variables entered into an independent significant relation with UCR-type serious offenses (see Table 7.3). Consistent with prior research, a liberated gender ideology is unrelated in a bivariate as well as in the multivariate analysis. In contrast, there are significant bivariate relationships for perceived impunity and mother's supervision but both are unrelated to delinquency in the multivariate analysis. The effect of supervision is indirect through its links with self-conceptions and either beliefs or delinquent peers. The relation between perceived impunity and delinquency appears to be spurious due to shared links with gender.

Similar analyses were conducted for number of offenses in police records, common and serious property crime, serious offenses by gang members and vandalism. As summarized in Table 7.4, gender-linked self-images, attitudes towards the law and interaction with delinquent friends reduces the relation between gender and delinquency to insignificance for official delinquency

**Table 7.2**
**UCR-Type Self-Reported Offenses [a]—Regression Models**

|   |   | Beta | t |   |
|---|---|---|---|---|
| A. | Gender | -.158 | -6.240 | $R^2$=.025 |
| B. | Gender | -.107 | -3.937 | $R^2$=.093 |
|   | Delinquent Peers | +.212 | +7.533 |   |
| C. | Gender | -.055 | -1.950 | $R^2$=.121 |
|   | Delinquent Peers | +.212 | +7.533 |   |
|   | Self-Image | +.191 | +6.592 |   |
| D. | Gender | -.046 | -1.332 | $R^2$=.133 |
|   | Delinquent Peers | +.358 | +6.393 |   |
|   | Self-Image | - +.147 | +4.701 |   |
|   | Negative Beliefs | +.123 | +3.596 |   |

[a]Includes armed robbery, aggravated assault and major property crimes as listed in Appendix.

**Table 7.3**
**UCR-Types Self-Reported Offenses [a]**

|   | Beta | t | $R^2$=.133 |
|---|---|---|---|
| Gender | -.041 | -1.430 |   |
| Delinquent Peers | +.-185 | +6.408 |   |
| Self-Image | +.144 | +4.613 |   |
| Negative Beliefs | +.120 | +3.910 |   |
| Maternal Supervision | -.028 | -0.318 |   |
| Perceived Impunity | +.001 | -0.032 |   |
| Liberation | -.008 | -0.318 |   |

[a] Includes armed robbery, aggravated assault and major property crimes as listed in Appendix.

and common and serious property crime. Gender variation in serious offenses by gang youth appears to be a product of delinquent peers and macho self-image alone.

Gender has a significant impact on vandalism despite controls for the three mediating mechanisms, although the relationship with gender is reduced considerably (see Table 7.4, Panel D). The independent effects of gender on vandalism may be a product of other variables that were not anticipated

Table 7.4
Officially Recorded Offenses and Self-Report Indices

### A. Officially Recorded Offenses

|                  | Beta   | t        |           |
| ---------------- | ------ | -------- | --------- |
| Gender           | -.040  | -1.466   | $R^2$=.160 |
| Self-image       | +.085  | +2.831   |           |
| Negative Beliefs | +.079  | +2.690   |           |
| Delinquent Peers | +.312  | +11.217  |           |

### B. Self-reported Common Property Offenses

|                  |        |        |           |
| ---------------- | ------ | ------ | --------- |
| Gender           | -.024  | -0.868 | $R^2$=.142 |
| Self-Image       | +.138  | +2.921 |           |
| Negative Beliefs | +.131  | +7.040 |           |
| Delinquent Peers | +.182  | +6.397 |           |

### C. Self-reported Major Property Offenses

|                  |        |        |           |
| ---------------- | ------ | ------ | --------- |
| Gender           | -.046  | -1.615 | $R^2$=.109 |
| Self-Image       | +.114  | +3.668 |           |
| Negative Beliefs | +.097  | +3.168 |           |
| Delinquent Peers | +.199  | +6.909 |           |

### D. Offenses by Gang Identifiers

|                  |        |          |           |
| ---------------- | ------ | -------- | --------- |
| Gender           | -.044  | -1.509   | $R^2$=.176 |
| Self-Image       | +.065  | +2.035   |           |
| Negative Beliefs | +.034  | +1.079   |           |
| Delinquent Peers | +.333  | + 10.685 |           |

### E. Self-reported Vandalism

|                  |        |        |           |
| ---------------- | ------ | ------ | --------- |
| Gender           | -.122  | -4.297 | $R^2$=.152 |
| Self-Image       | +.127  | +4.155 |           |
| Negative Beliefs | +.132  | +4.420 |           |
| Delinquent Peers | +.179  | +6.319 |           |

[a] See the Appendix for offenses included in these self-report indices.

or were unmeasured in this analysis. Numerous additional variables were considered, including grades earned at school, time spent on homework, time spent driving around in cars and attitudes towards school and teachers. No combination of such variables reduced the gender gap in vandalism to insignificance.[6]

Other possibilities for explaining resilient gender variation have been suggested in the two recent studies that statistically eliminated the gender effect. Heimer (1995) and Bartusch and Matsueda (1996) suggest that the differential relevance of variables to delinquency by gender may help to explain gender differences that are not fully explained by differences in mean levels on variables. For example, there may be a foundation for expecting the measure of delinquent friends to have differential relevance by gender. Since the item used to measure delinquent friends asks about friends "picked up by the police" and does not differentiate the gender of friends, it may be a more relevant variable for males than females. If boys who are close friends are those most likely to be picked up the police, then that variable may be more consequential for male respondents' own behavior than for the behavior of female respondents.

In fact, an analysis of covariance did yield evidence of a significant difference in slopes and intercepts for males and females in the sample. The slope relating the delinquent friends measure to vandalism for boys was .585 as compared to .091 for girls. Moreover, when the interaction between delinquent friends and gender was introduced into the analysis together with self-image, attitudes towards the law, and delinquent friends, the direct effect of gender on vandalism was reduced to insignificance (see Table 7.5).

### Further Tests

While some theories dealing with gender variation are supposed to apply better to some forms of delinquency than others (e.g., "common delinquency" or a "party subculture" in power-control theory), the social learning-interactionist theory has been shown to explain behaviors as diverse as smok-

**Table 7.5**
**Model for Vandalism [a] with Peer-Gender Interaction**

|                    | Beta   | t       | $R^2=.166$ |
|--------------------|--------|---------|------------|
| Gender             | -.045  | -1.395  |            |
| Self-Image         | +.129  | +4.272  |            |
| Negative Beliefs   | +.124  | +4.204  |            |
| Delinquent Peers   | +.532  | +6.556  |            |
| Peer x Gender      | -.362  | -4.639  |            |

[a] Items used are listed in the Appendix

ing, elderly drinking, rape and sexual aggression (see Akers 1998). The fact that the three key mediating mechanisms were relevant to indices of both serious and common property crimes suggests that the theory is a "general" theory applicable to the explanation of gender differences across a wide range of offenses. To provide further evidence relevant to social learning-interactionist theory as a general theory of gender variation, three very common forms of adolescent activity (drinking beer, using marijuana and shoplifting) and three very serious and uncommon forms of delinquency (robbery, aggravated assault and breaking and entering) were examined.

The bivariate correlations with gender were negative and significant for all six types of offenses. However, as summarized in Table 7.6, controls for gender-linked self-image, negative beliefs and delinquent peers reduced the gender difference to insignificance in each and every instance. In contrast, each of the three mediating mechanisms was a significant independent correlate for the full range of common and serious forms of delinquency.

The results reported, using measures of serious and common forms of delinquency, agency records of delinquency, serious offenses by self-identified gang youth and both common and very serious delinquent activities, are consistent with prior research testing social learning-interactionist theory. Given such robust findings, it is quite appropriate to propose that social learning-interactionist theory has a stronger claim to the status of an empirically verified, general theory than any of the competing theories proposed over the last several years.

## Conclusions

This analysis of gender variation in delinquency suggests several tentative conclusions that can shape future inquiry. For one, survey data yield patterns of gender variation by offense that are very close approximations to the patterns observed in national arrest or juvenile court data. Gender ratios are small for status offenses and common larceny but increase with the seriousness and/or destructiveness of offenses. The inclusion of status offenses in total indices minimizes the gender gap and gives the impression of greater disparities between official and self-report data than actually exist.

Second, the gender variation in serious offenses and property crime is easier to explain than the gender variation in vandalism although the introduction of a gender interaction in the impact of delinquent friends did the job for vandalism as well. However, the fact that acts of vandalism all involve destructive and aggressive action against passive objects may generate some of the gender gap for that offense. Measures of respect and care of property were not available and may have explained some portion of gender variation.

Since a variety of theories would imply that variations in self-image and beliefs about law and authority are relevant to the explanation of delin-

Table 7.6
Additional Self-Report Indices

### A. Drinking Beer

|  | Beta | t |  |
|---|---|---|---|
| Gender | +.024 | +0.852 | $R^2$=.138 |
| Self-Image | +.067 | +2.184 |  |
| Negative Beliefs | +.150 | +5.045 |  |
| Delinquent Peers | +.266 | +9.430 |  |

### B. Using marijuana

| Gender | -.045 | -1.716 | $R^2$=.271 |
|---|---|---|---|
| Self-Image | +.095 | +3.369 |  |
| Negative Beliefs | +.253 | +9.083 |  |
| Delinquent Peers | +.301 | +11.526 |  |

### C. Shoplifting

| Gender | -.003 | -0.104 | $R^2$=.087 |
|---|---|---|---|
| Self-IInage | +.101 | +3.215 |  |
| Negative Beliefs | +.150 | +4.874 |  |
| Delinquent Peers | +.136 | +4.641 |  |

### D. Robbery

| Gender | -.025 | -0.869 | $R^2$=.043 |
|---|---|---|---|
| Self-Image | +.096 | +3.020 |  |
| Negative Beliefs | +.076 | +2.419 |  |
| Delinquent Peers | +.333 | +3.037 |  |

### E. Aggravated Assault

| Gender | -.029 | -0.989 | $R^2$=.074 |
|---|---|---|---|
| Self-Image | +.136 | +4.304 |  |
| Negative Beliefs | +.107 | +3.469 |  |
| Delinquent Peers | +.101 | +3.447 |  |

### F. Breaking and Entering

| Gender | +.003 | +0.096 | $R^2$=.048 |
|---|---|---|---|
| Self-Image | +.103 | +3.223 |  |
| Negative Beliefs | +.043 | +1.368 |  |
| Delinquent Peers | +.141 | +4.776 |  |

[a] See the Appendix for offenses included in these self-report indices.

quency many of the findings reported above do not provide unique support for any one perspective. Such findings are consistent with the theory of reflected appraisals, social control and self-control theories, differential association and social learning theories. However, the mediating influence of delinquent friends is clearly more central to differential association theory and social learning theory than to social control theory.[7]

The fact that maternal supervision is only indirectly related to delinquency when other variables are introduced is consistent with differential association and social learning theory and contrary to the original formulation of social control theory. Social learning theory might be accorded the edge over differential association in this case since both delinquent friends and attitudes are each relevant to explaining the gender difference. In differential association theory attitudes are supposed to explain the impact of delinquent friends while social learning theory allows both normative (attitudinal) phenomena and interaction with delinquent peers to have separable consequences for delinquency (see Akers 1996; Stafford and Warr 1991).

The results are problematic for power-control theory in that two of the three variables measured in tests of that theory, parental supervision and perceptions of risk, were not the key variables mediating the effect of gender on delinquency. The importance of the third variable in that theory, "tastes for risk," cannot be determined in this study. Yet, were tastes for risk highly correlated with the self-image items, then these findings could be consistent with the claims about the impact of that motivational variable. However, in contrast to social control and social learning theories, power control theory does not include (theoretically or operationally) "moral" concepts such as values, norms and beliefs. Moreover, delinquent peers are no where to be found in the formal specification or tests of that theory. Since social learning theory includes both delinquent peers and the moral products of normative socialization, it is more consistent with these findings than either power control or social control theories.

"Reflected appraisals" theory has been proposed as an explanation of delinquency and the gender difference in delinquency and its relation to the concepts used in this study and in other theories should be addressed. While the gender-linked self-image items can be viewed as tapping similar phenomena to "reflected appraisals," reflected appraisals theory, as stated, does not include differentials in the degree to which male and female youth learn to accord moral authority to the law and/or its agents.

Such "attitudes" are encompassed in Heimer and Matsueda's "differential control" theory. Yet, when reflected appraisals and differential control theories are combined, the theory is nearly identical to Akers' social learning theory, albeit with a more specific symbolic interactionist flavor than many past presentations of social learning theory. As Akers notes in his most recent presentation of social learning theory (1998), variations in conventional moral socialization, differential association and the symbolic consequences of interaction are encompassed by his theory. Hence, we would once again have to accord a theoretical and empirical edge to a social learning-interactionist theory in the explanation of gender variation in delinquency since it includes variables that are not included in reflected appraisals theory and can encompass the impact of gender-linked appraisals or self-images as well.

The analysis has a bearing on the issues raised by Chesney-Lind and Shelden concerning the use of male values as the norm when discussing causes or correlates of delinquency. The findings in this paper might be viewed as evidence that girls are "constrained" by identities, beliefs and attitudes that limit their imagination and opportunities to hurt others (i.e., Tittle's control balance theory) or as support for the view that feminine self-images and values act as conscientious constraints, structuring choices among imagined alternatives. Girls are less involved in delinquency than boys because they are less likely to form identities as tough, mean and unforgiving and more likely to form identities as relatively caring, forgiving and nice. Such images may "handicap" girls in the pursuit of power within a patriarchal system and give males a competitive edge in some forms of economic and political activity. On the other hand, the "freedom" that such self-images accord males leads to high levels of interpersonal violence and destruction.

Girls are more likely to accord respect to conventional moral authority and less likely to learn beliefs excusing deviance. Again, such conventional commitments may constrain the range of activities acceptable in the pursuit of power and personal gain and may constitute a handicap in the pursuit of patriarchal goals. Yet, both differences in self-image and normative socialization point to something "positive" about the female world that inhibits the infliction of pain and suffering on other people.

This study provides strong support for the applicability of social learning-interactionist theory to the explanation of gender differences in delinquency but leaves a variety of issues involving gender and delinquency to further research. For example, Chesney-Lind and Shelden (1998) argue that status offenses, especially running away from home, constitute more consequential "gateway" activities for girls than boys. Indeed, they propose that the existence of such categories represents the "criminalization" of female strategies for survival in that female runaway is more likely than male runaway to reflect sexual abuse in the home. There were no significant differences in rates for status offenses or runaway in these data but the activities may have very different "meanings" and be generated by different circumstances for girls than for boys.

While social learning theory explained the gender difference in a wide range of offense types, the analysis does not explain why the gender ratios are more prominent for some offenses than others. It does not appear to be seriousness alone that structures gender ratios since the ratios are quite prominent for acts of vandalism. Ratios are quite prominent for offenses involving weapons, destruction and circumstances where risks of sexual assault may be high for girls (e.g., roaming the streets at night). Girls may be less inclined to enter into some situations than boys in the attempt to avoid risks that they would encounter in interaction with a male world where flirtation with danger and aggressive dominance may lead to victimization.

Another unexplored issue is the social origins of the gender-linked self-conceptions examined in this study. Discussions of the extreme versions of defiant individualism or the "bad ass" imply that such an attitude should be most exaggerated among youth who lack conventional sources of status and grow up in environments characterized by fierce competition for scarce resources (see Jankowski 1991). However, it is also an attitude that many would argue is facilitated in quite conventional contexts such as competitive male sports. Are "macho" self-images a product of socialization by fathers (and mothers) or a social character generated in the streets and on the courts in competitive interaction among young males? Since many of the features of a "feminine" identity are consistent with prominent religious belief systems, it is relevant to ask what role religion plays in shaping female and male identities? Since gender-linked variations in self-images constitutes a key intervening mechanism to a full explanation of gender variation in serious crime, research on the origins of such images may provide guidelines for reducing violence in American society.

## Notes

1.    Similar arguments about biases in classic sociological theories of crime and delinquency are discussed by Jensen (1987) in an article on "Mainstreaming and the Sociology of Deviance." In the effort to emphasize the normality of deviance and avoid the "evil causes evil" fallacy, many theorists transform the use of force and fraud into activities with positive connotations (e.g., innovation, loyalty to the gang, conformity to subcultural norms) and depict female deviance as secretive, escapist or ritualistic.

2.    The Seattle survey included three questions about gang membership: "Do you belong to what some people might call a youth gang? "Does the gang have a name?" "Does the gang have jackets or other things that let people know who they are?" Between 8 and 9 percent (8.6) of the Seattle sample indicated they belonged to a group that people might call a gang. When limited to respondents answering yes to the first and either the second or third questions the percentage dropped to 4.8 percent. Less than 2 percent (1.8) responded yes to all three items.

Of 137 Seattle respondents indicating that they belonged to a gang 53 (39 percent) were female. This figure is within the range of percentages reported in other survey research. Fagan (1990) reports that about 33 percent of gang members were girls in his study of gangs and Esbensen and Huisinga report that between 20 and 46 percent of self-identified gang members in their Denver research were female, depending on the time period considered. Recent survey research in Denver (Esbensen and Huisinga 1993) found that about 5 percent of inner-city, high risk, juveniles were gang members when membership was determined by acknowledgement in interviews that they were "members of a street or youth gang" and that the gang was involved in illegal activities. The measure of serious offenses by gang members was created by multiplying a gang member dichotomy (0 = No, 1 = Yes) by self-reported involvement in UCR type crime index offenses. Just over 5 percent (5.5 percent) of the sample identified as gang members and had committed at least one serious offense. See Jensen (1996) for research on the correlates of gang membership when measured in this fashion.

3.  A factor score based on principal components analysis was created based on these four items. Cronbach's alpha was relatively low for the score based on these items (.49). Each may be tapping a somewhat distinct but correlated dimension of macho attitudes. Analyses were conducted using the individual items as well as the factor score. The conclusions were unaffected by the use of single items as opposed to the factor score. Hence, for ease of presentation the factor score is used in this chapter.

4.  The items were factor analyzed using principal components and a score created with a high value indicative of criminogenic attitudes and beliefs. The alpha reliability was .54.

5.  The concepts "definitions favorable or unfavorable to the violation of law," "conventional moral beliefs," and "delinquent attitudes" are generally operationalized using some reference to law, legal authority or rationalizations for victimizing people. Yet, people also form definitions, beliefs or attitudes about "who they are" that can be favorable or unfavorable to law breaking. Heimer and Matsueda (1994) emphasize "role-taking" that can encourage or discourage delinquency and Bartusch and Matsueda (1996) focus on "reflected appraisals" as part of the same process. Normative socialization processes, including processes leading to self-conceptions, are included as one of four major learning mechanisms in Akers' social learning theory as well. In short, while self-images and moral beliefs are treated as conceptually distinct types of attitudes with different "referents," they are formed through the same processes of social interaction and social learning.

6.  The Seattle sample included youths in grades 10 through 12 and the relevance of the image, attitude and delinquent friends to the explanation of the gender gap in the different class cohorts was assessed, focusing on the total index and the gender difference in vandalism. The gender gap in total offenses was reduced to insignificance at each grade level. In contrast, the effect of gender on vandalism persisted among tenth and eleventh graders but was reduced to insignificance among twelfth graders. The addition of the one interaction term reduced it to insignificance for 10th graders but the direct effect persisted for eleventh graders (-.10). In race subcategories the gender gap in total offenses was eliminated by the same three variables for whites and by delinquent friends alone for blacks. The gender gap for vandalism was eliminated by the three variables together with the one interaction term for whites and by delinquent friends together with the interaction of friends and gender for blacks.

7.  Since this analysis is based on cross-sectional data there is reason to be concerned about issues of causal order involving self-images, attitudes and delinquent friends. However, since the Seattle survey included a "clean" high school sample with no delinquent or court records, we can assess whether the same results can be replicated when there should be minimal feedback loops from any official processing. Separate analyses were conducted using the clean sample for the same offense categories. In all instances the models applicable to the gender variation in self-reported delinquency in the clean sample were the same as in the sample with official offenders included.

## References

Adler, F. 1975. *Sisters in Crime: The Rise of the New Female Criminal*. New York: McGraw-Hill.

Agnew, R. 1991. "The Interactive Effects of Peers Variables on Delinquency." *Criminology* 29: 47-72.

Akers, R. L. 1985. *Deviant Behavior: A Social Learning Approach*. Belmont, CA: Wadsworth.

_____. 1996. *Criminological Theories: Introduction and Evaluation*. Second Edition. Los Angeles, CA: Roxbury Publishing Company.

_____. 1998. *Social Learning and Social Structure*. Boston: Northeastern University Press.

Akers, R. L., M. D. Krohn, L. Lanza-Kaduce, and M. Radosevich. 1978. "Social Learning and Deviant Behavior." *American Sociological Review* 44: 636-655.

Bartusch, D. J., and R. Matsueda. 1996. "Gender, Reflected Appraisals, and Labeling: A Cross-Group Test of an Interactionist Theory of Delinquency." *American Sociological Review* 75: 145-176.

Bjerregaard, B., and C. Smith. 1993. "Gender Differences in Gang Participation, Delinquency and Substance Use." *Journal of Quantitative Criminology* 4: 329-55.

Bonger, W. 1916. *Criminality and Economic Conditions*. Boston:    Little, Brown and Company.

Bowker, L. H., and M. W. Klein. 1983. "The Etiology of Female Juvenile Delinquency and Gang Membership: A Test of Psychological and Structural Explanations." *Adolescence* 18: 740-751.

Campbell, A. 1990. "Female Participation in Gangs." Pp. 163-182 in C. Ronald Huff (ed.), *Gangs in America*. Newbury Park, CA: Sage Publications.

Chesney-Lind, M., and R. Shelden. 1992. *Girls, Delinquency and Juvenile Justice*. Pacific Grove, CA: Brooks/Cole.

_____. 1998. *Girls, Delinquency and Juvenile Justice*. Second Edition. Pacific Grove, CA: Brooks/Cole.

Cohen, A. K. 1956. *Delinquent Boys*. New York: Free Press.

Cullen, F. T., K. M. Golden, and J. B. Cullen. 1979. "Sex and Delinquency: A Partial Test of the Masculinity Hypothesis." *Criminology* 17: 301-310.

Elliott, D. S.1994. "Serious Violent Offenders: Onset, Developmental Course, and Termination." *Criminology* 45: 95-110.

Erickson, M. L., and G.F. Jensen. 1977. "Delinquency is Still Group Behavior!" *Journal of Criminal Law and Criminology* 68: 262-273.

Esbensen, F., and D. Huisinga. 1993. "Gangs, Drugs, and Delinquency in a Survey of Urban Youth." *Criminology* 4: 565-589.

Fagan, J., 1990. "Social Processes of Delinquency and Drug Use among Urban Gangs." In C. Ron Huff (ed.), *Gangs in America*. Newbury Park, CA: Sage Publications.

Farnworth, M. 1984. "Male-Female Differences in Delinquency in a Minority Group." *Journal of Research in Crime and Delinquency* 21: 191-212.

Gilligan, C. 1982. *In a Different Voice*. Cambridge, MA: Harvard University Press.

Giordano, P. C. 1978. "Girls, Guys, and Gangs: The Changing Social Context of Female Delinquency." *Journal of Criminal Law, Criminology and Police Science* 69: 126-132.

Gordon, R. A., J. F. Short, Jr., D. S. Cartwright, and F. L. Strodtbeck. 1963. "Values and Gang Delinquency." *American Journal of Sociology* 69: 109-128.

Gottfredson, M. R., and T. Hirschi 1990. *A General Theory of Crime*. Stanford, CA: Stanford University Press.

Hagan, J. 1989. *Structural Criminology*. New Brunswick, NJ: Rutgers University Press.

_____. 1992. "Destiny and Drift: The Risks and Rewards of Youth." *American Sociological Review* 56: 567-582.

Hagan, J., A. R. Gillis, and J. Simpson. 1985. "The Class Structure of Gender and Delinquency: Toward a Power-Control Theory of Common Delinquent Behavior." *American Journal of Sociology* 90: 1151-1178.

_____. 1993. "The Power of Control in Sociological Theories of Delinquency." In Freda Adler and William S. Laufer (eds.), *New Directions in Criminological Theory*. New Brunswick, NJ: Transaction Publishers.

_____, J. Simpson, and A. R. Gillis. 1987. "Class in the Household: A Power-Control Theory of Gender and Delinquency." *American Journal of Sociology* 92: 788-816.

_____. 1990. "Clarifying and Extending Power-Control Theory." *American Journal of Sociology* 95: 1024-1037.

Heimer, K. 1995. "Gender, Race, and Pathways to Delinquency: An Interactionist Explanation." In John Hagan and Ruth D. Peterson (eds.), *Crime and Inequality*. Palo Alto, CA: Stanford University Press.

_____. 1996. "Gender, Interaction, and Delinquency: Testing a Theory of Differential Social Control." *Social Psychology Quarterly* 59: 39-61.

Heimer, K., and R. L. Matsueda. 1994. "Role-Taking, Role Commitment, and Delinquency." *American Sociological Review* 59 (June): 365-390.

Hindelang, M. J. 1973. "Causes of Delinquency: A Partial Replication and Extension." *Social Problems* 21 (Spring): 471-487.

Hindelang, M. J., T. Hirschi and J. Weiss. 1981. *Measuring Delinquency*. Beverly Hills: Sage Publications.

Hirschi, T. 1969. *Causes of Delinquency*. Berkeley: University of California Press.

Jankowski, M. S. 1991. *Islands in the Street*. Berkeley: University of California Press.

Jensen, G. F., 1987. "Mainstreaming and the Sociology of Deviance: A Personal Assessment." Karen Andersen et al., (eds.), *Changing Our Minds: Feminist Readings in the Transformation of Knowledge*. Albany: State University of New York Press.

_____. 1993. "Power Control versus Social Control Theories of Juvenile Crime." *Advances in Criminological Theory*, Volume 5: 365-382.

_____. 1997. "Setting the Record Straight." *Advances in Criminological Theory*, Volume 7: 343-349.

Jensen, G. F., and R. Eve. 1976. "Sex Differences in Delinquency." *Criminology* 13 (February): 427-448.

Jensen, G. F., M. L. Erickson, and J. P. Gibbs. "Perceived Risk of Punishment and Self-Reported Delinquency." *Social Forces* 57: 57-78.

Jensen, G. F., and K. Thompson. 1990. "What's Class Got to Do with It? A Further Examination of Power-Control Theory." *American Journal of Sociology* 95: 1009-1023.

Jensen, G. F., and D. G. Rojek. 1992. *Delinquency and Youth Crime*. Second Edition. Prospect Heights, IL: Waveland.

_____ 1998. *Delinquency and Youth Crime*. Third Edition. Prospect Heights, IL: Waveland

Katz, Jack. 1988. *Seductions of Crime*. New York: Basic Books.

LaGrange, T. C., and R. A. Silverman. 1999. "Low Self-Control and Opportunity: Testing the General Theory of Crime as an Explanation for Gender Differences in Delinquency." *Criminology* 37 (November): 41-72.

Lauritsen, J. 1998. "The Age-Crime Debate: Assessing the Limits of Longitudinal Self-Report Data." *Social Forces* 77 (September): 127-154.

Liu, X., and H. B. Kaplan. 1999. "Explaining the Gender Difference in Adolescent Delinquent Behavior: A Longitudinal Test of Mediating Mechanisms." *Criminology* 37 (November): 195-215.

Matsueda, R. L. 1982. "Testing Control Theory and Differential Association." *American Sociological Review* 47: 489-504.

_____. 1989. "Moral Beliefs and Deviance." *Social Forces* 2: 428-457.

Matsueda, R. L., and K. Heimer. 1987. "Race, Family Structure, and  Delinquency: A Test of Differential Association and Social Control Theories." *American Sociological Review* 52: 826-40.

Miller, W. 1958. "Lower Class Culture as a Generating Milieu of Gang Delinquency." *Journal of Social Issues* 14: 5-19.

Minor, W. 1977. "A Deterrence-Control Theory of Crime." In R. F. Meier (ed.), *Theory in Criminology: Contemporary Issues*. Beverly Hills, CA: Sage Publications.

Morash, Merry. 1986. "Gender, Peer Group Experiences, and Seriousness of Delinquency." *Journal of Research in Crime and Delinquency* 23: 43-67.

Norland, S., R. C. Wessel, and N. Shover. 1981. "Masculinity and Delinquency." *Criminology* 19: 421-33.

Rainwater, L. 1970. "The Problem of Lower Class Culture." *Journal of Social Issues* 26: 133-48.

Rowe, D. C., A. T. Vazsonyi, and D. Flannery. 1995. "Sex Differences in Crime: Do Means and Within-Sex Variation Have Similar Causes?" *Journal of Research in Crime and Delinquency* 32: 84-100.

Shoemaker, D. J. 1996. *Theories of Delinquency: An Examination of Explanations of Delinquent Behavior*. New York: Oxford University Press.

Siegel, L. J., and J. J. Senna. 1997. *Juvenile Delinquency*. Sixth Edition. St. Paul, MN: West Publishing Company.

Simon, R. 1975. *Women and Crime*. Lexington, MA: Lexington Books.

Singer, S.I., and M. Levine. 1988. "Power-Control Theory, Gender and Delinquency: A Partial Replication with Additional Evidence on the Effect of Peers." *Criminology* 26: 627-647.

Sutherland, E. H., and D. R. Cressey. 1970. *Criminology*. Eighth Edition. Philadelphia: J.B. Lippincott.

Tittle, C. R. 1995. *Control Balance: Toward a General Theory of Deviance*. Boulder, CO: Westview Press.

Warr, E. M., and M. Stafford. 1991. "The Influence of Delinquent Peers: What They Think or What They Do?" *Criminology* 29: 851-866.

Traub, Stuart H., and Craig B. Little. 1994. *Theories of Deviance*. Itasca, IL: F. E. Peacock, Publishers.

# Appendix: Self-Reported Delinquency Items

## I. Common Property Crime (Tables 7.1 and 7.4)

...taken things from a wallet or purse (or the whole wallet or purse) while the owner wasn't around or wasn't looking?

...taken things you weren't supposed to from a desk or locker at school?

...kept money for yourself that you collected for a team, a charity (like the march of Dimes), or someone else's paper route?

...taken material or equipment from a construction site?

...taken gasoline from a car without the owner's permission?

...taken little things (worth less than $2) from a store without paying for them? (Shoplifting, Tables 7.1 and 7.6)

## II. Major Property Crime (Tables 7.1 and 7.4)

..broken into a parking meter or coin box of a pay phone?

...taken mail from someone's mail box and opened it?

...taken hubcaps, wheels, the battery, or some other expensive part of a car without the owner's permission?

...taken a tape deck or a CB radio from a car.

...broken into a house, store, school, or other building and taken money, stereo equipment, guns, or something else you wanted? (Breaking and Entering, Table 6)

...broken into a locked car to get something from it?

...taken a car belonging to someone you didn't know for a ride without the owner's permission?

...taken things of large value (worth more than $50) from a store without paying for them? (Shoplifting, Tables 7.1 and 7.6)

...taken things worth between $10 and $50 from a store without paying for them? (Shoplifting, Tables 7.1 and 7.6)

### III. Vandalism (Tables 7.4 and 7.5)

...broken into a house, store, school, or other buildings with the intention of breaking things or causing other damage?

...purposely broken a car window?

...broken the windows of an empty house or unoccupied building?

...broken windows of a school building

...let the air out of car or truck tires?

...helped break up chairs, tables, desks, or other furniture in a school, church, or other public building.

...slashed the seats in a bus, a movie house, or some other place

...punctured or slashed the tires of a car?

...destroyed mailboxes?

...destroyed things at a construction site?

...fired a BB gun at some person, at passing cars, or at windows of buildings.

### IV. Status

...cursed or threatened an adult in a loud and mean way just to let them know who was boss?

...run away from home and stayed overnight? (Runaway in Table 7.1)

...gone out at night when your parents told you couldn't go?

...stayed away from school when your parents thought you were there?

...hit one of your parents?

## V. Violence

...used a club, knife, or gun to get something from someone? (UCR Type: Armed Robbery)

...grabbed a purse from someone and run with it? (Robbery)

...used physical force (like twisting an arm or choking) to get money from another person? (Robbery)

...threatened to beat someone up if they didn't give you money or something you wanted? (Robbery)

...beat someone up so badly they probably needed a doctor? (UCR Type: Aggravated Assault)

...pulled a knife, gun, or some other weapon on someone just to let them know you meant business? (Assault)

...jumped or helped jumped somebody and then beat them up? (Assault)

...hit a teacher or some other school official? (Assault)

...picked a fight with someone you didn't know just for the hell of it? (Assault)

## VI. Common Substance Use

...drunk beer or wine (Beer in Table 7.6)

...smoked marijuana, grass or pot (Marijuana in Table 7.6)

# 8

# Social Structure-Social Learning (SSSL) and Binge Drinking: A Specific Test of an Integrated General Theory [1]

*Lonn Lanza-Kaduce and Michael Capece*

In the last decades we have seen a trend toward integrative general theories of crime and deviance. Many such efforts have focused on what Liska, Krohn, and Messner (1989) refer to as conceptual integration—locating and meshing the common meanings and operations of concepts from different theories (see for example Elliot, Huizinga, and Ageton 1985; Lanza-Kaduce and Klug 1986; Thornberry 1987; Agnew 1992; Sampson and Laub 1993; Bartusch, Jeglum, Lynam, Moffitt, and Silva 1997). One of the most systematic efforts to demonstrate conceptual integration has been advanced by Akers (1973, 1977, 1985, 1997). He has long argued that social learning theory can subsume the operative variables from many other theories of crime and deviance, including deterrence, social bonding, and neutralization theories.

Krohn (1999) has recently pointed out that Akers has also relied on a form of conceptual absorption in his social learning theory to identify, from structural and cultural conditions, those contingencies that will be generally rewarding or punishing for individuals. This is one way in which Akers (1977) responds to concerns about tautology in the operant conditioning principles that lie at the center of his learning theory. It involves turning to more macro levels of analysis to specify how the learning process could work. Akers has been conscious of the need to integrate across levels of analysis from the outset of his theory construction.

Differential association-reinforcement spells out the *mechanisms* by which environmental stimuli produce and maintain behavior and the structural theories explicate the type of *environments* most likely to sustain norm and law-violating behavior. (Akers, 1968: 458, emphasis in the original)

179

...[S]ocial learning is complementary to other sociological theories and could be used to integrate extant formulations to achieve more comprehensive explanations of deviance. (Akers, Krohn, Lanza-Kaduce, and Radosevich 1979:637)

Akers' (1998) most recent contribution, *Social Structure Social Learning Theory*, is a systematic effort to integrate the social learning process with social structural variables. Although others of us (e.g., Morash 1999; Krohn 1999; Alden, Lanza-Kaduce, and Capece 2000) may wish that he had tried to advance propositional linkages between social learning and structural theories, his stated purpose is more modest: "The purpose ... is to integrate across levels by linking the variables, causes, and explanations at the structural/ macro level ... to probable effects on individual behavior through social learning variables" (Akers 1998: 329).

## Statement of Social Structure-Social Learning Theory

The Social Structure-Social Learning Theory (SSSL) tested here is summarized from Akers (1998: 322-341). SSSL assumes that social learning is the primary (not the only) process linking social structure to individual behavior:

Its main proposition is that variations in the social structure, culture, and locations of individuals and groups in the social system explain variations in crime rates, principally through their influence on differences among individuals on the social learning variables... (Akers 1998: 322)

The integrative theory maintains the four dimensions basic to the social learning process: differential association, differential reinforcement/punishment, imitation, and definitions favorable and unfavorable to crime/deviance (as discriminative or cue stimuli to which behavior will be paired because of reinforcement contingencies). These dimensions represent the learning process that is thought to mediate the effects of social structure.

Akers introduces four dimensions of social structure in SSSL. The first is differential social organization. It focuses on larger, more macro group processes and includes societal, community, cultural, institutional, and regional differences in social organization.

The second dimension is differential location in the general social structure. It concentrates on background characteristics that place or locate people in macro social organization, including gender, race, religion, age, and socioeconomic status or class.

A third dimension shifts to more meso levels of social organization. The focus is on the recognized groups with which individuals deal as well as reference groups with which they identify. The dimension remains structural in that it focuses on the location of individuals in families, work groups, school groups, church groups, reference groups, etc. rather than on the inter-actions in those groups (which would be part of the learning process itself). The differential organization (structural) aspect is reflected in the different groups to which people belong and the different positions they occupy in those groups rather than the quality or nature of the interactions.

The final structural dimension introduced by Akers refers to variables de-rived from structural theories. Akers is least specific in his discussion of this structural dimension. He refers abstractly to theoretical issues of social orga-nization and integration versus disorganization and conflict; he does not try to incorporate a particular structural argument into his theorizing. Hence, he has opened himself to the criticism that his integrative effort fails to generate propositional linkages between structure and process.

Akers is not particularly bothered by such criticism. Recall that his main proposition argues that differences in social structure will have an effect because they produce differences in social learning variables. In fact, Akers (1999: 485 citing Akers 1998: 340) has responded to his critics by reiterating his mediation hypothesis: "the social learning process ... mediate[s] a *sub-stantial portion* of the relationship between *most* structural variables" and behavior.

The SSSL formulation provides a blueprint for research. Although the theory does not specifically identify which indicators of the respective di-mensions of social structure will bear a relationship to deviant or criminal behavior, it expects that some of them will. Any test of SSSL, therefore, needs to begin by examining which social structural indicators relate to deviance or crime.

The second step in testing SSSL involves examining the respective rela-tionships between social learning variables and deviance. SSSL specifically incorporates the basic differential association, definitions, operant condi-tioning, and imitation elements of social learning theory. We expect that association with others who deviate, definitions favorable to deviance, rein-forcement for deviance, and imitation of deviant models will all predict an individual's propensity to engage in the deviance.

Neither of the first two steps is unique. The third and critical step in testing SSSL is to see whether, in a multivariate analysis, the effects of the social structural variables on deviance are mediated by the learning processes. If Akers is correct, those relationships between structural indicators and devi-ance that occur in an analysis limited to structural variables should be mark-edly diminished or eliminated when the social learning variables are added to the analysis.

The challenge is to find a data set on deviance that contains both suffi-cient indicators of the various levels of social structure and social learning process variables. The long form of the Core Alcohol and Drug Survey pro-vides such an opportunity. It has been administered at various institutions of higher education (an institutional level variable), it gathers background information (social structural locators), it includes questions about participation in various campus groups (group associations), and it asks questions about integration into the larger university environment (social integration). The Core survey also contains questions relevant to reinforcement/ punishment and definitions—two major social learning constructs. Because the Core survey was not constructed with SSSL in mind, the operationalizations for the social structural and social learning variables are neither as extensive nor as exacting as would be desired. Nevertheless, the survey collects information relevant to all four of the social structural dimensions laid out by Akers and permits us to examine the theoretical linkages he predicted.

The Core survey consists of four pages of self-report questions. Unfortunately, many of the items contain double-barreled wording and ask about both alcohol and drugs in the same question. Fortunately, enough of the questions regarding alcohol use do not suffer from this shortcoming so that the impact of process and structure on binge drinking can be examined. Binge drinking is defined as having five or more drinks at a single sitting. It is an indicator of heavy drinking.

Binge drinking occurs with regularity on many college campuses and is distributed differently along such structural dimensions as gender and participation in Greek organizations (Wechsler, Kuh, and Davenport 1996). For example, Wechsler (1996) points out that of 84 percent of all students in his sample drink 44 percent qualify as binge drinkers; 19 percent are classified as frequent binge drinkers. Wechsler indicates that there are a number of student characteristics that are associated with binge drinking. Binge drinking occurs more often among men, those under the age of twenty-four, students who live in fraternity and sorority houses, whites, those involved in athletics, and students who are more social.

The college population at highest risk for heavy alcohol use are the fraternity and sorority members, especially house residents (Wechsler 1996; Wechsler et al. 1996). Wechsler et al. (1996) report that 86 percent of fraternity house residents and 71 percent of fraternity non-resident members in a national sample engaged in binge drinking. This compares with 45 percent of college men who were not in fraternities. This same study reports that 80 percent of resident sorority members engaged in binge drinking at least once in the two weeks preceding the survey, compared with 35 percent of non-sorority members. The authors report that students independent of Greek affiliation were most likely to abstain from alcohol: 16 percent of independent men and 17 percent of independent women. They also find that students with no history of binging or heavy alcohol abuse became more likely to engage in binge or heavy drinking after they joined a fraternity or sorority.

## Methodology

*Sample and Procedure*

The data are from eight colleges and universities where the long form of the Core Alcohol and Drug Survey was administered to students in the mid-1990s. Each of the colleges/ universities gave permission to the researchers to obtain its data from the Core Institute at Southern Illinois University so long as the colleges were not identified.

The colleges vary markedly. They are spread throughout the United States from the Northeast to the Southeast to the Midwest and West. They include public and private institutions that vary in size. The majority of the student respondents (and students) in one school are African American; the plurality in another school are Asian; and a third school has a mix of Hispanic, white, and Asian students. While no claims can be made that either the students in the study are representative of their respective universities or that the Core samples are representative of U.S. college students generally, the schools and the students are diverse—diverse enough to permit examining the theoretical linkages among social structural variables, social learning ones, and binge drinking.

Because the structural variables available on the Core survey are anchored in the university setting, we restrict the analysis to that subsample of student respondents whose lives are most likely to be dominated by these structural arrangements rather than by other social organizational features. So we analyze only full-time students who are single (never married), who are of traditional college age (17-23), and who do not have full-time work obligations. Part-time students, married students, students of nontraditional ages and those working full-time in addition to school operate in more complex social structural environments—environments in which many important extra-university variables come into play. These extra-university structural variables are not measured in the Core survey so we simplify the analysis by restricting the sample. The sample, after cases with missing values are eliminated, includes 2,782 cases.

### Measurement of Variables

*A. Social Structural Dimensions*

The most macro-level differential social organizational variable that is available in these data is the university. To include university as a variable in an overarching multivariate analysis, we dummy-code each of the eight universities and include seven of the dummy variables in the analysis (UNIV1 through UNIV7). The last university serves as the reference category. The number and diversity of university environments in this data set allow us to examine whether the institution has an impact on binge drinking and whether that impact can be mediated by social learning variables. We expect different levels of binge drinking across the eight institutions.

The differential location of individuals in the larger social structure is measured by two background variables: gender and race. Males and whites have historically been involved in heavier alcohol use (Goode 2001). Even if the differences in the relationships between social locations and deviance are not large, Akers argues that the effects should be mediated by social learning variables. He makes this argument explicit in the case of gender: "the question is the same whether there is a greater (as in the case of most crime and deviance) or smaller (as in the case of smoking, some other drug use, and some minor offenses) gender difference in the dependent variable" (Akers 1999: 484). GENDER is dummy coded (males 0 and females 1). Race is measured through two dummy coded categories. WHITE is coded 1 for white respondents and 0 for everyone else. BLACK is coded 1 for black respondents and 0 for everyone else. The reference category is other (not white or black).

Several indicators of university group memberships are available in the Core survey. One is involvement in Greek organizations (dummy coded as yes or no). This GREEK involvement is singled out because of the relationship between participation in Greek organizations and alcohol use, especially binge drinking (Wechsler et al.1996). Another group indicator is involvement in such extracurricular activities as intramural sports, political organizations, journalistic groups, and groups dedicated to various performing arts. These affiliations are combined into a single measure (EXTRA) and dummy coded (yes the respondent participates in one or more of the extra-curricular activities or no the respondent does not participate in any of them).

Two structural theoretical variables can be derived from the Core data. One involves integration into academics. The grade-point average is a rough indicator of integration into scholarly endeavors. BGRADE is dummy coded, separating those having at least a B grade average (coded 1) from those having less than a B average (coded 0). We dummy code grade point rather than use the full range of grade averages because we want it to indicate integration with the university's official mission rather than individual performance or achievement.

The other structural theoretical variable involves the larger cultural climate surrounding alcohol on the campus. Although Akers and his associates have previously categorized norm qualities of intimate associates (family members and friends) as social learning definitions with which individuals are in differential association, he now recognizes that more distant cultural normative environments (like that of the larger university institution) are properly designated as a structural variable (Akers 2000). Akers (1998) insists that his is not a theory of cultural deviance, but he readily accepts the position that culture is important to the learning process. "Since the general conventional culture in modern society is not uniform and there are conflicts and variations among subgroups ..., the individual is likely to be exposed to different and perhaps conflicting cultural definitions..." (Akers 1998: 102). To get at the campus cultural CLIMATE regarding alcohol, respondents to the Core survey indicate whether or not alcohol is central to each of the following groups: male students, female students, faculty/staff, alumni, and athletes. A count is made across these groups (range of 0 through 5).

## B. Social Learning Dimensions

The Core survey yields only a few measures of the social learning process that are not tainted by double-barreled questions mixing responses to both alcohol and drugs. We do not use the imitation variable in the survey for that reason. We also avoid one other measurement controversy in social learning. Krohn (1999) argues that the differential association variable should be omitted because its more global conceptualization blurs measurement of other more specific learning processes like definitions and reinforcement/punishment (see also Lanza-Kaduce and Klug 1986). No good measure of differential peer associations is in the survey.

The survey does contain several good reinforcement/punishment variables. One is the anticipated reaction of friends to binge drinking: How do you think your close friends feel (or would feel) about you having five or more drinks in one sitting? The response alternatives for this PUNISHMENTS variable are (1) don't disapprove, (2) disapprove, and (3) strongly disapprove.

The survey also includes a series of items that assess positive consequences of alcohol use. Respondents are asked whether or not alcohol has the following positive effects: breaks the ice, enhances social activity, makes it easier to deal with stress, facilitates a connection with peers, gives people something to talk about, facilitates male bonding, facilitates female bonding, allows people to have more fun, gives people something to do, makes food taste better, makes women sexier, makes men sexier, makes me sexier, and facilitates sexual opportunities. A count of the "yes" responses across these items indicates the number of positive consequences (REWARDS) each respondent associates with alcohol use (range of 0 through 14).

The survey also includes one, rather weak, question about definitions favorable to alcohol. Students are asked whether they do or do not want to have alcohol available. This DEFINITIONS variable is dummy coded (1 they want alcohol available and 0 they do not).

## C. The Dependent Variable

Binge drinking is measured on the survey by an item that asks respondents to report how many times in the prior two weeks they had five or more drinks at a single sitting. The response alternatives for the binge drinking variable are none (0), once (1), twice (2), 3 to 5 times (3), 6 to 9 times (4), or 10 or more times (5). A drink is defined as a bottle of beer, a glass of wine, a wine cooler, a shot glass of liquor, or a mixed drink.

## The Social Structure Social Learning Model

The model advanced by Akers is straightforward. The effects on crime or deviance of the four levels of social structure should be mediated by the social learning variables. That basic path is diagramed at the top of Figure 8.1. The more precise ways in which the four levels of social structure and the

**Figure 8.1**
**Social Structure-Social Learning and Binge Drinking on College Campuses**

Social Structure ——————————> Social Learning ——————————> Deviance

Differential Institutional
Organization:
    UNIV1-7 vs. Other
                        DEFINITIONS
                             favorable to alcohol

Location in General
Social Structure:
    GENDER

    WHITE vs. Other
    BLACK vs. Other
                        Anticipated REWARDS        BINGE
                              of alcohol            DRINKING
Location in
Meso-level Groups:
    GREEK involvement

    EXTRA-curricular
    activities
                        Anticipated PUNISHMENTS
                            by friends for binge drinking
Integration into
the University:
    BGRADE

CLIMATE on campus
    regarding alcohol

social learning process have been operationalized in this application to binge drinking are also displayed in the figure.

*Method of Analysis*

Statistical analyses are dependent on the level of measurement. Most of the social structural variables are dummy coded—UNIV1 through UNIV7, GENDER, WHITE, BLACK, GREEK, EXTRA-curriculars, BGRADE. The exception is the CLIMATE variable regarding the centrality of alcohol to campus groups. This variable is a count across five campus groups; its level of measurement is interval. One social learning variable is measured in intervals; it counts the number of positive consequences that are associated with alcohol (REWARDS). Another (PUNISHMENTS) is measured on an ordinal scale. The DEFINITIONS variable is dummy coded. The dependent variable, binge drinking, is measured on an ordinal scale. Its five categories range from none (0) to 10 or more (5).

A series of least squares regression analyses is performed. Such analyses routinely incorporate independent variables that are dummy coded, and research indicates that analyses are robust when ordinal variables are used (Labovitz 1970; Kim 1975). The zero-order correlations indicate no problems with multicollinearity (presented upon request).

In an analysis that is not reported, we examine the relationships between binge drinking and the social structural variables. The social structural variables are entered simultaneously into a regression analysis to see how well they relate to binge drinking. Although the data are not from a probability-based sample, a significance level of .05 is used as a rough indicator of which relationships should be pursued. Given the sample size, this decision rule should not exclude any variable that may be related to binge drinking. Those variables that do not meet this minimal threshold are eliminated from the remaining analyses.

The second analysis focuses on the "significant" social structure variables and the social learning variables. In the first block, binge drinking is regressed on the significant social structure variables (entered simultaneously). Then the social learning variables are added with the social structural ones in a second block (the variables are entered simultaneously). Akers predicts three patterns: (1) the social learning variables should relate to binge drinking, (2) the strength of the social learning-binge drinking relationships should be stronger than that of the relationships between binge drinking and social structural variables (as indicated by the standardized regression coefficients or betas), and (3) the strength of the relationships between binge drinking and social structural variables should be markedly attenuated if Akers' mediation hypothesis were correct.

This stage of the analysis is further specified by looking at those university settings that are significantly related to binge drinking even after the social learning variables are added in the second block of the regression. Both the social structure block and the combined social structure and social learning block are included in separate regression analyses for the respective universities to see whether and how much the other structural relationships with binge drinking in each university are reduced (i.e., mediated) when the social learning variables are added.

We also employ a strategy used in the original test of social learning theory (Akers et al. 1979) to examine how much of the variance in binge drinking can be explained by the social structure and social learning subsets. If the social structural variables are explaining a unique part of the total variation in binge drinking, the R square (explained variance) statistic should drop markedly when the social structure variables are removed from the regression analysis. Akers' mediation hypothesis suggests that little will be lost in explained variance as social structure variables are eliminated because their impacts on binge drinking are not unique but are mediated by social learning variables.

## Findings

### The Relationship of Social Structure with Binge Drinking

We start with the results from the regression analysis that include all the social structure variables that are significantly related to binge drinking. The first column of Table 8.1 presents the standardized regression coefficients (betas) for those variables (all the relationships have a probability of less than .05).

As to the university institutional setting, only five of the seven dummied university variables bear relationships with binge drinking—all five have less binge drinking. Attending any of these five universities (UNIV1, UNIV3, UNIV4, UNIV5, and UNIV7) is negatively related to binge drinking, but the relationships are very weak (the betas range from -.04 to -.08).

Of the race variables, only WHITE is related to binge drinking (beta =.16). Whites binge a little more often than those in other racial categories.

GENDER is weakly related to binge drinking (beta = -.16). Females binge somewhat less often; males binge somewhat more often.

Two variables examine how campus group involvement relates to binge drinking. Participation in GREEK organizations is related to binge drinking (beta =.23) more than any other structural variable. [Involvement in other extra-curricular activities (EXTRA) is unrelated to binging and so is omitted from Table 8.1.]

Some structural theories suggest that social organization affects crime and deviance. Two indicators of these theoretical concerns are examined. Integration into the academic culture (as indicated by having a B or higher grade

Table 8.1
Binge Drinking Regressed on SSL: Significant Relationships (.05 Level)
between Binge Drinking and Both Social Structure and Social Learning
Variables N=2,782

| | Block 1<br>Social Structure<br>Variables Only | Block 2<br>Both Social Structure<br>and Social Learning |
|---|---|---|
| **Differential Organization**<br>**of Institutions:** | **Beta*** | **Beta** |
| UNIV1 | -0.07 | -0.04 |
| UNIV3 | -0.05 | -0.08 |
| UNIV4 | -0.04 | -0.06 |
| UNIV5 | -0.05 | -0.01 (not sign.) |
| UNIV7 | -0.08 | -0.06 |
| | | |
| **Location in**<br>**Social Structure:** | | |
| GENDER | -0.16 | -0.09 |
| WHITE | 0.16 | 0.06 |
| | | |
| **Location in**<br>**University Groups:** | | |
| GREEK | 0.23 | 0.13 |
| | | |
| **Integration**<br>**in Campus:** | | |
| BGRADE | -0.08 | -0.06 |
| CLIMATE | 0.12 | 0.04 |
| | | |
| **Social Learning:** | | |
| DEFINITIONS | | 0.13 |
| PUNISHMENTS | | -0.28 |
| REWARDS | | 0.20 |

* Standardized Regression Coefficient

average—BGRADE) is negatively related to binge drinking. The relationship is very weak (beta = -.08). On the other hand, the more that alcohol is
seen as being central to the university cultural CLIMATE, the more likely the
respondents are to report binge drinking. The relationship between binge
drinking and the campus CLIMATE about alcohol is a bit stronger (beta =.12)
but is still weak.

## The Interrelationship of Social Structure and Social Learning with Binge Drinking

Although the relationships between binge drinking and the structural variables are not strong, they do exist. Recall that Akers explicitly recognizes that even weak relationships between deviance and structural variables will be mediated by social learning processes. We can, therefore, proceed to an examination of what happens when the social learning variables are introduced into the regression equation.

The second column of Table 8.1 presents the results. We first note that, consistent with Akers predictions, each of the social learning variables is related to binge drinking. The DEFINITIONS variable (a weak operationalization) shows the lowest relationship (beta = .13), but still the relationship indicates that respondents who define alcohol more favorably are more inclined to binge. The more positive consequences (REWARDS) that are associated with alcohol, the more often respondents engage in binge drinking (beta = .20). The most important social learning variable proves to be the anticipated disapproval of friends. The beta for PUNISHMENTS is -.28; the stronger the disapproval, the less often the respondent binges.

The magnitudes of the betas for the social learning variables (displayed on the bottom of the second column of Table 8.1) can be compared with those of the social structure variables, either in the model that only enters social structure variables (Block 1) or in the model that combines both social structure and social learning (Block 2). The betas for the social structure variables are generally lower than those for any of the social learning variables, especially when both kinds of variables are included in Block 2. The pattern is consistent with Akers' predictions. Although GENDER (beta = -.16), WHITE (beta = .16), and GREEK (beta = .23) have higher betas in Block 1 than does the DEFINITIONS variable (beta = .13), in Block 2 the betas for GENDER and WHITE drop to -.09 and .06, respectively. In Block 2, the beta for GREEK (beta = .13) is reduced to match that of DEFINITIONS. None of the social structure variables are as strongly related to binge drinking as is PUNISHMENTS (beta = -.28).

The second column of Table 8.1 also provides the first evidence relevant to Akers' mediation hypothesis. The results are a bit mixed but generally support mediation. Only one structural variable (UNIV5) is mediated by social learning variables so that it is no longer significantly related to binge drinking. All the other structural variables survive the addition of the social learning variables to the regression analysis. They remain statistically significant at the .05 level despite weak betas in the original social structure regression. (The significance of the low betas probably reflects the fact that we have a large sample.) The question is whether there is substantive or theoretical significance in addition to statistical significance.

One way to examine this is to compare the betas for the structural variables that are presented in column two (when social learning variables are included in the analysis) with those in column one. Akers argues that they should be reduced substantially. The betas for four of the universities (UNIV1, UNIV3, UNIV4, and UNIV7) are not reduced substantially, but they were very small to begin with. The beta for GENDER is more substantially reduced (from -.16 to -.09) as is that for CLIMATE (from .12 to .04). That for WHITE is reduced even more (from .16 to .06) as is that for GREEK (from .23 to .13). The general pattern is for substantial, but not complete, attenuation for social structural variables, except for the dummied university variables. Akers' position is partially substantiated.

The fact that social learning variables do not mediate the effect that attending any of these four universities has on binge drinking warrants more scrutiny. The results from separate analyses for each of the four universities are presented in Table 8.2. These results clearly show that the relationships of the other structural variables are attenuated by social learning variables in each of the universities. When only social structure variables are included in the regressions (the SS columns), only 12 of the possible 20 relationships between social structure and binge drinking are statistically significant. When the social learning variables are entered with the social structure variables in the regressions (the SSSL columns), the betas for all 12 of the original significant relationships involving social structure variables are attenuated. In eight instances (for GENDER, WHITE, and CLIMATE in UNIV3 and in UNIV4 and for WHITE and GREEK in UNIV7) the betas are reduced below the level of statistical significance. This pattern is consistent with the mediation position Akers adopts.

The exceptions are also worth noting. The structural theory indicators of integration remain significant in UNIV1. BGRADE remains inversely related to binge drinking (beta = -.16) and cultural CLIMATE is still positively related to binging (beta = .15) even with the social learning variables in the regression equation. GREEK participation in UNIV3 is related to binging (beta = .22). The magnitudes of the relationships for all three structural variables are reduced, however. The beta diminishes from .22 to .15 for CLIMATE in UNIV1, from -.20 to -.16 for BGRADE in UNIV1, and from .31 to .22 for GREEK in UNIV3. So even when the social structural variables still relate to binge drinking, their importance is reduced once the social learning variables are included in the regression runs.

One other strategy is available to examine how much attenuation occurs when social learning theory is added to social structural analyses. We can compare the amounts of explained variance (R squares). Table 8.3 does just that. The first column presents the explained variances for the social structural variables as a single block for all the campuses combined and for each of the four universities for which social learning did not mediate the impact of the university itself. The second column presents the R square for the social

Table 8.2

**Binge Drinking Regressed on Social Structure (SS) and Social Structure-Social Learning (SSSL) Variables for Four Universities (Standardized Regression Coefficients)**

|  | UNIV1: | | UNIV3: | | UNIV4: | | UNIV7: | |
|---|---|---|---|---|---|---|---|---|
|  | SS | SSSL | SS | SSSL | SS | SSSL | SS | SSSL |
| Locations in Social Structure |  |  |  |  |  |  |  |  |
| GENDER | -.22 | -.15 | -.14 | -.09* | -.18 | -.07* | -.07* | -.00* |
| WHITE | .07* | .05* | .13 | -.01* | .11 | -.01* | .13 | .07* |
| Locations in University Groups |  |  |  |  |  |  |  |  |
| GREEK | -.04* | -.03* | .31 | .22 | -.07* | -.06* | .15 | .09* |
| Integration in Campus |  |  |  |  |  |  |  |  |
| BGRADE | -.20 | -.16 | -.08* | -.08* | -.01* | .03* | -.03* | -.04* |
| CLIMATE | .22 | .15 | .12 | .02* | .13 | .03* | .02* | .02* |

* indicates the relationship is NOT significant at the .05 level.

learning variables as a single block for the entire sample and for the four selected university subsamples. The third column presents the explained variance when social structural and social learning variables are combined.

Although the social structural variables by themselves can explain some of the variance in binge drinking for the overall sample and in each university subsample (R squares range from .04 to .18), the social learning variables explain much more (R squares range from .16 to .34). The differences between what the social learning variables explain (presented in the second column) and the total explained by both blocks (the combination of social structure and social learning variables presented in the third column) indicates how much of the variance is unique to the social structural variables (i.e., the variance that is not mediated when social learning variables are added to the analysis).

For all campuses, 37 percent of the variance can be explained with both social structure and social learning variables (SSSL) in the regression (see column 3). The social learning variables by themselves (SL VARS.) can explain 32 percent (column two) leaving only 5 percent of the total explained variance attributable to social structural variables. That is considerably lower than the 18 percent explained variance reported when just the social structure variables (SS VARS.) are in the regression (column one).

Table 8.3
Amount of Variance in Binge Drinking Explained (R Sq.)
by Social Structure Variables (SS), Social Learning Variables (SL),
and Their Combination (SSSL) for All Campuses and Selected Campuses

|  | SS VARS. R Sq. | SL VARS. R. Sq. | SSSL R. Sq. |
|---|---|---|---|
| ALL CAMPUSES: | .18 | .32 | .37 |
| SELECTED CAMPUSES: | | | |
| UNIV1 | .14 | .19 | .25 |
| UNIV3 | .18 | .34 | .43 |
| UNIV4 | .07 | .31 | .32 |
| UNIV7 | .04 | .16 | .18 |

The same pattern is seen in Table 8.3 for the four selected university campuses. For UNIV1, the SSSL model accounts for 25 percent of the variance in binge drinking. The social learning variables (SL VARS.) account for 19 percent of it so the remaining 6 percent is attributable to social structural variables. That is much lower than the 14 percent that is reported in the first column for just the social structure variables (SS VARS). For UNIV3, the respective numbers are 43 percent variance explained by SSSL with 34 percent of it due to social learning variables (SL VARS.) leaving 9 percent unique to the social structural variables (down from 14 percent in the SS VARS. regression reported in column one). For UNIV4, 32 percent of the variance in binge drinking is explained in the SSSL model, and almost all of it (31 percent) is due to the social learning variables (SL VARS.). Less variance (18 percent) in binge drinking is explained in the SSSL model in UNIV7, but it is almost all due to the social learning variables (16 percent for SL VARS.).

This consistent pattern indicates that much of the variance in binge drinking that can be explained by social structure is absorbed by the social learning variables. Relatively little of the total explained variance is unique to social structure; social learning theory accounts for most of it. Akers' mediation hypothesis receives its strongest support when explained variance is examined.

## Summary and Conclusion

These results comport with the patterns Akers expected. The social learning variables are related to binge drinking. The social learning variables tend to be more strongly related to binge drinking than are the structural variables.

Most importantly, the results support Akers' mediation hypothesis. Probably because of the large number of cases across the eight campuses, only one structural relationship disappears altogether when social learning variables are added to the multiple regression analysis (one of the university dummy variables). Most of the other relationships, however, are attenuated as is evidenced by comparing the standardized regression coefficients from an analysis that includes only the social structural variables with those from an analysis that adds the social learning ones. Greek participation, gender, race, and campus climate regarding alcohol all show substantial diminution. When the smaller subsamples at four universities are analyzed separately, many of these relationships disappear. The amount of explained variance that is unique to the social structural variables also indicates that their effects are mediated by social learning variables.

Because this "test" of SSSL relies on secondary data, the operationalizations of the social structure and social learning constructs are neither as extensive nor as exacting as they should be. Thus, these results are far from conclusive. Nevertheless, they are highly suggestive that the social learning process mediates many structural effects.

These survey data came from diverse campuses—campuses that have different organizational structures, different mixes of students, and different levels of binge drinking. These data contain measures that fit with each of the four social structure dimensions Akers outlined and two of the major social learning constructs. The pattern of relationships that emerge between binge drinking and social structure is consistent with other research. Males binge drink more than females, Greeks more than independents, whites more than blacks, and those with lower grades more than those with higher grades. The pattern of relationships between binge drinking and the social learning measures is also consistent with prior research. Rewards, punishments, and definitions about alcohol are related to drinking across campuses. Consequently, the substantial mediation of the social structural effects through social learning variables is probably not due to aberrant samples. Arguably, the mediation may be less if other structural variables are included. Still, the Core data provide more structural variables than social learning variables (and one of these is weakly operationalized). Our hunch is that better or more social learning operationalizations are likely to increase the mediation effect.

What remains to be done is to locate data that both capture broader structural arrangements than those involving university milieus and operationalize the learning process better. Such research should also examine deviant or criminal behaviors other than binge drinking. In other words, this study needs to be replicated and extended to see if other research also finds that "the social learning process mediate[s] a *substantial portion* of the relationship between *most* structural variables" and behavior (Akers 1998: 340).

## Note

1. An earlier version of this paper was presented at the 2000 Annual Meeting of the American Society of Criminology in San Francisco. The authors wish to acknowledge the cooperation of oith of the univerities which permitted the use of the data collected at their institutions and the Core Institute at Southern Illinois University which made the data available. The analysis and conclusions contained in this chapter are those of the authors and not those of the cooperating universities or the Core Institute.

## References

Agnew, Robert. 1992. "Foundation for a General Strain Theory of Crime and Delinquency." *Criminology* 30:47-88.

Akers, Ronald L. 1968. "Problems in the Sociology of Deviance: Social Definitions and Behavior." *Social Forces* 46:455-465.

_____. 1973. *Deviant Behavior: A Social Learning Approach.* Belmont, CA: Wadsworth.

_____. 1977. *Deviant Behavior: A Social Learning Approach.* Second Edition. Belmont, CA: Wadsworth.

_____. 1985. *Deviant Behavior: A Social Learning Approach.* Third Edition. Belmont, CA: Wadsworth.

_____. 1997. *Criminological Theories: Introduction and Evaluation.* Second Edition. Los Angeles: Roxbury.

_____. 1998. *Social Learning and Social Structure: A General Theory of Crime and Deviance.* Boston, MA: Northeastern University Press.

_____. 1999. "Reply to Sampson, Morash, and Krohn." *Theoretical Criminology* 3:477-493.

_____. March 6, 2000. Personal Communication. Gainesville, FL

Akers, Ronald L., Krohn, Marvin D., Lanza-Kaduce, Lonn, and Marcia Radosevich. 1979. "Social Learning and Deviant Behavior: A Specific Test of a General Theory." *American Sociological Review* 44:635-655.

Alden, Helen, Lanza-Kaduce, Lonn, and Michael Capece. 2000. "Liquor is Quicker: Gender and Social Learning among College Students." Presented at the Annual Meeting of the American Society of Criminology, San Francisco, CA, August 2000.

Bartusch, Dawn, R. Jeglum, Donald R. Lynam, Terrie E. Moffitt, and Phil A. Silva. 1997. "Is Age Important? Testing a General Versus a Developmental Theory of Antisocial Behavior." *Criminology* 35:13-48.

Elliot, Delbert E., David Huizinga, and Suzanne Ageton. 1985. *Explaining Delinquency and Drug Use.* Beverly Hills, CA: Sage Publications.

Goode, Erich. 2001. *Devant Behavior.* Sixth Edition. New Jersey: Prentice-Hall.

Kim, Jae-On. 1975. "Multivariate Analysis of Ordinal Variables." *American Journal of Sociology* 81:261-298.

Krohn, Marvin. 1999. "Social Learning Theory: The Continuing Development of a Perspective." *Theoretical Criminology* 3:462-476.

Labovitz, Sanford. 1970. "The Assignment of Numbers to Rank Order Categories." *American Sociological Review* 38:530-543.

Lanza-Kaduce, Lonn, and Mary Klug. 1986. "Learning to Cheat: The Interaction of Moral Development and Social Learning Theories." *Deviant Behavior* 7:243-259.

Liska, Allen E., Marvin D. Krohn, and Steven F. Messner. 1989. "Strategies and Requisites for the Theoretical Integration in the Study of Crime and Deviance." Pp. 1-19 in S. Messner, M. D. Krohn, and A. Liska (eds) *Theoretical Integration in the Study of Deviance and Crime: Problems and Prospects*. Albany, NY: SUNY Press.

Morash, Merry. 1999. "A Consideration of Gender in Relation to Social Learning and Social Structure: A General Theory of Crime and Deviance." *Theoretical Criminology* 3:452-461.

Sampson, Robert J., and John H. Laub. 1993. *Crime in the Making: Pathways and Turning Points Through Life*. Cambridge, MA: Harvard University Press.

Thornberry, Terence P. 1987. "Toward an Interactional Theory of Delinquency." *Criminology* 25:863-891.

Wechsler, Henry. 1996. "Alcohol and the American College Campus: A Report from the Harvard School of Public Health." *Change* 28: 20-25, 60.

Wechsler, Henry, George Kuh, and Andrea E. Davenport. 1996. "Fraternities, Sororities and Binge Drinking: Results from a National Study of American Colleges." *National Association of Student Personnel Administrators (NASPA) Journal* 33: 260-279.

# 9

# Occupational Structure, Social Learning, and Adolescent Violence[1]

*Paul E. Bellair, Vincent J. Roscigno, and María B. Vélez*

Research dealing with the spatial patterning of violence has ignored the relationship between local occupational structure and social learning processes related to violence. In this chapter, we draw from Akers' (1998) recent social structure and social learning (SSSL) model of delinquency and address this gap by developing a more explicit conceptual and operational focus on labor market opportunity, adolescent violence, and potentially mediating social learning and family processes. Findings, derived from multilevel analyses of adolescents drawn from the National Educational Longitudinal Survey, reveal a negative effect of higher wage and professional sector concentration on adolescent violence among males. Consistent with Akers (1998) SSSL model and our extension of it, these patterns are largely mediated through family well-being and social learning processes. Interestingly, these patterns vary little between males and females. Also noteworthy, given traditional subcultural perspectives, is that concentration of disadvantage does not positively impact violent attitudes once labor market opportunities and mediating family and social learning factors are accounted for. We conclude by discussing the implications of these results and our model for the study of adolescent delinquency specifically, and for theories pertaining to structural opportunity, social learning processes, and violence generally.

## Occupational Structure, Social Learning, and Adolescent Violence

The spatial patterning of violence has been a major issue in the sociological literature throughout the last century, with debates centering around two key questions. First, what are the structural covariates of violence? The second question, about which there is considerable theoretical debate, asks *why* violent behavior is more or less likely in some contexts, and under certain structural circumstances, than others. While a number of analyses have attempted to address empirically these questions, few have focused on adolescents specifically. Yet, a more developed focus on adolescents is warranted, given what appear to be increasing rates of teenage violence over the previous decade and concerns regarding the decreasing ages of first-time and persistent offenders (Cook and Laub 1998). It is also the case, according to developmental criminologists, that stable patterns of involvement in delinquency and violence emerge by the adolescent years, particularly for "life-course persistent offenders" (Moffit 1993).

Researchers have addressed the structural covariates of violence generally, denoting the potentially influential role of local socioeconomic and demographic characteristics such as unemployment, poverty, racial composition, and racial residential segregation, to name but a few. Indeed, Land, McCall, and Cohen's (1990) review of this literature suggests that many of these effects are invariant across levels of aggregation such as city, Standard Metropolitan Statistical Area (SMSA), and state. More recent community studies, extending on prior work, have been somewhat more concrete in their findings, delineating the importance of neighborhood social ties (Bellair 1997; Rountree and Warner 1999) and informal control structures such as "collective efficacy" (Sampson, Raudenbush, and Earls 1997; see also Sampson, Morenoff, and Earls 1999).

The more pressing question of why violence might emerge, given the confluence of certain structural attributes, is central to traditional sociological theories of crime. The social disorganization model, which has more recently been reformulated in structural terms (for a more thorough review of the current reformulation, see Bursik and Grasmick 1993), is concerned with the structure and functioning of local networks and institutions, and their role in stimulating the formation and maintenance of social capital (see Coleman 1990). Strain models, which have been utilized to explain higher rates of crime and violence among the lower class (Merton 1938) and racial/ethnic minorities (Blau and Blau 1982), focus on the social sources of, and adaptions to, stress resulting from inability to achieve material wealth or other societally desired goals.[2] Lastly, subcultural accounts focus on the development of unconventional values, attitudes, and lifestyles, and the process by which individuals are socialized into them (e.g., Sutherland 1939; Cohen 1955; Miller 1958).[3]

While each of the aforementioned perspectives inform our understanding of spatial criminological patterns, social learning (Akers 1998) and differential association theory (Sutherland 1939), with their explicit effort to link structure, cultural transmission, and action, hold largely unexplored promise for addressing both *how* and *why* violence varies across place. Sutherland

(1939), for instance, integrated key insights from social disorganization (which he later termed differential social organization) and subcultural perspectives, and described formally the process by which transmission of values and attitudes occurs. He suggested that delinquency is more likely when children and adolescents are exposed to a higher ratio of attitudes favorable to violating the law versus those that do not (weighted by frequency, duration, priority, and intensity). Akers (1998), who has more recently developed this perspective by using social learning concepts (see also Burgess and Akers 1966; Akers 1985), offers a social structure and social learning (SSSL) model. This contextual framework posits a causal sequence whereby structural features of communities, such as poverty or unemployment, alter the level of community violence through their effect on social learning processes among individuals.

In this chapter, and following the recent work of Akers (1998), we extend the literature by testing a social learning model of subcultural formation and violence among adolescents that has its roots in local labor market conditions and opportunity. Our approach is conceptually similar to and, indeed, is informed by Akers' (1998) recent SSSL formulation, although we expand upon it by explicating the mechanisms through which the occupational structure of a community may pattern social learning processes and, hence, the spatial concentration of violence among adolescents in the U.S. As such, our offering departs from much prior research, which tends to conceptualize subculture solely as a community-level property. In contrast, we examine whether structural constraints such as limited prospects for job mobility pattern social learning outcomes among individuals. This focus is important because anti-

**Figure 9.1**
**Social Structure and Social Learning (SSSL) Model of Violence (Akers)**

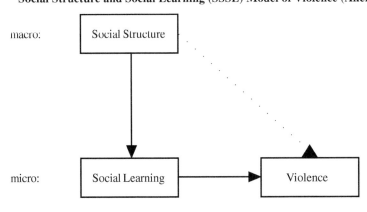

*Note:* Dashed arrow reflects reduction in effect of social structure on violence once social learning processes are controlled.

social learning, reflected in part by prior involvement in violence, negative peer influences, limited involvement in prosocial activity, internalization of violent attitudes, and low employment expectations are building blocks and logical precursors of community-level subcultural processes such as street gang formation and proliferation (Howell 1998). We begin with a brief review of key issues that have hindered subcultural perspectives and analyses, and then describe the conceptual model that underlies our research. Finally, we test our model on a nationally representative sample of adolescents.

## Background and Limitations of Subcultural Research

There are at least four interrelated issues that have impeded theoretical growth and empirical attention towards macro-level subcultural models. First, critics have argued that the internal theoretical logic of perspectives incorporating subcultural patterns is flawed, because they tend to view humans as having no "essential" nature, assume that socialization into subcultures is always successful, and apply solely to group (rather than individual) variations in delinquent involvement (Kornhauser 1978). Responding to these criticisms, Akers (1998) has argued, and we largely concur, that this critique, at least as it has been applied to differential association and social learning variants, is based on mis-interpretation and mis-representation. As we discuss below, our theoretical extension of Akers (1998) SSSL model assumes that local labor market structure shapes social learning processes in a probabilistic rather than deterministic fashion. Moreover, we interpret and apply Akers' (1998) SSSL formulation as an explanation of individual differences in violence outcomes, and present our elaboration of it in this context. At the same time, we emphasize that our conceptualization may be useful for explaining group differences in violent behavior, particularly if "group differences" refer to variations in adolescent violence that exist, on average, across geographical space.

A second problematic issue involves measurement of subculture. Although there are many definitions from which to draw, most define subculture as a set of beliefs, values, and normative patterns that exist within, but are unique to those of the larger society, and that typically emerge or persist as a function of structural conditions (i.e., see Ball-Rokeach 1973). A violent "subculture" can thus be defined and measured, at least in part, as the spatial concentration of pro-violent values, attitudes, or normative patterns. Unfortunately, with few exceptions, researchers rarely incorporate indicators of subculture into their models. Empirical work examining the southern subculture of violence thesis serves as a case in point. Rather than measuring specific spatial variations in subculture, such research tends to assume that regional (southern) differences in homicide that exist after structural conditions are controlled reflect subcultural processes (for instance, see Gastil 1971; Huff-Corzine,

Corzine, and Moore 1986). Subculture is not measured, nor are its effects on violence tested. The same applies to research that interprets racial differences in violence as evidence of subcultural processes (e.g., Wolfgang and Ferracuti 1967; Messner 1983). Although subcultural processes cannot be definitively ruled out, neither can they be established in the absence of direct measures included in regression equations.

There is one exception to the general pattern we note above. Felson, Liska, South, and McNulty's (1994) innovative contextual analysis links a school-level subculture measure, formed by aggregating student responses to questions about violence-related beliefs and attitudes within each school, to violent and property delinquency among individual students. We find merit in their strategy of measuring subcultural processes as values, attitudes, or beliefs that approve of the use of violence. Yet, given the arguments we are making, their analysis remains limited because it does not include explicit theoretical discussion or analyses of the context within which such cultural patterns emerge (Bruce, Roscigno, and McCall 1998; Sampson and Wilson 1995)— an important issue and oversight in much subcultural work, classic and contemporary, and a third limitation to which we now turn.[4]

Theoretical ambiguity and neglect surrounding the antecedents of subcultural patterns and processes is the third weakness of prior work. That is, many subcultural theories fail to provide a detailed description of where and why subcultures might emerge (e.g., Wolfgang and Ferracuti 1967). They also tend to assume that subcultural manifestation and exposure to delinquent behavior are a natural consequence of institutional patterns, such as in female-headed families, or something simply inherent in lower-class communities (Miller 1958). Indeed, one often gets the impression that subcultural processes originate from thin air among poor, minority inner-city residents, rather than as the result of structural constraints on economic opportunity and mobility that are created by inequality in local labor market conditions, and reinforced by residential segregation (Bruce, Roscigno, and McCall 1998; Massey and Denton 1993). As a consequence, researchers have tended to assign analytic priority to disadvantage indicators such as poverty or racial composition (as proxies for subculture), rather than constraints pertaining to local labor market opportunity—a central aspect of place, as has been established in spatial stratification literature (Hodson 1978, 1983; Tomaskovic-Devey 1987; Kasarda 1987; Wilson 1987). In an effort to address this, our theoretical explication and analyses of social learning and its implications for violence distinguish between the concentration of disadvantage such as poverty, female-headed households, unemployment or the prevalence of minority group members, on the one hand, and local labor market opportunity such as the availability of higher paying and stable employment opportunity in professional and managerial occupations, on the other.

Finally, virtually all macro-level subcultural research is carried out using a sample of major cities or neighborhoods drawn from them. Given the well-known relationship between extreme deprivation and violence, this sampling strategy, almost by definition, leads to the conclusion that subcultural processes arise in extremely poor, minority communities. This is because most large urban areas contain very few, if any, extremely poor, white communities. Yet, in those cities where poor, white communities are more common, rates of violence are comparable to those in extremely poor minority communities (Alex-Assensoh 1995; Krivo and Peterson 1996). Thus, the largely urban, major metropolitan area samples used in prior work have perhaps mistakenly created the impression that subcultural processes associated with violence are solely characteristic of inner-city, minority communities. The foregoing comment should not be interpreted to mean that we deny the existence of subcultural processes in underclass areas, such as those documented by Anderson (1990) or Wilson (1996). Rather, there is no reason to assume that subcultural processes arise solely in urban areas. Adolescents residing in suburban, and, in particular, rural poor areas—areas with substantial white populations and increasing crime rates through the 1990's—may also perceive limited opportunities, with consequences for antisocial learning. Thus, to draw general conclusions regarding social structure and social learning, it is important to employ broad samples that include rural, suburban, and urban communities to ensure adequate variability across context. This sampling strategy provides an additional analytical advantage as well—it allows for the inclusion of disadvantage and labor market indicators in the same equation while minimizing the collinearity concerns that have plagued city- and community-level research (for a review of this issue, see Land, McCall, and Cohen 1990).

## Social Learning of Violence within a Local Labor Market Context

Social learning processes are well-established predictors of adolescent delinquency and violent behavior at the micro level (Akers 1998; Matsueda 1982, 1988; Warr and Stafford 1991). Unfortunately, there has been surprisingly little empirical investigation of the community conditions that may pattern such learning (for an exception, see Heimer 1997). In this section, we discuss and elaborate on differential association and social learning theories. These perspectives provide theoretical discussion of the micro-level, social-psychological mechanisms by which violence is learned. We then ground this understanding within a local labor market context.

Differential association (DA) theory focuses on the cognitive processes that give rise to criminal attitudes (Sutherland 1939). To understand why someone engages in violence, it is suggested, one must understand why that person views a situation as an occasion for violent behavior. Individuals learn attitudes, rationalizations, techniques, and motives that define the meaning of violence, definitions that are either favorable or unfavorable, in the context of interaction within intimate primary groups, such as family, peer groups, school, and community. Definitions of violence to which an individual is exposed early in life (priority), from a person who is admired or looked up to (intensity), for longer durations, and with greater frequency have greater weight. Internalized violent attitudes, rationalizations, and motives eventually lend themselves to violent acts, particularly when the individual continues to be exposed to favorable, as opposed to unfavorable, definitions of violence (Akers, Krohn, Lanza-Kaduce, and Radosevich 1979).

Social learning theory, drawing from psychological principles involved in operant conditioning, extends DA theory by providing a more complete explanation of the mechanisms by which individuals acquire behavior (see Figure 9.2 ). Retaining a strong symbolic interactionist component, social learning theory emphasizes that social interaction consists of the exchange of meanings and symbols. Thus, individuals have the capacity to imagine themselves in the role of others and incorporate these images into their conception of self. Beyond learning definitions favorable towards the use of violence, social learning theory suggests that violent behavior can be initiated through the process of imitation (Bandura 1986), or through the anticipation of future rewards (Rotter 1954). Moreover, the theory posits that violent behavior, once initiated, will be repeated over time insofar as it is rewarded, and/or it goes unpunished (Akers 1985, 1998; Burgess and Akers 1966) .

Akers' (1998) recent reformulation of SSSL theory extends the social learning model by positing that social structural characteristics pattern the distribution of crime through their effect on individual-level social learning processes (see Figure 9.1). Our extension of Akers (1998) SSSL model relies on the SSSL conceptualization of causal linkage among structural character-

**Figure 9.2**
**Social Learning Model of Violence (Akers)**

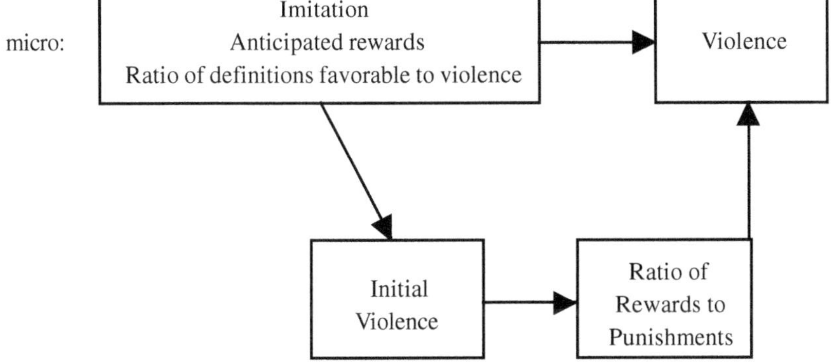

istics and crime, but expands it by elaborating on the interconnectedness of occupational structure, family well-being, social learning processes, and violent behavior. Indeed, we distinguish between local labor market conditions, such as the availability of professional and managerial occupations that provide exceptional opportunities for social mobility, and more often utilized disadvantage measures such as poverty or racial composition. Rather than associating the emergence of subcultural processes solely with the concentration of certain kinds of people (poor, minorities), we view them as the partial outcome of local opportunity structures that offer diminished prospects for social mobility.

Figure 9.3 offers our conceptualization. Establishing links between social learning processes and violence is not the main offering of our model. Rather, our contribution lies in conceptualizing relationships between occupational structure, social learning processes, and violence. Note that this argument does not rely on the assumption that adolescents are direct participants in the labor market. Some certainly are, and we account for these individuals with appropriate controls in our analyses. Rather, most adolescents will be *indirectly* affected by local labor market opportunities through family well-being and social learning processes, and possibly *directly* affected through their own observations and perceptions of adults in close proximity, such as parents or community residents.

We begin with the potential effect of local labor market structure on social learning and, consequently, adolescent fighting—a clear-cut manifestation and indicator of violence. Social learning theory suggests that adolescent perceptions of their economic future are formed, in part, through an assumption that their future lifestyle will be very similar to their average neighbor.

**Figure 9.3**
**Effect of Occupational Structure on Adolescent Violence through**
**Family Well-Being and Social Learning Processes**

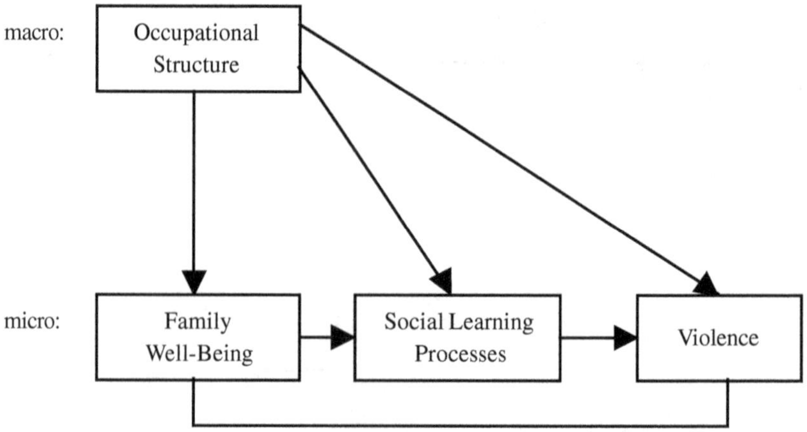

Thus, when adolescents perceive that adults in their community are being rewarded financially through participation in the mainstream economy, they are more likely to conclude that their future is positive and to model what they believe to be relevant or related behavior (Wilson 1996). Examples include devaluing and avoiding the use of violence by employing social skills and practicing anger management, avoiding negative peer influences, and immersing oneself in prosocial activity such as participating in extracurricular activity in school. More recent reviews of the contextual delinquency literature support our suppositions, indicating that variation in the concentration of adults employed in professional occupational sectors is the most robust contextual predictor of a range of developmental outcomes such as violent delinquency (Brooks-Gunn, Duncun, and Aber 1997).

What this means is that the presence of adults employed in high-wage sectors of the economy may directly reduce the likelihood of violence, in part by shaping the pattern of imitation and role modeling that local adolescents adopt. Conversely, some research suggests that adolescents who have no positive role models and who perceive that opportunities are constricted may be more likely to seek out status in peer groups (Fagan 1993; Klein 1995). Status, in such a scenario, may be attained by demonstrating courage and physical prowess by being ready and willing to fight, including adopting an oppositional and defiant attitude set (Cohen 1955). Adolescents in low-opportunity locales may also be more likely to observe that adults in the community are not economically secure and may infer that their future opportunities are quite limited. Here, adolescents are modeling, imitating, and internalizing values, attitudes, and expectations through processes outlined in social learning theory, including differential association.

The processes we are discussing may not be generalizable in a strict sense, but instead may take on a gendered character. Indeed, Messerschmidt's (2000) recent analyses of violence among working-class youth suggests that delinquency in general, and processes leading to violent behavior more specifically, may vary. Agnew and Brezina (1997) similarly explore the consequences economic and interpersonal strain on males and females, while others analyze whether educational expectations (Triplett and Jarjoura 1997), family interactional patterns (Coughlin and Vuchinich 1996; McCarthy, Hagan, and Woodward 1999), and peer associations (Liu and Kaplan 1999) differentially affect delinquency levels across sex groups. Findings from these studies suggest moderate and significant differences across groups. They also imply a danger in assuming general processes without first disaggregating group-specific patterns.

Local labor market effects, which may also have a gendered character, will be directly influential for adolescents by shaping social learning processes. We suspect, however, that a portion of the labor market impact will manifest itself indirectly through family well-being. Depressed family income and single-parent households, often viewed as institutional features of lower-class communities that give rise to a distinctive culture (Miller 1958), are conceived of here as shaped, at least in part, by labor market characteristics—a linkage clearly established in the stratification literature (e.g., Tomaskovic-Devey 1987; Hodson 1978, 1983). Indeed, Wilson (1996) makes the case that the decline in manufacturing employment and increasing disappearance of core and service sector employment have resulted in concentrated pockets of poor and unstable families (Wilson 1996). Anderson (1990) concurs, noting that when traditional sources of masculinity, such as breadwinner, are systematically absent, family disintegration is more likely and unconventional attitudes which encourage young males to avoid marriage unfold. Generally speaking, local labor markets that offer good-paying occupations, such as professional employment, will produce higher average incomes and greater family stability. Adverse effects on family well-being, in contrast, will be evident in locales characterized by low-wage job structures and, consequently, heightened disadvantage.

Family poverty and broken homes have long been viewed as precursors to delinquency. However, little empirical research has focused on their association with social learning processes. Recent analyses by Heimer (1997) are an exception, and her findings are consistent with our supposition that adolescents in poorer, disrupted households will be more likely to be exposed to violence and to antisocial learning. This will be a function of inferences and judgments about future life chances, dictated by observing the lives of their neighbors. Adolescents are also likely to make such judgments based on what occurs in their own households. "Given that perfect information regarding future opportunities is virtually impossible to acquire, it is likely to be the case that this type of information is supplied to a particular adolescent by his or her perceptions and observations regarding the current economic and occupational status of adults in close proximity" (Roscigno 1995:149). Thus, we expect antisocial learning to be more common among adolescents in low income, and single-parent households. Rather than an inherent characteristic of underclass communities or merely "cultural" in some obscure sense, family well-being and its consequences for adolescent experiences, perceptions, and actions are viewed here as shaped by local economic conditions (Alex-Assensoh 1995; Anderson 1990; Bruce, Roscigno, and McCall 1998).

## Study Design

*Data.* We draw from three waves of the National Education Longitudinal Survey (NELS) and U.S. zip-code data on local labor market opportunity in addressing the relations discussed above.[5] NELS represents a large, nationally representative data set with student, parent, teacher, and principal components. During the first wave in 1988, the National Center for Education

Statistics (NCES) drew random samples of about 25 eighth graders in each of about 1,000 middle schools. Students were then traced to high school in 1990 (wave 2) and 1992 (wave 3), with high follow-up response rates (see NCES 1992).

Exogenous and intervening variables are drawn from the first and second waves of NELS (1988, 1990), and we take advantage of the longitudinal nature of the data by predicting fighting among adolescents at a later time point (1992) in order to bolster confidence in causal ordering. We also employ a sample weight that takes into account racial representation and sample attrition across the first, second, and third waves. Rather than lose cases or artificially reduce variation through general mean substitution, regression imputation with random error components was used to replace missing items for explanatory measures (Jinn and Sedransk 1989).[6] Individual data was then matched with zip-code level labor market data derived from the U.S. Census.

Our geographic definition of neighborhood is based in part on data availability—NCES does not release data for smaller geographic aggregates such as census tracts. Zip-code areas (mean population of 25,127 in our data), however, are perhaps more appropriate than census tracts given our theoretical focus on adolescent perception of opportunity. We assume that many adolescents routinely cross tract boundaries in the course of their daily rounds and thus that conclusions drawn about their future are based on observation of adults in this wider geographical area. It is also the case that zip-code areas, because they are larger and more heterogeneous, may be more reflective of the range of opportunities available to adolescents in their local labor markets. Because of attrition across the years (which our sample weight accounts for), our sample ranges from 7,037 to 7,870 male and 7,321 to 8,147 female adolescents across 3,135 locales. Table 9.1 reports definitions, means and standard deviations for our outcome and explanatory variables, and descriptives disaggregated by sex are presented in Appendix 1.

*Measurement.* Our key outcome is a straightforward indicator of adolescent violence—fighting. This indicator is derived from two items which ask adolescents in the third wave (1) whether they had been in a fight at school or (2) been in a fight on their way to or from school over the previous half year. We combine these items and code fighting as a binary response with 1 indicating the respondent was in a fight in either context. We acknowledge the limitation of focusing on fighting to the exclusion of other forms of violence (i.e., such as involvement in shootings). Yet, fighting is perhaps the most common expression of violence among adolescents and more serious forms of violence are extremely rare. Nevertheless, we expect that our efforts will stimulate future research and evaluation of our model. Approximately 22 percent of the sample reports having been in a fight over the previous six months.

## Table 9.1
## Descriptive Statistics, National Education Longitudinal Study (NELS)

| Endogenous Variables | Variable Description | Mean | S.D. |
|---|---|---|---|
| Family Income [a] | 15 categories: 1=$0 ... 15 >= $200,000. | 41,341.98 | 38,466.39 |
| Biological Parents [b] | Dummy coded 1 if respondent lives with both biological parents. | .65 | .48 |
| Prior Fighting [c] | 10th grade - In the past 12 months, how many times have you gotten into a physical fight in school? (0=never ; 1= once or more) | .16 | .37 |
| Negative Peer Influence [c] | 10th grade – How many of your close friends have dropped out of school? (0=none,some; 1=most,all) | .02 | .13 |
| Pro-Social Activity [c] | 10th grade – Hours per week spent on extra-curricular activities? (0=none; 1= <1, 2=1-4; 3=5-9; 4=10-19; 5= >19) | 1.35 | 1.46 |
| Violent Attitude [c] | 10th grade -- Do you feel its OK to get into physical fights? (0=rarely,never; 1=sometimes,often) | .09 | .28 |
| Professional Expectation [c] | 10th grade – What type of occupation do you expect to have at age 30? (1=professonal; 0=other) | .53 | .50 |
| Fighting [d] | 12th grade - In the past 12 months, how many times have you gotten into a physical fight in school or on your way to or from school? (0=never ; 1= once or more) | .14 | .35 |
| **Exogenous Variables** | | | |
| Community Context: [e] | | | |
| % Professional | % employed in an executive, administrative, managerial, or other professional occupations. | 15.22 | 7.41 |
| % Service | % employed in retail, handler, cleaner, helper or private occupations. | 9.45 | 2.62 |
| Disadvantage | Principal components scale combining, %below poverty line, % female-headed households, % of labor force unemployed, % African American. | .06 | 1.09 |
| % Urban | % of zip-code population within an urbanized area. | 57.82 | 46.52 |
| Individual Level: | | | |
| Race/Ethnicity [b] | Dummy coded. Reference category is white. | reported in text. | |
| Moved [b] | Dummy coded 1 if respondent moved in the prior 2 years. | .17 | .37 |
| Violence Exposure [b] | Scale (0-4) combining yes responses to 4 items: (1) Has someone threatened to hurt you at school, and are (2) physical conflicts (3) physical abuse of teachers and (4) verbal abuse of teachers a problem in your school? | .61 | .88 |
| Employed [c] | Dummy coded 1 if respondent is currently working. | .24 | .43 |
| Contact Sports [b] | Dummy coded 1 if respondent participated in varsity, intramural, or non-school team sports. | .71 | .46 |
| School Attachment [b] | Dummy coded 1 if respondent talks to his/her teachers in school. | .43 | .49 |
| Cut Class [c] | Dummy coded 1 if respondent has cut class in current school year. | .35 | .48 |
| Smoke Pot [c] | Dummy coded 1 if respondent has smoked pot in the last 30 days. | .11 | .31 |
| Drinking [c] | Dummy coded 1 if respondent drank alcohol in the last 30 days. | .42 | .49 |

*Note:* [a] Source: 1988 parent survey. [b] Source: 1988 student survey. [c] Source: 1990 student survey. [d] Source: 1992 student survey. [e] community context is measured using 1990 census data for zip-codes.

We include a range of indicators that reflect the respondent's exposure to prosocial and antisocial learning. Social learning variables are treated as precursors to fighting, but also as being partially shaped by local labor market opportunity and its implications for family processes. As a proxy for social learning of the rewards (versus punishments) of violence, we include a measure of fighting in the tenth grade (also as a binary response). Negative peer influence, an indicator of differential association with more antisocial peers, is measured as a dichotomy with a value of 1 indicating that most or all of the respondent's close friends have dropped out of school. Prosocial learning is reflected by a Likert scaled item (ranging from 0 to 5) indicating the number of hours per week the respondent spends in extracurricular activity. Violent attitudes, an indicator of antisocial learning, is derived from a question asking respondents in the second wave whether they feel that it is okay to get into physical fights (1 = sometimes/always, 0 = seldom/never). Ideally, we would utilize multiple measures of violent attitudes. Unfortunately, data constraints limit us to the use of one. It is, however, directly related and most relevant to our outcome of concern. Relatedly, literature on the attitude-behavior consistency controversy (Liska 1975) suggests that attitude measures that correspond closely to the behavioral outcome of interest, such as the one we employ, offer the most effective test of the relationship between attitude and behavior. The development of positive employment expectations for the future rounds out our measurement of social learning. Respondent's indicating that they expect to be employed in a professional occupation by age 30 are coded one and other expectations serve as the referent.

Family well-being is reflected by two indicators. Family income falls into a 15 category ordinal income scale ranging from 1 (none) to 15 ($200,000 or more). This variable has been recoded to reflect midpoints of each category. Parental structure is measured as a biological, two-parent family, with single-parent and single/step-parent households as the referent. These deviations from the traditional, two-parent family have been shown in prior research to be consequential for children due to turmoil/disruption, depressed resources, and a less than ideal socialization environment (e.g., Hess and Camara 1979; Hetherington, Cox, and Cox 1978; McLanahan and Sandefur 1994; Menaghan 1996; Sandefur, McLanahan, and Wojtkiewicz 1992).

Measurement of labor market attributes is largely consistent with current research on labor market opportunity, economic development, and related patterns of stratification (e.g., Tomaskovic-Devey and Roscigno 1996). Professional sector size is arguably the most important indicator of labor market opportunity, with likely implications for family well-being and social learning. Similarly, low-wage, service sector size is important given the emphasis of Wilson (1987, 1996) and criminological work that incorporates a labor market focus (Shihadeh and Ousey 1998; Crutchfield and Pitchford 1997). Low-wage, service sector size is comprised of the percentage of the civilian labor force employed in retail trade and other services such as cleaners or private security.

We also include two additional contextual measures in our models based on consistent effects demonstrated in prior research and to minimize the possibility of spurious results. Disadvantage is a principal components factor scale combining percent below the poverty line, percent female-headed households, percent of the labor force unemployed, and percent African American. Disadvantage also reflects aspects of inequality, racial competition, or cultural manifestation not adequately accounted for by labor market indicators. Percent urban reflects the percent of the community that resides within an urbanized area. Adjusting for urbanicity is important because it establishes that we are capturing effects of occupational structure as opposed to variations due simply to geographic residence or population density. Indeed, a good deal of prior theorizing attempts to tie subcultural formation to urban, poor, and non-white populations, rather than occupational structure. Because respondents are approximately evenly distributed across the rural/suburban/urban continuum, intercorrelations among structural variables are not excessively high and, hence, collinearity concerns are minimized. The highest variance inflation factor (VIF) in any equation presented is 2.6—which is considerably below typical levels of concern (i.e., VIF's > 4).

Along with labor market, family, and social learning variables, we include important controls that more fully reflect the respondent's demographic characteristics and social environment found to be predictive of delinquency in prior studies and whose exclusion may bias results.[7] Race and sex at the individual level have been shown elsewhere to be important correlates of adolescent delinquency. Relative to the involvement of white adolescents in violence, Asians generally exhibit lower levels, and African Americans, Latinos, and Native Americans higher levels (Hawkins, Laub, Lauritson, and Cothern 2000). Our data is reasonably distributed across racial/ethnic subgroups: 3.5 percent are Asian, 12.8 percent African American, 10 percent Latino, 1.3 percent Native American, 71.7 percent White, and .7 percent report "other race." We also include an indicator of whether or not the student has moved in the past two years. This selectivity control affords some confidence that the main effects we find are not biased by movement in and out of labor markets areas. This control also likely captures potential disruption and the breaking of social capital ties for adolescents, both of which tend to have negative consequences for adolescent well being (Ingersoll, Scamman, and Eckerling 1989; Reynolds 1991). Along with these more common controls we also include measures that take into account a wide range of common adolescent activities and experiences: exposure to violence in school, employment status, involvement in contact sports, school attachment, class attendance, and whether respondents currently use alcohol or marijuana. A more complete description of these variables is provided in Table 9.1.

*Analytic Strategy.* To produce correct estimates of standard errors and hence accurate hypothesis tests, standard OLS or logistic regression techniques rely on the assumption that error terms are uncorrelated across observations. This assumption is violated in multilevel data because of the clustering of observations within sampling units. As a result, standard errors are likely to be underestimated thus inflating t-values (point estimates remain unaffected). To address this issue, we undertake a hierarchical modeling procedure, available in Stata 6.0, that adjusts standard errors for clustering within zip-code areas.[8]

The analyses proceed in several steps. First, in Table 9.2, we examine effects of occupational structure on family income and structure for the entire sample. In Tables 9.3 and 9.4, we disentangle the effects of occupational structure on social learning for males and females. These models, which control for an individual's race, residential mobility, and social environment delineate varying processes across group and help us establish linkages to potentially mediating social learning processes in the occupational structure-adolescent violence relationship. Consistent with the causal ordering specified in our earlier theoretical discussion, we add family income and structure to the modeling of social learning processes.

The second portion of the analysis (Tables 9.5 and 9.6) examines adolescent male and female fighting. The first equation introduces labor market indicators and relevant controls. We add indicators of family well-being, and then successively include each social learning variable separately in equations 2 through 7. Equation 8 considers the combined effects of social learning indicators. In concert with relations established in Tables 9.2, 9.3 and 9.4, declining labor market effects across equations reflect mediation through more proximate family and social learning mechanisms.[9]

## Results

*Family Well-Being, Exposure, and Violent Attitudes as a Function of Labor Market Opportunity*

Table 9.2 reports the effects of local labor market opportunity and controls on family income and family structure. Consistent with what one would expect, family income is higher, and two-parent, biological families are more likely in contexts with greater professional-sector concentration. This is in contrast to effects pertaining to concentrated disadvantage. Disadvantage depresses overall family income and destabilizes traditional family structure ($p < .01$).

Influential among controls are urbanicity, race/ethnicity and whether the adolescent's family has moved over the past couple of years. Urbanism positively affects income, but decreases the likelihood that traditionally structured families will form or persist. Those families who have moved within the prior two years are more likely to have experienced instability. African Ameri-

Table 9.2
Hierarchical Regression Models of Occupational Structure on Family Well-
Being for Entire Sample (metric coefficients)

| Variables | Income (Ln) (1) B | Biological Parents [a] (2) B |
|---|---|---|
| Community Context | | |
| % Professional | .032** | .027** |
| % Service | -.001 | -.004 |
| Disadvantage | -.114* * | -.072* |
| % Urban | .001** | -.002** |
| | | |
| Individilal-level/colltrols | | |
| Asian | -.095** | .839** |
| African American | -.530** | -1.039** |
| Latino | -.517** | .117 |
| Native American | -.235* | -.137 |
| Other | -.376** | -.646** |
| Moved | -.097** | -.855** |
| | | |
| constant | 9.868 | .593 |
| R² orPsuedoR² | 186 | .062 |
| N | 16,017 | 16,017 |

*Note:* ** p < .05, two-tailed test. * p < .10, two-tailed test. a logistic model, logits presented. b coefficient multiplied by 10 to reduce places to the right of the decimal.

can, Latino, and Native Americans have less in the way of family income per year than do whites and Asians, and black families are less likely, and Asian families more likely, to be intact, on average.

Analyses of labor market opportunity effects on our indicators of social learning are reported in Table 9.3 for males and Table 9.4 for females. Throughout the remainder of the analysis, our discussion of findings will focus on the effect of community context on social learning processes and violence. Consistent with expectations, living in an area with an abundance of professionals reduces the likelihood of prior fighting, negative peer influences, and the development of a violent attitude, and increases the likelihood of participation in prosocial activity and internalization of professional expectations for the future. These findings are markedly consistent among males and females. Interestingly, however, service sector concentration, a labor market sector which is more likely to be occupied by females and that is characterized by lower wages and job instability, is inversely associated with negative peer influence among males and positively associated with negative peer influence for females. It may be the case that the close friends of female respondents are more likely to drop out of school in a context of significant service sector employment. Indeed, the stigma associated with working in the service sector is arguably less pronounced for females relative to males.

## Table 9.3
## Hierarchical Regression Models of Occupational Structure and Family Well-Being on Social Learning Processes for Males (unstandardized) [a]

| Variables | Prior Fighting | | Negative Peer Influence | | Pro-social Activity [a] | | Violent Attitude | | Professional Expectation | |
|---|---|---|---|---|---|---|---|---|---|---|
| | (1) | (2) | (3) | (4) | (5) | (6) | (7) | (8) | (9) | (10) |
| | B | B | B | B | B | B | B | B | B | B |
| **Community Context** | | | | | | | | | | |
| % Professional | -.024** | -.027** | -.062** | -.051** | .019** | .011* | -.024* | -.021 | .045** | .034** |
| % Service | -.035 | -.030 | -.067* | -.085** | .012 | .019 | .004 | -.001 | .020 | .030 |
| Disadvantage | -.079 | -.078 | -.076 | -.093 | -.099** | -.085** | -.139** | -.142** | .063 | .076 |
| % Urban | .0001 | .0002 | -.001 | -.0003 | -.002** | -.002** | .001 | .001 | .001 | .0004 |
| **Family Background** | | | | | | | | | | |
| Family Income | | [b] .002 | | [d] -.001** | | [b] .005** | | [d] -.004** | | [d] .008** |
| Biological Parents | | -.137 | | -.188 | | .252** | | .144 | | .041 |
| **Individual-level/controls** | | | | | | | | | | |
| Asian | -.407** | -.380** | .902 | .906 | -.184* | -.205* | -.346 | -.376 | .227 | .249* |
| African American | .295 | .298 | .969** | .775** | -.089 | .028 | .029 | .013 | -.208 | -.094 |
| Latino | -.169 | -.130 | .738** | .603* | -.081 | -.031 | -.266 | -.322* | -.088 | .016 |
| Native American | .133 | .149 | .846 | .781 | -.007 | .044 | .053 | .029 | -.242 | -.172 |
| Other | .727** | .727** | -.114 | -.266 | -.008 | .094 | .418 | .405 | -.446 | -.353 |
| Moved | .074 | .049 | .149 | .142 | -.006 | .048 | -.035 | -.009 | .297** | .324** |
| Violence Exposure | .213** | .215** | -.105 | -.128 | -.055** | -.042 | .132** | .128** | -.065* | -.052 |
| Employed | .259** | .271** | .157 | .148 | -.061 | -.061 | .242** | .229** | -.240** | -.230** |
| Contact Sports | -.154 | -.160 | -.061 | -.018 | .579** | .557** | -.019 | -.013 | .339** | .315** |
| School Attachment | -.012 | .014 | .052 | .051 | .247** | .241** | -.058 | -.059 | .225** | .224** |
| Cut Class | 1.024** | 1.019** | 1.207** | 1.217** | -.136** | -.134** | .925** | .932** | -.089 | -.093 |
| Smoke Pot | .515** | .517** | .789** | .753** | -.283** | -.262** | .439** | .437** | -.299** | -.288** |
| Drinking | .416** | .407** | .531** | .552** | .019 | .003 | .525** | .538** | .075 | .049 |
| constant | -1.321 | -1.326 | -3.798 | -3.255 | .719 | .389 | -2.457 | -2.416 | -1.278 | -1.584 |
| Psuedo $R^2$ or $R^2$ | .081 | .083 | .091 | .101 | .066 | .087 | .068 | .070 | .031 | .043 |
| N | 7870 | 7870 | 7870 | 7870 | 7870 | 7870 | 7870 | 7870 | 7870 | 7870 |

*Note:* **p<.05, two-tailed test. *p.10, two-tailed test. [a] equations 5 and 6 utilize multiple regression, other equations employ logistic regression (logits presented). [b] coefficient multiplied by 10,000 to reduce places to the right of the decimal. [c] coefficient multiplied by 100 to reduce places to the right of the decimal. [d] coefficient multiplied by 1,000 to reduce places to the right of the decimal.

## Table 9.4
### Hierarchical Regression Models of Occupational Structure and Family Well-Being on Social Learning Processes for Females (metric coefficients) [a]

| Variables | Prior Fighting (1) B | (2) B | Negative Peer Influence (3) B | (4) B | Pro-social Activity [a] (5) B | (6) B | Violent Attitude (7) B | (8) B | Professional Expectation (9) B | (10) B |
|---|---|---|---|---|---|---|---|---|---|---|
| **Community Context** | | | | | | | | | | |
| % Professional | -.037** | -.028** | -.055** | -.037 | .021** | .004 | -.066** | -.060** | .029** | .020** |
| % Service | -.025 | .024 | .107** | .103** | .016 | .023 | .001 | -.001 | .022 | .025 |
| Disadvantage | -.216** | -.227** | -.173 | -.191 | -.099** | -.074 | -.364** | -.371** | -.045 | -.046 |
| % Urban | -.001 | -.0003 | .007** | .008** | -.077 | -.003** | .002 | .002 | .002** | .002** |
| **Family Background** | | | | | | | | | | |
| Family Income | | [b].078** | | [b]-.168* | | [b].108** | | [b]-.044 | | [b].055** |
| Biological Parents | | .036 | | -.306 | | .421** | | -.049 | | .060 |
| **Individual-level/controls** | | | | | | | | | | |
| Asian | -.468 | -.439 | -.789 | -.758 | -.174 | -.256 | -.065 | -.042 | .408** | .396** |
| African American | 1.212** | 1.123** | -.025 | -.278 | -.215 | .049 | .527* | .465 | .141 | .239* |
| Latino | .497** | .407** | -.332 | -.472 | -.422** | -.292** | .242 | .202 | -.229* | -.156 |
| Native American | .878** | .833** | .164 | .039 | -.389 | .339 | .277 | .249 | .619** | .656** |
| Other | -2.272** | -2.337** | .146 | .085 | -.623* | -.468 | -.379 | -.394 | -.014 | .057 |
| Moved | .303* | .286 | .402 | .279 | -.014 | .116 | .103 | .075 | -.084 | -.048 |
| Violence Exposure | .356** | .340** | .008 | -.011 | -.103* | -.086** | -.069 | -.072 | .036 | .041 |
| Employed | .111 | .097 | .361 | .339 | .249** | .266** | -.065 | -.074 | .130 | .141* |
| Contact Sports | .044 | .061 | -.543* | -.479 | .564** | .537** | .193 | .209 | .189** | .171** |
| School Attachment | -.139 | -.129 | .018 | -.011 | .405** | .403** | -.468** | -.461** | .192** | .186** |
| Cut Class | 1.237** | 1.238** | .896** | .869** | -.234** | -.216** | 1.405** | 1.397** | -.206** | -.199** |
| Smoke Pot | .743** | .735** | 1.315** | 1.279** | -.649** | -.638** | 1.189** | 1.184** | -.328** | -.317** |
| Drinking | .197 | .194 | .293 | .269 | .023 | .027 | .139 | .133 | .068 | .066 |
| constant | -3.356 | -3.210 | -5.476 | -4.922 | -.291 | -.833 | -3.390 | -3.259 | -.597 | -.761 |
| R² or Psuedo R² | .120 | .124 | .099 | .114 | .052 | .075 | .115 | .117 | .023 | .028 |
| N | 8147 | 8147 | 8147 | 8147 | 8147 | 8147 | 8147 | 8147 | 8147 | 8147 |

*Note:* ** p<.05, two-tailed. * p<.10, two-tailed test. [a] equations 5 and 6 utilize multiple regression, other equations employ logistic regression (logits presented). [b] coefficient multipled by 10,000 to reduce places to the right of the decimal.

Noteworthy is the lack of a consistent influence of concentrated disadvantage on these outcomes.[10] There are two exceptions. First is an expected negative effect of disadvantage on respondents involvement in prosocial pursuits such as extracurricular activity. Second, however, is a negative effect of concentrated disadvantage on the adolescent feeling that its okay to fight—a relation that, if anything, runs counter to traditional arguments regarding "cultural deprivation" among racial or economic subgroups. This finding is important for at least two reasons. First, the community and city-level crime literature has documented a strong relationship between concentrated disadvantage and violent crime. Although scholars have debated the causes, subcultural processes are commonly assumed to partially underlie these effects. Our results suggest that disadvantaged contexts do not necessarily produce pro-violent attitudes. This conclusion is not necessarily contradictory to ethnographic accounts on street cultures in inner-city minority communities. Rather, our findings suggest that the primary reason for the emergence of violent normative structures in disadvantaged, inner-city contexts is that opportunities for professional employment are not available. It is within these contexts that illicit markets, such as drug dealing, encourage possession of firearms and the use of violence emerge.

The second equation of these models introduces potential mediating family economic and structural indicators. Although effects vary by social learning indicator and between males and females, coefficient magnitudes for professional sector effects generally decline, albeit modestly, suggesting some mediation through families. Among the family background measures, family income is more consequential in promoting prosocial and impeding antisocial learning (for males and females), whereas living with both biological parents facilitates involvement in extracurricular activity only. Although effects are largely parallel, it seems to be the case that family processes have a stronger general impact on females.

## Adolescent Fighting

Tables 9.5 and 9.6 report analyses of adolescent male and female fighting in twelfth grade. The first equation highlights the impact of local occupational structure, concentration of disadvantage, and relevant individual controls. Particularly noteworthy, given our predictions, is the negative effect of professional sector concentration ($p < .05$) on male adolescent violence (Table 9.5). Surprisingly, the professional sector coefficient is negative but does not attain statistical significance in the female equation ($t = -1.524$, $p<.128$), perhaps because of restricted variance in the fighting outcome among females. Notably, service sector concentration, disadvantage, and urbanism likewise exert no effect on either male or female fighting.

## Table 9.5

### Hierarchical Regression Models of Occupational Structure, Family Well-Being, and Social Learning Processes on Adolescent Fighting for Males (metric coefficients)

| | | | | Adolescent Fighting [a] | | | | |
|---|---|---|---|---|---|---|---|---|
| | (1) | (2) | (3) | (4) | (5) | (6) | (7) | (8) |
| Variables | B | B | B | B | B | B | B | B |
| **Community Context** | | | | | | | | |
| % Professional | -.024** | -.019* | -.020 | -.023* | -.023* | -.021* | -.021* | -.009 |
| % Service | -.069 | -.076* | -.064 | -.068 | -.068 | -.071 | -.068* | -.071 |
| Disadvantage | .101 | .093 | .132 | .102 | .095 | .124 | .107 | .138* |
| % Urban | c-.0001 | c.006 | c-.002 | c-.001 | c-.002 | c-.003 | .001 | c-.002 |
| **Family Background** | | | | | | | | |
| Family Income | | d-.004** | | | | | | d-.003* |
| Biological Parents | | -.177 | | | | | | -.138 |
| **Social Learning Process** | | | | | | | | |
| Prior Fighting | | | 1.375** | .714** | | | | 1.289** |
| Negative Peer Influence | | | | | | | | .538** |
| Pro-Social Activity | | | | | -.088** | | | -.069* |
| Violent Attitude | | | | | | .884** | | .529** |
| Professional Expectation | | | | | | | -.398** | -.283** |
| **Individual-level/controls** | | | | | | | | |
| Asian | -.381* | -.374* | -.285 | -.393* | -.406* | -.354 | -.356 | -.283 |
| African American | .264 | .176 | .223 | .257 | .251 | .267 | .250 | .133 |
| Latino | .038 | -.007 | .093 | .032 | .033 | .073 | .040 | .064 |
| Native American | .821** | .802** | .909* | .798** | .801* | .806** | .814* | .859 |
| Other | .148 | .099 | .025 | .147 | .155 | .108 | .091 | -.082 |
| Moved | -.106 | -.137 | -.115 | -.112 | -.109 | -.101 | -.082 | -.119 |
| Violence Exposure | .194** | .187** | .143** | .194** | .194** | .182** | .192** | .130** |
| Employed | -.039 | -.042 | -.102 | -.040 | -.052 | -.069 | -.062 | -.152 |
| Contact Sports | -.033 | -.013 | -.018 | .028 | .019 | -.025 | -.004 | .062 |
| School Attachment | -.135 | -.133 | -.137 | -.136 | -.118 | -.126 | -.111 | -.103 |
| Cut Class | .647** | .647** | .422** | .632** | .637** | .559** | .642** | .360** |
| Smoke Pot | .352** | .337** | .235** | .336** | .323** | .294** | .323** | .131 |
| Drinking | .269** | .278** | .177 | .264** | .267** | .214** | .273** | .154 |
| constant | -.736 | -.480 | -1.077 | -.770 | -.666 | -.827 | -.649 | -.769 |
| Psuedo R² | .046 | .050 | .105 | .048 | .049 | .063 | .052 | .121 |
| N | 7037 | 7037 | 7037 | 7037 | 7037 | 7037 | 7037 | 7037 |

*Note:* ** p<.05, two-tailed test. * p<.10, two-tailed test. [a] logistic model, logits presented. [b] coefficient multiplied by 10,000 to reduce places to the right of the decimal. [c] coefficient multiplied by 100 to reduce places to the right of the decimal. [d] coefficient multiplied by 1,000 to reduce places to the right of the decimal.

## Table 9.6
### Hierarchical Regression Models of Occupational Structure, Family Well-Being, and Social Learning Processes on Adolescent Fighting for Females (metric coefficients)

| Variables | Adolescent Fighting [a] | | | | | | | |
|---|---|---|---|---|---|---|---|---|
| | (1) B | (2) B | (3) B | (4) B | (5) B | (6) B | (7) B | (8) B |
| **Community Context** | | | | | | | | |
| % Professional | -.023 | -.014 | -.014 | -.022 | -.021 | -.019 | -.019 | -.001 |
| % Service | .001 | -.001 | -.003 | .001 | .006 | .001 | .004 | -.002 |
| Disadvantage | .008 | .002 | .095 | .008 | [c].004 | .031 | .007 | .090 |
| % Urban | .001 | .001 | [c].001 | .001 | [c].005 | .001 | .001 | [c].001 |
| **Family Background** | | | | | | | | |
| Family Income | | [d]-.068** | | | | | | [d]-.048 |
| Biological Parents | | -.124 | | | | | | -.107 |
| **Social Learning Process** | | | | | | | | |
| Prior Fighting | | | 2.065** | | | | | 1.943** |
| Negative Peer Influence | | | | .935** | | | | .706 |
| Pro-Social Activity | | | | | -.177** | | | -.078 |
| Violent Attitude | | | | | | 1.179** | | .449 |
| Professional Expectation | | | | | | | -.538** | -.437** |
| **Individual-level/controls** | | | | | | | | |
| Asian | .556 | .583 | .681 | .561 | .522* | .558 | .614 | .709 |
| African American | 1.161** | 1.038** | .873** | 1.167** | 1.132** | 1.147** | 1.174** | .796** |
| Latino | .690** | .611** | .617** | .694** | .647** | .691** | .682** | .559** |
| Native American | 1.098** | 1.038** | .903** | 1.103** | 1.097** | 1.109** | 1.149** | .939** |
| Other | -.093 | -.129 | .225 | -.086 | -.043 | -.057 | -.041 | .263 |
| Moved | -.139 | -.188 | -.264 | -.148 | -.171 | -.158 | -.137 | -.310 |
| Violence Exposure | .136* | .136* | .016 | .139* | .127 | .148* | .143* | .039 |
| Employed | -.078 | -.094 | -.119 | -.092 | -.069 | -.062 | -.064 | -.116 |
| Contact Sports | -.068 | -.044 | -.115 | -.055 | .001 | -.085 | -.049 | -.053 |
| School Attachment | .025 | .028 | .055 | .019 | .068 | .056 | .060 | .111 |
| Cut Class | .726** | .715** | .451** | .718** | .695** | .647** | .698** | .389** |
| Smoke Pot | .566** | .551** | .393* | .528** | .511** | .455** | .513** | .251 |
| Drinking | .103 | .097 | .053 | .093 | .081 | .092** | .117** | .031 |
| constant | -3.097 | -2.857 | -3.202 | -3.111 | -2.962 | -3.187 | -2.920 | -2.845 |
| Psuedo R² | .071 | .076 | .149 | .074 | .077 | .083 | .079 | .163 |
| N | 7321 | 7321 | 7321 | 7321 | 7321 | 7321 | 7321 | 7321 |

*Note:* ** p<.05, two-tailed. * p<.10, two-tailed test. [a] logistic model, logistic model, logits presented. [b] coefficient multiplied by 10,000 to reduce places to the right of the decimal. [c] coefficient multiplied by 100 to reduce places to the right of the decimal. [d] coefficient multiplied by 1,000 to reduce places to the right of the decimal.

Family income and family structure clearly mediate some of the professional sector effects, as is evident in coefficient declines across equations 1 and 2. The professional sector effect declines by 21 percent for males and even more so (39 percent) for females. This mediation should come as no surprise given our earlier findings in Table 9.2. Labor markets of enhanced opportunity are conducive to higher income and more intact families. Income in particular decreases the likelihood that violence will emerge (p < .05). Once family well-being is controlled, we find a negative, and significant effect of low-wage service sector concentration on the likelihood of adolescent fighting. We suspect that this influence is net of the negative effects of this sector (i.e., its high unemployment and negative effect on family income), and may reflect a positive impact of employment, generally speaking (see also Shihadeh and Ousey 1998).

Equations 3 through 7 of Tables 9.5 and 9.6 successively introduce social learning indicators to the model. The indicators behave empirically as one might expect, and the professional sector coefficient declines across equations, again indicating some mediation of community context through more proximate micro processes. Among males and females, prior fighting, negative peers, and a violent attitude increase the likelihood of adolescent fighting net of controls, and participation in prosocial activity and internalization of professional occupational expectations decreases it. The final equation (equation 8) includes all of the family background and social learning variables. Noteworthy is that these mechanisms combined mediate 62 percent of the effect of professional sector employment on fighting among males and virtually all of the effect among females (95 percent), and partially explain why family income is meaningful in shaping violence. Among males, each of the social learning process indicators are significant in the fully specified model. Female fighting is more directly influenced by prior fighting, which reflects in part social learning of the rewards of violence, and the development and internalization of professional occupational aspirations for the future.

These findings offer considerable support for our argument that local labor market context matters, and that its impact is partially mediated through family processes and social learning processes. Particularly important is that these effects hold up after accounting for important individual controls. Likewise, the effects remain with a concentrated disadvantage indicator included— long thought of as a fundamental feature of place that shapes subcultural tendencies and related behavioral manifestations.

## Discussion and Conclusions

Subcultural models have long been employed to explain the distribution of violence across locales, focusing on the development and internalization of violent values, attitudes, and lifestyles. Akers (1998), drawing from differential association theory, social learning, and structural criminological traditions, has recently proposed a variation—a social structure and social learning model—that posits that structural causes of violence are mediated through social learning processes. In this chapter, we drew from and built on the SSSL model by highlighting the importance of local opportunity for family well-being, pro and antisocial learning, and fighting. We then tested these relations on a representative sample, and by employing appropriate analytic techniques given the hierarchical nature of the relations described and the structure of the data. We also disaggregated findings for males and females with the assumption that influential mediating processes may differ.

Results are not only supportive of Akers' (1998) SSSL formulation and our extension of it, but they challenge conventional wisdom and traditional perspectives pertaining to subcultural emergence. Among males, concentration of professional sector employment is associated with enhanced family well-being, fewer prior encounters with violence and negative peers, a reduced risk of violent attitude internalization, increased participation in extracurricular activity and heightened occupational expectations, and a diminished likelihood fighting. Consistent with our elaboration, professional sector effects are mediated almost entirely through the processes outlined above.

We find no evidence that concentrated disadvantage is consistently associated with social learning processes promoting violence. Rather, it is the presence of adults employed in high-wage sectors of the economy that reduces the likelihood of violence by shaping, in part, the pattern of imitation and role modeling that adolescents adopt. Adolescents residing in areas of constricted opportunity appear to have a greater potential for antisocial learning and may, for instance, adopt an oppositional or defiant, pro-violent attitude or seek status among negative peers. Within such a context, status may be attained by demonstrating courage and physical prowess by being ready and willing to fight (Anderson 1999). Interestingly, the links we have specified, especially between family well-being and violence and between social learning and violence, are relatively consistent for males and females and, if anything, appear stronger for females. This throws some question on the assumption of distinct processes and raises important empirical and theoretical questions. Do males and females actually differ in the processes leading up to violence, as is often assumed? Has violent expression become more acceptable for females over time, leading to a closing of the processual gap between sexes? Our analyses shed some light on these possibilities, although further analyses (cross-sectional, comparative, and historical) are clearly warranted.

Aside from disaggregating by sex and specifying important linkages between labor market opportunity on the one hand and adolescent violence on the other, the findings reported complement and inform qualitative accounts of adolescent subcultural processes. Such work tends to tie delinquency-specific, adolescent processes to particular race or class groupings. Anderson (1990, 1999), for instance, documents the existence of street codes, which condone the use of violence as a strategy to survive on the street, in an inner-city, minority community. Our results suggest that the adolescent street cultures, such as those Anderson (1990, 1999) describes, emerge not necessarily because of the concentration of disadvantage, but rather because of the relative absence in the community of professional role models and a decline in employment opportunities—both of which may communicate to adolescents that their future holds no realistic possibility of mainstream economic success. Thus, rather than inherent to a population or place, the emergence of antisocial learning and behavior "must be viewed in its social and political context," as a "mean adaptation to blocked opportunities..." (Anderson 1990: 112-113).

We believe that extending the focus of research on adolescents and delinquency specifically, and subcultural theories more generally, to local labor market processes and opportunities will be important for those interested in examining the spatial patterning of violence. Moreover, we caution future research against the assumption that disadvantage indicators such as poverty rates or racial composition are reasonable proxies for, or precursors to, subcultural formation. Finally, and perhaps most important, is the lesson that local context is meaningful for spatial and individual-level outcomes, and that this influence is often indirect through more proximate, micro-level experiential and attitudinal processes.

## Notes

1.    An earlier version of this paper was presented at the 1999 meetings of the American Society of Criminology. Direct all correspondence to Paul Bellair, Department of Sociology, 300 Bricker Hall, 190 N. Oval Mall, The Ohio State University, Columbus, OH 43210.
2.    For an exception, see Agnew's (1992) "general strain theory," which is explicitly not tied to a class-crime relationship. Agnew argues that adverse community characteristics such as poverty, family disruption, or unemployment impede residents from achieving positively valued goals. As a result, residents are more likely to experience negative emotions such as stress, anger, and frustration, which may find expression in violent behavior. Other recent revisions refine and expand the perspective to explain cross-national and community differences. Messner and Rosenfeld (1994), for instance, argue that American culture is dominated by the pursuit of material wealth, rendering noneconomic functions and roles that otherwise exert social control less effective.
3.    Shaw and McKay (1942) were among the first U.S. sociologists to argue that criminal behavior patterns are passed across generations. They maintained that young children reared in delinquency areas are more likely to be exposed to, and thus more likely to model, associate with, and internalize the unconventional attitudes and behavior of older delinquent children, adolescents, and adults. A precursor to differential association and social learning models, their theory is useful for

understanding why violence remains an every day occurrence in some community areas over long periods of time despite substantial turnover in the population.

4. That analysis also uses an analytical technique (a maximum likelihood, LISREL) that does not account for clustering of observations within schools and thus underestimates the standard errors of contextual variables in the model (Goldstein 1995).

5. We also drew from the principal's survey and entered characteristics of schools into our models including: percent minority, percent receiving a free lunch (a proxy for poverty), and a range of measures reflecting the principal's perception of social and behavioral problems (drugs, violence, gangs, etc.) in the school. These measures did not emerge as significant predictors in any of our models. In the interest of parsimony, we therefore dropped them from our models.

6. Missing data is not a major issue in NELS. Of the variables examined in our models, family income was by far the least likely to be reported. We imputed income values for 1,544 cases, roughly 9.6 percent of our sample.

7. There is virtually no variation in the age of respondents because they are all in the same grade. Thus, a control for age, when included, is not significant.

8. We resort to the procedure available in Stata because it provides stable estimates and corrected standard errors for clustered data and for data with small within area samples. The majority of zip-code areas in our sample contain only one respondent. Stata also permits estimation of logistic models with sample weights—a limitation of alternative packages such as HLM or MLwiN. Estimates of unstandardized coefficients obtained using traditional OLS and logistic regression techniques are identical to those presented. However, consistent with statistical theory on hierarchical models (Goldstein 1995), traditional regression techniques produced estimates of standard errors which were 50 percent to 70 percent smaller, and thus yielded inflated t values.

9. The effects of family and social learning variables may vary across context. However, space limitations preclude the development of theory and hypotheses for expecting and predicting the direction of these effects. We therefore defer exploration of cross-level interactions for future research and focus on the primary goal of this chapter—evaluating the prediction of Akers social structure and social learning model and our elaboration of it that structural effects are *mediated* by family and social learning processes.

10. We also examine specifications that include a square term for disadvantage in all of the models as suggested by prior research (Krivo and Peterson 1996). This coefficient was not significant in any equation.

## References

Agnew, Robert. 1992. "Foundation for a General Strain Theory of Crime and Delinquency." *Criminology* 30:47-88.

Agnew, Robert, and T. Brezina. 1997. "Relational Problems with Peers, Gender, and Delinquency." *Youth & Society* 29:84-111.

Ainsworth-Darnell, J. W., and D. B. Downey. 1998. "Assessing the Oppositional Culture Explanation for Racial/Ethnic Differences in School Performance." *American Sociological Review* 63:536-553.

Akers, Ronald L. 1985. *Deviant Behavior: A Social Learning Approach, 3rd ed*. Belmont, CA: Wadsworth.

_____. 1998. *Social Learning and Social Structure: A General Theory of Crime and Deviance*. Boston: Northeastern University Press.

Akers, Ronald L., Marvin D. Krohn, Lonn Lanza-Kaduce, and Marcia Radovich. 1979. "Social Learning and Deviant Behavior: A Specific Test of a General Theory." *American Sociological Review* 44:636-655.

Alex-Assensoh, Yvette. 1995. "Myths About Race and the Underclass: Concentrated Poverty and 'Underclass Behaviors'." *Urban Affairs Review* 31:3-19.

Anderson, Elijah. 1990. *Streetwise: Race Class and Change in an Urban Community*. Chicago: University of Chicago Press.

_____. 1999. *Code of the Street: Decency, Violence, and the Moral life of the Inner City*. New York : W. W. Norton.

Ball-Rokeach, Sandra J. 1973. "Values and Violence: A Test of the Subculture of Violence Thesis." *American Sociological Review* 38:736-749.

Bandura, Albert. 1986. *Social Foundations of Thought and Action: A Social Cognitive Theory*. Englewood Cliffs, NJ: Prentice-Hall.

Bellair, Paul E. 1997. "Social Interaction and Community Crime: Examining the Importance of Neighbor Networks." *Criminology* 35: 677-704.

Burgess, Robert L., and Ronald L. Akers. 1966. "A Differential Association-Reinforcement Theory of Criminal Behavior." *Social Problem* 14:128-147.

Blau, Peter, and Judith Blau. 1982. "The Cost of Inequality: Metropolitan Structure and Violent Crime". *American Sociological Review* 47: 114-129.

Brooks-Gunn, Jeane, Greg J. Duncun, and J. Lawrence Aber. 1997. *Neighborhood Poverty, Volume 1: Context and Consequences for Children*. New York: Russell Sage.

Bruce, Marino A., Vincent J. Roscigno, and Patricia L. McCall. 1998. "Structure, Context, and Agency in the Reproduction of Black-on-Black Violence." *Theoretical Criminology* 2:29-55.

Bursik, Robert J., and Harold G. Grasmick. 1993. *Neighborhoods and Crime*. New York: Lexington Books.

Cantor, David, and Kenneth C. Land. 1985. "Unemployment and Crime Rates in the Post-WW II United States: A Theoretical and Empirical Analysis." *American Sociological Review* 50:317-332.

Chiricos, Theodore G. 1987. "Rates of Crime and Unemployment: An Analysis of Aggregate Research Evidence." *Social Problems* 34: 187-212.

Cloward, Richard, and Lloyd Ohlin. 1960. *Delinquency and Opportunity*. Glencoe, IL: Free Press.

Cohen, Albert. 1955. *Delinquent Boys*. Glencoe, IL: Free Press

Coleman, James S. 1990. *Foundations of Social Theory*. Cambridge, MA: Harvard University Press.

Cook, Philip J., and John H. Laub. 1998. "The Unprecedented Epidemic in Youth Violence." In Michael Tonry and Mark H. Moore (eds.), *Youth Violence*. Chicago: University of Chicago Press.

Cook, Philip J., and Ludwig Jens. 1998. "The Burden of 'Acting White': Do Black Adolescents Disparage Academic Achievement?" Pp. 375-400 in C. Jencks and M. Phillips (eds.), *The Black-White Test Score Gap*. Washington, D.C.: Brookings Institution Press.

Coughlin, C., and S. Vuchinich. 1996. "Family Experience in Preadolescence and the Development of Male Delinquency." *Journal of Marriage and Family* 58:491-501.

Crutchfield, Robert D., and Susan R. Pitchford. 1997. "Work and Crime: The Effects of Labor Market Stratification." *Social Forces* 76:93-118.

Fagan, Jeffrey E. 1993. "The Political Economy of Drug Dealing Among Urban Gangs." Pp. 19-54 in R. Davis, A. Lurgicio, and D. P. Rosenbaum (eds), *Drugs and Community*. Springfield, IL: Charles C. Thomas.

Felson, Richard B., Allen E. Liska, Scott J. South, and Thomas L. McNulty. 1994. "The Subculture of Violence and Delinquency: Individual vs. School Context Effects." *Social Forces* 73 (5): 155-174.

Gastil, Raymond D. 1971. "Homicide and a Regional Culture of Violence." *American Sociological Review* 36: 412-427.

Goldstein, Harvey. 1995. *Multi-Level Statistical Models*. New York: Halstead Press.

Hawkins, Darnell F., John H. Laub, Janet L. Lauritson, and Lynn Cothern. 2000. *Race, Ethnicity, and Serious and Violent Juvenile Offending*. Washington, D.C: U.S. Department of Justice, Office of Justice Programs, Office of Juvenile Justice and Delinquency Prevention.

Heimer, Karen. 1997. "Socioeconomic Status, Subcultural Definitions, and Violent Delinquency." *Social Forces* 75: 799-833.

Hess, Robert D., and Kathleen A. Camara. 1979. "Post-Divorce Family Relationships as Mediating Factors in the Consequences of Divorce for Children." *Journal of Social Issues* 35:79-98.

Hetherington, E.Mavis, Martha Cox, and Roger Cox. 1978. "The Aftermath of Divorce." Pp. 149-176 in Joseph H. Stevens and Marilyn Matthews (eds.), *Mother-Child, Father-Child Relationships* Washington, D.C.: National Association for the Education of Young Children.

Hodson, Randy. 1978. "Labor in the Monopoly, Competitive, and State Sectors of Production." *Politics & Society* 8:429-480.

_____. 1983. *Workers' Earnings and Corporate Economic Structure*. New York: Academic.

Hochschild, J. L. 1995. *Facing Up to the American Dream: Race, Class, and the Soul of the Nation*. Princeton, N.J.: Princeton University Press.

Howell, Jay C. 1998. *Youth Gangs: An Overview*. Washington, D.C: U.S. Department of Justice, Office of Justice Programs, Office of Juvenile Justice and Delinquency Prevention.

Huff-Corzine, Lin, Jay Corzine, and David C. Moore. 1986. "Southern Exposure: Deciphering the South's Influence on Homicide Rates." *Social Forces* 64:906-24.

Ingersoll, Gary M., James P. Scamman, and Wayne D. Eckerling. 1989. "Geographic Mobility and Student Achievement in an Urban Setting." *Educational Evaluation and Policy Analysis* 11:143-149.

Jinn, J. H., and J. Sedransk. 1989. "Effects on Secondary Data Analysis of Common Imputation Methods." Pp. 213-241 in Clifford Clogg (ed.), *Sociological Methodology, 1989*. Oxford: Basil Blackwell.

Kasarda, John D. 1987. "Urban Industrial Transition and the Underclass." *Annals of the American Academy of Political and Social Science* 501:26-47.

Klein, Malcolm W. 1995. *The American Street Gang*. New York: Oxford University Press.

Kornhauser, Ruth. 1978. *Social Sources of Delinquency: An Appraisal of Analytic Models*. Chicago: University of Chicago Press.

Krivo, Lauren, and Ruth Peterson. 1996. "Extremely Disadvantaged Neighborhoods and Urban Crime". *Social Forces* 75:619-648.

Land, Kenneth C., Patricia L. McCall, and Lawrence E. Cohen. 1990. "Structural Covariates of Homicide: Are There Any Invariances Across Time and Space?" *American Journal of Sociology* 95: 922-963.

Liska, Allen E. 1975. *The Consistency Controversy: Readings on the Impact of Attitude on Behavior*. New York: Wiley.

Liska, Allen E., and Paul E. Bellair. 1995. "Racial Composition and Violent Crime: Convergence over Time." *American Journal of Sociology* 101: 578-610.

Liu, X.R., and H. B. Kaplan. 1999. "Explaining the Gender Difference in Adolescent Delinquent Behavior: A Longitudinal Test of Mediating Mechanisms." *Criminology* 37:195-215.

Massey, Douglas S., and Nancy A. Denton. 1993. *American Apartheid*. Cambridge: Harvard University Press.

Matsueda, Ross L. 1982. "Testing Control-Theory and Differential Association—A Causal Modeling Approach." *American Sociological Review* 47: 489-504

_____. 1988. "The Current State of Differential Association Theory." *Crime and Delinquency* 34:277-306.

McCarthy, B., J. Hagan, and T. S. Woodward. 1999. "In the Company of Women: Structure and Agency in a Revised Power-Control Theory of Gender and Delinquency." *Criminology* 37: 761-788.

McLanahan, Sara, and Gary Sandefur. 1994. *Growing Up With A Single Parent: What Hurts, What Helps*. Cambridge, MA: Harvard University Press.

Menaghan, Elizabeth G. 1996. "Family Composition, Family Interaction, and Children's Academic and Behavior Problems: Interpreting the Data." Pp. 185-196 in Alan Booth and Judith F. Dunn (eds.), *Family-School Links: How Do They Effect Educational Outcomes?* Hillsdale, NJ: Erlbaum.

Merton, Robert K. 1938. "Social Structure and Anomie." *American Sociological Review* 3:672-682.

Messerschmidt, James W. 2000. *Nine Lives: Adolescent Masculinities, the Body, and Violence*. Boulder, CO: Westview.

Messner, Steven F. 1983. "Regional and Racial Effects on the Urban Homicide Rate - The Subculture of Violence Revisited." *American Journal of Sociology* 88:997-1007.

Messner, Steven F., and Richard Rosenfeld. 1994. *Crime and the American Dream*. Belmont, CA: Wadsworth.

Mickelson, Roslyn A. 1990. "The Attitude-Achievement Paradox Among Black Adolescents." *Sociology of Education* 63:44-61.

Miller, Walter B. 1958. "Lower Class Culture as a Generating Milieu of Gang Delinquency." *Journal of Social Issues* 14:5-19.

Moffitt, Terrie E. 1993. "Adolescence-Limited and Life-Course-Persistent Anti-Social Behavior: A Developmental Taxonomy." *Psychological Review* 100: 674-701.

National Center for Education Statistics (NCES). 1992. *First Follow-Up: Student Component Data File User's Manual*. Washington, D.C.: U.S. Department of Education.

Reynolds, Arthur J. 1991. "Early Schooling of Children at Risk." *American Educational Research Journal* 28 (2):392-422.

Rotter, Julian. 1954. *Social Learning and Clinical Psychology*. Englewood Cliffs, NJ: Prentice-Hall.

Roscigno, Vincent J. 1995. "The Social Embeddedness of Racial Educational Inequality: The Black-White Gap and the Impact of Racial and Local Political-Economic Contexts." *Research in Social Stratification and Mobility* 14:135-165.

Rountree, Pamela W., and Barbara D. Warner. 1999. "Social Ties and Crime: Is the Relationship Gendered?" *Criminology* 37: (4) 789-813.

Sampson, Robert J., Jeffrey D. Morenoff, and Felton Earls. 1999. "Beyond Social Capital: Spatial Dynamics of Collective Efficacy for Children." *American Sociological Review* 64:633-660.

Sampson, Robert J., Stephen W. Raudenbush, and Felton Earls. 1997. "Neighborhoods and Violent Crime: A Multilevel Study of Collective Efficacy." *Science* 277:918-924.

Sampson, Robert J., and William Julius Wilson. 1995. "Toward a Theory of Race, Crime, and Urban Inequality." In John Hagan and Ruth D. Peterson (eds.), *Crime and Inequality*. Stanford, CA: Stanford University Press.

Sandefur, Gary D., Sara McLanahan, and Roger A. Wojtkiewicz. 1992. "The Effects of Parental Marital Status During Adolescence on High School Graduation." *Social Forces* 71:103-121.

Shaw, Clifford, and Henry McKay. 1942. *Juvenile Delinquency and Urban Areas.* Chicago: University of Chicago Press.

Shihadeh, E. S., and G. C. Ousey. 1998. "Industrial Restructuring and Violence: The Link Between Entry-Level Jobs, Economic Deprivation, and Black and White Homicide." *Social Forces* 77:185-206.

Sutherland, Edwin. 1939. *Criminology.* Philadelphia: J. B. Lippincott.

Tomaskovic-Devey, Donald. 1987. "Labor Markets, Industrial Structure, and Poverty: A Theoretical Discussion and Empirical Example." *Rural Sociology* 52:56-74.

Tomaskovic-Devey, Donald, and Vincent J. Roscigno. 1996. "Racial Economic Subordination and White Gain in the U.S. South." *American Sociological Review* 61:565-589.

Triplett, R., and G. R. Jarjoura. 1997. "Specifying the Gender-Class-Delinquency Relationship: Exploring the Effects of Educational Expectations." *Sociological Perspectives* 40:287-316.

Warr, Mark, and Mark Stafford. 1991. "The Influence of Delinquent Peers: What They Think or What They Do?" *Criminology* 4:851-866.

Wilson, William J. 1987. *The Truly Disadvantaged: The Inner City, The Underclass, and Public Policy.* Chicago: University of Chicago Press.

_____. 1996. *When Work Disappears: The World of the New Urban Poor.* New York: Alfred A. Knopf.

Wolfgang, Marvin E., and Franco Feracuti. 1967. *The Subculture of Violence.* London: Social Science Paperbacks.

# 10

# Confessions of a Dying Thief:
# A Tutorial on Differential Association

*Darrell Steffensmeier and Jeffery Ulmer*

Our purpose in this chapter is to clarify and broaden key elements of differential-association/social-learning theory, using illustrative quotes from the life history of "Sam Goodman"—a longtime "thief" and quasi-legitimate businessman who died in the 1990s following a four-month bout with lung cancer. Sam was the principal subject of Darrell Steffensmeier's *The Fence: In the Shadow of Two Worlds*. His lengthy criminal career spanned fifty years and encompassed burglary, fencing, and rackets, and he maintained extensive network ties in both the underworld and the world of legitimate small business. We are especially interested in illuminating the nuances and details of differential social organization, as well as the processual shifts and oscillations of the differential-association/social-learning process. Sam Goodman's life history narratives reveal crime and criminal careers not so much as discrete events or series of events, but as a process that can be marked by amplification spirals, shifts, and oscillations, and waxing and waning commitments to crime and criminal others. We use the interview material from Sam Goodman to argue nine critical points about criminal specialization vs. generalization, crime and the life course, the conceptualization of criminal careers, and assumptions about human nature upon which criminological theories are based.

Since his first meeting with Sam in the 1970s, Darrell Steffensmeier maintained regular contact with him and also met many of his associates both in the underworld and on its edge. Steffensmeier is now completing a monograph entitled: *Confessions of a Dying Thief: Sam Goodman—Burglar, Conman, Dealer in Stolen Goods, (Illicit) Entrepreneur*. A culmination of many years of contact with Sam, *Confessions* draws heavily from *deathbed* interviews with Sam not only about the underworld and his place in it, but also about death, God, and religion; about women, family, and relationships; and about Sam's initial wariness but eventual acceptance of Steffensmeier, whom Sam called "the professor." The Friday morning interview began with a "real wake-up" and is quoted in some detail here, since it sets the stage for our application of *Confessions* toward an understanding of differential-association/social-learning theory, as well as themes from labeling theory.

### Sam Assesses His Situation

*I'm going to lick this fucking cancer. Get my legs back, be back at running my shop. Get on Donnie and Benny's asses. They need that. Before I didn't care. Now my mind is on getting fucking better. No doubt I'm gonna get better.*

 . . . 15 minutes later

*I do know I am not going to make it. Asked the Doc about seeing another specialist. He gave it to me plain, very Goddamn plain: "Sam, there ain't time for that. Get your house in order, with your grandchildren, with Melody. It's too late. If you had started treatment when it was first spotted, then maybe." I says, "How long?" He tells me, "Give or take a little, six weeks, three months. Maybe sooner."*

*That hit home like a ton of bricks fell on my nuts. Kicked right in the belly is the way it felt. Whew, I am thinking how fast this year went by and bang here it is already. A year ago the doctor told me I had a dark spot on my lung, that we should do some tests to check it out. That was in April. I thought right away, fuck, it is cancer. But I ignored him. Kept right on smoking. I'm thinking, people with cancer live a long time—5, 6, 10 years. No big deal—have to die sometime anyway. Didn't worry about it, not realizing how quick it can be and what you have to go through. I thought, you get the cancer, take pills and that, and then you just die. But it don't work that way. That year went so awful fast. At that time I didn't care. But as it got closer, Goddamn, you know you wanna live.*

*I was ready to go. I had made my peace. My will and the shop stuff were taken care of. So much goes to my daughter, so much goes to my grandchildren. So much to Wanda and to Donnie to keep the shop going. Benny will get the shop but if he gives it up, then it goes to Donnie and Wanda. Wanda is the best woman I've met in my life. Has stuck with me the most. But I don't think I've found that woman yet who meant a lot to me.*

*It's funny how me and Wanda got hooked up, as honest as she is. Listen to this. Just before I went into the hospital, we're leaving a restaurant and Wanda finds a $20 bill on the floor by the cash register. She picks it up and gives it to the lady behind the cash register, "Here, you musta dropped this." Holy fuck, I could've rung her neck. But that is the way she is.*

*Looking back, whew, so damn much has happened. I pulled a lotta rank shit in my life, lotta rank shit. But helped a whole lotta people, too. If somebody needed something, came into my shop, I more or less gave it away. Was very fair that way. How did it all start? It is hard to remember all the twists and turns...*

## Key Elements of Differential-Association/Social-Learning Theory

That delinquent/criminal behavior, like most social behavior, is learned and that it is learned in the process of social interaction are at the core of differential association and social learning theory. In Sutherland's (1947) classic statement, criminal or delinquent behavior involves the learning of (a) techniques of committing crimes and (b) orientations (motives, drives, rationalizations) and attitudes favorable to violation of law.

Akers (1985, 1998; Akers et al. 1979) combines Sutherland's ideas with Sykes and Matza's (1957) theory of vocabularies of motive and crime, and developments in social psychology that post-dated Sutherland to articulate a social-learning theory of crime that specifies the process of differential association in more detail and specificity. According to Akers, crime is learned through three conceptually distinct—but potentially interrelated—social processes: differential association, differential reinforcement, and imitation.

The behaviors of peers or associates may be as or more important than the attitudes of peers in influencing an individual's own delinquency (Warr and Stafford 1991), just as one's past delinquency is likely to forecast greater risk for future delinquency. In sum, socialization favorable to crime involves learning definitions, attitudes, behaviors, skills, and vocabularies of motives favorable to given forms of deviance (Sutherland 1947; Akers et al. 1979; Sykes and Matza 1957), as well as forming of relationships with deviant others (Warr 1993) and self-definitions in terms of deviant identities (Glaser 1956; Matsueda 1992).

For both Sutherland and Akers, the key principle is that criminality and especially *systematic* or repetitive criminality is learned—"it is learned in direct or indirect association with those who already practice criminal behavior; and that those who learn this criminal behavior are segregated from frequent and intimate contacts with law-abiding behavior" (Sutherland 1940: 10-11). Unfortunately, both the specific content of what is learned and the process by which it is learned has received some, but not enough, attention in either theory or research. Additionally, some prominent treatments of differential association provide incomplete, even inaccurate, accounts of the theory that hamper its application. In addressing these shortcomings, we consider the following as key, often neglected elements of differential association.

The concept of normative conflict frames the theory. *Normative conflict* is simply the notion that various groups and subgroups in society differ in terms of definitions of right and wrong, and in their definitions of whether individuals are obligated to follow laws (either particular ones or laws in general). These groups can include subcultures, professions and occupational groups, ethnic groups, voluntary associations, religious groups, neighborhoods, and other collectivities. This normative conflict, in turn, is played out at both the individual and group levels.

The structural, group level manifestation of normative conflict is *differential social organization*. The norms, values, meanings, skills, and definitions found within these groups can be favorable to particular kinds of crime, or crime in general. In addition, cultural, subcultural, or group messages or definitions can be *supportive, neutral, hostile,* or *mixed* toward crime. Furthermore, many groups draw a thin line between legitimate and illegitimate activities. The thinner this line, the more the potential for criminality, and the line is thinner in some groups than in others. Groups are organized differently (e.g., in terms of skills, status orders, philosophies of life, vocabularies of motives or neutralizations, and network relationships), so that some are more organized for crime or exposed to crime-favorable messages than are others. Group organization (the social and cultural organization of various groups or settings) can be potentially favorable for crime in general, and/or for specific kinds of crimes, or for specific kinds of crimes in specific circumstances (for example, see Athens 1997). Therefore, differential-association/social-learning theory is both a theory of general criminality and offense specific behavior; of both generalized criminal propensity or *versatility and specialization* in crime. In sum, Sutherland (1940: 12) describes the effect of differential social organization this way: "The law is pressing in one direction, and other forces are pressing in the opposite direction."

It is important to note that differential social organization need not entail or imply *oppositional culture*, as Kornhauser's (1978) and Hirschi's (1996) caricatures of differential-association theory argue. First, differential-association theory does not assume an overarching dominant culture characterized by consensus, and instead treats the existence of dominant cultural norms and the degree of consensus around them as variable. Second, while oppositional cultures are possible, they are but one potential manifestation of differential social organization. More accurately, subcultures and their messages vary in the degree to which they contradict legal norms, and how overtly or subtly they may contradict them. Sometimes subcultural messages can be largely congruent with dominant culture, but can contain themes or subthemes that subtly encourage law-breaking. Furthermore, dominant cultures often contain contradictory messages, as Merton (1938) noted long ago. For example, American culture values honesty and trust, but also values shrewdness and what Charles Dickens called "the love of smart dealing."

The individual-level manifestation of normative conflict is the *process of differential association*. Criminal behavior becomes more likely to the extent that individuals learn and internalize pro-criminal norms, values, meanings, skills, and definitions through socialization and social-learning processes within the kinds of pro-criminal group contexts described above. "Whether a person becomes a criminal or not is determined largely by the comparative frequency and intimacy of his contacts with the two types of behavior [i.e., "criminal or law-abiding"] (Sutherland 1940: 11). Pro-criminal definitions will have varying degrees of influence on individuals depending on the source, emotional intensity, priority, frequency, and duration of the individual's contact with the definitions.

Differential association is also a theory of both criminal versatility and specialization. That is, one may be exposed to and learn messages and skills favorable for crime in general or for varied kinds of crime. For example, one may learn to "make a buck" from widely varying criminal activities whenever various opportunities present themselves (as members and associates of La Cosa Nostra apparently do). Or, one might learn messages favorable to using violence to get what one wants, whether it be settling disputes, emotional satisfaction, or money (Athens 1997). Alternatively, one may be exposed to and learn messages and skills favorable to one kind of crime but not others. For example, one may learn messages and skills favorable to embezzlement, taking bribes, or burglary that do not translate into a willingness or ability to deal drugs or pimp.

Ulmer (2000), drawing from Becker (1960, 1963) has described differential association as a process of developing structural, personal, and/or moral commitments to crime or deviance—a process that can also be triggered or aggravated by criminal sanctions (Ulmer 1994). These commitments can produce continuity in criminal behavior both by fostering a *desire* for criminal activities and choices, and/or by *constraining* individuals from terminating criminal careers. For example, personal commitment to criminal activities develops through learning positive attitudes toward criminal activities and criminal others, and adopting criminal self-definitions. Moral commitment constrains individuals from terminating criminal lines of action once one has become involved in them through internalized cultural and subcultural norms of exchange and obligation. Structural commitment constrains the termination of criminal careers, and is produced by the relative availability and attractiveness of conventional and criminal opportunities, irretrievable investments in criminal activity, and social reactions from criminal associates. The differential-association/social-learning process described earlier potentially entails developing all of these kinds of commitments, and the concept of structural commitment also embeds the individual in contexts of differential social organization.

Although Sutherland did not spell it out, the notion of *opportunity* is central to his conceptualization of criminal careers (see especially *The Professional Thief* 1937). In fact, Sutherland admitted later in his life that opportunity was a key missing ingredient in his original formulation (Merton 1997). He was gratified to see that Cloward and Ohlin produced a theory of criminal opportunity to complement differential association (Merton 1997). Opportunity is also central to Akers' social-learning theory. Building on Steffensmeier's (1983) extension of *ill*egitimate opportunity, access to crime opportunities entails differences across individuals and groups in access to *civil or technical knowledge useful for committing crime as well as access to* (a) places or victims, (b) tools and hardware, and (c) contacts or networks suitable/facilitative for actual crime commission. In turn, crime opportunities can be distinguished relative to whether they encompass: (1) underworld vs. upperworld forms of criminality, (2) solo, partnership, or more organized forms of criminality, and (3) minor, less serious or lucrative, more serious forms (see Steffensmeier 1983).

Differential association and labeling theory also have a symbiotic relationship with one another (Ulmer 1994). One basic contention of labeling theory is that sanctions against crime/deviance can inadvertently contribute to continuity in deviant activity and careers. This occurs in that sanctions can potentially: (1) restrict opportunities for conventional employment and relationships, (2) open up illegitimate opportunities and access to deviant networks or subcultures, (3) lead to the development of deviant self-identities and a sense of estrangement from conventional society (Ulmer 1994; Braithwaite 1989). The other contention of labeling theory is an emphasis on *careers and process* (Ulmer and Spencer 1999), in particular the notion that the original causes of criminal behavior may not be the same as the eventual causes that reproduce or sustain criminal behavior (or, as Becker [1963] says, the deviant behavior in time produces its own set of deviant motivations).

In the following narrative by Sam, we identify key features of differential-association/social-learning theory. We are especially interested in illuminating the nuances and details of differential social organization, as well as the processual "shifts and oscillations" (Adler and Adler 1983) of the differential-association/social-learning process. Sam Goodman's life history narratives reveal crime and criminal careers not so much as discrete events or series of events, but as a process that can be marked by amplification spirals, shifts, and waxing and waning commitments to crime and criminal others (see Ulmer and Spencer 1999). We present Sam's narrative in full context where feasible. The presentation to some extent also tracks Sam's criminal career chronologically.

### Differential Social Organization: Settings and Groups Where Sam Was Exposed to Messages and Skills Favorable to Crime

Key themes in this section center around differences across individuals in extent to which they associate with groups, collectivities, situations where they are exposed to messages and performance opportunities favorable to law violation more generally or to specific forms of violation. Conventional norms may also exist in these settings, and even be more pervasive, but coexist with mild to considerable tolerance for deviance—especially tolerance for some forms of deviance. The tolerance quotient for crime in general, or for this or that form or variety of crime, varies across structural and situational contexts—i.e., across groups, settings, and situations.

*Gas Station as Hangout*

> *By the time I was fifteen I was running my own life. I am at my mom's or grandparents, just to hang my hat. I was always on the go. Working, trading cars, horsing around. Hustling pussy was the big thing in my life at that time. I'm working six days a week, long hours. After work, I would bum around, maybe go to the skating rink—which was known as a place to find a woman. Or I hanged around the gas station. Always be guys there, maybe some girls too. The gas station crowd was older. When I was sixteen, they were maybe eighteen, nineteen, twenty. Some of them like my Uncle Howie was a lot older.*
>
> *Uncle Howie helped me learn the ropes you might say. Was maybe fifteen years older than me. Nice looking guy. Kind of a gambler, hustler type. Did time in the penitentiary for a hot car. Was always out for chasing women, especially the younger ones. I hooked him up with a lot of younger girls who were more my age. He took me to my first whorehouse. That was something. I still today have to laugh about that place. Uncle Howie was a lot of fun, lot of fun. It was a "live and learn" thing for me.*
>
> *The burglaries I pulled with Ronnie, Marge's cousin, were my first "real" crimes you might say. [Sam was about 16 years old at the time, Marge was his occasional girlfriend, and Ronnie was Marge's cousin.] Before that it was little shit, stuff that most kids will do. Steal apples from somebody's orchard or knock over mailboxes. Most serious thing was stealing candy, candy corn, from this guy's car. Guy drank a lot, would have his car parked at one of the local taverns. Would leave bags of candy corn on the seat. After we started clipping him, he would hide some under the seat. Off and on we'd steal the candy. Myself and a couple of other guys who hung at the gas station did it for devilment and to hear him gripe about it cause he would often stop there for gas or to pick-up milk and eggs, then complain to Al about somebody stealing his candy [Al was the gas station owner]. We got a kick out of this cause Al would tell us what he was saying. Just guys wanting to be part of something, to show off to each other, and wanting to get away with something.*

*After-Work "Hanging Out" Group*

Sam and Ronnie were arrested for burgling gas stations, and Sam was sentenced to a juvenile reformatory. After his release, Sam worked at a paper mill and hung out with a group of workmates who "horsed around" after work.

*It wasn't too long, maybe three or four years, I get popped for burglary again. A whole group of guys were involved, maybe twelve, fourteen of us. I am working at this big paper mill, the evening shift mostly, and we'd be going out after work—drinking beer, horsing around, guys showing off to one another, and one thing leads to something else. It started little but got bigger and bigger. If a guy wanted a tire, couple of us would go out and get a tire. Might steal a car, take the tires off and then let the car sit. We'd bullshit about it a work, get a laugh out of it. It was more devilment than anything. But then later it got to be more for the money, too. It was a little bit of everything—burglaries, stealing cars, even a couple of gas station robberies.*

*Then, a couple of 'em got caught in the act and they started talking. See, it wouldn't be all twelve guys breaking into an empty house. Maybe three or four one night and another three guys a different night. We all got picked up at work. I was the only one to do time on account of my record. See, at that time having a juvenile record counted against you. I was given two years in the county jail. That's where I broke the queer's jaw and got hit with more time. Not long after that, me and my buddy O'Keefe took off in the warden's car [escaped from jail]. I'm on the run for like three years, then got popped. Ended up doing a lotta time, seven years and eight days.*

## American City (Boonesboro and Tylersville)

After his release from prison for the assault and escape charges, Sam heads for American City where his burglary and fencing involvement hit full stride. Twenty years later, after serving time for fencing stolen goods, Sam ends up in Boonesboro and then Tylersville. Each town offered a somewhat distinctive setting, or differential social organization, for criminal activity.

*Ended up in American City as soon as I got out, for the escape and the assault bullshit. I don't know for sure why. Except I knew some guys from prison who moved there. Heard it was a good place to find work. Too, that the cops weren't hard-asses, didn't go around busting the balls of ex-cons. So, I took a shot at it.*

*American City is a pretty loose town. Big for gambling, for prostitution. Helluva nightlife. Lotta good burglars. If you look over the years, has been a main area for turning out decent burglars and for getting rid of the warm stuff [stolen goods]. Most of your secondhand places will buy. Has always had some very big dealers, guys who can unload truckloads if that is what is being peddled. Be surprised at how many of the store people [merchants] would buy from a dealer like me if they see the coast is clear.*

*Three, four weeks after I hit American City, I ran into some guys I done time with. They were breaking into gas stations, small businesses. Were after cash. These guys were half decent—not good burglars but not penny-ante either. If they needed another guy they'd ask me to go along. I did whatever was needed—driver, lookout, some scouting. Altogether, I'd say over the next year I pulled about twelve, fifteen jobs with them.*

*Then the burglary really takes off, cause I met Jesse. Jesse Tate. We became partners. He comes into my little upholstery shop I had opened up. Is shopping for a partner. Jesse heard I was solid, that I didn't scare easy. His brother or somebody recommended me, that he check me out. I knew his brother from hanging out at the same places.*

*I heard Jesse was good people, a good safeman. Was careful who he worked with. I'd say all the better burglars in that area knew of Jesse, respected him for what he was. Whew, it would be hard to believe how many places Jesse and I clipped. . . . But I just wasn't into burglary. In the meantime, I'm getting more and more into the fencing and my legit business [in upholstery and secondhand goods] is doing good.*

*Once I got in with the local clique, once I got rolling, I had more leeway from the local police and the local magistrates than I really needed. It all fell into place like you wouldn't believe. Every city will have its share, but as far as the local cops and the district attorney go, and then throw in having a good lawyer go to bat for you, different ones have a license to operate. In gambling, in the fencing, in the higher-up drug dealing, in the shady land deals. It is all joined together. Lots of people are involved. Is something in it for everybody.*

*Tylersville is pretty corrupt, but it doesn't run as deep. Has more in the way of dope and gangs, the street bullshit. The cops especially aren't as shady. But the magistrates are just as bad, maybe worse. One just got kicked out of office for letting prostitutes go if they will blow him. Is a clique in American City and a clique in Tylersville which more or less controls what you call the rackets. Each one [i.e., clique member] has his fingers into different things that are illegal or just on the edge. Do favors for each other but still try to outdo the other guy. Have a license to operate if don't go overboard.*

*In-between American City and Tylersville, I settled in Boonesboro. Horseshit little town. A chief and two cops. The Chief was a nice guy, on the lazy side. So knew he'd pretty much leave me alone. Wasn't any real gambling, prostitution, or major fencing going on. Not even any street crime to speak. Mostly guys getting drunk and getting into fights, or this or that group of kids breaking windows or shooting somebody's cat. Was a good place for me to clear my head, see if I could get my secondhand business going and start operating at the auctions again. Made my parole guy happy, too, on account it was a good distance from American City. He was leery I'd be drumming up my old contacts and fall back into the fencing. Which, in a way, I was itching to do.*

*Gambling Club and Local Clique*

*The fencing really took off. . . . For one thing, Jesse decided to pack it in—get out of the burglary altogether. And in some ways I am thinking, too, that I am getting too old for crawling in windows. Another thing, the local clique in American City is more and more opening its doors. I am pulling but in many ways they are pushing on me. Angelo [local racketeer] and me is doing a lot of business. He doesn't want to be out front anymore, so I'm handling the warm stuff for him. I would deal with the thieves or whomever and have the stuff taken to such and such a place. I am a layer-in-between cause Angelo wants to stay in the background. A lot of Angelo's connections came from his old man who was in the mafia. I mean really "in." Angelo was always someone I could go to if I needed a contact or for quick cash if I was short. Had his fingers into a lot of things. Very high up.*

*The gambling hookup was a big help, was like a club or a clique that got together on a Friday or Sunday night. A bunch of regulars. If not a regular, then show up once in awhile. That's how I got to be buddies with some of them. If I needed an outlet for something, I could go to one of them cause you're running in a circle of free spirits and guys that will be at least a little shady. Could they recommend somebody? This is how I met Ciletti, the food importer. We hit it off, became pals. Would stop at my shop almost every day. Maybe go for coffee or a sandwich. He was a big help cause he knew everybody. I would ask him, is so-and-so strictly legit or will they close an eye?*

*Hookup came from Louie [local fence and racketeer whom Sam became friends with and co-offended with]. One time he just asked me if I wanted to come to their card game. Some nights they play cards, other times it'll be rolling dice. Not anybody could come. It was only if one of the main ones—like Louie or Angelo or Nicky—invited you. Was like a clique and everybody had his fingers into something, were connected with city hall or with the money downtown. I wouldn't say all the main operators in town were part of the club. Some of the Jews weren't. But they were still connected with the Italians and others who were.*

*A big boost with the cops came from my getting in with the gambling club. With Duggan and his buddy, Lorenzo, who later became captain of the detectives. Duggan's brother was in the gambling club and must've passed the word to his brother cause he was in my shop almost like the next day. Week or so later, Lorenzo is with him and has his hands open, too. Didn't pull any punches. "Hey Sam, what are you selling cheap? I need a TV, need a refrigerator, can you help me out? Got any snow tires coming in?"*

*Auctions and Secondhand Shops*

*In my shop or if I peddled at the auction, I didn't come right out and say, hey, my prices are cheap cause I'm selling hot stuff. But I would give them an opening, play on the larceny that is them. Create a trust so they will feel it is safe, that they can get away with it. Play on the greed that is there. Ninety-nine out of a hundred will go for it.*

*Making contacts with the auction people and the antique dealers is a lot easier than with your ordinary business man. The auction people are shadier and they're not as afraid of taking a little risk. Don't ask many questions. Are figuring, what they don't know won't hurt them, so don't ask many questions. Another thing, your antique dealers and secondhand people hang at the same places, run in the same circle. If you stop at one secondhand place, you might bump into other dealers or private collectors. When I was operating in American City and taking stuff to Scottie in Ocean City, I would run into dealers there. Just killing time and talking business. You get to know them that way first, then later on it might develop into something more.*

*Criminal Networks and "Grapevines" as Differential Social Organization*

*Getting the connections is the hardest part. For burglary, too, but especially for the fencing. This will depend on the kind of dealer one is. Operating the way I was in American City, whew, you have to have contacts with a lotta people, and different kinds of people. Not just with the thieves now, but with other dealers, with the local clique, and with the legit business guy too. And don't forget about the cops—you will need their help too.*

*I had a helluva "spider web" in American City. Helluva spider web. And connected with other spider webs—with Louie's, with Angelo's, with Cooper's with Scottie's, with guys in the clique. A lotta of the people I was dealing with knew each other or at least were acquainted. Other ones didn't know each other but they are connected to different ones I am dealing with but don't even know it.*

*This time in Tylersville, not sure you'd call it a spider web. Pretty half-assed. Enough for me to operate but the comparison would be like night and day. Needed a couple more good spokes in wheel to really get it rolling.*

*Word of mouth is the best advertisement cause there is a helluva grapevine out there. One buddy to his buddies, one dealer to another dealer. Not one grapevine, now, but different grapevines. There is the street grapevine, there is the grapevine the better thieves have, the grapevine the businessman has, and your fences and secondhand dealers have their own grapevine. Same with your truckers and warehouse guys, they may hear from the street grapevine or from a better thief, but they will have their own grapevine. Is some overlap, but less then you would think.*

*Most dealers in an area will know one another, will bump into each other here and there. Same is true of burglars and guys in the rackets. It's only natural that you will rap about things. Not that you say, "hey, teach me about burglary or about fencing." But you can watch how the guy handles himself and some things will come up in conversation.*

*It goes back and forth. A lot of the people I did business with also did business with Angelo and Louie. Same with Scottie. We knew a lot of the same people, helped make contacts for each other. Woody knew people up here and I was acquainted with people in Southstate. If I couldn't handle something I would send the guy to Louie, and he was sending people to me. Louie and me palled together, had lunch or saw each other almost every day. Not always now, but some fences are buddies. Other ones will know and trade with one another but won't go out of their way to help out the other guy, say, by making a contact. Then, too, some fences will play dirty and snitch on other dealers to give themselves some slack. It isn't black and white, same as the legit world.*

*What you need are a couple of good spokes in the wheel, to get the wheel rolling. It would be fucking hard to name them all, to rank them. Jesse I would say was the most important spoke cause he helped the most to get me started in American City. . . . Jesse stayed to himself, didn't hang with the local clique but they respected him. Jesse connected with me a number of fences—good fences now —and with the good lawyers in town. Hooking up with Jesse put out the word that you can do business with Goodman.*

*Maybe Louie was the next biggest. Was a main spoke in the beginning for getting the wheel rolling. Angelo and Phil rank right up there. And Scottie was big, which is still going cause his son has taken over and will handle some pieces for me. . . . That is why a hookup with somebody like Angelo who is part of the Mafia is a big boost. The Mafia guy is normally better connected. That is his strength. Not just in the local area but connected into other areas as well. This was a real plus for Angelo and for Louie, too. The Italians and some of the Jews have the contacts, which is very hard for somebody else to get. Someone like Rosen [large jeweler] keeps to himself but is connected like you wouldn't believe. With the Italians, with the old Jewish clique, and with jewelry people in places like Oceantown and Franklinburg.*

*This last time, no way. I would not even call it a spider web. It was one but pretty puny.*

### Jail/Prison as Differential Social Organization

From age seventeen (first incarceration) to his early fifties (last incarceration) Sam was incarcerated five different times and altogether spent about fourteen years in jail or prison. During the last decade-plus of his life, Sam was arrested several times for fencing involvement but was not incarcerated. For both amateurs and veteran offenders, the prison setting represents one of the more active centers, or type of *differential social organization*, for active recruitment and tutelage into the underworld of more varied and more skillful criminal practitioners. Even seasoned offenders like Sam may become acquainted with new skills and rackets there, as well as contact with thieves both inside and outside of their usual spheres of activity.

## Incarceration in Juvenile Reformatory

Sam served one year in a juvenile reformatory at age 17 for involvement in gas station burglaries with Ronnie, a cousin of Marge, whom Sam was dating at the time.

*Doing time in the reformatory wasn't that bad. Lots of fights. Took up boxing. I was always pretty strong and with the boxing, I could handle myself pretty well. The "jailbirds," the ones who done time before, were the worse for the needling shit, see if they can get under skin. They pretty quick left me alone. I wasn't one to pick fights, but I wouldn't back away either. See, I wasn't jail-wise but I had already been in jail about two months before my juvenile hearing 'cause I couldn't make bail. Yeh, you can get all you want, but you got to take what comes with it. That, and it don't take me long to make friends. Never did.*

## County Jail

Sam served about 10 months in a county jail for involvement in an after-work burglary group. While serving his term, Sam fought with and broke the jaw of another inmate and escaped from jail. Sam was "on the run" as a fugitive for the next three years.

*The county jail was in-between your ordinary jail and a regular penitentiary. Was a pretty big place, held maybe 400-500 guys. Other counties sent their people to do time there too. Mostly, it was guys who were there for shitass crimes—writing checks, assaulting someone, dumb burglaries. Lotta guys had drinking problems. Your ordinary "joe blow" who fucked up. No lifers or the hardened criminals you might say.*

*I didn't run into any really good thieves or con men, but there were some decent thieves. They were the ones I hung with. There was a lotta bullshitting about burglary and that, to impress each other. Mostly guys blowing wind outta their asses but there was some learning on my part. Some contacts, too, with guys that ended up working in warehouses or on the docks which down the road would become part of my life, especially with the fencing.*

*I was in jail for maybe ten months when I broke this queer's jaw. He was making the rounds—wanted to blow me. They charged me with assault and bang, bang, the judge gave me two more years. No questions were asked. That was the routine way at the time. Now you got to have lawyers, a trial, and everything. About a month later, my buddy O'Keefe and I escaped. Took money out of the jail safe and took off in the warden's car. See, we both worked for the warden, in the jail office. He ran a pretty loose operation.*

*On the Run*

*It's hell being on the run. In the beginning you're always looking over your shoulder. I lasted several years by moving a lot and by getting tied up with women, mostly older women, for a place to eat and sleep. But I hustled money off of them, too. The only crime I did was checks and one burglary. I would take the woman's checkbook I was living with and write checks at different stores. Then I'd leave town.*

*The burglary was a fluke. I am in this city eating a bowl of soup. Only had a couple of bucks in my pocket. Guy comes in and after awhile starts rapping with me. Asks me where I did time. I didn't answer. Then, he tells me he had a job to pull and needed somebody to drop him off. How he could tell how I was an ex-con, I don't know. I finally went for it. He was cool, knew what he was doing. The job went off very smoothly. He gave me a handful of money that turned out be about $1600. Flat broke and then that happens. That always stuck in my mind, how cool this guy was, how easy the whole thing was pulled off.*

*Being on the run, escaping from jail, changed things for me. I had to pull a lotta shit to make it. I got more cockiness, more brazen. Gave me a lotta confidence in myself that I could do what I had to do, to survive. In some ways I enjoyed it because there was an excitement in it, a certain kick I was getting out of it.*

*"Big Time" in State Penitentiary*

Sam served "big time," seven years in a state penitentiary, following his capture and arrest for jail assault and escape.

*I finally got popped and ended up doing seven years altogether—for the old sentence, taking the warden's car, the assault in jail, and for the escape. The escape was the serious one cause the cops and the penitentiary people are pushing the judge to hammer you. This time my stay in the penitentiary is a different ballgame for me. On account of all the charges, I know I am going to be there awhile.*

*I came across some half-decent thieves in the county jail but nothing like you find in the regular penitentiary. You will still meet a lotta assholes but also will be meeting a better class of criminal and some good thieves too. The hardened criminal and a lotta lifers.*

*Main thing is, I'm hanging with the burglars and the con men. I met a lot of safecrackers. Guys who were a whole lot better than what I'd seen before. They would talk about different things—how to scout out a job, how to break into a place. That you needed to have a dropoff driver, a good partner to take inside and back you up, a good lawyer, and places to unload what you was stealing. Even how to crack a safe. It sounded easy and it sounded good.*

*Then, I'm assigned to the furniture factory. Turns out I am good at it and before long I am put in charge of showing other prisoners how to upholster. Looking back, this paved the way for my fencing because I learned a lot about different kinds of furniture, different pieces of wood—cherry, oak, maple, walnut. It got to where I am even going to the penitentiary library and reading up on the subject.*

*I would have to say that when I got out of the penitentiary that time, in a way I was itching to get into burglary. No doubt. Into safes, really. Cause I feel I got a helluva education. Not that I'm planning to fall back into crime but more an inkling.*

Sam served 18 months in a state prison for burglary of a "house full of antiques" committed with Jesse, his longtime burglary partner. Later, Sam served three years at the same prison for fencing stolen goods.

*When I got to the Midstate Penitentiary this last time, it was a shocker how the penitentiaries have changed. This time, holy fuck, you got the counselors, the teachers, the psychologists, the psychiatrist. You got programs for this and that, you got furloughs for good behavior, you got hearing boards for misconduct shit. A lot more kids, a lot of dopers and penny-ante thieves in prison now. A lot more assholes. Guys come in with radios and TVs. I'm thinking, holy fuck, is this really a penitentiary? The older prisons were tougher, a lot tougher in terms of doing without. Just the bare essentials was all you got.*

*But doing time is harder now cause today you got all this psychological bullshit, all the assholes who are in prison, and the code is weaker. There used to be a helluva code in prison. That is weaker now. Myself, I just skated by. Go by the rules on the outside, get along with everybody but don't kiss anybody's ass. There's a borderline there.*

*I did a little more than three years. Was known as an "old head." As a solid con but one who skated by. A lot of the younger inmates looked up to me. After I got out, different ones contacted me or I would bump into them. But I mostly kept my distance, shied away from them. Didn't want to aggravate my parole officer and didn't see any point to it. Sure, if I was to get back into the fencing on big scale again, then I might have encouraged it. But I was taking a different path—do some fencing but keep it small.*

*Effects of Doing Time (including labeling effects)*

*I really believe this. Once you do time, you're never the same as the guy who didn't do time. See, no one knows what loneliness is until you enter the goddamn penitentiary, looking out the window at 2 o'clock in the morning, rainy or whatever it may be and no where to go. That is lonely. When you lose your freedom you lose something else with it. Except for someone like Jesse or Steelbeams, everybody forgets you in prison. I sat down and thought about it a lot of times. Prison takes something out of you. I can't explain it. You come out a different person. I don't know if it makes you bitter, hard, or whatever. You learn to trust only yourself.*

*Doing time, the fact that I'd been in the penitentiary, helped in little ways. Looking back, it is hard to believe the different guys from prison I bumped into, got hooked up with. My main connections on the docks were guys I knew from jail. One ran the fork lift. Was a mob-connected job. Other guys from jail got jobs driving truck or working in warehouses, in the shipping departments of this or that large store.*

*But the main thing is, your name carries from prison. People can find out if you're an asshole or not. I was known as a good con, could hold my own but also did my time without hassles. That's why when I first came to American City, my name got there before me. This was added to, when Jesse and me got popped for the antiques. Cause after I got of jail for that, the local gang and them were really coming my way and giving me the openings. They could see we didn't take anybody down with us and that we got off so easy. Even with my record I only did eighteen months. Jesse only did six months. Our lawyers did a helluva job. This really made it known I was good people, and that I had some connections, too. I'm not saying doing time is necessary but it can help. Not too much time cause then you will be seen as a loser.*

## Underworld Code and Pecking Order

The underworld refers broadly to the culture, setting, or social organization associated with criminal activities and more general rule-violating behavior. Burglary crews, auto thieves, gamblers, prostitutes, drug dealers, fences, illicit gun dealers, forgers, the syndicates, and corrupt police all have actual and potential relationships with one another that are different from those they have with people not in the underworld. These individuals and groups form a kind of *loosely coupled system*—in the sense of being linked to one another and to crime activities, while still maintaining independent identities and some evidence of physical and logical separateness. The underworld culture also both reflects and exacerbates values and identities of the blue-collar working class. The embeddedness of Sam's burglary and fencing involvement in the setting and culture of the underworld is reflected in the themes of trust, safety, reputation, toughness, and "carrying oneself right" that he uses to portray his experiences.

*The Code*

*The rule is that everybody on a job gets the same, that the score is split equally. But it don't always happen that way. The main guys in a crew will split it evenly amongst themselves but will chisel the other ones. Take Jesse and me, we would fill our pockets before we came out of a place. Or, if we had to unload the stuff, we would chisel the other by telling him the price was lower than it actually was.... But had to be careful cause it may come out in the paper how much was taken.*

*They [Bowie and Gordon, two good burglars] don't really get along, personally. They would both bitch to me about the other one. Don't like each other. That is unusual. In my eye, they were both whiners and got on one another's nerves. Most burglary partners like each other, are comfortable with one another. Me and Jesse was. Normally, that is what you want.*

## An Undisclosed Murder

*I don't know if I should tell you this. Cause I have never told anybody. Never, never. Not even Jesse. Never mentioned this to anybody. I had to put a motherfucker to sleep. I did it because I had to. I would've ended up with a lotta time otherwise. I put him to sleep. It was in American City.*

*Came up twice in my mind since I've been sick. I don't even want to bring it up now, cause I don't want to remember it. Afraid I will say something in my sleep or if I'm delirious. All these years I have buried it—has only been a few times it has popped into my mind. Always afraid it might come out. Not that it was painful or that I felt bad about it. But somebody hearing it, then asking: "Hey, you were talking the other night about putting someone away."*

*I had to snuff him out. Guy I knew from jail. Wanted me to wait in the car while he robbed a bookmaker. Bookie was making the rounds, picking up his money. I should wait in the car on the next street. But the bookie didn't go along with it as planned. Carried a gun and fired shots at this guy when he was running back to where I was parked. Got him in the neck and leg. Bleeding bad, very bad. I was over a barrel, so I had to snuff him. I don't really want to say more cause it will just refresh my mind, make me more likely to repeat it when I shouldn't.*

*[Darrell brought up the matter the following morning and Sam elaborated]*

*I did it with my hands. Choked him. Dumped his body in a quarry that had filled with water. Tied rocks, weighted him down. The car I burnt. They never found him. About two years ago, I heard they drained the quarry. I wondered if they had found the body, the bones. But never heard anything.*

*Wasn't really a decision on my part. Knew what I had to do. He was hurt bad. Needed to go to the hospital, get sewed up. But then questions would be asked. It would come out what happened and I'm back doing time. The other thing was, the bookie was connected, tied up [with the local mafia]. So I'd be on their bad side too.*

*I don't feel bad about it. Not good either. Know what I mean. Snuffing somebody out like that is accepted. Not by the cops and the ordinary Joe Blow. But among thieves and them, yes. You have to do what you have to do. I wish there had been another way. There was no hesitation on my part. I knew what had to be done. With my hands, "Gag, gaaggh." It was over.*

(Then later that day...)

*I do not feel bad for snuffing that guy out. There is murder and there is murder. Not all murders are the same. If you're wife is causing you grief, that is no reason to snuff her out. Know what I mean. You should get big time. That one life is done with. It ain't like you replace one television with another one. I'm not saying the death penalty, not necessarily. For a baby rapist, yes. He deserves the chair. I'd pull the switch myself. I am a strong believer in the death penalty for that.*

*It is different if a guy is ratting or the chance is there he will rat. Then you're protecting your own life. If he is putting me away for years and years, by doing the motherfucker in, that is eliminated. Let's just suppose Jesse and me is in a place and somebody comes in on us and we could get hurt. I'm going to take care of him. I wouldn't feel guilty about it at all. That is accepted. Is part of the code you might say.*

### Don't be a whiner, carry yourself right, be a stand-up guy

*I don't think I ever made anybody do something he himself didn't want to do. Know what I mean? Same as nobody made me do something I didn't want to do. You hear this bullshit, so and so came from a broken take care of it? Even if I wasn't sure of myself, I would always let the thieves and them think I was, that I was on top of things family, he was raised poor, blah, blah, blah. That is blowing wind out your ass.*

*I could point to this or that which made me a burglar or a fence. Blame it on my mother, on my stepdad cause he was a real asshole. Or that I didn't get a fair shake from the judge who sent me to the juvenile reformatory. That Angelo and the local clique were pushing on me to do the fencing. You see this in prison. Guys whining, crying it wasn't their fault. They are blowing wind out of their asses. What I did, I did because I wanted to. Nobody got me to steal, nobody made me be a fence. All the rank shit I pulled—I, Sam Goodman, did it.*

*How you carry yourself means a whole lot. Is the man an asshole or not? Is the man honest or not? Will he hold up his end of the deal? Does he know what is going down and can he? I would not show a weakness that way.*

### Don't break into occupied places

*The rule is, don't break into a place if you know or surmise somebody is there. Unless the person is drunk or is on his deathbed, most burglars will not touch a place that's occupied. The risks are too great. What if the fucker has a gun and is so fucking scared he just starts firing. He is a witness, too, has seen your face. Don't forget that. And what if you have to hurt him or snuff him out. Then, there will be heat on the police to solve it and you're facing big time.*

*Now, if it turns out there is somebody in the place and they surprise you, you have to be ready to get rough. Be able to hit someone across the side of his head. To do what needs to be done, but that is a last resort.*

*Don't gossip or show off*

*Hard to be a thief and not want to blow yourself up to your buddies and to your lady friends. Your girlfriend or whatever. Guys will wear jewelry they've stolen or keep a good antique in their house, just to show off to their buddies or to get some pussy. Then run out of money and have to peddle the stuff anyway.*

*Not letting it go to your head, not become a big shot and come across as better than you are. I was always very careful that way, not to act cocky and not to badmouth one thief to another thief, behind his back. You got to figure, too, the guy is thinking, "hey, if he talks about this guy this way, what the hell does he say to others about me?" I was always very careful not to run somebody down that way.*

*Racket values about "fairness" and "understandings" with other dealers*

*Not that I didn't try to outdo Louie or some of the smaller secondhand dealers. There was some of that. But you also help each other, work together in some ways. . . . There can be understandings, where fences won't buck each other. You handle this and I'll handle that. I'm talking about your bigger fences, now. For a long time, Louie was the main one for guns in American City. If guns came my way, I sent the business to Louie. Same with liquor and cigarettes—that business mostly went to Angelo, to the Mafia. You didn't want to buck that. It worked the other way, too, Louie and Angelo were sending antiques my way.*

*You're doing it as a courtesy and to avoid hassles. But not all the way now. Even on the guns, I am bypassing Louie as my operation got rolling. Run the guns down South or to Oceantown. There was tension between Louie and me when I started doing that. With the liqour and cigarettes, no, once I was peddling that to Angelo, I stayed with him. There's a helluva grapevine and I didn't want to take that risk. Not that I feared Angelo but didn't want to be on his bad side either.*

*As a rule, though, one dealer isn't gonna pass up a good deal on account of another dealer. They're too greedy and there ain't that kind of honor among fences. There's more honor among thieves—well, among your better thieves anyway.*

*Another thing, the thief don't want to risk harming that relationship, what each side is doing for the other. Buying from Rocky over the years, he would feel he owes it to me to give me first shot at any good antiques he runs across.*

### Be ready to play hardball

*The thief has to know you can play hardball. I was always a firm believer of that. Can lean on the guy if you need to. Say that cops have a thief who is fingering you, are making him promises. I am going to lean on the guy or have someone else lean on him. Do whatever needs to be done. It was well known I was a nice guy in most ways but could be nasty. There was a threat there that was well known.*

*Leaning on somebody doesn't mean there is revenge. You do that to keep the guy from snitching or from testifying if it has gone that far. Take Bobby Hoyle. He snitched on me but then backed down, wouldn't testify. After the case was settled, no, I didn't go after him. Thought about it but figured what is done is done. Unless you want to send a message all the way down the line that you're not to be fucked with, but normally no—whacking him or working him over would bring me hassles. Just don't do business with him again and spread the word he was no damn good.*

*Say you're shopping for a partner. May want someone who can hold his own, will get rough if he has too. Isn't a pussy. But you don't want someone who is blowing people away. Someone who has his hand on the trigger. Will bring you nothing but headaches. Comes down to it you start blowing people away, you will get blown away. More than anything you want a guy that is solid, which can mean different things. Does he have heart? Can you depend on him to do what needs to be done? Can he keep his mouth shut?—that is the biggest thing. Ask Jesse, he will tell you—if you like the guy and you trust him, that is more important than anything.*

### Snitching

*Myself, I never snitched. The police in American City did try to open me up but never really pushed on me, "Just tell us if we're on the right track." Couple of times in Tylersville this one detective would come in my shop, had an envelope with a bunch of mugshots: "have you seen these guys, have they come in here." In my eye I would have a hard time looking at myself in the mirror if I did that. Another thing, the thieves and them saw me as "solid." I didn't want to undermine that. The snitching will hurt you in the long run, especially with the better thief. You also got to figure, once the snitching starts and the police got their foot in the door, they can squeeze you in different ways. The police can play dirty, too. That doesn't mean I have never thought about snitching. If you are dealing with dopers and asshole thieves, the temptation is there.*

*Underworld Pecking Order*

The crime world is differentially organized or stratified by type of criminal involvement and on the bases of the offender's character, contacts, immunity from the law, and skill level—all of which contribute to variable capacity to practice crime safely and profitably. Run-of-the-mill thieves, street hustlers and doper thieves are near the bottom of the status hierarchy (but above child molesters and baby rapists), racketeers and background operators are at the top, and are ranked higher than good thieves/burglars and dealers in stolen goods. Also, large-scale fencing ranks higher than burglary, which ranks higher than shoplifting or low-level drug dealing.

*I shot for the decent or so-so thief, between the good burglar and the asshole thieves and hustlers. I catered to the in-between burglar but off and on I bought from the penny-ante thieves and the "walk-in" trade. The doper thief I was always leery of. Can be good at the stealing but will do anything for a fix. The bottom-barrel thief is just that—bottom barrel. Too lazy to work, too dumb to be good at stealing.*

*A good burglar like Jesse has a lot of heart and a lotta skill. I don't want to take anything away from that. But the fence is in a different league. Has to push and pull in a lotta different ways, and always be looking ahead. For an opening, for making a contact, and for covering his ass. The burglar needs an eye for clipping but doesn't have to scheme, to wheel and deal in the same way. Doesn't need to know people from all walks of life.*

*The fence has to hustle, but it is different than the street hustling, what the dopers and street types do. They will do anything to turn a buck, really lower themselves and beat anybody. How can I say it. There's more honor in the hustling a fence does. It is more like that of a businessman or a salesman. Playing on the greed of the person looking for a bargain. Being shrewd, being a shyster. Getting over on somebody to make a buck, give you information or make a contact. A good conman, really.*

*The fence is more than just a thief. Will have his legit business as a cover. Is a businessman, really. There is hustling, but it's more wheeling and dealing. The fence has to take the openings that come his way, but even more so, he has to make his own openings. Is really a schemer, an operator. It's more like what Angelo or somebody in the rackets does, cause they are schemers too.*

*Guys like Angelo that are in the rackets or that stay in the background are more or less at the top. Are pulling the strings and bringing in good money, and are keeping a layer-in-between. Are both ways—shady but legit, too. Are operating where the line is thin between the two. In their eye and in the public's eye, they are more a businessman than a thief or a crook.*

## Specialists vs. Generalist Offenders

Differential association/social learning implies that criminal versatility or specialization will vary across settings and criminal subcultures, across population subgroups like age and race-ethnicity, over time (e.g., perhaps less specialization today than in Sutherland's time), across offender's skill-level and experience, and by type of criminal involvement. Key Elements for addressing the issue of versatility versus specialization center around differential access to messages and opportunities that encourage or discourage either versatility or specialization. Also, here and elsewhere in Sam's narrative, we get a close-up view of Sam's definitions, neutralizations, and "apologia" and how these reflect messages linked to the broader culture as well as to criminal subcultures.

*I always hated the dope and the dopers. The opportunity has been there, many times now, to get into peddling dope. Not on the street, but to be a layer-in-between for the guys bringing the stuff in. Could not look at myself in the mirror if I was peddling dope, especially if it ends up with kids. I was always leery of buying from the doper thief. It's a fact that a doper can't be trusted. Will do anything for a fix, to get his dope. Really lower themselves.*

*In my legit business, I did buy from your blacks and your Hispanics. A lot, really. If buy on credit, had no worries bout getting the money. But buying what's warm, where there's some risk involved, I did buy from some black thieves but just felt safer dealing with your white thief. In my eye, they don't believe in trust like a lot of your white thieves. Your black thief is more into hustling—hustling dope, women, and doing almost anything to make a buck. I'm thinking, too, your black thief is more likely to be a doper, into drugs.*

*If a guy has an eye for clipping for one kind of crime, you have to figure the eye can be there for other crimes. The know-how and being able to spot the openings for doing this or that crime will be a help for doing other crimes. Will depend on the crime. My burglary helped with the fencing. Was an overlap there.*

*It is only common sense that if somebody has larceny in the heart for one kind of crime, then the larceny [in the heart] for another crime is more likely to be there. Break the law one way, more likely than the ordinary Joe Blow to break it another way. But that doesn't mean the thief will do any goddamn thing. May break into houses but won't rob old ladies. Same as the store guy who is buying stolen goods from me or cheating Uncle Sam. He is comfortable with that. But couldn't look at himself in the mirror if he was on the other end, the one who is selling the warm stuff or the one breaking into places. Would upset him if you said, "hey, you're a thief, you're a fence."*

*It'd be the same with heart—if have it to clip one way, then more likely to have the heart to clip other ways, say, compared to the average Joe Blow. Not all the way now. Can have the heart for one crime but are chicken for doing other crimes. Same way, can lose the heart for a crime like burglary but can pull off other crimes like writing checks or selling dope outta your house.*

*Some of your students are dealing in drugs, right? Say its pot for their friends and other students. Will have some of the know-how for dealing in other drugs. Maybe the contacts, too. Are gonna be part of the partying crowd, so can get into other kinds of trouble. But do they have the heart to move into dealing dope all the way? Can they get the contacts? Can they look at themselves in the mirror? Maybe yes, maybe no. Sure, more so than someone who is naive or the guy who's a nerd—cause a nerd is a nerd, no matter how you cut it. But many will stop with dealing dope at that level cause that is what they know and are comfortable with, cause the opportunity is handed to them on a silver platter. But very few would have the heart and the contacts to go all the way. Even more so, they would be in a different league if we're talking about getting into burglary, stealing cars, or the fencing. Wouldn't have the know-how and your decent thieves wouldn't clip with them. Wouldn't have confidence in them.*

*I feel bad about very few things. Maybe the one old guy who I hit. Put him in la-la land. Me and Jesse got this tip, that this guy had all kinds of money in his house. Kept it under the bed in a metal box. But he never left the house. This is a seventy- year-old man. So we decided to pull the job at Halloween. I would dress up as Batman, do the trick or treat bit. I knocked at the door and when he opened it, I said "ho ho ho" and hit him. Boom. Wanted to put his lights out for a little awhile. Jesse goes in and gets the box. Some good bills but not big money. Then when the guy wakes up, he tells the police that Batman hit him. Batman got in the window and robbed him. In a way it was funny, cause we got a kick out of hearing that story. But he was always weird after that. That I do feel bad about. Same with Jesse—wanted no part of that again. Stick to breaking into places.*

*Myself, I have never shoplifted. I'd be scared or whatever. Just wouldn't be me. Know what I mean. Don't get me wrong, there are some good shoplifters and that, and who are respected. But not the same way as a decent burglar. Is it a sissy thing on account so many women are doing it? Can't say. Really, they have a lock on shoplifting, are better at it than men. A lotta guys—a Rocky, a Steelbeams, a Bowie, a Jesse—would see it as lowering themselves, as not being what they really are.*

*Hard to answer that—if you mean by "specialize" that someone who is into crime does the same crime his whole life or even for years and years, then the answer is "no." Even more so today this is true. Jesse comes close. And Steelbeams and Bowie. It is more that this becomes your main thing, maybe your only thing, but that may lead to other things that are similar or different avenues may open up. Theft is theft and hustling is hustling, know what I mean. If you have larceny in heart for this, you are more likely to have larceny in the heart for that. Jesse was into burglary, that was his thing. But he would not hesitate to cheat Uncle Sam [on taxes] or buy stolen goods if the good opportunity was there. But he wouldn't sell dope or rob people with gun, or steal from old ladies, or be a baby rapist. Know what I mean.*

*Guys like Angelo or Lenny, the Lebanese guy, are involved in different things but stay in the background. Are bringing the drugs in you might say but aren't peddling to the doper or the street thief, not direct anyway. Mafia guys, or the guys in local clique in American City, have their fingers in lots of things. Have the contacts and the money to go into different things, go where the money is—whether it's legit, strictly shady, or in-between. Have limits but are out to make money anyway they can. Same as the street hustler but each is in a different league and the mafia guy would not stoop as low.*

*The opportunity is there for guys in burglary like Rocky and Steelbeams to go into dealing dope, at the higher levels. On account of their contacts and the reputation for being solid and knowing their way around. Rocky tried this, was the contact, the go-between for Angelo for drugs coming in from Florida. Would take the train down. Was good money but Rocky didn't feel comfortable. Wasn't him and was putting himself too much in somebody else's hands. But I know other decent burglars who have pretty much packed in the burglary and are now selling dope as a go-between for the higher-ups.*

*Most thieves are nickel and dime, will do almost anything to make a buck. If the opportunity is there, will take it. The younger guys and especially your kids [juveniles] will do almost any goddamn thing. Sell dope, break into cars, grab somebody's purse, even peddle their girlfriend's ass on the street if they run low on money to party. Are hustlers as much as they are thieves. But if stay in crime, like the Beck boys, will prefer doing this crime over other crimes. But other ones like Chubbie will clip whichever way they can.*

*Most better thieves will stick to one or a couple of things. Not that they never done other crimes or wouldn't if the good opportunity is there. If into burglary, might break into a van or might steal a car if he has a ready outlet for it. Not exactly the same as burglary but there is a lotta similarity, say, compared to shoplifting or passing checks. Will feel more comfortable just doing burglary or just doing shoplifting. Then get to be known by their buddies or even the cops for being a "burglar" and may take pride in being that. Take Rocky, saw himself as a burglar, wanted to be seen that way. Would be upset if you said he was an all-around thief.*

*Bobby Porter was into shoplifting. Very good at it. He did pull a few burglaries. But shoplifting was his thing. Now, if you look at Bobby's record, you will see some other offenses—like assault and carrying a weapon, some disorderly conducts, and using some dope. But those aren't crimes the same way. He didn't do those to make money, know what I mean. Crimes like those in many ways are part of being in the criminal world, are part of the places you hang out, the people you associate with, and from being watched by the cops and the parole people.*

### Chronic Offending, Rewards/Risks, and Opportunities

Sam's narrative confirms the importance of aging, the wear and tear of crime, good legitimate jobs, and stable romantic relationships as factors contributing to desistance, or at least a slowing down in one's criminal involvement. But his career also points to the importance of variable access to criminal opportunities as a pivotal factor in both chronic offending and desistance, and argues for a broader view of desistance and chronic offending. In addition, Sam's narrative reminds us that deviants, even persistent criminals, are seldom deviant in all or even most aspects of their lives. Sam comfortably rubs shoulders with thieves, gamblers, and quasi-legitimate businessmen but also courts respectability and pledges allegiance to some major normative standards. From Sam, we also learn that many offenders who should have "matured out" of crime (according to conventional criminal careers wisdom) still find crime morally acceptable, continue to justify crime and commit crimes sporadically when the opportunity presents itself and the risks are small. We also learn that one particular subset of the larger criminal population—good burglars, small-time as well as large-scale fences, bookmakers, pimps, corrupt cops, shady businessmen, local racketeers, mafioso, and so forth—actively persist in their criminality until they are too old or feeble to do otherwise. Finally, Sam's account strongly cautions against the static view of crime opportunity that prevails in the criminological literature. Offenders like Sam not only respond to crime opportunities, they construct and sustain them. Motivation and opportunity complement one another. What is objectively possible is more likely to become subjectively acceptable, and vice versa.

*Funny thing is, a lotta thieves look down on guys that work and puff themselves up with their buddies by not having a regular job. Want to get up when they want to, come and go as they please, and don't have to listen to some asshole tell you what to do. But generally it is better to have a regular job. That way you have money coming in and won't be under the gun to get cash quickly. Is a cover, too, cause the cops will be less suspicious and all the way down the line you're more likely to get a break. That is why I always told Rocky, the Beck boys, and different ones—get a job, even a part-time job. Will keep the parole people happy, too. That, and having a woman. Will think you're settling down and have somebody to get on your case.*

*I'm not saying that people don't change. No way. Looking back at American City, some of the people I was involved with are still at it but others have packed it in or they have slowed down. Take Jesse, he packed in the bur-*

*glary—that is what he told me. Then I find out later that he is still clipping places but is working alone. Maybe only does a job or two a year. Jesse has worked himself up to supervisor of maintenance in the county and he would not want to jeopardize that. The burglary is a very sideline thing for him, when before it was his main thing. A lot of the ones I bought from, the walk-in thieves and the in-between burglars, have pretty much quit. That is what I hear. Not that they quit all the way—cause if the opening is there and it is safe, very safe, most won't walk away. But they really aren't thieves anymore.*

*I don't know how to explain it. When you get older you get tired of the hassles, all the bullshit you have to put up with. When you're young, you don't think about prison—doesn't really concern you. When you're older, it's not that you fear prison but that you don't want to waste your time there. There's more to lose when you get older. This last time I lost my shirt—my business, just about everything. Look at what I would lose now. When I did time in my twenties, I didn't lose shit.*

*Lotta guys lose the heart for clipping. Get too shaky. Then use dope or alcohol for a spark, but it is a false courage. Just as well pack it in, get a legit job or clip in other ways cause the decent thief and different ones will shy away from doing business with them.*

*Most thieves are penny-ante. They're not getting rich off of stealing. No way. So with all the hassles and bullshit, why not pack it in. A big thing is, who the fuck they gonna work with? When you're a kid, yes, you can hook up with others, is no big deal cause there are lots of kids and other assholes out there. But once you've done time, not just once but maybe several times, the choices aren't there. Lotta the other assholes are doing time, too, or have packed it in. It gets harder to find a good partner as you get older. That is a very big part of it. The losers will find it very, very hard. Especially if they have snitched, which quite a few will have done. The name carries. Who will work with them? Another loser, maybe. Or some woman who's on dope or feels sorry for the guy.*

*The higher-ups, like Angelo and Nicky, are making good money and there are fewer hassles. If they are careful, stay in the background, don't get too greedy, there is very little risk for them. May have to pay a horseshit fine once in awhile, for gambling and that, but that's about it. With one foot in the grave, they will still have their fingers in it.*

*Same with Steelbeams and Bowie and Gordie. Steelbeams is in his forties, Bowie and Gordie are close to fifty, maybe older. Are still clipping [burglary]. If Bowie gets popped, he is facing big time on account of his prior record. Has gotten himself jammed up a couple of times from opening safes with other crews. Now he works with Gordie, that's it. Work on tips, pull inside jobs. I would like to make what they are making. The last couple of times I saw Bowie, he bitched about the physical side, that he was getting too old. Just quit altogether. I told him he was blowing wind out of his ass, will believe it only when I see it.*

It is very hard to nail a burglar if he is careful and nobody snitches. Very hard to get a conviction. Jesse and me only got nailed, were sent away, for that one burglary—the antique job. Never got nailed for a safe job, for stealing metals, for all the other burglaries we pulled. Unless you can catch the guy on the job, really catch him, it is hard to get a conviction. If the guys are careful, know what they are doing, and keep their mouths shut—your chances of doing time from burglary is very slim. But it is easy to slip up, to think you got it made. Even believe you have a license to steal. The law of averages is there, can catch up with anybody.

## Who's a Thief, Who's a Crook, Who's a Chronic Offender?

To me the people who buy [stolen goods] are as guilty as the ones who steal. The public and the ordinary businessman is buying from me, surmising the stuff is hot. The cops are shopping at my store, looking for bargains and asking me to keep my eyes open for something they needed. The cops I have known in my life were always looking for a handout. There are some very crooked cops who have pulled a lotta rank shit. Take Duggan, if he and me made a list of all the shit we pulled, I don't think mine would be longer.

Your fence is more crooked than your average businessman, a little more anyway, but are some very shady businessmen and store people. Chisel or clip in one another. If not buying stolen goods from me, are chiseling in other ways. You ever watch the preachers on TV? Being in that goddamn hospital I got my fill. Is a good racket, playing on old ladies and people on their deathbed. They are the ones that ought to be locked up.

I'm a smoker, right? That's how I got the cancer. Nobody made me do it. I bought the Camels, I lighted the match, right? But still, the tobacco people are pushing me. Tried quitting but then I was very nasty. Irritable as a son-of-a-bitch. I'm not making excuses. Don't feel sorry for me but what about all the kids that are lighting up? They are being hustled, conned is what it comes down to. To become dope heads, only it isn't called that. The hell many of these kids will be going through, cause it's a bitch [the cancer] that I can tell you. All the rank shit I pulled, who should find it harder to look at himself in the mirror? I don't think I'm blowin wind outta my ass when I say that.

The guy who runs a store, legit now, is buying from a dealer like me—who is buying direct from the thieves. His chances of hassles with the police are small, and he doesn't have to put up with the thieves. To me, this store guy is a businessman looking for an easy buck. Nothing more than that. He ain't a fence. Is he a crook? Sure as hell doesn't see himself that way. But comes down to it, some of them were pretty shady.

*Sam's Risk Assessment, Temptation to Expand, and Shrinking Access to Crime Opportunities*

When I first got out of Midstate penitentiary [about 1980], I would go back to American City. It was a longing, like I was being pulled back there. Saw some of the guys I did business with. To say "Hi" but also to let them know I was back. On the one side, I'm telling myself not to get involved again but still wanting too. Angelo approached me early on. Whatever I can do Sam, to help you out let me know . . . . On the other side, I was leery. I'm past 50 years old. Maybe it's time to stay legit.

Many times I thought about it. Should I go for it again? Should I take on Rocky or Steelbeams as a middleman for my operation? Advise them, pull the strings, but keep a layer-in-between? Was I willing to put up with the hassles? Be on the go all the time? Did I still have it in me? Had I gotten too soft? Because something comes up, somebody has to be leaned on. Bing, bing, you have to do it. Then, there was my record. If I got popped again, that was all she would write. They would bury me in prison.

I did get approached by a main guy in Tylersville. I would do the buying, he would have the contacts for the unloading. Very big locally. Into gambling, fencing, shylock loans, you name it. On the order of Angelo in American City. I can't say how he knew of me but I feel certain that him and Angelo were well acquainted. He would back me. I had the knowledge, all-around knowledge, of what different things are worth and knew how to handle myself. We'd each get a percentage. He would send people to me—drivers, burglars, and that. I would buy and handle the stuff. He had the outlets for unloading the stuff but I could use my contacts if I wanted. He wanted that layer-in-between. I told him I wasn't into that [fencing] anymore but I would keep it in mind. Fuck, I needed that like a hole in the head, to be a layer-in-between for somebody else. If I'm gonna take the risk, I'm gonna do it for my own pocket.

Still the temptation was always there. Many times I wished I was back in it, like the way it was before. To tell you the truth, I would've liked to have gotten a younger guy to be the fence but I would be in the background, more supervising. My knowledge to somebody is worth quite a bit. I put a lot of hours in getting the contacts, running to the auctions and meeting people. That don't come overnight. The contacts, knowing how to get the confidence of someone, to read people. Who's buying, what's the stuff going for? It takes hours and hours, a lot of time consumed to get all that. I didn't want the hassles but I still wanted to keep my fingers in it.

It was hard not to fall into the fencing much deeper, go for it in a big way. Cause the larceny [in my heart] is still there and the know-how. I still have the heart, too. Not leery of dealing with the thieves and your other dealers. The cops are a concern, not a fear. I ain't got the contacts I once had but I do *believe I could build them back up. Really, it is my record that is holding me back, that I can't stand another pop [arrest]. And the dope scared me, that the quality of thief is less today. All the assholes out there today. Here is my thinking when I got out this last time. As long as I keep it small, don't overdo it, I don't think they will want to send me to prison. On account of my age and cause I am supporting 5-6 families. What will the guys in my shop do if I'm sent away? But the itching to get back into it, all the way now, was always there. Just knowing I could do it but couldn't let myself go would gnaw at me.*

*As far as the fencing—there's three periods, really. First period, you might say I am a burglar, a half-assed fence, and a small businessman. All three, but more than anything I am a burglar. Jesse and me is clipping something fierce and most of my time is spent finding places to clip and scouting them. Jesse and me spent days doing that. The second period I am a fence and a businessman, with some burglaries mixed in. The fence and the businessman are about even but I was more a fence I would say. This last period I am a businessman and a smalltime fence. The fencing is a sideline, very much so. If I was to live life over, I would want to be a fence. Only get into it sooner. Or be a guy in the rackets, like an Angelo.*

## Discussion

Current treatments of criminal careers have made many useful contributions to our understanding of criminality over the life course. These include improved understanding of types kinds of career trajectories for some kinds of offenders (Blumstein et al. 1986; Greenberg 1991; Nagin and Farrington 1992; D'Unger et al. 1998), recognition of both stable criminal propensity and changes in criminality across the life course, and better understanding of the careers of street offenders and "bottom-barrel" thieves and hustlers (Jacobs 1999; Shover 1996). But life in general and the world of crime in particular is far more complex and has more "grey areas" than the contemporary literature on criminal careers likes to admit. If Sutherland were alive today, what advice would he give and how would he respond to current developments in criminal career research? We think he would make nine important suggestions/corrections to the field today, and we illustrate these nine points with the material presented above from Sam Goodman's final interviews.

I. He would remind us that both generality/versatility and specialization in offending are congruent with his theory. The key factor in producing either empirical possibility is differential access to messages and opportunities that either encourage or discourage versatility or specialization.

1.  The potential transference of criminal skills and contacts, which makes a variety of crimes objectively possible;

2. "Larceny in the heart"; willingness to violate conventional standards in one area (e.g., burglary) sometimes indicates willingness to violate standards in another area (e.g., fencing, rackets). In addition, "since crime/deviance is defined by conventional standards for behavior, we would expect the overlap between general deviance and any particular behavior to fluctuate with variations in those standards" (Osgood et al. 1988: 91);
3. Norms in some underworld subcultures encourage specialization, while in other parts of the underworld the do not. For example, an all-around hustler or jack-of-all-trades offender is an admired status in some underworld circles (e.g., a member of La Cosa Nostra is an entrepreneur on the prowl to make money anyway he can);
4. Having the "heart" for one kind of crime will contribute to heart for another type of crime, leading to some versatility. Conversely, one can have or lose the heart for one type of crime but not have it for another type of crime, thus leading to specialization. Relatedly, there is the *background operator* who may support or direct a variety of criminal activities. This underworld role is played especially by older offenders who "mature" in the position at which time being a background operator is their *speciality*.
5. The lifestyle of criminal subculture as a whole (Jacobs 1999), and specific criminal behavior systems in particular, involve access to settings and people involved in other kinds of deviant activities, and a kind of contagion effect. This will contribute to versatility and arrest records showing involvement in multiple forms of crime or antisocial behavior. Street criminals in particular are often part of the "partying scene" (Hagan 1991; Jacobs 1999) and come in contact with persons on society's fringe much more than the average person, and much more so than many seasoned offenders like Sam or Jesse.
6. Skills and contacts cannot be infinitely stretched, and one can only be really good at one or a few types of crime. Also, opportunities are constrained by existing contacts and reputations. These are factors that can produce specialization.
7. One's rationalizations and neutralizations may foster specialization. One may try to maintain one's respectability by pointing to even less respectable behaviors. Sam did this, as did Jesse and many of the merchants to whom Sam sold stolen goods.

II. Sutherland would recognize that stable criminal propensity and change in criminality over the life course are both empirically possible (see Ulmer and Spencer 1999; Akers 1998). On one hand, delinquent behavior developed in early childhood may persist throughout life (Sutherland 1947: 7). In other words, exposure to criminal influences in early life can have a long-lasting influence on behavior. Also, exposure to criminal influences over prolonged periods of time has a greater effect on behavior than exposure over more limited periods. Both of these patterns, especially the latter, can be seen in the life of Sam Goodman.

On the other hand, criminal careers empirically exhibit both consistency and change and transitions (Ulmer and Spencer 1999). As abundant literature shows (see reviews in Sampson and Laub 1993; Ulmer 2000), many pathways into and out of crime across the life course exist, and criminal propensity is not *inherently* stable over time. Sutherland would point out, and some of the themes from Sam Goodman illustrate, that much of the change in criminal careers stems from the variations over time in differential-association processes, and access to attractive criminal opportunities and networks. Furthermore, labeling processes can heavily influence deviant career trajectories ( Ulmer 1994), as can luck, and situational and other factors (Adler and Adler 1983; Becker 1963). In addition, the original causes of behavior (e.g., bad companions, poverty, neuropsychological deficit) may not be the same as the later causes that sustain or entrench criminal behavior, but the generic role of association/learning processes will be similar.

III. We are certain that Sutherland would be very skeptical of the almost extreme emphasis on "pathology"—either in terms of personality (e.g., lack of self control, neuropsychological deficit) or the social environment (e.g., poverty)—found in some of the criminal careers literature. In fact, it is well known that he was highly critical of emphases on either psychological or social pathologies as generic explanations of all crime. For example, how well does Moffit's (1997; Moffit and Silva 1988) theory of neuropsychological deficit fit offenders like Sam, Jesse, Howie, Louie, Burkette (business merchant who regularly bought stolen goods), or Rosen (jeweler who also fenced stolen jeweler)? We suspect that it would not hold up very well. Furthermore, Moffit's theory also does not hold up very well even when the focus is on ordinary street offenders (see Lipsey and Derzon's [1998] meta-analysis of longitudinal studies of serious delinquency). Sam's interviews suggest that many chronic and serious offenders aren't "losers" either socially or psychologically.

IV. We think Sutherland would not agree with the image of human nature that self-control and predispositional theories depict; that one is bad from childhood onward, one is bad in nearly every way, one is bad most of the time, and one will always be bad. In our view, this image of human nature in self-control and propensity theories reflects more of a moral stance than a social scientific viewpoint with a sound empirical basis. Perhaps self-control theories and predispositional theories require criminals to have low self-control or psychological deficits because they engage in "bad" behavior, are morally reprehensible, and deserve to be negatively imaged.

Differential association, in seeing criminal offending as learned behavior, removes some of the stigma from criminals. Criminals are no longer intrinsically evil people; they are products of the same generic sociological processes that characterize every person who learns the innumerable tasks that people use throughout life. Sutherland's is also a more optimistic view of human nature. If crime is learned in the context of differentially organized groups, then if the criminal socialization is not too entrenched and the individual is not too embedded in criminal networks and relationships, crime can be replaced with more useful learning in the context of more conventional groups.

At the same time, there also are countervailing cultural pressures and contradictory messages even within dominant cultures. Subcultural values and identities, and subterrainian traditions and beliefs in the general culture condone or encourage "dishonesty." For example, mainstream American culture values honesty and trustworthiness, but also makes folk heroes (real and fictitious) out of Jesse James, Al Capone, and Don Corleone. Indeed, many readers found Sam Goodman in *The Fence* to be a sort of admirable rogue. Furthermore, even deviants are conforming in most aspects of their lives most of the time, and people are often deviant in some but not in most aspects of their lives and activities. Both of these situations characterized Sam Goodman. Sutherland recognized each of these possibilities, but some later criminologists have not (e.g., Kornhauser 1978; Gottfredson and Hirschi 1990; Hirschi 1996).

V. Sutherland made room for personality and predispositional variables in his theory of differential association (i.e., their possible effects on messages or opportunities), but was skeptical of their significance and empirical validity. Nonetheless, neither differential association nor Akers' social-learning theory deny that personality or neuropsychological predispositions (or even pathologies) play a role in at least some kinds of crime, and for some kinds of criminals.

VI. We believe Sutherland would be critical of the narrow view of his theory and the criminal landscape found in most of criminology, as well as the restricted view of crime and "chronic criminal offending." First, many contemporary researchers treat differential-association/social-learning theory as if it were synonymous with, and limited to, "peer influence." Instead, it is a theory of *differences in association with messages and opportunities favorable vs. unfavorable to crime.* Peers are *only* important insofar as associations with them are the carriers of messages and opportunities favorable to crime. However, peers are only one possible source of associations. Associations with parents (Hagan and Palloni 1990), relatives, teachers/mentors, and others, as well as real and imaginary role models (Glaser 1956; Akers 1998) can also be the carriers of criminal or deviant messages and opportunities. An example of this from Sam Goodman's life is the strong role of associations with Uncle Howie in Sam's criminal learning early in life.

Second, sophisticated quantitative studies of variations in criminal career trajectories like D'Unger et al. (1998), well done and informative ethnographies like those by Jacobs (1999) and Shover (1996), and overviews of the literature like Benson (2002) are valuable, but focus almost exclusively on street offenders and "losers." This focus ignores empirical material on offenders, including chronic and serious offenders, whose careers, networks, opportunities, and commitment to crime as a way of life are probably quite different than those of the ordinary, "bottom of the barrel" street offenders that are the focus of most criminology.

For example, Adler and Adler (1983), Bryant (1974), Letkemann (1973), Prus and Sharper (1977), Klockars (1974), Miller (1978), Steffensmeier (1986), and Ulmer (1994) provide studies that depart from the usual focus on bottom-level street offenders. In addition, the 1990 Pennsylvania Crime Commission Decade Report on Organized Crime essentially identified and provided mini-case studies of a very sizable number of racketeers, illicit entrepreneurs, professional criminals, moonlighting specialists, and background operators involved in gambling, loansharking, drug-dealing, the sex trade, theft, fencing stolen goods, political corruption, and other illicit scams and hustles. Most had lengthy criminal careers going back to adolescence or early adulthood, but did not necessarily have much in the way of an official criminal record. Most were between their mid-forties and mid-sixties, but some practiced their criminal trades well into their seventies. Similar findings are reported in some analyses of chronic or systematic involvement in lucrative kinds of white-collar criminality (Clinard 1952; Shapiro 1984).

Most criminologists working in the life course tradition ignore or deny almost completely a substantial portion of chronic, serious offenders. These chronic offenders, as reflected in the material from Sam Goodman include white-collar offenders and business merchants, secondhand dealers, and racketeers. By contrast, Sampson and Laub's (1993) reanalysis of the Glueck's data is sophisticated and valuable, but limited in scope. The Glueck's data came from very disadvantaged and abused boys who were mostly "bottom-barrel" street offenders. No matter how sophisticated Sampson and Laub's analysis, it cannot overcome this limitation in sampling, and the resulting problems for generalizability to other kinds of offenders. What is remarkable about their results is the high percentage who eventually desisted, apparently because of adult social bonds such as marriage and good jobs. However, an alternative explanation is that these men were so lacking in skills and sophistication ("losers"), that they owe their desistance to the lack of opportunity to do otherwise (i.e., were lacking in opportunity for lucrative crime or access to networks of reliable or skillful co-offenders). In any case, the key question we want to raise is whether, or to what extent, findings from contemporary studies of criminal career offending can be generalized to the full population of chronic offenders like Sam Goodman (and a sizable number of his colleagues or co-offenders).

VII. We believe Sutherland would be puzzled by the dichotomous view of desistance found in much of the criminal careers literature. In this literature, desistance is usually taken to mean "successful" disengagement from criminal behavior (Meisenhelder 1977). Offenders either desist or not. However, many criminal careers, like Sam Goodman's are marked by shifts and oscillations (Adler and Adler 1983). Thus, one lesson from the life of Sam Goodman is that the focus on complete desistance is too narrow. Some offenders do not so much terminate criminal activity, but may instead: (1) reduce or slow down the frequency of offending, perhaps even "moonlighting" in criminal activity to supplement one's legitimate income, (2) reduce the variety of offending, that is, specialize more, (3) reduce the type or seriousness of offending, or (4) switch to less visible forms of offending, to become more of a "background operator." Also, the causes and processes of desistance are likely to vary across distinct offender categories (such as street offenders vs. white-collar criminals; see Benson 2002).

Additionally, some approaches (Gottfredson and Hirschi 1990; Samspon and Laub 1993) emphasize either self-control or social bonds, but implicitly assume that opportunities for crime are ubiquitous and play little, if any, role in desistance. By contrast, we argue differences in access to crime opportunities, especially safe and profitable ones, play a key role in explaining desistance or continuation in crime. The greater the criminal opportunities that become or remain available, the greater the inclination to continue in crime. Furthermore, objective factors like criminal opportunity and subjective factors like criminal motivation, skills, definitions, and personal commitment to crime feed each other and complement one another (see Steffensmeier 1983, 1986; Ulmer 2000).

Sam Goodman never completely desisted from crime, but he did markedly reduce his offending frequency, roles, and seriousness. His career does show some support for contemporary portraits of desistance (see Benson 2002; Shover 1996) in that the effects of stable conventional work, marriage/stable partnership, transformation of identity, aging, and tiring of the "wear and tear" or "hassles" of criminal life all contributed to his criminal ebbing and slowdown. Additional potential factors in decline or desistance in criminal careers include changes in expectations of gratification from crime (or lack thereof), differential-association processes that favor conventional activity (including those that produce a loss of "heart" or "larceny in the heart"), and declining skills (which accompanies aging for some crimes) and importantly, perceptions of diminished attractive criminal opportunities or diminished criminal network contacts.

VIII. We think Sutherland would agree with Akers (1998) that rational choice theories are consistent with, and actually are a component of the more general theory of differential association/social learning. Social-learning theory brings in more clearly than perhaps Sutherland did that criminal behavior is determined by the results anticipated by the offenders (excitement, possessions/money, power, admiration of peers, and the defense of essential interests). In fact, some kinds of criminal decision making, like that of Sam

Goodman resembles the kind of "strategic analysis" described by Cusson (1983).

Offenders like Sam continue in crime (even as moonlighters later in life) because they judge it to be rational. As with most realms of human behavior, this kind of rationality is circumscribed by limitations such as lack of information, errors in judgment, and nonrational factors such as moral limitations (that is, there were activities that Sam refused to engage in, like drug dealing, because of his moral qualms about them, no matter how profitable they were or how available the opportunities were). For Sam, the opportunities were plentiful, the risks were manageable, the rewards were attractive (e.g., money, excitement, pride in his skill), and the criminal behavior was a part of his sense of self. At the height of his career, Sam (and many of his co-offenders) believed he would gain income from crime, would not get caught, would not serve much prison time if he got caught (e.g., because his business employs workers who provide economic support to families), and was not afraid to serve time because life in prison, while unpleasant, was not threatening to him.

We reiterate that opportunity is often key for understanding criminal careers and desistance—many offenders are "driven out" of crime by a lack of attractive opportunites. Alternatively, lack of opportunities for one kind of crime may drive offenders out of that crime into another, where pastures look greener. After all, it is hardly remarkable that criminals—like conventional workers—might reach a point in their lives when they seek less arduous careers, choose to move on to less demanding activities, and seek opportunities in related fields (e.g., switching from burglary to fencing, like Sam Goodman did).

IX. We believe Sutherland would encourage a stronger emphasis on networks as a feature of differential social organization. Criminal networks, like conventional ones, are forms of social organization made up of actors that pursue exchange relations with one another of varying duration (Podolny and Page 1998), though unlike conventional networks, they lack a legitimate organizational authority to arbitrate and resolve disputes that may arise during exchange.

We would also note that the ability to operate effectively in a network (what Sam called his "spider web") is a skill that must be learned. As Podolny and Page (1998: 72) argue, "the ability to exploit the substantive knowledge gained through network relationships without killing the proverbial goose can be viewed as an important capability in its own right." As Sam Goodman repeatedly says, the importance of trust in the viability in crime networks cannot be overemphasized. Contrary to the arguments of Kornhauser (1978), Hirschi (1996), and Gottfredson (1999), such viable criminal networks apparently do exist, and provide participants with many advantages for criminal enterprise. This, of course, would be no surprise to Sutherland.

We have presented Sam Goodman's career as a case study to illustrate differential-association/social-learning theory, and we derived nine points of critique that Sutherland might make of criminology today. Sutherland was the first to propose a truly viable general theory of crime. We believe that pursuing these nine suggestions in theorizing and empirical research would enrich criminology's understanding of the whole criminal landscape, and would demonstrate just how powerful Sutherland's legacy really is.

## References

Adler, Patricia, and Peter Adler. 1983. "Relations Between Dealers: The Social Organization of Illicit Drug Transactions." *Sociology and Social Research* 67:260-278.

Akers, Ronald. 1998. *Social Learning and Social Structure: A General Theory of Crime and Deviance.* Boston: Northeastern University Press.

Akers, Ronald. 1985. *Deviant Behavior: A Social Learning Approach.* Belmont, CA: Wadsworth.

Akers, Ronald, Marvin Krohn, Lonn Lanza-Kaduce, and Maria Radosevich. 1979. "Social Learning and Deviant Behavior: A Specific Test of a General Theory." *American Sociological Review* 44:635-655.

Athens, Lonnie. 1997. *Violent Criminal Acts and Actors Revisited.* Urbana: University of Illinois Press.

Becker, Howard. 1960. "Notes on the Concept of Commitment." *American Journal of Sociology* 66:32-40.

_____. 1963. *Outsiders.* New York: Macmillan.

Benson, Michael. 2002. *Crime and the Life Course.* Los Angeles: Roxbury.

Blumstein, Alfred, Jaqueline Cohen, J. Roth, and Christy Visher. 1986 *Criminal Careers and "Career Criminals."* Vols. 1 and 2. Washington, DC: National Academy Press.

Braithwaite, John. 1989. *Crime, Shame, and Reintegration.* Cambridge: Cambridge University Press.

Bryant, Clifton (ed.). 1974. *Deviant Behavior: Occupational and Organizational Bases.* Chicago: Rand McNally.

Clinard, Marshall. 1952. *The Black Market.* New York: Rinehart.

Cloward, Richard, and Lloyd Ohlin. 1960. *Delinquency and Opportunity.* Glencoe, IL: Free Press.

Cusson, Maurice. 1983. *Why Delinquency?* Toronto: University of Toronto Press.

D'Unger, Amy, Kenneth Land, Patricia McCall, and Daniel Nagin. 1998. "How Many Latent Classes of Delinquent/Criminal Careers? Results from Mixed Poisson Regression Analyses." *American Journal of Sociology* 103:1593-1630.

Glaser, Daniel. 1956. "Criminality Theories and Behavioral Images." *American Journal of Sociology* 61:440-441.

Gottfredson, Michael. 1999. Review of *Social Learning and Social Structure*, by Ronald Akers. *American Journal of Sociology* 105:283-284.

Gottfredson, Michael, and Travis Hirschi. 1990. *A General Theory of Crime.* Stanford, CA: Stanford University Press.

Greenberg, David. 1991. "Modeling Criminal Careers." *Criminology* 29:17-46.

Hagan, John. 1991. "Destiny and Drift: Subcultural Preferences, Status Attainments, and the Risks and Rewards of Youth." *American Sociological Review* 56:567-581.

Hagan, J., and A. Palloni. 1990. "The Social Reproduction of a Criminal Class in Working-Class London, circa 1950-1980." *American Journal of Sociology* 96: 265-299.

Hirschi, Travis. 1996. "Theory without Ideas: Reply to Akers." *Criminology* 34 (2):249-256.

Jacobs, Bruce. 1999. *Dealing Crack: The Social World of Streetcorner Selling*. Boston: Northeastern University Press.

Klockars, Carl. 1974. *The Professional Fence*. New York: Free Press.

Kornhauser, Ruth. 1978. *Social Sources of Delinquency*. Chicago: University of Chicago Press.

Letkemann, Peter. 1973. *Crime as Work*. Englewood Cliffs, NJ: Prentice-Hall.

Lipsey, Mark and James Derzon. 1998. "Predictors of Violent or Serious Delinquency in Adolescence and Early Adulthood: A Synthesis of Longitudinal Research." In Rolf Loeber and David Farrington (eds.), *Serious & Violent Juvenile Offenders: Risk Factors and Successful Interventions*. Thousand Oaks, CA: Sage.

Matsueda, Ross. 1992. "Reflected Appraisals, Parental Labeling, and Delinquency: Specifying a Symbolic Interactionist Theory." *American Journal of Sociology* 97:1577-1611.

Meisenhelder, Thomas. 1977. "An Exploratory Study of Exiting from Criminal Careers." *Criminology* 15:319-334.

Merton, Robert. 1938. "Social Structure and Anomie." *American Sociological Review* 3:672-682.

_____. 1997. "On the Evolving Synthesis of Differential Association and Anomie Theory: A Perspective from the Sociology of Science." *Criminology* 35:517-525.

Miller, Gale. 1978. *Odd Jobs: The World of Deviant Work*. Englewood Cliffs, NJ: Prentice-Hall.

Moffitt, Terrie. 1997. "Adolescence-Limited and Life-Course Persistent Offending: A Complementary Pair of Developmental Theories." In T. Thornberry (ed.), *Developmental Theories of Crime and Delinquency*. New Brunswick, NJ: Transaction Publishers.

Moffitt, Terrie, and Phil Silva. 1988. "Neuropsychological Deficit and Self-Reported Delinquency in an Unselected Birth Cohort." *Journal of the American Academy of Child and Adolescent Psychiatry* 27:233-240.

Nagin, Daniel, and David Farrington. 1992. "The Stability of Criminal Potential from Childhood to Adulthood." *Criminology* 30:235-60.

Osgood, D. Wayne, Lloyd Johnston, Patrick O'Malley, and Jerald Bachman. 1988. "The Generality of Deviance in Late Adolescence and Early Adulthood." *American Sociological Review* 53:81-93.

Pennsylvania Crime Commission. 1991. *1990 Decade Report on Organized Crime in Pennsylvania*. Conshohocken, PA: Commonwealth of Pennsylvania.

Pistone, Joseph. 1987. *Donnie Brasco*. New York: Penguin Books.

Podolny, Joe, and Karen Page. 1998. "Network Forms of Organizations." *Annual Review of Sociology* 24:57-140. Palo Alto, CA: Annual Reviews.

Prus, Robert, and C. R. D. Sharper. 1977. *Road Hustler*. Toronto: Gage.

Sampson, Robert, and John Laub. 1993. *Crime in the Making: Pathways and Turning Points through Life*. Cambridge, MA: Harvard University Press.

Shapiro, Susan. 1984. *Wayward Capitalists: Target of the Securities and Exchange Commission*. New Haven, CT: Yale University Press.

Shover, Neal. 1996. *Great Pretenders: Pursuits and Careers of Persistent Thieves*. Boulder, CO: Westview Press.

Steffensmeier, Darrell. 1983. "Organization Properties and Sex-Segregation in the Underworld: Building a Sociological Theory of Sex Differences in Crime." *Social Forces* 6:1010-1032.

_____. 1986. *The Fence: In the Shadow of Two Worlds.* Totowa, NJ: Rowman and Littlefield.

Sutherland, Edwin. 1937. *The Professional Thief.* Chicago: University of Chicago Press.

_____. 1940. "White Collar Criminality." *American Sociological Review* 5:1-12.

_____. 1947. *Principles of Criminology.* Philadelphia: J. B. Lippincott.

Sykes, Gresham, and David Matza. 1957. "Techniques of Neutralization: A Theory of Delinquency." *American Sociological Review* 22:664-670.

Ulmer, Jeffery T. 1994. "Revisiting Stebbins: Labeling and Commitment to Deviance." *The Sociological Quarterly* 35:135-157.

_____. 2000. "Commitment, Deviance, and Social Control." *The Sociological Quarterly* 41:315-336.

Ulmer, Jeffery T., and J. William Spencer. 1999. "The Contributions of an Interactionist Approach to Research and Theory on Criminal Careers." *Theoretical Criminology* 3:95-124.

Warr, Mark. 1993. "Age, Peers, and Delinquency." *Criminology* 31:17-40.

Warr, Mark, and Mark Stafford. 1991. "The Influence of Delinquent Peers: What They Think or What They Do?" *Criminology* 29:851-866.

# 11

# Exploring the Relationship between Social and Non-Social Reinforcement in the Context of Social Learning Theory

*Timothy Brezina and Alex R. Piquero*

In recent years, criminologists have given more attention to the idea that juveniles engage in delinquency because such behavior is a source of intrinsic pleasure and reward. Greater attention to this idea appears to be warranted. Several studies indicate that participation in delinquency is often associated with immediate gratification—mainly in the form of positive emotional sensations such as "fun," "thrills," and "excitement" (e.g., Agnew 1990; Katz 1988; Wood et al. 1994, 1995, 1997). Consequently, a number of theorists have concluded that, for some individuals, delinquency/drug use may be "rewarding in and of itself, independent of any extrinsic rewards such behavior might produce" (Grasmick and Bursik 1990:857; Gove and Wilmoth 1990; Katz 1988; Wood et al. 1995; also see Gottfredson and Hirschi 1990). Moreover, some theorists contend that the expectation of intrinsic reward is a major motivating force behind delinquent involvement (Katz 1988; Wood et al. 1994, 1995, 1997).

Certain theorists also suggest that, in the context of social learning theory, greater attention to the intrinsic rewards of crime and delinquency (or *nonsocial* reinforcement) will be important for the further development of the theory. In principle, social learning theory encompasses the role of nonsocial reinforcement in the learning of criminal and delinquent behavior. With few exceptions, however, social learning theorists have focused mainly on processes of social reinforcement, with special attention to such factors as attitudes, beliefs, and delinquent peer influences. It is possible that processes of nonsocial reinforcement—in the form of immediate pleasures and powerful emotional sensations—may play a larger and more direct role in the etiology of delinquency and drug use (see Katz 1988; Wood et al. 1997). Moreover individuals may vary in the extent to which they derive intrinsic pleasure from delinquency, and this fact may help to explain why some youths exhibit relatively high levels of delinquent involvement. According to Wood and his colleagues (1995:188), "social learning theory traditionally fails to consider individual differences in finding thrills and excitement intrinsically rewarding." Greater consideration of such differences, they argue, may help to enhance and expand the theory in important ways.

In light of the above observations and suggestions, we give further consideration to the role of nonsocial reinforcement in social learning theory. In this chapter, we examine the role of nonsocial reinforcement as stated in Akers' social learning theory of crime and deviance. We also examine the ability of the theory—as currently formulated—to account for individual differences in the propensity to derive intrinsic rewards from delinquency and drug use. Ultimately, we find that the processes of "nonsocial" reinforcement described above are not as independent or distinct from traditional social learning processes as some theorists have claimed or implied. Rather, processes of social and nonsocial reinforcement appear to be intimately related (also see Akers 1977:55; 1998:70-72; 2000:78).

In particular, processes of social reinforcement appear to play an important role in shaping the immediate experience of delinquent involvement, including the extent to which delinquent acts produce direct positive effects in the eyes of the offender. Thus, social learning theory, with its current emphasis on social reinforcement, may already be equipped with the conceptual tools necessary to incorporate an emphasis on "intrinsic rewards" and to account for individual differences in the propensity to derive intrinsic pleasure from delinquent involvement. The theory, however, would benefit from a detailed statement on this issue.

Toward this end, we conduct a theoretically informed examination of the relationship between social and "nonsocial" reinforcement and articulate an initial statement. We also derive several hypotheses which we test with exploratory data from a large sample of adolescents. To illustrate our points, we focus mainly on adolescent drug and alcohol use. However, we also relate our arguments to more general forms of criminal/delinquent involvement and show how these arguments can facilitate future research.

## Nonsocial Reinforcement and Delinquency

The history of positive criminology can be summarized in simple terms as the search for the biological, psychological, and socio-environmental factors that increase the probability of—and logically precede—criminal and delinquent involvement. As Katz (1988) describes, "The study of crime has been preoccupied with a search for background forces, usually defects in the offenders' psychological backgrounds or social environments" (p. 3).

Thus far, this search has yielded moderate success. Contemporary criminology texts tend to highlight a standard set of key "risk factors" involving such variables as delinquent peer associations, aspects of the social bond, certain individual traits, and other psychosocial factors. To be sure, there is much debate over *how* and *why* these background factors increase the probability of delinquent involvement (Agnew 1995) and the causal status of many factors remains tentative. These problems alone, however, are not likely to change criminologists' preoccupation with background risk factors. Rather, criminologists will likely respond to these problems by intensifying their examination of such factors—in an effort to refine our understanding of their influence and operation.

Yet, there are compelling reasons to believe that this focus on background risk factors, by itself, is not likely to yield a complete or satisfactory account of criminal/delinquent behavior—especially criminal and delinquent conduct that is habitual or reoccurring. What is lacking is adequate attention to the specific qualities of the deviant experience, the manner in which these qualities affect the offender, and the power of such qualities to motivate future criminal and delinquent behavior.

With a few important exceptions, the bulk of criminological theory and research has treated delinquency as a dependent variable and relegated it to the very end of the causal chain. Yet there is reason to believe that involvement in delinquent behavior is itself a key factor in the etiology of persistent offending and, indeed, a more important determinant of future offending than any other background factor. As Gottfredson and Hirschi (1990:107) observe, "competent research regularly shows that the best predictor of crime is prior criminal behavior." Moreover, longitudinal studies typically reveal that the effects of other background factors are substantially reduced in size after prior levels of criminal and delinquent behavior are controlled, leading some researchers to conclude that the effects of these other factors have been exaggerated in previous theory and research (e.g., see Agnew 1985, 1991; Matsueda 1989; Matsueda and Anderson 1998).

The strong effect of prior delinquency has been explained in a number of different ways. According to some theorists, a high level of prior delinquency is likely to foster negative labeling, generate additional interpersonal strain, weaken inhibitions, or further erode social controls, and thereby strengthen a delinquent orientation (Agnew 1997; Nagin and Paternoster 1991; Sampson and Laub 1997; Thornberry 1987). According to Gottfredson and Hirschi (1990), a high level of prior delinquency indexes a time-stable propensity to offend which, in their view, is a function of low self-control. Akers (1998), on the other hand, interprets the effect in terms of his social learning theory of crime and deviance—asserting that a high level of prior delinquency indexes previously learned behavior patterns, resulting from differential association with delinquent peers, modeling and imitation, and social and nonsocial reinforcement. In the words of Akers (1998:159), "The more behavior has been shaped through differential reinforcement in the past, the more likely it is that it has developed habit strength, and the more likely it is to be repeated in the future."

A related possibility, which is theoretically consistent with Akers' social learning interpretation, is that something about the experience of delinquency itself is highly rewarding and is therefore likely to motivate future delinquent involvement (Gove and Wilmoth 1990; Wood et al. 1994, 1995, 1997). As noted above, Akers' learning account recognizes the possible roles of both social and nonsocial reinforcement and, thus, conceptually it encompasses feedback from the social environment as well as nonsocial feedback in the form of physiological arousal produced by drugs and alcohol, sensations of thrill and excitement resulting from participation in deviant and risky acts, or other intrinsic rewards. The main focus of social learning theory, however, is on social reinforcement (see Akers 2000:78-79). Yet, if the possibility raised above has merit, the role of nonsocial reinforcement in the etiology of crime and delinquency requires further consideration. In the words of Katz (1988:3), criminologists would do well to consider the *foreground* of crime and to explore the seductive qualities of the deviance, including "what it means, feels, sounds, tastes, or looks like" to commit a delinquent or criminal act.

It would not be correct to say that the foreground of crime has been overlooked by earlier criminologists. Rather, it has largely been taken for granted and, for this reason, not subjected to extensive scientific scrutiny (also see Gove 1994). The idea that offenders are motivated by the intrinsic pleasures of crime is, in fact, a core underlying assumption of social control theory. So strong is this assumption that, in the view of social control theorists, crime requires no further explanation (Hirschi 1969; also see Gottfredson and Hirschi 1990). It is also true, however, that social control theorists further assume that the attraction to crime and its pleasures is universal, and that the strength of this attraction is constant across groups and individuals. Although this assumption of constant motivation is highly questionable (e.g., see Elliott, Huizinga, and Ageton 1985), it has served nonetheless to direct the attention of researchers away from the real or anticipated pleasures of crime. The attention of researchers is drawn instead to variation and, in the view of social control theorists, this is to be found in the strength of the individual's bond to society. The assumption of constant motivation has also discouraged consideration of (if not denying all together) the possibility that individuals may differ in terms of the amount of pleasure they ultimately derive from criminal and delinquent involvement.

Ironically, the intrinsic pleasures of crime and delinquency have received more attention from researchers who have rejected—implicitly or explicitly—the assumptions of social control theory. Matza and Sykes (1961:713-714) identified some of the specific pleasures of delinquency and also raised the possibility of individual differences by highlighting the sheer thrill and excitement of much delinquent behavior, pointing to these sensations as a "major motivating force," and describing delinquents as "deeply immersed in a restless search" for the kind of thrills offered by a deviant lifestyle (also see McCarthy 1995; Nagin and Paternoster 1993; Piquero and Tibbetts 1996). In more recent years, Akers (1998) and his colleagues have examined—theoretically and empirically—the contributing role of nonsocial reinforcement to the learning of deviant behavior, primarily in the context of substance use and abuse. Nonetheless, the examination of nonsocial reinforcers has been largely overshadowed by learning theorists' focus on social reinforcers and other background risk factors.

In his groundbreaking work, *Seductions of Crime*, Katz (1988) provides what we believe to be the most notable departure from the traditional criminological focus on background factors and, indeed, the most comprehensive examination of the "foreground" of crime, including the specific pleasures associated with various kinds of criminal and delinquent acts. Drawing on personal accounts and other materials, Katz attempts to view deviance through the eyes of offenders and discovers a range of sensual dynamics operating outside the boundaries of conventional life. Offenders are shown to revel in the "sneaky thrills" of property crimes; to reap a sense of power, control, and significance from their ability to inspire fear and dread in others; and to achieve a sense of accomplishment from their ability to navigate social chaos and, ultimately, transcend the ordinary limitations of the conventional world. In fact, these enticements can be so compelling and powerful that at times offenders may feel drawn or propelled to crime and thus "lose themselves" in the sensuality of their own criminality.

Following the publication of *Seductions of Crime*, Gove and Wilmoth (1990) specify the possible biological bases of these sensual dynamics. Drawing on a substantial body of neurophysiological research, they conclude that, for some people, challenging and risky behaviors such as crime and delinquency activate a dopamine-dependent reward process in the brain, leading to the experience of an intrinsically pleasurable "neurophysiologic high."

A series of quantitative self-report studies conducted by Peter B. Wood and his colleagues lend further support to this conclusion. When asked to report their primary reason for using drugs and alcohol, the vast majority of adolescent respondents in a study by Wood et al. (1995) referred to either the direct pleasurable effects of substance use ("it felt good") or to the fun, thrills, and excitement associated with substance use and the ability to "get away with it." No more than 10 percent of the respondents identified peer modeling or influence (e.g., because "my friends were doing it too")—or any other social reinforcement—as the primary reason for their substance use.

In another study, Wood and his colleagues (1997) obtained reports from incarcerated offenders and college students who were asked to either describe or anticipate the kind of "feelings" associated with various criminal acts. These reports suggest that theft and violence are also associated with positive sensations, especially among the more experienced offenders who claimed to be "very familiar" with such crimes. It appears to be the experience of these offenders that criminal involvement often generates pleasurable emotional sensations such as feelings of being "intensively alive," "powerful," "pumped up," "on a high or rush," and "on top of the world" (Wood et al. 1997:355; also see Agnew 1990; Wood et al. 1994). Based on the accounts of habitual offenders, it also appears that pleasurable sensations of this sort are "very important" motivations for crime, especially violence (Wood et al. 1994).

Due to the self-report nature of the studies, these findings must be viewed as tentative. Although the findings obtained by Wood and his colleagues are highly consistent with numerous ethnographic studies of crime, the validity of offender accounts can be challenged on the grounds that offenders may not possess sufficient awareness of personal motivations, experiences, or related internal processes; they may have trouble engaging in accurate recall or may find it difficult to articulate their motivations and experiences; and/or they may feel compelled to rationalize or justify their criminal involvement and therefore provide distorted information. These challenges, however, may best apply to studies that ask offenders to account for their general predisposition to criminality, especially in terms of background risk factors. These challenges may have less merit when dealing with the concrete moods and feelings associated with specific criminal and delinquent acts (Agnew 1990).

It can also be noted that self-gratification—both as a motivator and product of crime—is a prevalent theme in the offender accounts collected by Wood and his colleagues, suggesting that the offenders under study did not feel a strong need to rationalize or justify their involvement (Wood et al. 1994:81; also see Agnew 1990). Moreover, in the 1997 study by Wood and his colleagues, it appears that offenders with the most extensive criminal histories—those who presumably would have the strongest need to rationalize and justify criminal involvement—are, in fact, the most likely to associate the offending experience with self-gratification. In particular, individuals who say they are "very familiar" with crime (habitual offenders) are more likely than others to associate criminal involvement with positive emotional sensations such as excitement and pride, and less likely to associate crime with feelings of guilt or remorse.

The existence of individual-level variation in the experience of crime-associated pleasure deserves special attention because it may have broader implications for understanding crime and delinquency. If some individuals are more likely than others to reap neurophysiologic highs from crime and delinquency, and if such variation can be explained, then we may better understand why some persons exhibit a relatively strong propensity to offend.

## Explaining Individual Differences in the Experience of Delinquency-Derived Pleasures and Rewards

Previous researchers have noted the strong possibility that some individuals are "particularly responsive to the neurological reward" associated with risky and dangerous behaviors, including crime and delinquency (Gove and Wilmoth 1990:263). Yet attempts to explain individual differences in this regard have not been a major focus of criminologists in this area.[1] Perhaps the most complete account available is provided by Baldwin's (1990) "sensory stimulation" account of adolescent delinquency, described below.

### The Role of Sensation-Seeking Motives

As individuals move from childhood to adolescence, they tend to habituate to increasing levels of sensory stimulation, as prior levels of stimulation lose their ability to arouse or excite (Baldwin 1990). This process of habituation leads most youths to seek out new and more novel experiences. In the words of Baldwin (1990:207), over the years young people "come to find higher and higher levels of sensory input to be optimally stimulating and rewarding." By the time they reach adolescence, most young people are strongly attracted to the "buzzing" adolescent subculture.

While these processes of habituation and sensation-seeking apply to youths in general, youths nonetheless habituate to different levels of sensory stimulation due to variation in reward-punishment contingencies and to individual differences in the ability to manage highly stimulating activities. Some youths may find the ratio of reinforcers to punishers to be particularly high for their sensation-seeking behavior, thereby promoting habituation to relatively high levels of sensory input. In their search for new and exciting activities, these youths may be especially likely to discover the thrills of criminal and delinquent involvement and "get hooked on such illegal behavior as a way of obtaining the rewards of optimal levels of sensory stimulation" (Baldwin 1990:208). According to Baldwin (1990:208), youths who "love high levels of sensory stimulation are more likely to find crime an optimally stimulating and reinforcing sensory high."

Baldwin (1990), however, does not specify the exact nature of the social rewards and punishments (or lack of punishments) that would lead some youths to find crime and delinquency optimally stimulating and intrinsically rewarding. We believe insights drawn from Akers' social learning theory of crime and deviance can point us to some of the more relevant processes and, ultimately, can help us to better understand why some individuals are particularly responsive to the neurophysiologic highs of criminal and delinquent involvement.

*Insights from Akers' Social Learning Theory*

As stated earlier, social learning theory places explicit emphasis on processes of social versus nonsocial reinforcement. In light of recent research on the intrinsic rewards of crime, this emphasis on social reinforcement may appear to reflect an unjustified bias. In fact, it has substantial grounding in theory and observation. As Akers (2000:78) describes, social learning theory recognizes the possible role of nonsocial reinforcers (intrinsic rewards), but the emphasis of the theory is on social reinforcers because it is partly through social reinforcement that "one learns to interpret the effects [of crime, delinquency, or drug use] as pleasurable or enjoyable or as frightening and unpleasant." In the view of social learning theory, processes of social and nonsocial reinforcement are intimately related and, for this reason, it may be difficult to isolate processes that are truly nonsocial in nature. The direct physiological effects of drugs and alcohol may provide the best example of nonsocial reinforcement but, even in this case, "whether or not these effects are experienced positively or negatively is partially contingent upon previously learned expectations" (Akers 1998:71).

Becker's (1953) classic study of marijuana use provides a good illustration of this argument. Becker (1953:239) observes that "marijuana-produced sensations are not automatically or necessarily pleasurable." In fact, novice users frequently do not experience any apparent effects from the drug. Others may find the effects to be confusing or frightening. Whether or not the novice user reaps intrinsic pleasure from marijuana, and thus acquires a taste for the drug, often depends on the user's exposure to others who call attention to its positive effects. In particular, other users may talk the novice user out of being afraid; reassure the novice that unpleasant sensations are only temporary; convince the novice that eventually "one learns to like it"; and provide concrete referents to assist the novice in interpreting the overall effects of marijuana as a pleasurable "high." In short, how a person experiences the effects of a drug depends greatly on the way others define those effects for him or her (also see Becker 1967).

We suspect that the same conclusion also applies to more general forms of criminal and delinquent involvement. Because many delinquent acts are committed in groups, much criminal and delinquent behavior is social in nature, and thus similar processes of definition and redefinition may occur. Through association with peers who approve of delinquent activities, individuals become more likely to interpret the actual *experience* of delinquent involvement as overwhelmingly positive in nature. For example, other offenders may help the individual to minimize the seriousness of various offenses and to see that nothing horrible is likely to happen. They may also talk the individual out of being afraid and therefore reduce anxiety; build confidence; call attention to the more enjoyable aspects of offending (including intrinsic thrill and excitement); and ultimately shape the symbolic meanings the individual comes to attach to deviant behavior. For these reasons, extensive exposure to delinquent peers may help to explain why some individuals are particularly responsive to the "intrinsic" pleasures of criminal and delinquent activity.

Peer influences, however, are not likely to be the only forces shaping the individual's experience of delinquency. Due to effective prior socialization in the form of moral beliefs or definitions, and to the symbolic meanings and associations individuals have previously attached to criminal and delinquent conduct, many individuals may associate such behavior primarily with feelings of guilt and shame. Moreover, for such individuals, real or anticipated feelings of guilt and shame may be so strong that they outweigh the positive sensations potentially derived from participation in criminal and delinquent acts. Thus, while delinquent peers can reinforce and—to a certain extent— make possible delinquent sensation-seeking, received punishments are also likely to affect the immediate experience of deviant behavior. The most important punishments in this regard may be those arising from internal processes.

While some criminologists view internalized moral beliefs or definitions as "nonpunitive" controls (Paternoster 1989), we believe there is merit in the suggestion made by Grasmick and Bursik (1990:840) that moral beliefs can make possible a kind of "self-imposed, or reflective, punishment." As they describe:

> The internalization of a norm poses another kind of potential cost or punishment for violating the law—the threat of guilt feelings or shame for doing something which the actor considers morally wrong.... The most immediate adverse consequence of such guilt feelings probably is a physiological discomfort, but more long-term consequences might include a damaged self-concept, depression, anxiety, etc., which could impede normal functioning in one's social environment (Grasmick and Bursik 1990:840).

The fact that strong moral beliefs may generate physiological discomfort is important because, if correct, this would suggest that the neurophysiologic pleasures of crime must compete with potential physiological distress associated with feelings of guilt or shame. Ultimately, physiological discomfort generated by strong moral beliefs may detract from the "neurophysiologic highs" of crime. Thus, among individuals with strong moral beliefs, criminal and delinquent involvement (to the extent that such behavior is undertaken) is not likely to be reinforcing. For individuals who lack strong moral beliefs, the overall balance of pleasure taken from crime should be relatively great, and this fact may help to explain why some individuals are particularly responsive to the intrinsic rewards of illegal behavior.

In sum, social learning processes are seen to play an important role in shaping the extent to which one associates criminal and delinquent acts with intrinsic pleasure and reward, especially processes involving differential association (exposure to delinquent peers and peers' norm qualities) and definitions (moral beliefs). Although other social or nonsocial (biological) factors may also play a role, we suspect that the factors highlighted above are among the factors having the most direct, and therefore strongest, influence on the amount of intrinsic pleasure individuals come to associate with criminal and delinquent involvement.

In the section below, we report the results of an initial, exploratory attempt to test our social learning account, drawing on drug and alcohol data from a large sample of adolescents.

*Data and Methods*

To examine the influence of various social learning factors on the experience of intrinsic reward, we draw on data from the first two waves of the Youths and Deterrence (YD) study. The YD study is a multiwave panel survey based on a sample of public high school students located "in and around a mid-sized southeastern city" (Paternoster 1989). The data are available to member universities through the Inter-University Consortium of Political and Social Research (ICPSR). The survey contains measures of delinquency and drug use, differential association (exposure to delinquent peers and peers' norm qualities) and definitions unfavorable to delinquency and drug use (moral beliefs). Although the survey does not measure the level of intrinsic reward respondents associate with general forms of crime and delinquency, it does contain items that index the extent to which alcohol and marijuana have positive effects on the respondent. Thus, these data permit an initial test of our social learning account in the context of adolescent drug and alcohol use.

The initial wave of data collection took place during the beginning of the 1981-82 school year. Confidential questionnaires were administered to all tenth-grade students attending nine different high schools in the city. The composition of the student bodies in these schools is said to reflect the demographic characteristics (gender, race, and social class) of the surrounding metropolitan area. According to the author of the study, "over 99 percent of the approximately 2,700 attending students agreed to participate in the study" (Paternoster 1989).

A follow-up questionnaire containing identical items was administered to the same students approximately one year later, as they were beginning the eleventh grade. Approximately 1,600 of the original students (60 percent) completed the follow-up questionnaire, with most of the sample attrition due to student absences on the day of questionnaire administration or other "essentially random" factors (Paternoster 1989:15). Data presented by Paternoster (1989:15) indicate that, with respect to key variables, respondents lost to attrition did not differ substantially from respondents who continued in the study (for additional details, see Paternoster 1989).

*Measures of Variables*

*Alcohol and Marijuana Use.* Measures of self-reported substance use include an item that asks respondents to report the number of times they "drank liquor" during the previous twelve months, and another item that asks them to report the number of times they used marijuana during the previous twelve months. These items were administered during both waves of data collection.[2]

*Effects of Alcohol/Marijuana.* Two items in the survey index the amount of pleasure respondents obtain from substance use. If a respondent in the survey had used alcohol more than once, he or she was asked to report "the effects" that alcohol "usually has on him or her." A similar item asked respondents to report the usual effects of marijuana. Responses to each item (recoded) range from 1 ("mainly bad effects") to 2 ("mixed or no effects") to 3 ("mainly good effects"). A potential limitation of these measures is that they do not index the exact nature of the positive or negative effects. Thus, it is possible that these items tap effects that are not strictly "nonsocial" (or physiological) in nature. However, it seems clear from the wording of these items that they are intended to refer to the direct effects of alcohol and marijuana on the user. For this reason, we believe these items are suitable as rough measures of the amount of intrinsic pleasure (i.e., "good effects") derived from drug and alcohol use (also see Paternoster and Triplett 1988:602). Thus, they should be suitable for purposes of exploratory analyses.[3]

*Differential Association.* Two measures of differential association were employed: peer substance use and peer approval of substance use. Many delinquent acts, especially those related to the consumption of alcohol and marijuana, are committed in the company of peers (Reiss 1988). Respondents were asked about the proportion of their friends who (a) "drink liquor under age" and (b) have "used marijuana." Response options range on a four-point continuum from "none" to "all." In addition, each respondent was asked to report how his or her best friends would most likely react if they knew that he or she had (a) "drunk liquor" and (b) "used marijuana." Responses to these items range on a five-point continuum from "strongly disapprove" to "strongly approve."

*Definitions Unfavorable to Alcohol/Marijuana Use (Moral Beliefs).* Respondents in the survey were asked to judge the moral unacceptability of alcohol and marijuana use. In particular, each respondent was asked to state "how wrong" it is to (a) "drink liquor under age" and (b) "smoke marijuana." Responses to each item range on a five-point continuum from "never wrong" to "always wrong."

*Control Variables.* Our analyses control for a number of variables that have been linked to general delinquency and substance use including the following dummy variables: race (scored 1 for nonwhite respondents), sex (scored 1 for male respondents), and family structure (scored 1 for respondents who live with both their mother and father). A single-item measure of family involvement indexes the average number of hours the respondent spends with his family each week. A two-item measure of parental attachment indexes the extent to which the respondent feels it is important that his or her mother and father approve of the respondent's activities (alpha reliability = .63). A three-item measure of commitment to school indexes the extent to which the respondent feels it is important to "get good grades," finish high school," and "get a college degree" (alpha = .74). Finally, a pair of two-item measures index the extent to which the respondent believes his or her mother and father would disapprove if they knew that the respondent had (a) "drunk liquor under age" (alpha = .78) and (b) "used marijuana" (alpha = .80). To adjust for skew in the distributions of the parental disapproval measures, each was dichotomized into "low" and "high," with the latter category representing strong parental disapproval (also see Paternoster 1989:18).

In the section below, we report the results of exploratory cross-sectional and longitudinal OLS regression analyses. Where appropriate, we also report the results of supplementary bivariate and structural equations analyses. Because our measures of intrinsic pleasure (i.e., positive effects derived from alcohol and marijuana) apply only to respondents who have used alcohol or marijuana "more than once," these respondents are the focus of our analyses. All other respondents are excluded from the analyses reported below.

### Results

*Cross-Sectional Regression Analyses*

Table 11.1 shows the cross-sectional impact (OLS regression estimates) of the social learning measures on self-reported effects of alcohol and marijuana, controlling for parental attachment, commitment to school, frequency of substance use, and other variables. Consistent with expectations, the social learning measures exert significant effects on the amount of pleasure respondents derive from alcohol and marijuana. Moreover, these effects are in the predicted direction. Differential association factors (peer substance use and peers' approval of substance use) are associated with an increase in the amount of pleasure (or "good effects") respondents derive from alcohol and marijuana, while adherence to moral beliefs against substance use is associated with a decrease in such pleasure (p < .05).

In addition to social learning factors, frequency of substance use and race have significant associations with the self-reported effects of alcohol and marijuana. Nonwhite respondents tend to report fewer positive effects from substance use, while frequent users tend to report more positive effects (p <

## Table 11.1
### The Cross-Sectional Effects of Social Learning Variables on the Self-Reported Effects of Alcohol and Marijuana

*Dependent Variables:*

| | Alcohol has Good Effects | | | | Marijuana has Good Effects | | | |
|---|---|---|---|---|---|---|---|---|
| | b | (B) | S.E. | t-value | b | (B) | S.E. | t-value |
| *Independent Variables* | | | | | | | | |
| Peer Use | .078 | (.110) | .021 | 3.661* | .063 | (.080) | .032 | 1.969* |
| Peer Approval | .073 | (.100) | .021 | 3.518* | .110 | (.159) | .027 | 4.029* |
| Moral Belief | -.082 | (-.167) | .014 | -5.936* | -.134 | (-.275) | .020 | -6.762* |
| *Control Variables* | | | | | | | | |
| Family Structure (1 = intact) | .008 | (.007) | .032 | .265 | .020 | (.014) | .047 | .426 |
| Family Involvement | -.001 | (-.049) | .000 | -1.998* | -.001 | (-.026) | .001 | -.792 |
| Parental Attachment | -.001 | (-.003) | .008 | -.120 | .008 | (.025) | .011 | .723 |
| Parental Disapproval | .016 | (.010) | .041 | .387 | .024 | (.011) | .073 | .328 |
| Commitment to School | -.009 | (-.040) | .006 | -1.568 | .006 | (.024) | .009 | .701 |
| Sex (1 = male) | .008 | (.006) | .029 | .260 | .036 | (.026) | .045 | .800 |
| Race (1 = nonwhite) | -.319 | (-.173) | .046 | -6.951* | -.182 | (-.093) | .064 | -2.845* |
| Drinking Behavior | .002 | (.124) | .000 | 4.453* | — | | — | — |
| Marijuana Use | — | | — | — | .005 | (.165) | .001 | 3.793* |
| R Squared | .204 | | | | .307 | | | |
| N (listwise deletion) | 1,390 | | | | 695 | | | |

*Note:* Analyses include respondents who have used alcohol/marijuana "more than once." Unstandardized effects shown, with standardized effects in parentheses.

* p<.05 (one-tailed test)

.05). High levels of family involvement are associated with fewer positive effects from alcohol (p < .05), but not marijuana.[4]

Although the findings described above are consistent with our social learning account of delinquency-derived pleasures and rewards, they should be viewed with caution due to the cross-sectional nature of the analyses. Time 1 measures of social learning have been used to explain time 1 self-reported effects of alcohol and marijuana. It might be argued that the relationship between social learning and drug-associated pleasure is not due to the effect of social learning on drug-associated pleasure, but to the effects of drug-associated pleasure on social learning. For example, individuals who reap mainly positive effects from alcohol and marijuana may be drawn to substance-using peers. They may also develop more accepting attitudes toward substance use. It is therefore important to verify the above cross-sectional results with longitudinal data.

*Longitudinal Regression Analyses*

Table 11.2 presents the results of exploratory longitudinal OLS regression analyses, showing the lagged effects of time 1 social learning measures on time 2 self-reported effects of alcohol and marijuana, controlling for time 1 self-reported effects and other variables. The pattern of results in Table 11.2 is similar to the pattern observed in cross-sectional analyses. Peer approval of substance use and moral beliefs at time 1 exert significant effects on the amount of drug-associated pleasure reported at time 2 (p < .05). Once again, these effects are in the predicted direction. Peer use, however, does not exhibit significant lagged effects.[5] Race has a significant effect on time 2 self-reported effects of alcohol, but not marijuana. Unexpectedly, time 1 parental disapproval has a *positive* effect on the amount of marijuana-associated pleasure reported at time 2 (p < .05), but an insignificant effect in the alcohol equation.[6]

Overall, the longitudinal results increase confidence in the causal assumptions we have made regarding the impact of social learning on the experience delinquency-derived pleasures and rewards. Nonetheless, the longitudinal results should also be interpreted with caution. Due to the one-year lag that exists between the two waves of data collection, the longitudinal analyses may provide conservative estimates of the true impact of social learning factors. Serial correlation may also be a problem in the longitudinal analyses. In particular, the errors between time 1 and time 2 measures of drug-associated pleasure may be correlated. The most likely result of serial correlation, however, is the overestimation of stability effects (i.e., the effects of time 1 drug-associated pleasure on time 2 drug-associated pleasure) and the underestimation of other effects in the model, such as the effects of social learning variables on the self-reported effects of alcohol and marijuana (see Kessler and Greenberg 1981).

## Table 11.2
## The Lagged Effects of Social Learning Variables on the Self-Reported Effects of Alcohol and Marijuana

*Dependent Variables:*

| | T2 Alcohol has Good Effects | | | | T2 Marijuana has Good Effects | | | |
|---|---|---|---|---|---|---|---|---|
| | b | (B) | S.E. | t-value | b | (B) | S.E. | t-value |
| *T1 Independent Variables* | | | | | | | | |
| Peer Use | -.033 | (-.046) | .029 | -1.119 | -.085 | (-.098) | .060 | -1.416 |
| Peer Approval | .099 | (.134) | .030 | 3.260* | .087 | (.115) | .051 | 1.720* |
| Moral Belief | -.044 | (-.087) | .019 | -2.260* | -.079 | (-.154) | .035 | -2.270* |
| *Control Variables* | | | | | | | | |
| Family Structure (1 = intact) | -.062 | (-.046) | .046 | -1.341 | .107 | (.071) | .081 | 1.319 |
| Family Involvement | -.000 | (-.011) | .000 | -.311 | .001 | (.052) | .001 | .970 |
| Parental Attachment | .009 | (.030) | .011 | .832 | -.023 | (-.068) | .020 | -1.182 |
| Parental Disapproval | -.020 | (-.011) | .060 | -.328 | .327 | (.127) | .138 | 2.367* |
| Commitment to School | .005 | (.020) | .008 | .587 | .016 | (.055) | .016 | 1.019 |
| Sex (1 = male) | .031 | (.027) | .040 | .797 | .078 | (.056) | .074 | 1.057 |
| Race (1 = nonwhite) | -.186 | (-.096) | .067 | -2.776* | -.004 | (-.002) | .113 | -.035 |
| Drinking Behavior | .001 | (.044) | .001 | 1.188 | --- | --- | --- | --- |
| Marijuana Use | --- | --- | --- | --- | .003 | (.116) | .002 | 1.644 |
| T1 Alcohol Effects | .320 | (.317) | .037 | 8.714* | --- | --- | --- | --- |
| T1 Marijuana Effects | --- | --- | --- | --- | .313 | (.296) | .062 | 5.037* |
| R Squared | .200 | | | | .226 | | | |
| N (listwise deletion) | 748 | | | | 307 | | | |

*Note*: Analyses include respondents who have used alcohol/marijana "more than once." Unstandardized effects shown, with standardized effects in parentheses.

* p<.05 (one-tailed test)

*Supplementary Analyses*

Having observed significant effects of social learning factors on drug-associated pleasure, we conducted additional analyses to determine whether the amount of pleasure derived from substance use is in turn associated with frequency of substance use. First, we examined the bivariate relationship between time 1 self-reported effects of alcohol/marijuana and time 2 frequency of substance use. The results of ANOVA's (not shown) indicate that time 1 self-reported effects of substance use are related to time 2 frequency of substance use in ways anticipated by social learning theory. For example, when we examined the mean level of time 2 alcohol use by time 1 self-reported effects of alcohol, we found that the mean frequency of alcohol use at time 2 varied across the three possible categories of alcohol-related effects: (1) mainly bad effects (mean = 28.74), (2) mixed or no effects (mean = 30.69), and (3) mainly good effects (mean = 49.46), with the third group mean significantly different from groups 1 and 2. Similar results were obtained when we examined the mean level of time 2 marijuana use by time 1 self-reported effects of marijuana. The mean frequency of marijuana use at time 2 varied from a low of 4.96 (for those reporting mainly bad effects) to 10.58 (for those reporting mixed or no effects), to 28.95 (for those reporting mainly good effects). As can be seen, the motivation to continue substance use varies considerably by the amount of pleasure respondents derive from substance use.[7]

The results of additional cross-sectional and longitudinal OLS regression analyses also indicate a significant effect of drug-associated pleasure on frequency of substance use. The results of these analyses are presented in Tables 11.3 and 11.4. In both the cross-sectional and longitudinal analyses, the self-reported effects of alcohol and marijuana (i.e., "good effects") exhibit a significant impact on the frequency of alcohol and marijuana use, controlling for other relevant variables ($p < .05$). These results correspond to earlier findings on the effects of nonsocial reinforcement on adolescent substance use (e.g., Akers et al. 1979; Krohn et al. 1985; Paternoster and Triplett 1988).

Finally, in an effort to determine whether the theoretical model tested with OLS provides a good fit to the data, we used LISREL v8.30 to estimate a structural equation model for alcohol and marijuana use separately. The estimated models contained the same pattern of effects found in the OLS estimation section. The key difference between the structural equation models and the OLS estimation was the inclusion of both endogenous variables (self-reported effects of substance use and frequency of substance use) simultaneously in a full-information fashion.

Across both substance use outcomes, the model provided a very good fit to the data. The chi-square for alcohol use was .0029 with 1 degree of freedom, while for marijuana use, the chi-square was .0022 with 1 degree of

## Table 11.3
### The Cross-Sectional Effects of Social and Nonsocial Learning Variables on Frequency of Substance Use

*Dependent Variables:*

| Independent Variables | Alcohol Use b | (B) | S.E. | t-value | Marijuana Use b | (B) | S.E. | t-value |
|---|---|---|---|---|---|---|---|---|
| Good Effects | 6.678 | (.114) | 1.500 | 4.453* | 3.952 | (.125) | 1.042 | 3.793* |
| Peer Use | 11.413 | (.276) | 1.159 | 9.849* | 7.961 | (.291) | .832 | 8.607* |
| Peer Approval | 2.137 | (.051) | 1.160 | 1.842* | -.150 | (-.014) | .312 | -.479 |
| Moral Belief | -3.758 | (-.131) | .779 | -4.823* | -4.268 | (-.278) | .538 | -7.938* |
| *Control Variables* | | | | | | | | |
| Family Structure (1 = intact) | -2.810 | (-.037) | 1.793 | -1.567 | -3.602 | (-.081) | 1.290 | -2.792* |
| Family Involvement | .010 | (.008) | .031 | .336 | .038 | (.046) | .024 | 1.608 |
| Parental Attachment | .999 | (-.057) | .442 | -2.262* | -.150 | (-.014) | .312 | -.479 |
| Parental Disapproval | -11.311 | (-.120) | 2.291 | -4.937* | -3.880 | (-.057) | 1.997 | -1.943* |
| Commitment to School | -.497 | (-.036) | .347 | -1.434 | -.386 | (-.046) | .253 | -1.525 |
| Sex (1 = male) | 1.472 | (.021) | 1.635 | .900 | 1.650 | (.038) | 1.226 | 1.346 |
| Race (1 = nonwhite) | -6.593 | (-.061) | 2.616 | -2.521* | 1.145 | (.019) | 1.772 | .646 |
| R Squared | .268 | | | | .474 | | | |
| N (listwise deletion) | 1,390 | | | | 695 | | | |

Note: Analyses include respndents who have used alcohol/marijuana "more than once." Unstandardized effects shown, with standardized effects in parentheses.

* p <.05 (one-tailed test)

# Table 11.4
## The Lagged Effects of Social and Nonsocial Learning Variables on Frequency of Substance Use

*Dependent Variables:*

| | T2 Alcohol Use b | (B) | S.E. | t-value | T2 Marijuana Use b | (B) | S.E. | t-value |
|---|---|---|---|---|---|---|---|---|
| *T1 Independent Variables* | | | | | | | | |
| Good Effects | 4.250 | (.066) | 2.168 | 1.960* | 3.184 | (.105) | 1.667 | 1.910* |
| Peer Use | 5.387 | (.119) | 1.713 | 3.144* | 1.502 | (.061) | 1.573 | .955 |
| Peer Approval | -.810 | (-.017) | 1.785 | -.454 | 1.240 | (.057) | 1.298 | .955 |
| Moral Belief | -1.347 | (-.043) | 1.149 | -1.172 | .015 | (.001) | .939 | .016 |
| *Control Variables* | | | | | | | | |
| Family Structure (1 = intact) | -.509 | (-.006) | 2.737 | -.186 | .876 | (.019) | 2.223 | .394 |
| Family Involvement | .042 | (.030) | .044 | .952 | -.014 | (-.017) | .038 | -.357 |
| Parental Attachment | .170 | (.009) | .656 | .259 | .765 | (.075) | .532 | 1.439 |
| Parental Disapproval | 4.052 | (.037) | 3.535 | 1.146 | 2.502 | (.033) | 3.684 | .679 |
| Commitment to School | -.313 | (-.020) | .505 | -.619 | -.365 | (-.043) | .423 | -.862 |
| Sex (1 = male) | 5.371 | (.072) | 2.338 | 2.298* | 7.143 | (.173) | 1.977 | 3.614* |
| Race (1 = nonwhite) | -2.750 | (-.022) | 3.960 | -.695 | 3.164 | (.051) | 3.045 | 1.039 |
| T1 Alcohol Use | .504 | (.440) | .040 | 12.653* | — | — | — | — |
| T1 Marijuana Use | — | — | — | — | .427 | (.420) | .064 | 6.642* |
| R Squared | .285 | | | | .307 | | | |
| N (listwise deletion) | 762 | | | | 327 | | | |

*Note:* Analyses include respndents who have used alcohol/marijuana "more than once." Unstandardized effects shown, with standardized effects in parentheses.

* p <.05 (one-tailed test)

freedom. For both outcomes, the chi-square/df ratio was less than 5.0 (Smith and Patterson 1985), RMSEA for both outcomes was .00, and the GFI for both outcomes was 1.0. These three different fit measures indicate that the model provides an adequate fit to the data.

For alcohol, significant predictors of time 2 self-reported effects include time 1 self-reported effects, time 1 peer approval of alcohol use, and race—with white respondents more likely to report "good effects" from alcohol use (results not shown). Significant predictors of time 2 alcohol use included time 2 self-reported effects, sex (with males reporting more frequent alcohol use), time 1 alcohol use, and time 1 peer alcohol use. For marijuana, significant predictors of time 2 self-reported effects include time 1 self-reported effects, time 1 moral beliefs, and time 1 marijuana use. Significant predictors of time 2 marijuana use include time 2 self-reported effects, time 1 marijuana use, and sex—with males reporting more frequent marijuana use (complete set of results available from the first author on request). In general, the results of the structural equation analyses for the experience of drug-associated pleasure suggest the importance of social learning mechanisms. For alcohol and marijuana use, the results suggest the importance of nonsocial and—with the possible exception of continuity in marijuana use—social learning mechanisms.

## Conclusion

The results of previous research indicate that some individuals are particularly responsive to the intrinsic pleasures and rewards of criminal and delinquent behavior. Some individuals, for example, tend to associate criminal and delinquent acts mainly with positive emotional sensations, while others tend to associate such behavior with negative emotions in the form of guilt or shame (Wood et al. 1997). In this chapter, we have argued that processes of social learning can help to explain individual differences in this regard.

Especially in the context of drug and alcohol use, social learning theorists have noted that the experience of intrinsic reward/reinforcement is a "variable phenomenon" that is influenced by the characteristics of individuals and their life situations (Simons, Conger, and Whitbeck 1988:303; see also Becker 1953; Brezina 2000). Drawing on related research (Baldwin 1990; Becker 1953, 1967), we attempted to specify the relevant characteristics and situations that are most likely to affect processes of nonsocial reinforcement. We argued that how an individual experiences the effects of criminal and delinquent involvement (i.e., the amount of intrinsic pleasure and neurophysiologic reward derived from such behavior) is partly dependent on the way others—especially delinquent peers—define those effects for him or her. There is reason to believe that the individual's own definitions (moral beliefs) are also important in this regard. The presence of strong moral beliefs against criminal and delinquent involvement is likely to generate physiological discomfort (Grasmick and Bursik 1990) and, thus, reduce the overall amount of intrinsic reward that might otherwise be obtained from crime and delinquency.

The results of exploratory regression analyses lend initial empirical support to our social learning account as applied to adolescent drug and alcohol use. Drawing on data from a large sample of adolescents, we found that social learning factors (especially peers' norm qualities and moral beliefs) exert significant cross-sectional and longitudinal effects on the amount of intrinsic pleasure respondents derive from alcohol and marijuana. (Exposure to substance-using peers exhibited significant effects in cross-sectional analyses, but not in longitudinal analyses.) Consistent with the results of previous research (e.g., Akers et al. 1979; Krohn et al. 1985; Paternoster and Triplett 1988), we also found that the self-reported effects of alcohol and marijuana on the respondent, in turn, predicted frequency of substance use.

Thus, the results of the analyses suggest that a social learning account may have much promise. Individual differences in the propensity to derive intrinsic pleasure and reward from substance use appear to be related to social learning factors in ways predicted by the theory. These findings lend additional support to the assertion made by social learning theorists that processes of social and nonsocial reinforcement are intimately related and that, in fact, it may be difficult to isolate processes of reinforcement that are truly nonsocial in nature (Akers 1998).

We hasten to add that the findings we observe should be viewed as tentative at this time. Future examinations of the relationship between social and nonsocial reinforcement should be based on more refined measures of the relevant processes. Ideally, subsequent studies will employ detailed measures of nonsocial reinforcement that index the extent and intensity of pleasurable emotional sensations (or other neurophysiologic highs) that individuals derive from drugs and alcohol. Also, in future studies, researchers should examine the relationship between social and nonsocial reinforcement in the context of different types of criminal and delinquent involvement, such as theft and violence.

Although the social learning account we outline emphasizes the importance of differential association (delinquent peer exposure and peers' norm qualities) and definitions (moral beliefs), it is possible that other processes related to social learning also affect the immediate neurophysiologic effects of crime, delinquency, and drug use. According to Akers' (1998) social structure and social learning model, four principle types of social structures influence social learning processes including: (a) differential social organization, including society, community, and social institutions, (b) differential location in social structure, including age, gender, race, class, and religion, (c) social disorganization and conflict, and (d) differential social location in primary, secondary, and reference groups, including family, peers, school, work, and media. As such, individual differences in criminal and delinquent orientation are a function of the extent to which cultural traditions, norms, social organization, and social control systems provide socialization, learning environments, reinforcement schedules, opportunities, and immediate situations conducive to conformity or deviance. It is our hope that future research will explore the relationship between nonsocial reinforcement and a more complete range of social learning processes and, ultimately, how each set of processes vary according to different elements of the social structure as well as different types of criminal behavior.

We believe future research in this area will be important. If it is possible to explain individual variation in the amount of intrinsic pleasure and reward derived from crime and delinquency, then we will be in a better position to understand why some individuals develop a relatively strong propensity to offend.

## Notes

1. In his study of sneaky thrill property crime, McCarthy (1995) attempts to explain individual variation in the likelihood of succumbing to criminal temptations (i.e., of being "seduced" by crime). He explains such variation in terms of rational choice considerations, demographic characteristics, and other background factors. As such, McCarthy's research is related in some ways to the questions that are the central focus of this study. However, his study is more clearly concerned with the attraction to crime, rather than the amount of intrinsic pleasure or reward (nonsocial reinforcement) that is derived from actual participation (see McCarthy 1995:527).

2. The number of times respondents self-reported alcohol and/or marijuana use is positively skewed, with a small percentage of youths reporting very high frequencies. Following the procedure used in earlier studies employing the YD data (e.g., Paternoster and Piquero 1995:284), higher frequencies were truncated to the frequency corresponding to the 90th percentile.

3. Because the nonsocial reinforcement variables (i.e., the self-reported effects of alcohol and marijuana use) select on those individuals who have previously engaged in substance use, some concern about potential tautology may be raised. Two facets of our analysis however, mitigate against this concern. First, having selected only on those individuals who have engaged in substance use restricts the sample to only those individuals who have the ability to experience "good effects." Second, in explaining time 2 substance use, our analyses include controls for prior (time 1) substance use. In sum, we believe that while prior substance use is somewhat necessarily confounded with our measures of nonsocial reinforcement, the measurement protocol is in line with prior theoretical and empirical work on the measurement of nonsocial reinforcement (see Akers et al. 1979; Krohn et al. 1985; Paternoster and Triplett 1988).

4. One might suspect that respondents who score high on measures of differential association, and who score low on the moral belief items, would be especially likely to reap intrinsic pleasure from alcohol and marijuana. We tested for such interactions, but did not observe significant effects. Thus, the effects of differential association and moral beliefs on the self-reported effects of substance use appear to be, at least in the YD data, additive in nature.

5.    In helping the individual to define the effects of drugs and alcohol, it is possible that the expressed attitudes and beliefs of one's peers may play a larger role than peers' substance-using behavior. This fact would not be inconsistent with Becker's (1953) account of marijuana use. For example, experienced users model the proper techniques of marijuana use for the novice, but these techniques alone are not necessarily sufficient for the novice to experience a pleasurable high from marijuana intoxication. Experienced users assist the novice mainly by providing encouragement, cognitive strategies, and promoting certain attitudinal orientations toward marijuana use. It should be noted, however, that the failure to observe significant effects for peer use in the longitudinal analyses may also be related to the one-year lag that separates the waves of data collection, or to problems involving serial correlation. These issues are discussed further in the text.

6.    To account for the positive effect of parental disapproval, it may be that adolescent marijuana use expresses a defiant rejection of parental expectations and, in this sense, provides important symbolic rewards (also see Akers 1992).

7.    We observed similar effects when we compared the respondents' time 1 level of exposure to substance-using peers and time 2 substance use. As respondents reported more exposure to substance-using friends, so too did they report a higher frequency of substance use for both alcohol and marijuana.

## References

Agnew, Robert. 1985. "Social Control Theory and Delinquency: A Longitudinal Test." *Criminology* 23:47-61.

_____. 1990. "The Origins of Delinquent Events: An Examination of Offender Accounts." *Journal of Research in Crime and Delinquency* 27:267-294.

_____. 1991. "A Longitudinal Test of Social Control Theory and Delinquency." *Journal of Research in Crime and Delinquency* 28:126-156.

_____. 1995. "Testing the Leading Crime Theories: An Alternative Strategy Focusing on Motivational Processes." *Journal of Research in Crime and Delinquency* 32:363-398.

_____. 1997. "Stability and Change in Crime Over the Life Course: A Strain Theory Explanation." In Terence P. Thornberry (ed.), *Advances in Criminological Theory, Volume 7: Developmental Theories of Crime and Delinquency.* New Brunswick, NJ: Transaction Publishers.

Akers, Ronald L. 2000. *Criminological Theories. Third Edition.* Los Angeles, CA: Roxbury.

_____. 1998. *Social Learning and Social Structure: A General Theory of Crime and Deviance.* Boston: Northeastern University Press.

_____. 1992. *Drugs, Alcohol, and Society: Social Structure, Process, and Policy.* Belmont, CA: Wadsworth.

_____. 1977. *Deviant Behavior: A Social Learning Approach.* Second Edition. Belmont, CA: Wadsworth.

Akers, Ronald L., Marvin D. Krohn, Lonn Lanza-Kaduce, and Marcia Radosevich. 1979. "Social Learning and Deviant Behavior: A Specific Test of a General Theory." *American Sociological Review* 44:636-55.

Baldwin, John D. 1990. "The Role of Sensory Stimulation in Criminal Behavior, with Special Attention to the Age Peak in Crime." In Lee Ellis and Harry Hoffman (eds.), *Crime in Biological, Social, and Moral Contexts.* New York: Praeger.

Becker, Howard S. 1953. "Becoming a Marihuana User." *American Journal of Sociology* 59: 235-242.

_____. 1967. "History, Culture, and Subjective Experience: An Exploration of the Social Bases of Drug-Induced Experiences." *Journal of Health and Social Behavior* 8:163-176.

Brezina, Timothy. 2000. "Delinquent Problem-Solving: An Interpretive Framework for Criminological Theory and Research." *Journal of Research in Crime and Delinquency* 37:3-30.

Elliott, Delbert S., David Huizinga, and Suzanne S. Ageton. 1985. *Explaining Delinquency and Drug Use*. Beverly Hills, CA: Sage.

Gottfredson, Michael R., and Travis Hirschi. 1990. *A General Theory of Crime*. Stanford, CA: Stanford University.

Gove, Walter R. 1994. "Why We Do What We Do: A Biopsychosocial Theory of Human Motivation." *Social Forces* 73:363-394.

Gove, Walter R., and Charles Wilmoth. 1990. "Risk, Crime, and Neurophysiologic Highs: A Consideration of Brain Processes That May Reinforce Delinquent and Criminal Behavior." In Lee Ellis and Harry Hoffman (eds.), *Crime in Biological, Social, and Moral Contexts*. New York: Praeger.

Grasmick, Harold G., and Robert J. Bursik, Jr. 1990. "Conscience, Significant Others, and Rational Choice: Extending the Deterrence Model." *Law and Society Review* 24:837-861.

Hirschi, Travis. 1969. *Causes of Delinquency*. Berkeley, CA: University of California Press.

Katz, Jack. 1988. *Seductions of Crime*. New York: Basic Books.

Kessler, Ronald C., and David F. Greenberg. 1981. *Linear Panel Analysis*. New York: Academic Press.

Krohn, Marvin D., William F. Skinner, James L. Massey, and Ronald L. Akers. 1985. "Social Learning Theory and Adolescent Cigarette Smoking: A Longitudinal Study." *Social Problems* 32:455-473.

Matsueda, Ross L. 1989. "The Dynamics of Moral Beliefs and Minor Deviance." *Social Forces* 68:428-457.

Matsueda, Ross L., and Kathleen Anderson. 1998. "The Dynamics of Delinquent Peers and Delinquent Behavior." *Criminology* 36:269-306.

Matza, David, and Gresham M. Sykes. 1961. "Juvenile Delinquency and Subterranean Values." *American Sociological Review* 26:712-719.

McCarthy, Bill. 1995. "Not Just 'For the Thrill of It': An Instrumentalist Elaboration of Katz's Explanation of Sneaky Thrill Property Crimes." *Criminology* 33:519-538.

Nagin, Daniel S., and Raymond Paternoster. 1991. "On the Relationship of Past to Future Participation in Delinquency." *Criminology* 29:163-189.

_____. 1993. "Enduring Individual Differences and Rational Choice Theories of Crime." *Law and Society Review* 27:467-496.

Paternoster, Raymond. 1989. "Decisions to Participate in and Desist from Four Types of Common Delinquency: Deterrence and the Rational Choice Perspective." *Law and Society Review* 23:7-40.

Paternoster, Raymond, and Alex Piquero. 1995. "Reconceptualizing Deterrence: An Empirical Test of Personal and Vicarious Experiences." *Journal of Research in Crime and Delinquency* 32:251-286.

Paternoster, Raymond, and Ruth Triplett. 1988. "Disaggregating Self-Reported Delinquency and Its Implications for Theory." *Criminology* 26:591-625.

Piquero, Alex, and Stephen Tibbetts. 1996. "Specifying the Direct and Indirect Effects of Low Self-Control and Situational Factors in Offenders' Decision Making: Toward a More Complete Model of Rational Offending." *Justice Quarterly* 13:481-510.

Reiss, Albert J. 1988. "Co-offending and Criminal Careers." In M. Tonry and N. Morris (eds,), *Crime and Justice: A Review of Research, Volume 10*, 117-170. Chicago: University of Chicago Press.

Sampson, Robert J., and John H. Laub. 1997. "A Life-course Theory of Cumulative Disadvantage and the Stability of Delinquency." In Terence P. Thornberry (ed.), *Advances in Criminological Theory, Volume 7: Developmental Theories of Crime and Delinquency*. New Brunswick, NJ: Transaction Publishers.

Simons, Ronald L., Rand D. Conger, and Leslie B. Whitbeck. 1988. "A Multistage Social Learning Model of the Influences of Family and Peers Upon Adolescent Substance Abuse." *Journal of Drug Issues* 18:293-315.

Smith, Douglas A., and E. Britt Patterson. 1985. "Latent-variable Models in Criminological Research: Applications and a Generalization of Joreskog's LISREL Model." *Journal of Quantitative Criminology* 1:127-158.

Thornberry, Terence P. 1987. "Toward an Interactional Theory of Delinquency." *Criminology* 25:863-891.

Wood, Peter B., Walter R. Gove, and John K. Cochran. 1994. "Motivations for Violent Crime Among Incarcerated Adults: A Consideration of Reinforcement Processes." *Journal of the Oklahoma Criminal Justice Research Consortium* 1:75-93.

Wood, Peter B., John K. Cochran, Betty Pfefferbaum, and Bruce J. Arneklev. 1995. "Sensation-Seeking and Delinquent Substance Use: An Extension of Learning Theory." *Journal of Drug Issues* 25:173-193.

Wood, Peter B., Walter R. Gove, James A. Wilson, and John K. Cochran. 1997. "Nonsocial Reinforcement and Habitual Criminal Conduct: An Extension of Learning Theory." *Criminology* 35:355-366.

# 12

# Theory-Mapping in Social Research: An Application to Social Learning Theory[*]

*Patrick M. Horan and Scott Phillips*

Objectivity in science requires that theoretical elements employed in research be available for public scrutiny. We offer a strategy for mapping the theoretical components of social research applications. Following Blalock (1968), we argue that much social research rests upon two theoretical components: a set of hypothesized measurement relationships and a set of hypothesized causal relationships. We elaborate this interpretation of the theoretical character of causal and measurement relationships, showing how the analytical framework associated with Structural Equation Modeling (SEM) can be used as a conceptual tool to map both explicit and implicit theoretical structures in research applications. After developing the conceptual elements of our mapping strategy, we apply this strategy to Akers' and colleagues' research applications of social learning theory to adolescent substance use. We use social learning research for our illustrative effort because it represents a compact and theoretically coherent body of work. However, we contend that our theory-mapping strategy can be applied to a wide range of theoretically motivated empirical research in the social sciences. The results of our illustrative effort suggest that this strategy can illuminate important theoretical issues, as well as reveal new insights about and questions for the research literature being mapped.

## Introduction to Theory Mapping

The "new philosophy of science" literature (Brown 1977) has focused increased attention on the role of theory in scientific research. The classical empiricist maintained that scientific knowledge is that which is known to be true through the systematic application of scientific methods to observational data (Hempel 1965; Nagel 1961). However, some philosophers have noted that scientific research necessarily involves cognitive elements that are not readily interpretable as known-to-be-true (see e.g., Hanson 1958; Kuhn 1962; Quine 1953). For example, Hanson (1958) argued that scientific observation is necessarily theory-laden, while Kuhn (1962) proposed that scientific research takes place within a paradigm that contains unrecognized and untested assumptions as essential components, and Quine (1953) emphasized the importance of auxiliary theories for the process of empirically evaluating scientific theories.

The inclusion of theoretical elements in the practice of scientific research raises serious problems for those who view science as providing true knowledge that is totally empirical in origin. (For a review of some of these problems, see Hunt 1993.) In a sense, the classical empiricist view of science that seeks to extract absolute knowledge from an empirical base, and the relativist view that denies the attainability of such absolute knowledge, both rest on an *objectivist* conception of science (Lakoff and Johnson 1980; Bernstein 1983). Lakoff and Johnson define *objectivism* as the position that: "There is an objective reality, and we can say things that are objectively, absolutely, and unconditionally true or false about it" (1980: 187). Thus, while empiricists seek new methodological techniques that will purge scientific practice of dependence on prior theoretical assumptions (Glymour et al. 1987), relativists use the inability to guarantee such absolute knowledge as a springboard for denying that scientific knowledge is different from other forms of human knowledge or activity (Bernstein 1983).

But by using objectivity rather than objectivism as the defining characteristic of science, we can retain a conception of science as an empirically grounded discipline in which theory plays important roles (Greenwood 1990). Objectivity in science does not guarantee the truth of scientific knowledge. Rather, objectivity provides an empirical evaluation process for scientific theories that is both public and intersubjective: "Science strives for objectivity in the sense that its statements are to be capable of public tests with results that do not vary essentially with the tester" (Hempel 1970:195). Shapere (1982) and Greenwood (1990) argue that objectivity in science is compatible with the inclusion of theoretical elements in the practice of scientific research. But such compatibility has an important condition: theoretical elements must also be "public." That is, those who utilize a research literature must be able to recognize the theoretical components that are encompassed in an empirical research effort. The alternative to "public" or "explicit" theoretical elements is "hidden" or "implicit" theoretical elements, which have been a source of concern in sociology for several decades (Blalock 1979; Carter 1971).

Thus, a commitment to objectivity in science requires greater attention to the role of theory in research (Shapere 1982; Greenwood 1990). Although the literature on objectivity in science does not provide a uniform delimitation of the types of theoretical content that are employed in scientific research, several authors have offered insights. For example, Shapere (1982) characterizes such theoretical content as "background information," while Greenwood (1990) differentiates between elements of what he calls "explanatory theory" and "exploratory theory." In the social sciences, Hunt (1993) interprets Greenwood's distinction as follows:

> On one side are theories that specify relationships among our concepts. These explanatory theories are the ones we test empirically. On the other side, testing explanatory theories required accessing a great amount of background information, or what we will call "measurement theory." (1993: 85)

While much more detailed classifications of the theoretical elements of scientific research are possible (see e.g., Wagner 2000), the distinction between explanatory and measurement components is crucial for understanding the interplay between theory and observation in scientific research and is widely utilized in sociological theory construction (see, e.g., Blalock 1982).

Our presentation will develop this distinction between explanatory and measurement components of theory in light of a particular set of contemporary research practices, called structural equation modeling (Jöreskog 1977), that are widely used in quantitative research applications in the social sciences. It is not our premise that structural equation modeling (SEM) procedures offer a mechanical way to avoid reliance on theory in a research environment. Instead, we argue that SEM procedures offer an analytical template that can be used to "map" the presence and utilization of theory across a broad range of research situations.

The use of a structural equation modeling framework to identify theoretical content will doubtless strike some as backward, in that theory should be used to specify methods, rather than vice versa. However, our use of structural equation modeling emphasizes its conceptual, rather than methodological, characteristics. Specifically, we will use this analytical framework to map the theoretical foundations of research applications in terms of two systems of relationships—one involving explanatory or causal relations, the other involving measurement relations—that together are essential to any empirical research effort. Such a theoretical interpretation of research operations is obviously helpful in planning a new empirical research effort. But it can also be applied to research that has already been completed. When applied to existing research, this theory-mapping strategy can be used to create theoretical maps of a research effort, to identify differences between explicit theory (theory proposed to motivate an analysis) and implicit theory (theory embedded in a research application) and even to help evaluate the implications of different theoretical formulations for substantive research efforts.

Our effort to first motivate and then illustrate the theory-mapping strategy begins by examining the critical role of causal and measurement models in Blalock's approach to sociological theory construction and research. Next, we show how the representation of causal and measurement models in SEM can be used to map the theoretical foundations of research practice. After developing the elements of our theory-mapping strategy, we apply this strategy to Ronald Akers' and colleagues' application of social learning theory to research on adolescent substance use. We use social learning research for our illustrative effort because it represents a compact and theoretically coherent body of theory and research. However, our mapping strategy can be applied to a wide range of research literatures in the social sciences. The results of our illustration show that our proposed mapping strategy is not just a mechanical exercise, but a technique that can provide important insights for the interplay between theoretical and research elements in an existing research literature.

### Causal and Measurement Relationships: A Dual Theoretical Structure

Causal modeling is sometimes viewed as a computational strategy for applying regression analysis techniques to the construction and estimation of models for social structures and processes. In principle, the logical foundations for causal modeling in sociological research could be traced to the work of Lazarsfeld (1955), who pioneered the use of causal relationships in his three-variable elaboration typology for the analysis of contingency tables. But in practice most causal modeling advocates (Blalock 1971; Duncan 1975) have emphasized the statistical origins of causal models in the econometric (Goldberger 1972) and path analysis (Wright 1960) literatures.

In addition to the conventional emphasis on the statistical properties of causal modeling, early advocates of the causal modeling approach such as Hubert M. Blalock (1961) and Otis Dudley Duncan (1975:150-152) have also noted the critical interplay between theory and method that is central to causal modeling applications. For most research applications, the specification of a hypothesized system of causal relationships must precede any empirical estimation of causal parameters. Thus, empirical estimates of causal parameters must be understood as conditional on a prior theoretical specification (Leamer 1983). This theoretical interpretation of causal relationships in nonexperimental research helps to maintain the viability of the causal modeling approach in the face of the truism that empirical correlation cannot be used to prove causation or to establish the direction of causal influence among variables. Because causal modeling cannot be justified on purely statistical criteria (Freedman 1987), Blalock's (1961) statement of the theoretical nature of causal-modeling frameworks is of critical importance:

One admits that causal thinking belongs completely on the theoretical level and that causal laws can never be demonstrated empirically. But this does not mean that it is not helpful to think causally and to develop models that are indirectly testable. (1961: 6)

The recognition that causal analysis could be interpreted as the empirical evaluation of a causal theoretical model—one in which the direction of causality is theoretically specified, but the existence, magnitudes and signs of the hypothesized relationships are subject to empirical estimation—has transformed sociological research practice in many substantive areas. The status attainment model for social stratification research represents one early exemplar for such a research transformation (Blau and Duncan 1967; Horan 1978). Status attainment research employed the strategy of generating causal theoretical models by first stating substantive theory in terms of a process model and then representing this process as a causal sequence of relationships among a set of theoretical concepts. In this way, the status attainment model demonstrated the potential power of the interplay between a causal theoretical specification and a multivariate empirical estimation strategy.

But, causal structure is only one component of the theoretical structure that underlies research employing causal modeling strategies, and by itself it is insufficient to permit empirical analysis of explanatory theories. In his classic paper on "bridging the gap" between theory and research, Blalock (1968) notes that the effort to bring empirical information to bear on theory also requires another necessary component. This second component, which Blalock characterized as "auxiliary theory" (1968: 21), consists of a set of measurement linkages that the researcher constructs to link theoretical concepts to empirical information. Once such measurement linkages have been constructed, then the combined system of causal and measurement components provides a framework for obtaining empirical answers to theoretically motivated questions.

Blalock's recognition (1968) that causality and measurement are theoretically distinct, yet also interdependent, was one of his earliest and most important contributions to sociological theory and research. Unfortunately, his later endorsement of a causal interpretation of measurement (1971, 1979, 1982) has served to attenuate the clarity of this original distinction between causal and measurement models, and to direct attention away from the different roles played by causal and measurement models in both social theory construction (Horan 1989) and empirical estimation.

Bailey's (1984a, 1984b, 1986, 1988) extensive work representing Blalock's conceptualization of measurement in terms of a three-level model provides an important insight for understanding the interplay between theory and research (for other examples of three-level representations of measurement, see Horan 1987, 1989, and Wagner 2000). Because of the importance of measurement for this interplay, and for the theory-mapping strategy presented below, we will give special attention to Blalock's (1968) original interpretation of the role of measurement in social theory construction and research and to the three-level representation of measurement.

In his 1968 paper, Blalock interprets measurement as involving relationships between two different kinds of concepts, one defined in words and the other defined in terms of a set of operations involving empirical entities or indicators. For the former, Blalock's *conceptual definition* of a theoretical concept serves to "establish its meaning in terms of other theoretical and abstract terms" (1968: 9). For the latter, his *operational definition* of a concept involves a set of procedures or operations on empirical data that define the concept in empirical terms. But in order to draw any theoretical inference from an empirical analysis, both *conceptual* and *operational* elements must necessarily be involved. Blalock presents this bridge between the conceptual and operational levels as critical to the theoretical foundations of research:

> In a sense we seem to have two distinct languages, each composed of concepts defined in a very special way. Tests of hypotheses are made in the one language; our thinking is done in the other. (1968: 8)

Blalock's conceptualization of measurement as bridging the gap between theoretical and empirical languages requires the establishment of links between *conceptual* and *operational* concepts. But such *operational concepts* contain several different components. In explicating these components, Bailey (1984a, 1984b) proposes a three-level representation of measurement. In Bailey's elaboration of Blalock's model, operational measures are an intervening link between theoretical concepts and empirical information. Panel A of Figure 12.1 presents this three-level representation of Blalock's approach. (For more on the implications of the three-level measurement model for social research, see Bailey op. cit. and Horan 1987, 1989).

The three-level measurement model specifies that a theoretical concept is linked to empirical information (and empirical information is imputed to the theoretical level), by way of an intervening (operational) step that is constructed by the researcher. Recognizing this intervening step is important because it allows us to understand the interplay between theory and empirical information in the measurement process. For example, it reminds us that the "variables" that we employ in our empirical analysis are also "constructs" which include both theoretical and empirical content (Carter 1971). The use of such measurement constructs constitutes an essential element of theory construction, as well as a prerequisite for the empirical analysis of hypothesized theoretical relationships among concepts. The recognition that measurement involves a theoretical component is consistent with a theory-laden interpretation of measurement (Horan 1978; Hanson 1958). But the existence of a theoretical component in measurement need not

**Figure 12.1**
**A Comparison of Blalock and SEM Models for Measurement**

A.  The Blalock/Bailey
    Measurement Model

B.  The SEM Measurement
    Model

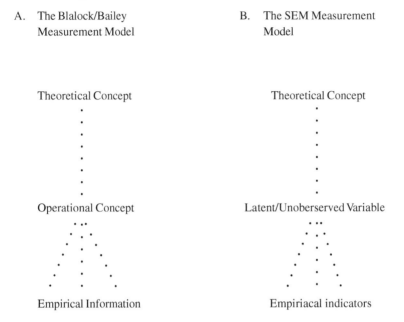

Theoretical Concept

Operational Concept

Empirical Information

Theoretical Concept

Latent/Unoberserved Variable

Empiriacal indicators

invalidate the potential objectivity of an empirical research effort, so long as that theoretical content is recognized.

In sum, causal and measurement relationships play important roles in many empirical research areas. However, the theoretical foundations of specific research efforts may not always be clearly recognized or presented. Indeed, Blalock (1979) refers to unacknowledged theoretical elements in a research application as "hidden assumptions." We share Blalock's interpretation that such "hidden assumptions" are widespread, often unintentional, and of great potential importance for objectivity in science. The question that we seek to address is how to identify and represent such "hidden assumptions" in a relatively simple, yet analytical fashion.

## Structural Equation Modeling and Theory-Mapping

In recent decades, much attention has been given to a new structural equation modeling approach that seeks to "integrate" elements of the psychometric research tradition and the econometric research tradition into a single analytical framework. While structural equation modeling (SEM) is generally viewed as a statistical estimation strategy, we will show that it also provides a useful conceptual framework for representing the construction and utilization of theory in a research setting. Specifically, in providing an analytical framework that includes both measurement and causal relationships, SEM provides a template for mapping the utilization of these theoretical elements in a research application. And it is these theory-mapping applications of SEM that will be the primary focus of attention here.

Most readers will be familiar with the representation of a theory in terms of a set of theoretical concepts linked together by arrows representing hypothesized causal directions. But, as indicated by the discussion above, there is a necessary duality between the representation of theory in terms of a set of hypothesized theoretical relationships between concepts and the parallel representation of the theory in terms of a set of empirical relationships among variables. While these two representations—one theoretical, the other empirical—are clearly connected to one another, the connection cannot be one of identity. But, what is the alternative? We have argued that the three-level measurement model (Bailey 1984b; Horan 1987) which connects each concept to its empirical referent(s) by way of a constructed research variables provides the answer to this question.

The SEM approach provides a conceptual framework that both differentiates causal and measurement relationships and explicitly represents their interdependence in the research process. In the SEM framework, the connection between theoretical and observational information is provided by an intervening level of empirical measures that are constructed by the researcher (see Panel B of Figure 12.1). The novelty of these measurement constructs is reflected in their SEM designation as *latent variables* or as *unobserved variables*. Whatever the terminology, it is these constructed variables that appear as the empirical actors in the estimation of an explanatory model. Thus the construction of these variables, which constitute the interface between theoretical and empirical levels, is of critical importance for the research effort.

A comparison of Panels A and B in Figure 12.1 illustrates important parallels and differences between the SEM approach to measurement and the approach derived from Blalock. Blalock's (1968) formulation refers to the middle-level elements linking theoretical concepts and empirical data as *operational concepts*—and hence presumably theoretical entities. Yet, in the SEM approach, the elements linking theoretical concepts and empirical data are called *latent variables*—and hence presumably empirical entities. These terminological disparities reflect Blalock's emphasis on theory construction as compared with the SEM emphasis on statistical estimation. In a sense, the two representations focus on different sides of the same coin, with Blalock emphasizing the conceptual side of measurement and SEM emphasizing the empirical side of measurement. While both are accurate in the sense that the measurement constructs used in research contain both theoretical and empirical content, in emphasizing one side, each tends to downplay the other, equally important, aspect of the theoretical/empirical connection provided by measurement. We can utilize the three-level measurement formulation that represents a measurement construct as the outcome of theoretically motivated operations on observed empirical information to understand both sides of the measurement model formulation.

It would be misleading to suggest that most SEM practitioners subscribe to the theoretical construct interpretation of the measurement process portrayed here. Because Jöreskog, a developer of SEM software (LISREL) used a causal "true score" representation to motivate his measurement model application (Jöreskog 1971), most practitioners have interpreted the relationships between latent variables and their empirical indicators as representing the causal influence of the former on the latter. However, this causal interpretation is a theoretical overlay which is *not* necessary for SEM estimation of measurement or confirmatory factor models.[1]

Once both causal and measurement models have been theoretically specified, structural equation modeling allows the researcher to estimate hypothesized causal relationships and hypothesized measurement relationships simultaneously, within a common analytical framework.[2] That is, SEM uses the prior theoretical specification of causal and measurement models as a foundation for multivariate estimation of hypothesized causal and measurement parameters. Equally important, the diagrams/equations associated with a SEM analysis provide a clear "map" for the theoretical assumptions—in both causal and measurement components—upon which an analysis rests. And, as we will demonstrate below, such a "map" can be readily compared across different research efforts, or even different parts of a single research effort.

We have argued that the use of multivariate causal modeling procedures, which are receiving increased attention in sociological research, rests on the utilization of two important theoretical components: causal models and measurement models. The causal model proposes theoretical relationships among concepts, and the measurement model proposes an empirical construct to represent each concept in empirical terms. From an empiricist perspective, in which research is seen as a purely empirical process, this dependence of research operations and outcomes on prior theoretical assumptions may suggest a fragile, or even whimsical character to scientific research (Leamer 1983). However, the recognition that empirical research is built upon such theoretical foundations suggests the need for a strategy to map the interplay between theoretical and empirical elements in the research process. As employed here, a theory-map consists of three basic components: (1) a set of theoretical concepts that are elements in the proposed explanatory scheme; (2) a set of measurement relationships linking each concept to empirical information; and (3) a set of explanatory relationships linking the concepts to one another.

## Creating Maps of "Explicit" Theoretical Statements:
## An Example Using Social Learning

We use the social learning research tradition of Ronald Akers and his colleagues to illustrate our strategy of mapping causal and measurement theories in a research literature. Although social science research literatures can be highly fragmented, our goal was to select a coherent body of theory and research. Social learning offers such coherence on both theoretical and research fronts. On the theoretical side it reflects the consistent intellectual leadership of Ronald Akers, and on the research side it has been characterized by regular and systematic data collection efforts aimed at testing the theory.

The social learning research literature also offers a broad range of applications. In addition to adolescent substance use (cf. Akers et al. 1979), social learning concepts have been applied to elderly drinking (Akers et al. 1989; Akers and La Greca 1991), sexual coercion among fraternity men (Boeringer, Shehan, and Akers 1991), and college cheating (Lanza-Kaduce and Klug 1986). Moreover, social learning concepts can be applied to several aspects of deviant behavior, including initiation, repetition, maintenance, and desistance (Akers 1998: 59). We have restricted our attention to the literature on the maintenance of adolescent substance use because it represents the most widely used research application of social learning theory.[3]

In this section, we create maps of the explicit theoretical formulations that have been presented to motivate the application of social learning theory to the maintenance of adolescent substance use. Creating a theory-map for such an application will require three steps: (1) identifying theoretical concepts; (2) deriving measurement models for all theoretical concepts; (3) deriving a causal model for the proposed linkages among theoretical concepts. In some research literatures, these tasks may be difficult due to the prevailing lack of theoretical clarity. Fortunately, the social learning research literature offers a relatively clear presentation of the explicit theoretical statements for both measurement and causal components.

Akers' social learning theory is a reformulation of Edwin Sutherland's (1947) classic differential association theory, which argues that crime and conformity are learned through interactions in intimate groups. Such groups present favorable and unfavorable definitions of crime. Sutherland suggests that crime occurs when the learning process results in "... an excess of definitions favorable to violation of law over definitions unfavorable to violation of law" (1947: 6). However, Sutherland did not specify the precise nature of this learning process.

Akers' revision of differential association theory sought to elaborate the learning process, and in doing so create a theoretical model that could be empirically tested (Burgess and Akers 1966; Krohn et al. 1985; Akers 1998). Akers presents his rationale as follows:

It was in response to this recognized need for specifying the learning process, and thereby enhancing the conceptualization and testability of the theory, that Burgess and I undertook a revision of differential association theory in 1965. (1998: 43)

The expanded version of the theory presents social learning as a process defined in terms of relationships among four theoretical concepts: differential association, imitation, definitions and differential reinforcement. Akers notes, "social learning theory proposes a process which orders and specifies the interrelationships among these variables [concepts]" (1979: 638). Each concept is involved in two sets of theoretical relationships, one set involving hypothesized causal relationships, the other involving the construction of empirical variables to represent that concept. To illustrate the construction of the map of explicit theoretical formulations, we will indicate the textual materials on which each of the linkages in the model is based. We will begin by considering our theory-map for the measurement of each of the four basic theoretical concepts, which is presented in Panel A of Figure 12.2.

The concept of differential association, the catalyst in the social learning process, refers to interactions with significant persons and groups. However, the composition of these significant groups varies over the life course: in childhood, the family is central; in adolescence, friends, peers, and school increase in importance; and, in adulthood, spouses, friends, and co-workers are salient. Significant groups provide the social context in which learning mechanisms operate. The influence of these significant groups varies according to the frequency, duration, priority, and intensity of associations (Akers 1998: 60-66). In the context of the study of adolescent substance use, Akers suggests that differential association be measured through indicators of how the respondent's family ($X^1$) and friends ($X^2$) feel about substance use, and the respondent's friends' own substance use ($X^3$) (for a summary of all indicators see Appendix A reproduced from Akers et al. 1979: 654-55).

The concept of definitions refers to "normative attitudes or evaluative meanings" attributed to a particular behavior (Akers 1998: 78). Social learning theory delineates three types of definitions: positive, neutralizing, and negative. Positive definitions portray a behavior as good and acceptable. Neutralizing definitions portray a behavior as justified. Negative definitions portray a behavior as wrong (Akers 1998: 77-87). In the study of adolescent substance use, Akers suggests that definitions be measured through indicators that reflect techniques of neutralization (X4), the respondent's attitude toward law ($X^5$), and the respondent's attitude regarding approval or disapproval of substance use ($X^6$).

The concept of differential reinforcement refers to the effects of rewards and punishments on behavior. Specifically, social learning theory maintains that the probability, frequency, and extent of anticipated or actual rewards and punishments serve as criteria for choosing between alternative behaviors (Akers 1985). Most rewards and punishments are social, but some, such as the

## Figure 12.2
## Theory Maps for Social Learning

### Panel A: Measurement Models for Social Learning Concepts

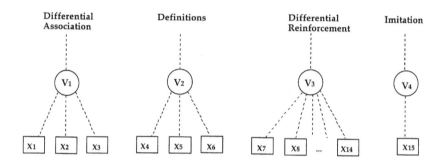

### Panel B: Casual Model of the Social Learning Process

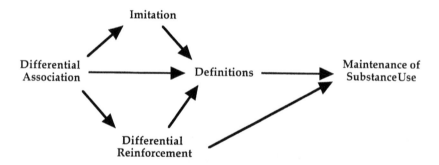

unconditioned physiological and neurological effects of drugs and alcohol, are nonsocial. Yet, even these effects are influenced by socially scripted expectations (Akers 1998). In the study of adolescent substance abuse, Akers suggests that differential reinforcement be measured through indicators that reflect the actual or anticipated reactions of family members and friends to substance use ($X^7$-$X^{10}$), the respondent's perception of the probability of being caught ($X^8$-$X^9$), and the respondent's perception of the general consequences of substance use ($X^{11}$-$X^{14}$).

The concept of imitation refers to behavioral modeling. Members of primary groups with whom one is in direct contact, such as parents, peers, and siblings, are the most important models. But, the increasing influence of mass media has transformed actors and sports figures into models as well (Akers 1998: 75-77). Imitation is not simply a case of "monkey see, monkey do" (Akers 1985: 46). Instead, imitation is a form of observational learning; observers experience "vicarious reinforcement" when a model's behavior is rewarded, and are therefore more likely to emulate the behavior (Akers 1985: 47). In the study of adolescent substance use, Akers suggests that imitation be measured through an indicator that examines the substance use of people the respondent admires ($X^{15}$).

Specification of measurement models for theoretical concepts provides the empirical content for such concepts that is necessary for research to proceed. But the object of such research is often the theoretical relationships among the concepts, and these must also be specified. One popular form of theoretical specification takes the form of causal linkages representing the elements of a proposed social process, and Akers' social learning theory offers such a process model.

To derive the causal relationships in Panel B of Figure 12.2, we draw on Akers and colleagues (1979) exposition of the process represented by social learning theory. The social learning process begins with differential association, and we posit causal theoretical linkages from differential association to definitions, imitation, and differential reinforcement on the basis of the following statement:

> Differential association, which refers to interaction and identity with different groups, occurs first. These groups provide the social environments in which exposure to definitions, imitation of models, and social reinforcement for use of or abstinence from any particular substance take place. (Akers et al. 1979: 638)

Next, we posit causal theoretical linkages from imitation and differential reinforcement to definitions based on the statement that "definitions are learned through imitation and social reinforcement of them" (1979: 328). Finally, we posit causal theoretical linkages from definitions and differential reinforcement (but not from imitation) to maintenance of substance use, based on the following statement:

> After the initial use, imitation becomes less important while the effects of definitions should continue (themselves affected by the experience of use). It is at this point in the process that the actual consequences (social and nonsocial reinforcers and punishers) of the specific behavior come into play to determine the probability that use will be continued and at what level. (1979: 638)

Having illustrated the creation of maps of the causal and measurement components derived from explicit theoretical presentations of social learning theory, we now turn to the process of mapping theoretical formulations of social learning theory, as reflected in the research literature. Creating maps of both explicit and hidden or implicit theoretical elements is critical to a better understanding of the interface between theory, data, and methods in a research literature. And, comparisons between maps for explicit and implicit theoretical formulations will often provide new insights for the research literature itself.

## Creating Maps of "Implicit" Theory: Social Learning Examples

While maps of explicit theory can be constructed using any explicit presentation of a theoretical perspective, it is also possible to map implicit theoretical frameworks that are embedded in research applications. And when the mapping strategy is applied to parallel theoretical and empirical presentations, it allows us to follow a theory from a theoretical presentation to the research setting, and to make comparisons across these settings. To continue our illustration of this mapping strategy, we examine several research applications in the social learning literature, seeking to map theoretical elements that are suggested in the research applications. While we believe that the selections employed here represent important contributions to the social learning research literature, we do not claim to offer a comprehensive map of that literature. Instead, our aim is to illustrate how the distinction between causal and measurement models can be used to construct theory-maps for specific research applications.

### Akers' And Colleagues' Early Research on Social Learning Theory

In 1979, Akers and colleagues published the first "test" of social learning theory based on self-report data regarding adolescent substance use. The well-known Boys Town project was used to collect data specifically designed to test this theory (Akers 1998). Describing the purpose of the research, Akers et al. (1979) note:

> We have presented a social learning perspective on deviant behavior which holds promise as a general theory of the process of coming to engage in deviant acts but which had not been tested with primary data collected in the community and subjected to multivariate analysis. We have tested it here on specific forms of adolescent deviance —drug and alcohol use and abuse. (651)

Akers' and colleagues' use of these data on adolescent substance use to test social learning theory is organized as follows: First, the authors present the four theoretical concepts (differential association, imitation, definitions, and differential reinforcement) discussed above. Next, one or more empirical indicators are presented for each of the four theoretical concepts, for a total of 16 indicators in all. Next, a multiple regression design is employed in which all 16 indicators are entered as predictors of adolescent substance use, estimating the "net effect" of each (note that Blalock (1961) refers to this common regression design as an "inventory of causes" model). Finally, the indicators are entered in sets, with each set containing the indicators corresponding to a particular theoretical concept. The latter analyses produce R-square figures that are used in an attempt to assess the relative explanatory power of the different theoretical concepts.

Efforts to interpret the results of these analyses as supportive of social learning theory prompted several critical responses. These criticisms focused on alternative causal specifications and estimation strategies, and on methodological problems (i.e., multicollinearity) raised by using regression to separate the effects of a set of predictors that were characterized by strong linear relationships with one another (Strickland 1982; Stafford and Ekland-Olson 1982).

Our theory-mapping approach will raise some similar concerns. But, we will argue that the source of these problems is more conceptual than methodological, involving a disjuncture between the explicit and implicit versions of social learning theory. Remember that in the explicit theoretical model derived above, the indicators are presented as empirical measures for the broader theoretical concepts (see Akers et al. 1979: 654-55). Yet, in the model implied by the accompanying analysis, the indicators are treated as separate predictors and used in a causal model estimating the impact of each indicator on a behavioral outcome. In short, the implicit theory represents as causal relationships what the explicit theory represented as measurement relationships. By considering the implications of this disjuncture in more depth, we hope to demonstrate how our theory-mapping strategy for the causal and measurement components can help to clarify what might otherwise seem to be purely methodological problems in a research literature.

We have argued that the distinction between the causal and measurement components of a theory is an important one, and so the present example that appears to lose track of that distinction in the transition from explicit theory to implicit theory is of potential interest beyond the confines of social learning, per se. Specifically, the recasting of measurement relationships as causal relationships led to an analysis design in which the researchers conflate causal and measurement components. While this is a conceptual problem, it also has methodological implications. Specifically, the use of multiple regression to "separate the effects" of a set of indicators is inappropriate when interest focuses on the common referent for the indicators. In other words, the analysis design applies a causal modeling estimation strategy, one that seeks to separate indicator variables from one another, to a measurement model situation involving sets of indicators that "belong together" according to the conceptual scheme.

Figure 12.3 elaborates the implications of the distinction between measurement and causal components for a simple research setting involving three empirical variables, denoted as X1, X2, and X3. The upper panel in Figure 12.3 differentiates between a measurement model representation and a causal model representation. The goal of the measurement model, on the left, is to use X1-X3 as set of empirical indicators to operationalize, or create an empirical construct for, a theoretical concept (see note 1 above). The goal of the causal model, on the right, is to separate the empirical effects of a set of

explanatory variables, X1-X3, on an outcome variable. These different purposes lead to different analytical operations, and different empirical results,
using the same empirical information.

The lower panel in Figure 12.3 provides a heuristic illustration of how this
analytical distinction guides the differential use of empirical information in
the estimation of causal and measurement models. The measurement model
approach uses information on the covariation among indicators to identify a
common area of empirical content. This common empirical content, designated by the shaded area, provides a basis for constructing an empirical measure of the theoretical concept that the indicators are posited to represent.
Causal model estimation, in contrast, uses areas of non-overlapping information among the variables to estimate the separate impacts of each on a crite-
rion variable Y.[4]

**Figure 12.3**
**The Logic of Causal and Measurement Models**

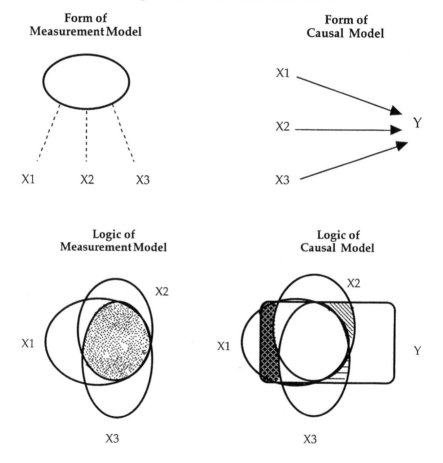

In sum, the application of our theory-mapping strategy to Akers' and colleagues' initial test of social learning theory exposes the existence of a disjuncture between explicit and implicit theoretical models. On one hand, we have an explicit theoretical presentation that delineates a set of empirical variables to be used as indicators to measure the distinct theoretical concepts. On the other hand, we have an implicit theoretical representation, suggested by the analysis design, which treats these same empirical variables as separate elements in a causal model. The strength of the mapping strategy that we employ here is in providing a means of identifying, rather than resolving, apparent conflicts between explicit and implicit theoretical models. We will continue with our examination of research applications of social learning theory before returning to the issue of how such conflicts between explicit and implicit theoretical models might be addressed or resolved.

## Akers' and Colleagues' Recent Research on Social Learning Theory

In the second phase of mapping implicit theoretical formulations, we examine several of Akers' and colleagues' more recent social learning applications to research on adolescent substance abuse. These recent research applications are based on the Iowa data, a longitudinal study of smoking (Akers and Lee 1996), and the original Boys Town data (Akers and Lee 1999). We consider the two papers simultaneously because both adopt a similar approach to measurement and causality, which is as follows: First, three theoretical concepts are introduced: differential association, definitions, and differential reinforcement.[5] Next, a series of empirical indicators are presented for each of the theoretical concepts. The indicators for each concept are then added together to form a single summative measurement scale for each concept. Finally, the three summative scales for differential association, definitions, and differential reinforcement are each used as indicators in a SEM estimation of a single measurement construct for social learning. The social learning construct is then used to predict smoking (Akers and Lee 1996) and marijuana use (Akers and Lee 1999).

Again, there appears to be a disjuncture between the explicit theoretical model derived above (Panel A of Figure 12.2) from Akers et al. (1979), and the implicit theoretical model represented in these analyses (Akers and Lee 1996, 1999). And, again, the disjuncture seems to involve a juxtaposition of causal and measurement model components. Specifically, the explicit model treats the theoretical concepts as elements in a hypothesized causal sequence. That is, each concept plays an important role in a *dynamic social learning process*, and the relationships among the concepts are central to the theory. In contrast, the implicit theoretical model uses empirical relationships among the theoretical concepts to construct a measurement model for the broader concept of social learning, thus eliminating any empirical examination of the *social learning process* hypothesized by the theory.

## Comparing Alternative Theoretical Models

The application of our theory-mapping strategy to early and recent examples of social learning research has revealed some interesting discrepancies between both explicit and implicit theoretical models, and between the implicit models involved in different research applications. The emergence of three different (and apparently incompatible) specifications of the same theory suggests the need for a discussion of how such theoretical discrepancies can be reconciled. Of course, one useful approach would be to compare the models on theoretical grounds, in search of the "correct" theoretical representation. However, the fact that our theory-mapping strategy derives from the analytical framework for SEM opens another interesting avenue for comparisons among alternative models, by comparing the research implications of these different theoretical specifications.

We begin by estimating the explicit measurement model presented in Panel A of Figure 12.2. To do so, we draw on correlation matrices published in Akers et al. 1979. The specific variables from the 1979 paper are reproduced in Appendix A of this chapter. However, we follow the lead of more recent social learning research (Akers and Lee 1996, 1999) by excluding imitation, which has no estimable parameters. The resulting measurement model, involving constructs for differential association, definitions and differential reinforcement, are estimated in a confirmatory factor analysis of this model using LISREL. The results of the confirmatory factor analysis are presented in Figure 12.4. The standardized weights or factor loadings linking indicators to constructs denote the empirical relevance of each indicator for its corresponding construct. These estimated parameters indicate a wide range of variability in the strength of the indicator/construct relationship. (For interpretation purposes, the squares of these standardized loadings can be interpreted as the proportion of variance in each indicator that is used in the empirical construct for the corresponding theoretical concept.) The results indicate that some of these indicators are only tangentially related to the concepts that they are used to measure, suggesting that there is room for improvement in the selection of indicators to represent the basic concepts of social learning theory.

But, despite variability in the connections between indicators and constructs, the confirmatory factor analysis also indicates a very high level of empirical association among the three separate measurement constructs. The estimated correlations among the constructs, presented in Figure 12.4, include a correlation of .92 between differential association and differential reinforcement, of .93 between definitions and differential reinforcement, and

Figure 12.4
A Confirmatory Factor Model for Social Learning Theory Concepts

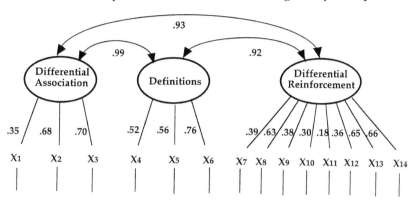

of .99 between differential association and definitions. In statistical terms, the constructs for differential association and definitions are probably not empirically distinguishable from one another, while the distinctions between these two and the construct for differential reinforcement may not be substantively distinguishable.[6] For all practical purposes, then, the three theoretical concepts in social learning theory are not empirically distinguishable from one another. This empirical indistinguishability precludes proceeding to the second step of estimating the explicit causal model in Figure 12.2. These results indicate the importance of examining the measurement issues that have been raised in more detail.

In their responses to earlier multicollinearity criticisms, Akers and his associates argued that "to oppose the variables to one another is to misunderstand the theory, for the variables are all integral parts of the same theory; they are dimensions of a single underlying learning process. Consequently, conceptual overlap and some multicollinearity were expected" (Lanza-Kaduce et al. 1982:170). But, this defense raises some interesting questions about what sort of expectations we may have about separating the concepts in a theory. Should the fact that the concepts are empirically indistinguishable be considered "good news," providing empirical support for the coherence of the theory? Or, does the failure to differentiate these "integral parts" pose a serious problem, making it impossible to test the dynamic social learning process posited by the theory?

While these results raise interesting problems for both the explicit and implicit theoretical models that we derived from Akers et al. (1979), they have different implications for the implicit theoretical model derived from the later social learning research efforts of Akers and Lee (1996, 1999). In those research applications, rather than estimating empirical constructs for the three theoretical concepts (differential association, differential reinforcement and definitions), the researchers instead summed the indicators within each construct to produce a single empirical measure, and then used these three summative scales as indicators for a single "social learning" construct. From the perspective of our CFA model presented in Figure 12.4, Akers and Lee define social learning as a second order factor in a confirmatory factor model. Thus, we use data from Akers et al. (1979) to estimate a second order factor model for the construct social learning based on estimated constructs for differential association, differential reinforcement and definitions. (A reviewer noted that our approach here parallels that employed in the Akers and La Greca (1991: 255-6) analysis of elderly drinking, in which social learning was represented as a second order construct, based on a set of first order social learning constructs.)

The results of the second order factor model are presented in Figure 12.5. In empirical terms, the second order factor model is quite effective. We noted above that the constructs for the separate dimensions of the social learning process are highly correlated. The intent of the second order model is to interpret that commonality as a single, higher-order entity, called social learning. The standardized coefficients presented in Figure 12.5 attest to the effectiveness of this empirical representation, with the social learning construct exhibiting loadings on the three first order constructs for definitions, differential association and differential reinforcement of 1.0, 1.0 and .93, respectively.

The analysis presented in Figure 12.5 supports the empirical contention that the three theoretical concepts can be used to represent a single phenomenon called social learning. However it raises problems for social learning, the theory. What is at issue here is the theoretical importance of the distinc-

**Figure 12.5**
**A Second Order Factor Model for Social Learning Theory**

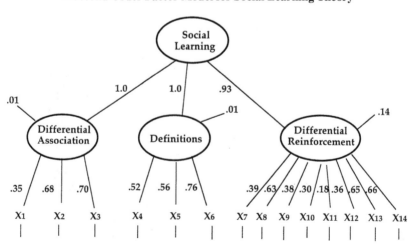

tions between the concepts of definitions, differential association, and differential reinforcement. In effect, these concepts, while conceptually distinct by construction, appear to be empirically indistinguishable from one another. One possible reaction would be to treat such redundancy as confirmation of the social learning concept, and abandon efforts to differentiate these "dimensions." However, such a reaction would jeopardize the original theoretical purpose of specifying the *dynamic social learning process*. After all, the authors themselves note that the concepts are "aspects of the same learning process," yet remain "conceptually distinct" (Akers et al. 1979: 638-39).

## Discussion

We began by noting that the presence of theoretical elements and assumptions in scientific research raises problems for empiricist conceptions about science. However, the maintenance of objectivity in science does not require that theoretical elements be eliminated from scientific inquiry. Instead, it requires that the presence and uses of these theoretical elements be recognized. We have argued that the general analytical framework that is associated with structural equation modeling can be used to represent the underlying theoretical structures employed in many areas of sociological research. Central to this analytical framework is the distinction between measurement models and causal models, and the recognition of the distinct roles that each plays in the research setting. In this chapter we have attempted to demonstrate how this analytical distinction can be used as a tool for constructing theory-maps, which can be applied both to explicit theoretical presentations, and to research applications where parts of the theoretical formulation may not be explicitly recognized.

We contend that this theory-mapping strategy can be a powerful tool in understanding sociological research literatures and evaluating and improving the coherence of the research efforts contained therein. To illustrate the strategy, we have drawn on the theoretical and research literature of social learning theory as applied to the maintenance of adolescent substance use. One element of the theory-mapping exercise involved developing a map of the explicit theoretical model, by converting the explicit presentation into a diagram of causal and measurement components (Figure 12.2). A second element of the theory-mapping exercise involved developing a map of implicit theoretical models, or reconstructing the theoretical models that were implied in the research design and estimation procedures of early and recent social learning research.

Our application of a theory-mapping strategy to the research literature on social learning, while intended primarily as an illustrative exercise, identified some potentially important issues for social learning theory and research. Comparing explicit and implicit theoretical models offers a useful strategy for identifying "hidden assumptions" as well as unintended discrepancies between theoretical intent and empirical implementation. Our review identified several interesting kinds of discrepancies. One was the application of regression methods appropriate to evaluating a causal theoretical model to a measurement model situation. Another was the problem of differentiating empirically between the distinct theoretical concepts of social learning theory. While the results indicating the indistinguishability of the concepts are not encouraging for the prospect of estimating the causal model suggested by the theory, recognizing the empirical redundancy among the theoretical concepts is a necessary first step toward solving this problem.

We believe that our mapping strategy has identified some important issues for the interplay between theory and research in the social learning research area. And, we hope that our efforts will encourage others to apply this theory-mapping strategy to other theoretical and research literatures. We do not claim that this mapping strategy is the only way to identify hidden assumptions or other aspects of the theory/method interface. We do contend that this theory-mapping strategy provides a systematic way to explore and identify elements of the theoretical specification of many sociological research literatures, whether or not the original researchers are aware of these theoretical elements. (See Britt 1997 for a parallel argument applied to qualitative research settings.) While we view the generalizability of the theory-mapping strategy presented here to other sociological research literatures as an open question, it is clearly applicable to a wide range of research applications that employ causal modeling techniques. Where it is applicable, this theory-mapping strategy offers an effective tool for identifying and systematizing both implicit and explicit theoretical structures upon which these research literatures depend. In this way it offers a potential solution to the important problem noted by Blalock of "bringing implicit assumptions out into the open" (1979: 893).

## Notes

*    Direct all correspondence to Patrick Horan, Institute for Behavioral Research, 117 barrow Hall, University of Georgia, Athens, GA, 30602 (phoran@arches.uga.edu). We would like to thank Jim Coverdill and Peggy Hargis for their comments on this chapter.
1.    Sutcliffe (1965) noted that the "platonic true score" interpretation, upon which a causal representation of measurement presumably rests, is "methodologically unsound" (1965:75). Lord and Novick (1968) have shown that such an interpretation is not necessary to the generic measurement models employed in SEM estimation. Further, Horan (1989) argued that imposing a causal interpretation of measurement conflates the important theoretical distinctions between causal and measurement relationships.
2.    Some have argued that the theoretical distinction between measurement and causal relationships provides a rationale for a two-step estimation in which measurement

relationships are estimated before causal relationships (see, e.g., Burt 1976; Anderson and Gerbing 1988).

3. For examples of social learning applications to adolescent substance use beyond those employed here see: Krohn et al. 1982; Krohn, Lanza-Kaduce, and Akers 1984; Lanza-Kaduce et al. 1984; Akers and Cochran 1985; Krohn et al. 1985; Spear and Akers 1988.

4. These heuristic diagrams are used to represent the logic, not the computational mechanics, of the estimation procedures involved here.

5. Akers and Lee (1996: 327) exclude the concept of imitation on the grounds that it is highly correlated with differential association. And, on theoretical grounds, imitation is more important in explaining the initiation of behavior than the maintenance of behavior (Akers et al. 1979; Akers and Lee 1996: 327; Akers 1998: 75), which is the focus of the analysis.

6. Our analyses are based on published data sources which provided correlations rather than the covariances needed for more definitive parameter estimates and associated significance tests. However, the general pattern of results reported here will be robust to alternative estimations.

## References

Akers, Ronald L. 1985. *Deviant Behavior: A Social Learning Approach*. Belmont, CA: Wadsworth.

_____. 1998. *Social Learning and Social Structure: A General Theory of Crime and Deviance*. Boston: Northeastern University Press.

Akers, Ronald L., and John K. Cochran. 1985. "Adolescent Marijuana Use: A Test of Three Theories of Deviant Behavior." *Deviant Behavior* 6:323-46.

Akers, Ronald L., and Anthony J. La Greca. 1991. "Alcohol Use Among the Elderly: Social Learning, Community Context, and Life Events." In D. J. Pittman and H. R. White (eds.), *Society, Culture, and Drinking Patterns Reexamined*. New Brunswick, NJ: Rutgers Center of Alcohol Studies.

Akers, Ronald L., Marvin D. Krohn, Lonn Lanza-Kaduce, and Marcia Radosevich. 1979. "Social Learning and Deviant Behavior: A Specific Test of a General Theory." *American Sociological Review* 44:636-55.

Akers, Ronald L., Anthony J. La Greca, John K. Cochran, and Christine Sellers. 1989. "Social Learning Theory and Alcohol Behavior Among the Elderly." *The Sociological Quarterly* 30:625-38.

Akers, Ronald L., and Gang Lee. 1996. "A Longitudinal Test of Social Learning Theory: Adolescent Smoking." *Journal of Drug Issues* 26:317-43.

Akers, Ronald L., and Gang Lee. 1999. "Age, Social Learning, and Social Bonding in Adolescent Substance Use." *Deviant Behavior* 19:1-25.

Anderson, James C., and David W. Gerbing 1988. "Structural Equation Modeling in Practice: A Review and Recommended Two-Step Approach" *Psychological Bulletin* 103:411-23.

Bailey, Kenneth D. 1984a. "On Integrating Theory and Method." Current Perspectives in Social Theory 5:21-44.

_____.1984b. "A Three-Level Measurement Model." *Quality and Quantity* 18:225-45.

_____.1986. "Philosophical Foundations of Sociological Measurement: A Note on the Three-Level Model." *Quality and Quantity* 20:327-37.

_____.1988. "The Conceptualization of Validity: Current Perspectives." *Social Science Research* 17:117-36.

Bernstein, Richard J. 1983, *Beyond Objectivism and Relativism*. Philadelphia: University of Pennsylvania Press.

Blalock, Hubert M. 1961. *Causal Inferences in Nonexperimental Research*. Chapel Hill: University of North Carolina Press.

_____. 1968. "The Measurement Problem: A Gap Between the Languages of Theory and Research." In H. M. Blalock and A. B. Blalock (eds.), *Methodology in Social Research*. New York: McGraw-Hill

_____. 1971. "Causal Models Involving Unmeasured Variables in Stimulus-Response Situations." In H. M. Blalock (eds.), *Causal Models in the Social Sciences*. Chicago: Aldine-Atherton.

_____. 1979. "Measurement and Conceptualization Problems: The Major Obstacle to Integrating Theory and Research." *American Sociological Review* 44:881-894.

_____. 1982. *Conceptualization and Measurement in the Social Sciences*. Beverly Hills, CA: Sage Publications.

_____. 1989. "The Real and Unrealized Contributions of Quantitative Sociology." *American Sociological Review* 54:447-60.

Blau, Peter M., and Otis Dudley Duncan. 1967. *The American Occupational Structure*. New York: Basic Books.

Boeringer, Scot B., Constance L. Shehan, and Ronald L. Akers. 1991. "Social Contexts and Social Learning in Sexual Coercion and Aggression: Assessing the Contribution of Fraternity Membership." *Family Relations* 40:58-64.

Britt, David. 1997. *Conceptual Modeling*. Mahwah, NJ: Lawrence Erlbaum.

Brown, Harold I. 1977. *Perception, Theory and Commitment*. Chicago: University of Chicago Press.

Burgess, Robert L., and Ronald L. Akers. 1966. "A Differential Association-Reinforcement Theory of Criminal Behavior." *Social Problems* 14:128-47.

Burt, Ronald S. 1976. "Interpretational Confounding of Unobserved Variables in Structural Equation Models." *Sociological Methods and Research* 5:3-52.

Carter, Lewis F. 1971. "Inadvertent Sociological Theory." *Social Forces* 50:12-25.

Duncan, Otis Dudley. 1975. *Introduction to Structural Equation Models*. New York: Academic Press.

Freedman, D. A. 1987. "As Others See Us: A Case Study in Path Analysis." *Journal of Educational Statistics* 12:101-28.

Glymour, Clark, Richard Scheines, Peter Spirtes, and Kevin Kelly. 1987. *Discovering Causal Structure*. New York: Academic Press.

Goldberger, Arthur. 1972. "Structural Equation Methods in the Social Sciences." *Econometrica* 40:979-1001.

Greenwood, John D. 1990 "Two Dogmas of Neo-Empiricism: The 'Theory-Informity of Observation and the Quine-Duhem Thesis." *Philosophy of Science* 57:553-574.

Hanson, N.R. 1958. *Patterns of Discovery*. London: Cambridge University Press.

Hempel, C. G. 1970. *Aspects of Scientific Explanation*. New York: Free Press

Horan, Patrick M. 1978. "Is Status Attainment Research Atheoretical?" *American Sociological Review* 43:534-41.

_____. 1987. "Theoretical Models in Social History Research." *Social Science History* 11:379-400.

_____. 1989. "Causal Models of Measurement: Some Problems for Theory Construction." *Quality and Quantity* 23:39-59.

Hunt, Shelby D. 1993. "Objectivity in Marketing Theory and Research." *Journal of Marketing* 57:76-91.

Jöreskog, Karl. 1971. "Statistical Analysis of Sets of Congeneric Tests." *Psychometrika* 36:109-33.

_____. 1977. "Structural Equation Models in the Social Sciences: Specification, Estimation and Testing." In P. R. Krishnaiah (ed.), *Multivariate Analysis III*. Amsterdam: North-Holland.

Krohn, Marvin D., William F. Skinner, James L. Massey, and Ronald L. Akers. 1985. "Social Learning Theory and Adolescent Cigarette Smoking: A Longitudinal Study." *Social Problems* 32:455-71.

Krohn, Marvin D., Ronald L. Akers, Marcia J. Radosevich, and Lonn Lanza-Kaduce. 1982. "Norm Qualities and Adolescent Drinking and Drug Behavior: The Effects of Norm Quality and Reference Group on Using and Abusing Alcohol and Marijuana." *Journal of Drug Issues* 12:343-59.

Krohn, Marvin D., Lonn Lanza-Kaduce, and Ronald L. Akers. 1984. "Community Context and Theories of Deviant Behavior: An Examination of Social Learning and Social Bonding Theories." *The Sociological Quarterly* 25:353-71.

Kuhn, Thomas. 1962. The Structure of Scientific Revolutions. Chicago: University of Chicago Press.

Lakoff, George, and Mark Johnson. 1980. *Metaphors We Live By*. Chicago: University of Chicago Press.

Lanza-Kaduce, Lonn, Ronald L. Akers, Marvin D. Krohn, and Marcia Radosevich. 1982. "Conceptual and Analytical Models in Testing Social Learning Theory: Reply to Stafford and Ekland-Olson and Strickland." *American Sociological Review* 47:169-73.

Lanza-Kaduce, Lonn, and Mary Klug. 1986. "Learning to Cheat: The Interaction of Moral. Development and Social Learning Theories." *Deviant Behavior* 7:243-59.

Lanza-Kaduce, Lonn, Ronald L. Akers, Marvin D. Krohn, and Marcia Radosevich. 1984. "Cessation of Alcohol and Drug Use Among Adolescents: A Social Learning Model." *Deviant Behavior* 5:79-96.

Lazarsfeld, Paul F. 1955. "Interpretation of Statistical Relations as a Research Operation." In P. F. Lazarsfeld and M. Rosenberg (eds.), *The Language of Social Research*. New York: Free Press.

Leamer, Edward. 1983. "Let's Take the Con Out of Econometrics." *American Economic Review* 73:31-43.

Lord, Frederic M., and Melvin R. Novick. 1968. *Statistical Theories of Mental Test Scores*. Reading, MA: Addison-Wesley

Nagel, E. 1961. *The Structure of Science*. London: Routledge & Kegan Paul.

Quine, W. V. O. 1953. "Two Dogmas of Empiricism," in his *From a Logical Point of View*. Cambridge, MA: Harvard University Press.

Shapere, Dudley. 1982. "The Concept of Observation in Science and Philosophy." *Philosophy of Science* 49:485-525.

Spear, Sherilynn F., and Ronald L. Akers. 1988. "Social Learning Variables and the Risk of Habitual Smoking Among Adolescents: The Muscatine Study." *American Journal of Preventive Medicine* 4:336-42.

Stafford, Mark C., and Sheldon Ekland-Olson. 1982. "On Social Learning and Deviant Behavior: A Reappraisal of the Findings." *American Sociological Review* 47:167-69.

Strickland, Donald E. 1982. "Social Learning and Deviant Behavior: A Specific Test of a General Theory: A Comment and Critique." *American Sociological Review* 47:162-67.

Sutcliffe, J. P. "A Probability Model for Errors of Classification. I. General Considerations." *Psychometrika* 30: 73-96.

Sutherland, Edwin H. 1947. *Principles of Criminology*. Philadelphia: J. B. Lippincott.

Wagner, David G.. 2000. "On the Irrationality of Rejecting Falsified Theories." *Sociological Focus* 33:27-39.

Wright, Sewall. 1960. "Path Coefficients and Path Regressions: Alternative or Complementary Concepts?" *Biometrics* 16:189-202.

# Appendix A
# Empirical Indicators for Social Learning Concepts*

Differential Association

x1    Respondents' perception of the approving-disapproving attitudes toward use held by adults whose opinions they value.

x2    Respondents' perception of the approving-disapproving attitudes toward use held by other teenagers whose opinions they value.

x3    A scale of three items measuring how many of respondents' best friends, friends with whom they associate most often, and friends whom they have known for the longest time use the substance.

Definitions

x4    A scale of three items measuring Sykes and Matza's (1957) "techniques of neutralization" or definitions justifying or excusing use by "denial of injury," "denial of responsibility," or "condemning the condemners."

x5    A scale of items measuring obedient or violating attitudes toward the law in general and alcohol and drug laws in particular.

x6    Respondents' own approval or disapproval of use.

Differential Reinforcement

x7    Respondents' report as to whether or not friends, parents or both encouraged them not to use.

x8    Respondents' report of anticipated or actual positive or negative sanctions of friends to respondents' use of the substance, ranging from encouraging their use to turning them in to the authorities.

x9    Respondents' report of anticipated or actual positive or negative sanctions of parents for respondents' use of the substance, ranging from encouraging their use to turning them in to the authorities.

x10   Respondents' perceived probability that their parents would catch them if they used the substance.

x11   Respondents' perceived probability that the police would catch them if they used the substance.

x12   Respondents' perception of the extent to which using the substance would interfere with their participation in activities (i.e. school work, athletics, etc.) important to them.

x13   The total good things from a list of positive drug effects and social outcomes which the using respondent checked as having actually experienced and the nonusing respondents checked as what they perceived they would experience as a result of using the substance minus the total bad things checked (there is an equal number of good and bad possible consequences in the list.)

x 14    Respondents' assessment of whether on balance mostly good things (such as "a good high or get along better with others") or mostly bad things (such as "a bad high or get into trouble") would (as perceived by nonusers if they were to use) or did (as reported by users when they used the substance) happen.

Imitation

x 15    Total of all the "admired" models (parents, friends, other adults, etc.) whom the respondent reports having observed using the substance.

*Reproduced from appendix of Akers et al. 1979: 654-655.

# 13

# Development of Antisocial Behavior and Crime across the Life-Span from a Social Interactional Perspective: The Coercion Model [1]

*Margit Wiesner, Deborah M. Capaldi, and Gerald R. Patterson*

Social learning theory contributes to the explanation of antisocial behavior and crime through the application of learning principles. This chapter gives a brief overview of the coercion model developed by Gerald R. Patterson and his colleagues at the Oregon Social Learning Center (for detailed overviews, see Patterson, Reid and Dishion 1992; Reid, Patterson, and Snyder, in press). The model originally was developed as a means for understanding children referred for treatment because of antisocial behavior, but later was thought to offer insights about the development of delinquent and criminal behavior in the general population. The chapter begins with a description of key assumptions of the coercion model. Next, some results from empirical research testing the validity of the model are reviewed. Finally, we outline how the developmental course of criminal behavior might be affected by contextual changes accompanying the transition from adolescence into adulthood.

## A Social Interactional Perspective on the Development of Antisocial Behavior

In the coercion model, criminal behavior and its childhood precursors (i.e., antisocial behavior) are conceptualized as complex outcomes of a history of reinforcing exchanges with the immediate social environment. This process starts within the family context but takes place in several stages and settings across the life course. The most important mechanism for learning antisocial behavior within the family context is hypothesized to be negative reinforcement, wherein a young child learns to use aversive responses (termed "coercive behaviors") to terminate the aversive behaviors of parents and siblings (Patterson 1982). Thus, when asked by a parent to do a chore, a child may ignore the parent. As the intensity of the parental request increases in tone and volume, the child refuses outright to do the chore, then yells at the parent to stop asking, and finally runs out of the front door. If these behaviors effectively stop the repetition of the undesired parental request, it is likely that the child will repeat them in the future (i.e., behaviors like this are negatively reinforced by the termination of an undesirable intrusion). The child learns aggressive techniques for avoiding complying with parental requests. In line with the matching law proposed by Herrnstein (1970), the relative rate of occurrence for coercive behaviors is posited to match the relative payoff for that behavior for each child. In sum, children learn through social interactions with their parents and siblings that coercive interaction styles and overt antisocial behaviors are functional because they maximize the overall payoffs available in those settings at that time. In addition, they may fail to develop prosocial behaviors, including problem solving, humor, or negotiation.

As children get older and experience developmental transitions, they gain access to new interaction partners, including peers. These new social contexts play an important role regarding the transformation of overt antisocial behaviors into more severe forms of offending and the maintenance of offending throughout the adolescent and young adult years. The coercion model proposes that the coercive interaction styles and antisocial behaviors learned through interactions with family members are generalized into new settings (e.g., Patterson 1996). Thereby, the children simply might continue to react with coercive and antisocial behaviors to terminate aversive behaviors from peers. In that sense, interactions with peers provide an additional source for negative reinforcement of coercive and antisocial behaviors. Antisocial children, however, do not merely react passively to environmental stimuli. As emphasized by most contemporary developmental-contextual theories (e.g., Brandtstädter 1998; Elder 1998; Lerner, Freund, De Stefanis, and Habermas 2001; Scarr and McCartney 1983; Zimmermann 1995), children are also proactive agents, with the capacity to regulate the course of their own life, to select developmental contexts, and to exert influence on their environment. Consistent with such models of human development, the coercion model posits that antisocial children also actively select friends who maximize the immediate payoffs for his or her repertoire of coercive skills and their limited repertoire of prosocial skills, namely, other antisocial peers (Snyder, West, Stockemer, Gibbons, and Almquist-Parks 1996). Negative reinforcement thus continues to be an important mechanism for the maintenance of coercive and antisocial behaviors, but is complemented by positive reinforcement of (increasingly) more severe forms of antisocial behavior, including stealing, lying, substance use, or truancy, provided by antisocial peers (e.g., Patterson 1996). Intensive interactions with peers who model and reinforce deviant behaviors, as indexed by higher relative rates of reinforcement for deviant talk, more time spent with peers, and a high proportion of antisocial youth in the peer group, are considered to be the driving mechanism for the maintenance of antisocial behavior during adolescence and for the development of more severe forms of offending (Dishion, Eddy, Haas, Li, and Spracklen 1997).

### Antisocial Behavior Evolves across the Life-Span: The Chimera Effect

Underlying this conceptualization of the development of antisocial behavior is the assumption that the manifestation of antisocial behavior evolves in an orderly and transitive progression across the life-span, with individuals at advanced stages having passed through each of the prior stages. During childhood, overt antisocial behaviors predominate, including defiance, temper tantrums, teasing, and hitting. From early adolescence onwards, such behaviors progress into more developmentally advanced forms, namely, covert antisocial behaviors such as truancy or stealing and, finally, adult crimes. This progression of antisocial behavior towards more severe forms of deviant behaviors has been labeled the "chimera effect" (Patterson 1993).

*Two Pathways of Offending*

Although the association of contextual risk factors such as poor parenting skills and antisocial peers with antisocial and delinquent behaviors during adolescence is ubiquitous, there also appears to be heterogeneity in the development of juvenile offending. Patterson (Patterson, Capaldi, and Bank 1991; Patterson, DeBaryshe, and Ramsey 1989; Patterson and Yoerger 1993, 1997; in press) has posited two heterogeneous subgroups, namely early-onset offenders who were arrested for the first time prior to age 14, and late-onset offenders who were arrested for the first time after age 14.

*Early-Onset Offenders*

Shown in Figure 13.1 is the model for early-onset offenders. The process is thought to begin during the preschool years. Poor family management skills of the parents are considered the primary determinant of the initiation of coercive interaction styles and antisocial behavior during childhood (Patterson, Reid, and Dishion 1992; Patterson 1996). In other words, ineffective parenting skills are a necessary prerequisite for the cycle of exchanges between the child and other family members that provides negative reinforcement of coercive interaction styles. The poor parenting skills are assumed to be related to various risk factors within the family context, including low socioeconomic status, poverty, divorce of the parents or other stressful family transitions, depressed parents, and antisocial parents (Patterson 1996; Patterson and Yoerger 1997). These high-risk factors within the family context themselves are embedded in a larger matrix of macro-contextual variables, such as economic conditions and neighborhood, that define the setting in which ineffective parenting occurs (Capaldi, DeGarmo, Patterson, and Forgatch in press).

Poor parenting might be related to high-risk contexts for two reasons. On the one hand, some parents with poor and ineffective family management skills are likely to live in higher-risk contexts. Antisocial parents are a case in point. They are likely to have learned coercive behaviors in the family of origin, as well as unskilled parenting behaviors such as neglectful supervision and harsh discipline. Later, these learned coercive behaviors and poor parenting skills are carried forward into interactions with their own children. Antisocial parents are further likely to start a family of procreation in higher-risk contexts (Hardy, Astone, Brooks-Gunn, Shapiro, and Miller 1998; Serbin, Cooperman, Peters, Lehoux, Stack, and Schwartzman 1998) because of other developmental failures associated with their antisocial behavior. Under these circumstances, high-risk contexts are not a contributor to the development of poor family management skills of the parents. Alternatively, high-risk contexts, such as parental separation, unemployment or other stressful events, might trigger a break-down in parenting skills. This is likely to occur in two ways: (1) through taking time and attention from parenting, and (2) by increasing irritability and negative affect which disrupts parenting.

Once established, poor parental family management skills can result in repetitive and possibly escalating negative interaction sequences with parents and siblings. This is especially the case with antisocial children who show difficult temperament, for instance, a high activity level and high levels of negative affect or anger. Therefore the child, in addition to the parents, affects the interaction patterns within the family, resulting in bi-directional effects. Early-onset children learn during these interaction sequences (in Figure 13.1 denoted as "reinforcing contingencies") that coercive and antisocial behaviors have functional value (i.e., maximize the immediate payoffs available at that time).

Once early-onset offenders have acquired a broad range of coercive and antisocial behaviors and only limited prosocial skills, they are at heightened risk to become involved with deviant peers very early in life (sometimes as early as age 6 or 7) for two reasons. Antisocial children and adolescents are likely to be rejected by prosocial peers. They also may actively select antisocial friends who share their interest in deviant activities and match their repertoire of coercive and antisocial skills. If their parents fail in effectively

**Figure 13.1**
**Early-Onset of Offending Model (from Patterson and Yoerger 1997)**

Temperament

X

Family Process
1. Discipline
2. Monitoring
3. Family Problem Solving

Reinforcing Contingencies

Socially Unskilled

Transition Frequency

Antisocial Child

Early Arrest (before age 14)

Context
1. Socioeconomic Status
2. Stress
3. Divorce
4. Antisocial Behavior
5. Depression

Early Involvement with Deviant Peers

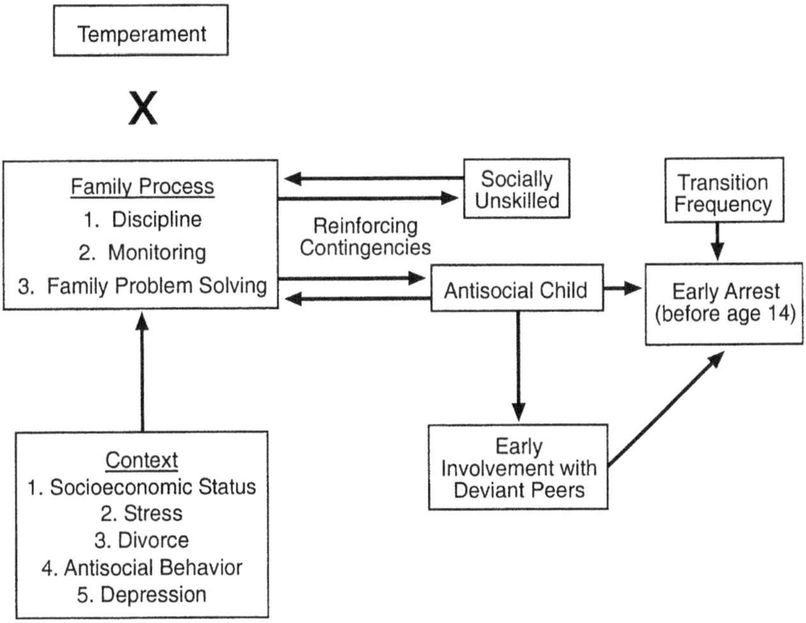

monitoring their behavior, they are likely to spend large amounts of unsupervised time together with deviant peers. Early and intensive involvement with deviant peers is considered to be the driving mechanism for rapid growth in and escalation of covert antisocial behaviors such as substance use, stealing, or truancy, ultimately leading to early arrest (before age 14) (Dishion, Eddy, Haas, Li, and Spracklen 1997; Patterson 1996). Co-occurring adversities in the family context such as numerous transitions of parental figures (e.g., intact to single status) during adolescence are posited to contribute to disengagement from the family and involvement in a deviant peer group (in Figure 13.1 labeled as "transition frequency.") Early onset of offending, as indexed by early arrest, in turn, heightens the risk for chronic offending and criminal behavior during adolescence and young adulthood (Patterson 1996; Patterson and Yoerger 1997).

*The Late-Onset Offenders*

As can be depicted from Figure 13.2, the mechanisms regarding the development of antisocial behavior and the more severe forms of offending are assumed to be somewhat similar for late-onset offenders. The training-cycle within the family, however, begins much later relative to early-onset offenders, namely in early to middle adolescence. Further, the family contexts and the family management skills of the parents may show deficits compared to those for families of non-offenders, but are better than for the families of early-onset offenders (i.e., show more moderate levels of risk compared to early-onset offenders). In addition, antisocial and coercive behaviors of the child presumably are not permitted to work quite so well in late-onset families as they do in early-onset families. Instead, the at-risk family contexts predominantly may lead to disrupted parental supervision. The late-onset offenders consequently acquire a more limited or less severe repertoire of antisocial behaviors and a more extensive repertoire of prosocial skills relative to early-onset offenders. For that reason the late-onset offenders also have been labeled as "marginal offenders" (Patterson and Yoerger 1997).

Because overt antisocial behaviors are learned later in life and occur at much lower levels compared to early-onset offenders, late-onset offenders are likely to become involved with deviant peers relatively late. The growth in and escalation of covert antisocial behavior consequently takes place during early and middle adolescence, leading to a later onset of serious offending (i.e., first arrest after 14 years of age) compared to early-onset offenders. Because prosocial skills are better developed, involvement with deviant peers is less intensive, and severe forms of offending are initiated later, the criminal careers of late-onset offenders are assumed to be shorter and to terminate at younger ages than those of early-onset offenders (Patterson 1996; Patterson and Yoerger 1997). Processes responsible for persistence and desistance of offending and criminal behavior during adulthood are described in more detail later in this chapter.

### Secondary Consequences of Antisocial Behavior: The Cascade Model

Antisocial behaviors are associated with (or produce) a cascade of secondary problems, including academic failure, substance abuse, depressive symptoms, health risking sexual behavior, and work failure (Capaldi and Stoolmiller

**Figure 13.2**
**Late-Onset of Offending Model**
**(adapted from Patterson and Yoerger 1997)**

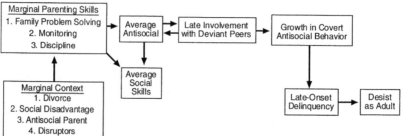

1999). Each problem then causes new detrimental consequences or developmental failures in later periods of life. This assumption of sequences of secondary consequences that are triggered by early antisocial behavior has been termed the cascade (Patterson and Yoerger 1993) or failure model (Patterson and Stoolmiller 1991; Capaldi 1991, 1992).

### Testing the Coercion Model: Longitudinal Studies and Intervention Trials

Most of the core assumptions of the coercion model have been tested in various longitudinal studies, spanning the period from childhood to late adolescence. A particular strength of these studies is that generally multiple methods (including observational data) as well as multiple agents were used for the measurement of key constructs. Space limitations do not permit an extensive review of the findings, but overall the results were favorable (for overviews, see Patterson 1996; Patterson and Yoerger 1993, 1997, in press). The interested reader is referred to Patterson (1993), Patterson, Forgatch, Yoerger and Stoolmiller (1998), and Patterson and Yoerger (1999) for examinations of the progression of antisocial behavior towards more severe forms such as adult crimes. Capaldi, DeGarmo, Patterson and Forgatch (in press), and Capaldi and Patterson (1991) studied the association of high-risk contexts with parental family management skills. Eddy, Leve, and Fagot (2001), Forgatch (1991), and Stoolmiller (1994) tested the association between disrupted parental family management skills and antisocial behavior of the children. Patterson, Dishion, and Yoerger (2000), and Stoolmiller (1994) examined the effects of deviant peer association on growth of antisocial behavior. Dishion, Andrews, and Crosby (1995), Dishion, Duncan, Eddy, Fagot, and Fetrow (1994), Dishion, Spracklen, Andrews, and Patterson (1996), and Snyder and Patterson (1995) conducted in-depth explorations of interactions between children and their parents and peers, respectively. For research on early-onset offenders and late-onset offenders, see Patterson, Forgatch, Yoerger, and Stoolmiller (1998), and Patterson and Yoerger (1993, 1997). Dishion (1990) and Patterson and Capaldi (1990) studied secondary consequences of antisocial behavior. Note that the studies just mentioned were selected from a larger body of empirical research on the coercion model.

Although the findings from those longitudinal studies were very encouraging, they are limited insofar as they cannot really establish causal effects. Controlled experimental manipulation is much better suited for this task. Hence, Patterson and his colleagues at the Oregon Social Learning Center conducted several intervention studies, thus subjecting the coercion model to a strong test of its causal hypotheses. It was demonstrated in an intervention study that used random assignment to parent training that changes in parental discipline practices were significantly related to changes in the child's antisocial behavior (Dishion, Patterson, and Kavanagh 1992). Findings from this and other experimental trials overall provided strong support for the coercion model (for more recent findings see Forgatch and DeGarmo 1999; Forgatch and Martinez 1999).

## Current Status and Future Challenges for the Coercion Model

The coercion model shares many assumptions of other theories of criminal behavior, but also has some unique features. They are briefly summarized before future extensions of the model are discussed. First, a basic premise shared by many other researchers (e.g., Elliott, Huizinga, and Menard 1989; Loeber and LeBlanc 1990) is that juvenile crime involves a developmental progression from relatively minor to more serious antisocial behaviors. A comprehensive understanding of adolescent and adult crime consequently requires an understanding of childhood misconduct that serves as a primary precursor to later delinquent acts.

Second, the need to distinguish distinctive subgroups within the offender population, each showing a prototypical trajectory of offending over time, has been emphasized by others as well (e.g., Catalano and Hawkins 1996; Farrington and Hawkins 1991; Loeber 1996; Moffitt 1993). Investigators disagree, however, regarding the number and specific characteristics of offending pathways. Third, in opposition to ontogenetic or static approaches (e.g., Gottfredson and Hirschi 1990), different causal mechanisms are proposed for different stages of a criminal career (i.e., onset, transformation into more serious forms of offending, maintenance, termination). Similar hypotheses also have been proposed by others (e.g., Farrington and Hawkins 1991).

Fourth, antisocial children and juvenile or adult offenders are viewed as being embedded into several social contexts that partly change throughout the life course (e.g., nuclear family, peers, teachers, coworkers, romantic partners). Such age-graded, environmental discontinuities, or dynamic factors, provide opportunities for changes in offending behavior in later developmental periods. It is, however, the interplay of person and context characteristics that is crucial for understanding stability and change in offending behavior. Offenders are not merely reacting passively to context stimuli, but also influence and change their environment, and actively seek environments that maximize their own payoff. Sampson and Laub (1997) have employed very similar concepts in their research on stability and change in offending across the life-span, pursuing a more general theory of crime that does not recognize distinctive offender pathways.

Fifth, other investigators (e.g., Akers, 2000; Krohn, Massey, and Skinner 1987) also considered delinquent and criminal behavior to be a consequence of reinforcing contingencies, with the model pursued by Conger and colleagues (e.g., Conger and Simons 1997) probably coming closest to the coercion model. The specific merit of the coercion model, however, is the zeal and effort invested in the in-depth exploration of the processes by which antisocial behavior and its more adult forms are learned and maintained during social interactions with parents, siblings, and peers.

In the future, the challenge for the coercion model is at least fivefold. First, a goal is further to define the developmental aspects of the model, in particular regarding development in very early childhood and age-related differences in behaviors (e.g., temper tantrums have a very different developmental meaning when they occur at two versus ten years of age). A second goal is to integrate other important developmental mechanisms into the model, as well as the interplay between social learning and these other factors at different developmental stages. Thus, the role that emotions and cognitions play in the learning process at different stages of development is not well understood. The potential contribution of temperamental and genetic or biological factors also needs to be specified more precisely. Consideration of such factors might shed additional light on the reasons why some antisocial children later do not progress into chronic offending (i.e., drop out of the offending pathway). Third, our understanding of the development of antisocial behavior would benefit from progressing from a focus on interactions between the antisocial child and a single agent towards more complex and systemic models that examine interactions and reciprocal influences between multiple agents (e.g., antisocial child, mother, father, and siblings together). Fourth, the extent to which coercive and aggressive behaviors are carried across relationships of the same type (e.g., from one romantic relationship to another), or of different types (e.g., from a peer relationship to a romantic relationship) is still not well understood. Finally, mechanisms responsible for desistance or persistence of antisocial behavior and offending in adulthood need to be explored and specified in more detail than before. None of these tasks will be easy to accomplish, but efforts in these directions are currently under way (see Capaldi, Shortt, and Crosby, 2001; Shortt, Capaldi, Dishion, Bank, and Owen, 2001; Reid, Patterson, and Snyder, in press).

In the remainder of this chapter, we outline very briefly how the two pathways of offending proposed in the coercion model might be affected by developmental and contextual changes during the transition from adolescence into adulthood. Note that most of the following ideas are speculative because the participants in our longitudinal studies have not yet reached the age necessary for hypothesis testing (i.e., 30+ years of age).

## The Transition from Adolescence into Adulthood

Pursuing a life-span approach, we propose that persistence and desistance of offending in adulthood cannot be explained fully by individual characteristics and environmental influences in early childhood or adolescence. Age-graded changes during adulthood have to be considered as well. Neither is the length and termination of criminal careers entirely determined by early-onset or late-onset of offending, although, for various reasons that are outlined below, early-onset offenders generally are expected to persist in offending during adulthood more often and longer than late-onset offenders. However, the overall association between timing of onset of offending and career length presumably is weakened because the completion of young adult developmental tasks (i.e., selection of a job or a romantic partner) is partly influenced by chance effects (e.g., the local economic situation; Sampson and Laub 1997) as well as by individual self-regulation (e.g., the decision to obtain a higher educational degree to increase chances on the job market; Brandtstädter 1998; Elder 1998). Pathways of some early-onset offenders thus can be "redirected" towards more normative developmental courses earlier than predicted by age-of-onset alone. The same argument applies to prolonged criminal careers of some late-onset offenders.

We suggest at least three major processes that are related to persistence in offending, namely, generalized coercive behavior patterns, developmental failures, and continued engagement in high-risk contexts. The first assumption is concerned with the coercive interaction styles that were learned within the nuclear family and later reinforced within the peer-group. According to the coercion model, much of this behavior is overlearned and consequently performed more or less automatically in differing settings (Patterson, Reid, and Dishion 1992). In other words, antisocial individuals carry the same underlying constellation of traits into adulthood that placed them at risk for offending when they were children (Caspi and Bem 1990; Moffitt 1993). If those coercive and abrasive interaction styles are displayed in new settings, they can ultimately lead to new failures and adverse consequences, such as job loss or weakened conventional relationships, that increase the risk for continued adult offending. Compared to late-onset offenders, early-onset offenders should be at increased risk for carrying overlearned coercive interaction styles into new social contexts (e.g., intimate relationships, work relationships) and for experiencing more adverse consequences, because their well-developed coercive behaviors combined with the absence of prosocial skills do not permit much variation and modification of their interaction styles in such relationship contexts.

The extent to which coercive behavior patterns generalize from the family of origin to young adult settings presumably depends on the nature of the relationships. Several researchers have argued that coercive and abusive behaviors of antisocial individuals are likely to be more frequent and intense in intimate relationships (Caspi and Elder 1988; Sroufe and Fleeson 1986) because of the necessity to negotiate interpersonal conflicts in such interdependent relationships. Relationships at work, in contrast, often are asymmetric with regard to power and deviant behavior is more likely to be sanctioned (i.e., coercive behaviors at work frequently minimize rather than maximize pay-offs). Coercive interaction styles thus should be less likely to carry over into the work place than into romantic relationships, in particular for late-onset offenders who can replace coercive behaviors with prosocial behaviors more easily than early-onset offenders.

The second major mechanism is derived from the "cascade model" (Patterson and Yoerger 1993). It posits that early antisocial behavior and juvenile offending trigger various developmental failures (Capaldi and Stoolmiller 1999) or negative cumulative consequences (Caspi and Bem 1990; Moffitt 1993), including academic failure and substance use. In line with the developmental psychopathology framework (e.g., Cicchetti and Schneider-Rosen 1986; Sroufe 1990), such secondary problems or early adaptational failures are considered to be associated with an increased likelihood of later failures, which themselves heighten the risk for continued offending. Particularly important in this regard are consequences that limit future environmental options. Adolescents who leave high school without a degree, for instance, are more than twice as likely to be unemployed than those who graduate, are more likely to find themselves in low-paid, low-level jobs, and are more likely to engage in other high-risk behaviors such as premature sexual activity, crime and delinquency, and alcohol and drug abuse (see Kushman and Heariold-Kinney 1996; Youth Indicators 1993). The consequences of incarceration might even be more detrimental. For instance, ex-prisoners are barred from literally hundreds of government-regulated private occupations, including apprentice electrician, billiards operator, barber, and plumber, as well as jobs where bonding is required, such as security guards and hotel workers; that is, precisely from the sort of low-skilled jobs that are compatible with the educational and work-history profiles of most offenders (see Sampson and Laub 1997). In short, poor educational attainment and incarceration restrict future opportunities for employment and a successful vocational career, thus providing a strong incentive for persistence in criminal activities. Preliminary results from our longitudinal research revealed that low academic achievement and number of arrests, together with mental health problems, differentiated the most negative career pathways (characterized by extended periods of unemployment) from more positive ones (Wiesner, Vondracek, Capaldi, and Porfeli 2001), thus lending some preliminary support to this hypothesis. Because early-onset offenders initiated antisocial behavior earlier in life, they are considered to be at elevated risk for secondary problems and developmental failures compared to late-onset offenders who had less time to trigger similar negative cumulative consequences.

Third, persistence in offending behavior during adulthood is presumed to be related to continued engagement in high-risk contexts, such as affiliation with delinquent peers and selection of an antisocial partner. Such contexts provide (mutual) positive reinforcement of delinquent behavior (Patterson,

Reid, and Dishion 1992) and are thus regarded as strong proximal risk factors for continued criminal involvement in adulthood. Continued engagement in high-risk contexts might be due to several factors. It might result from rejection by more normative peers and prosocial romantic partners. Prior adjustment failures and engagement in conduct problem related behaviors also might lead to unintended restrictions of environmental options (e.g., an adolescent who drops out of high school may not attend a four-year college and thus cannot meet well-educated young women in college classes; Capaldi and Stoolmiller 1999). According to the matching law, offenders also may actively select and keep friends and romantic partners with whom they can engage in behaviors they enjoy (e.g., partying, drug use) or who are similar to them (e.g., an adolescent boy who likes to party is likely to meet adolescent girls with the same social preferences at such activities and is likely to choose to date such girls; Capaldi and Gorman-Smith, in press). Capaldi and Crosby (1997), for instance, found evidence of assortative partnering of young couples by antisocial behavior. Because early-onset offenders are characterized by higher levels of coercive and antisocial behaviors, we predict they are at heightened risk for continued involvement with at-risk contexts relative to late-onset offenders.

Desistance from offending during adulthood primarily is considered a result of environmental discontinuities that lead to processes which shape or reinforce changes in behavior. The transition from late adolescence into young adulthood marks several psychosocial transitions and contextual changes. For instance, young adults move out of their parents' home, start postsecondary educations, go to the military, or directly enter the labor-force, establish stable relationships with a partner, and start a family of procreation. We assume that such age-graded environmental discontinuities lead to behavioral changes (i.e., desistance from offending), when they limit access to salient reinforcers of criminal behavior and reduce the pay-offs of offending behavior.

Establishment of a relationship with a prosocial romantic partner and starting a family of procreation are deemed to be particularly important dynamic factors in this regard (but other dynamic factors such as joining the military can have similar effects). Both can be subsumed under the macro concept social capital. It refers to those social relationships with family, peer or community members that provide access and control over various types of resources (Coleman 1988; Furstenberg and Hughes 1995; Sampson and Laub 1990). Individuals embedded in dense and bounded social networks are considered to be high in social capital (Coleman 1988). Furstenberg and Hughes (1995) found a strong help network for the family of origin to be associated with lower criminal activity at age 20. In another study, young men with histories of delinquent behavior and strong attachments to their partners were significantly less likely to be arrested in their 20s than those offenders who were only weakly attached to their partners (Sampson and Laub 1990).

Strong investment in close social relationships (e.g., with a partner or children) is hypothesized to relate to desistance from offending during adulthood in two ways. First, positive social bonds are increased (e.g., Sampson and Laub 1997). Second, by reducing the amount of leisure time spent with deviant peers (Warr 1998) who provide positive reinforcement of offending behavior. Young men engaged in such relationships, regardless of the prosocial or antisocial characteristics of their female partners, generally have less time to spend with criminal peers and experience more pressure to spend time with and to support their family. We assume that early-onset offenders generally are less likely to establish relationships with prosocial romantic partners or to invest considerable efforts in raising their own children compared to late-onset offenders, because of their poor social skills and other developmental failures that limit their attractiveness to prosocial partners. They are consequently less likely to desist from offending.

In Figure 13.3, the major factors related to persistence and desistance of offending in adulthood are summarized. As outlined, early-onset offenders are considered to be at heightened risk for (longer) persistence in offending during adulthood compared to late-onset offenders, because they have more obstacles to overcome (e.g., pronounced coercive interaction styles and less well-developed prosocial skills, more developmental failures, more involvement with high-risk contexts) and most likely will take longer, developmentally, to desist from criminal behavior. The association between timing of onset and length of criminal careers, however, will not be perfect because major normative (and non-normative) life events during adulthood sometimes can function as "turning points" and redirect pathways (Sampson and Laub 1997) of early-onset offenders and late-onset offenders earlier or later than predicted by age-of-onset of offending. That is, some early-onset offenders will terminate offending quite early in adulthood, and some late-onset offenders will become chronic long-term offenders.

This does not necessarily imply, however, that young adults who desist from offending and criminal activities terminate all forms of antisocial behavior. Nagin, Farrington and Moffitt (1995) found that men who completely refrained from committing criminal acts after adolescence, as indexed by absence of convictions, continued to show less visible (or less severely sanctioned) forms of antisocial behaviors, such as violent behaviors (fighting), substance abuse, and traffic violations. From a social learning or matching law perspective, this may be due to the fact that criminal behaviors become dysfunctional in many young adult contexts and limit access to resources or other pay-offs. It may be that these young adults improve enough to desist from more extreme behaviors, but not enough to desist from all antisocial behaviors. We will conclude this chapter with presenting a more detailed model of the way in which coercive interaction styles learned in the family of origin might carry over into relationships with partners.

Figure 13.3
Factors Associated with Persistence and Desistance of Offending in Adulthood

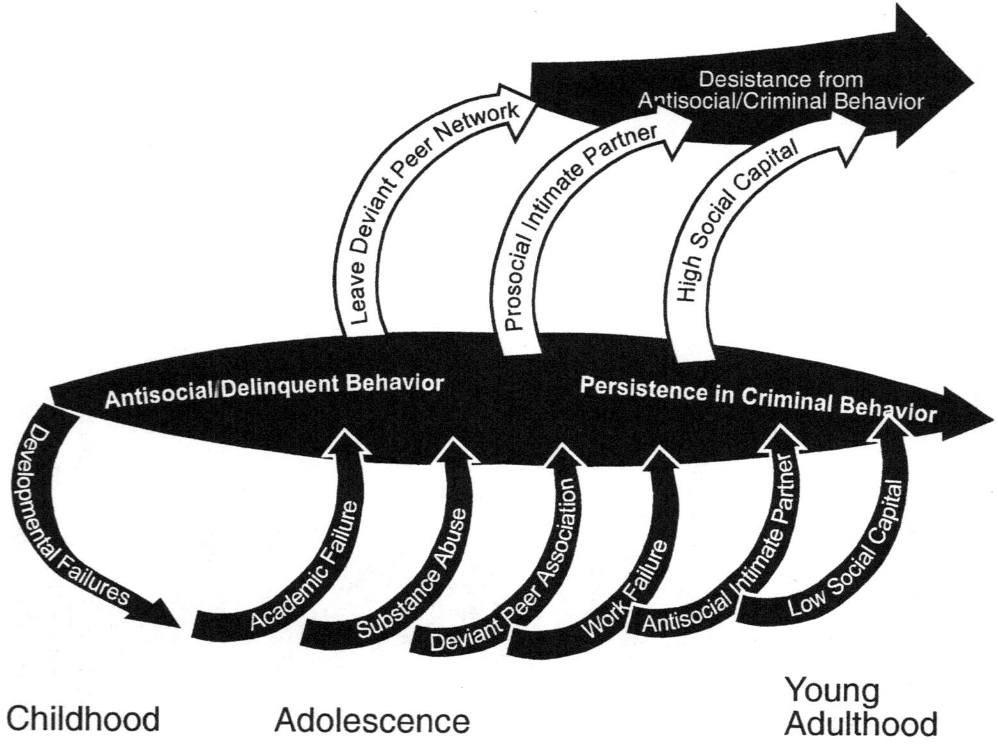

**Figure 13.4**
**Intergenerational Transmission of Aggression toward a Partner**

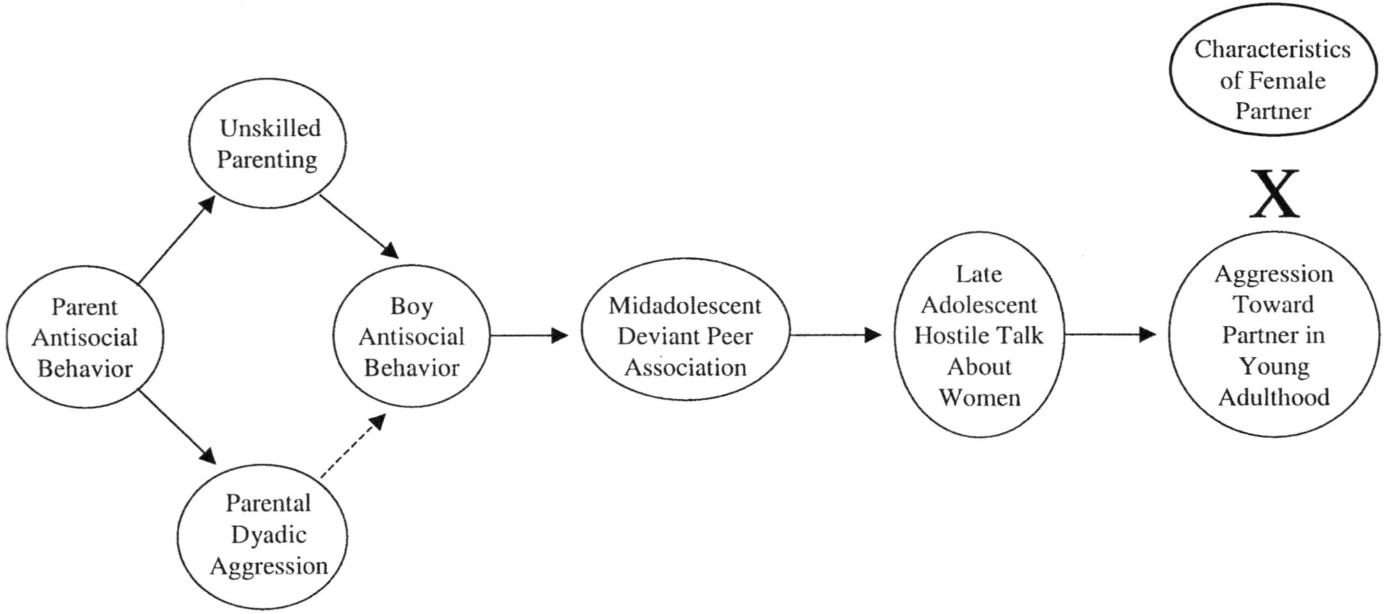

## Physical and Psychological Aggression toward the Partner

Social learning explanations of aggression toward a partner during adult-hood typically have employed an intergenerational transmission paradigm. At least two processes in the family of origin have been hypothesized to be associated with later aggression toward a partner (see Capaldi and Gorman-Smith, in press). Aggression between parents may be observed and directly modeled in later relationships with partners. Alternatively, aggression toward the children themselves might teach them that aggression is a tactic to use in family relationships.

The social-interactional model proposed by Capaldi and her colleagues from the Oregon Social Learning Center (see Capaldi and Clark 1998; Capaldi, Dishion, Stoolmiller, and Yoerger 2001; Capaldi and Gorman-Smith, in press) is summarized in Figure 13.4. It illustrates the processes responsible for the development of male aggression towards a female partner. In this model, parental antisocial behavior in interaction with individual characteristics of the child fosters learning of coercive and aggressive interaction strategies and the development of antisocial behavior. This effect is mediated by un-skilled parenting and parental dyadic aggression, with the direct treatment of the child by the parent being viewed as more central than observing aggres-sion between the parents (Capaldi and Clark 1998). These non-constructive problem-solving strategies and interaction styles are later reinforced during contacts with deviant peers. A particularly important element of this process might be mutual hostile talk about women (Capaldi, Dishion, Stoolmiller, and Yoerger 2001. Characteristics of the female partner, including use of coercive and aggressive behaviors that result in couple conflict and conflict escalation (Capaldi and Gorman-Smith in press), as well as environmental factors during young adulthood, such as the male partner's continued en-gagement in the deviant peer-group, or stressors such as school failure and unemployment, are additional factors that presumably contribute to the de-velopment and stability of aggression toward a female partner.

Recent findings from our studies (Capaldi and Clark 1998; Capaldi, Dishion, Stoolmiller, and Yoerger 2001) are congruent with this model and suggest that researchers and practitioners in the area of the intergenerational transmission of domestic violence have overemphasized the role of witness-ing aggression between parents and underestimated the role of unskilled parenting. More research with ethnically and culturally diverse samples is needed before firm conclusions can be drawn.

## Conclusion

In this chapter we have argued that a social learning or social interactional perspective provides a fruitful way for understanding the development of antisocial behavior and crime across the life-span. It was assumed that juvenile offending would explain some fairly large proportion of adult offending. Very recent findings from our studies regarding trajectories of arrest rates, however, suggested that some adult offenders do not have a history of juvenile offending. This issue clearly deserves more attention in future research.

## Note

1.  The writers gratefully acknowledge the support provided by Grant MH 50259 and Grant MH 37940 from the Prevention, Early Intervention, and Epidemiology Branch, National Institute of Mental Health (NIMH), U.S. Public Health Service (PHS). We also thank Sally Schwader for editorial assistance with the manuscript preparation.

## References

Akers, R. L. 2000. *Criminological Theories: Introduction, Evaluation, and Application.* Third Edition. Los Angeles, CA: Roxbury Publishing Company.

Bank, L., M. S. Forgatch, G. R. Patterson, and R. A. Fetrow. 1993. "Parenting Practices: Mediators of Negative Contextual Factors." *Journal of Marriage and the Family* 55, 371-384.

Brandtstäedter, J. 1998. "Action Perspectives on Human Development. In R. M. Lerner (ed.), *Handbook of Child Psychology: Theoretical Models of Human Development* Vol. 1. Fifth Edition. New York: John Wiley and Sons.

Capaldi, D. M. 1991. "The Co-Occurrence of Conduct Problems and Depressive Symptoms in Early Adolescent Boys: I. Familial Factors and General Adjustment at Grade 6." *Development and Psychopathology* 3, 277-300.

Capaldi, D. M. 1992. "The Co-Occurrence of Conduct Problems and Depressive Symptoms in Early Adolescent Boys: II. A 2-Year Follow-up at Grade 8." *Development and Psychopathology* 4, 125-144.

Capaldi, D. M., and Clark, S. 1998. "Prospective Family Predictors of Aggression toward Female Partners for At-Risk Young Men." *Developmental Psychology* 34, 1175-1188.

Capaldi, D. M., and L. Crosby. 1997. "Observed and Reported Psychological and Physical Aggression in Young, At-Risk Couples." *Social Development* 6, 184-206.

Capaldi, D. M., D. S. DeGarmo, G. R. Patterson, and M. S. Forgatch. (in press). "Contextual Risk across the Early Life-Span and Association with Antisocial Behavior." In J. B. Reid, G. R. Patterson, and J. Snyder (eds.). *The Oregon Model: Understanding and Altering the Delinquency Trajectory*. Washington, DC: APA.

Capaldi, D. M., T. J. Dishion, M. Stoolmiller, and K. Yoerger. 2001. "Aggression toward Female Partners by At-Risk Young Men: The Contribution of Male Adolescent Friendships." *Developmental Psychology* 37, 61-73.

Capaldi, D M., and D. Gorman-Smith. (in press). "Physical and Psychological Aggression in Male/Female Adolescent and Young Adult Couples." In P. Florsheim (ed.), *Adolescent Romance and Sexual Behavior: Theory, Research and Practical Implications*. Mahwah, NJ: Lawrence Erlbaum.

Capaldi, D. M., and G. R. Patterson. 1991. "Relation of Parental Transitions to Boys' Adjustment Problems: I. A Linear Hypothesis. II. Mothers at Risk for Transitions and Unskilled Parenting." *Developmental Psychology* 27, 489-504.

Capaldi, D. M., J. W. Shortt, and L, Crosby. 2001. *Stability and Change in Aggression for At-Risk Young Couples*. Manuscript in preparation.

Capaldi, D. M., and M. Stoolmiller. 1999. Co-Occurrence of Conduct Problems and Depressive Symptoms in Early Adolescent Boys: III. Prediction to Young-Adult Adjustment. *Development and Psychopathology* 11, 59-84.

Caspi, A., and D. J. Bem. 1990. "Personality Continuity and Change across the Life Course." In L. Pervin (ed.), *Handbook of Personality Theory and Research*. New York: Guilford Press.

Caspi, A., and G. H. Elder, Jr. 1988. "Childhood Precursors of the Life Course: Early Personality and Life Disorganization." In E. M. Hetherington, R. M. Lerner, and M. Perlmutter (eds.), *Child Development in Life-Span Perspective*. Hillsdale, NJ: Lawrence Erlbaum.

Catalano, R. F., and J. D. Hawkins. 1996. "The Social Development Model: A Theory of Antisocial Behavior." In J. D. Hawkins (ed.), *Delinquency and Crime: Current Theories*. New York: Cambridge University Press.

Cicchetti, D., and K. Schneider-Rosen. 1986. "An Organizational Approach to Childhood Depression." In M. Rutter, C. E. Izard, and P. B. Read (eds.), *Depression in Young People: Developmental and Clinical Perspectives*. New York: Guilford Press.

Coleman, J. S. 1988. "Social Capital in the Creation of Human Capital." *The American Journal of Sociology* 94, 95-120.

Conger, R. D., and Simons, R.L. 1997. Life-Course Contingencies in the Development of Adolescent Antisocial Behavior: A Matching Law Approach. In T. P. Thornberry (ed.), *Advances in Criminological Theory: Developmental Theories of Crime and Delinquency* (Vol. 7). New Brunswick, NJ: Transaction Publishers.

Dishion, T. J. 1990. "The Family Ecology of Boys' Peer Relations in Middle Childhood." *Child Development* 61, 874-892.

Dishion, T. J., D. W. Andrews, and L. Crosby. 1995. Adolescent Boys and Their Friends in Adolescence: Relationship Characteristics, Quality, and Interactional Process. *Child Development* 66, 139-151.

Dishion, T.J., T. E. Duncan, J. M. Eddy, B. I. Fagot, and R. Fetrow. 1994. "The World of Parents and Peers: Coercive Exchanges and Children's Social Adaptation. *Social Development* 3, 255-268.

Dishion, T. J., J. M. Eddy, E. Haas, F. Li, and K. M. Spracklen. 1997. "Friendships and Violent Behavior during Adolescence." *Social Development* 6, 207-225.

Dishion, T.J., G. R. Patterson, and K. A. Kavanagh. 1992. "An Experimental Test of the Coercion Model: Linking Theory, Measurement, and Intervention." In J. McCord and R. Tremblay (eds.), *The Interaction of Theory and Practice: Experimental Studies of Intervention*. New York: Guilford Press.

Dishion, T.J., K. M. Spracklen, D. W. Andrews, and G. R. Patterson. 1996. "Deviancy Training in Male Adolescent Friendships." *Behavior Therapy 27*, 373-390.

Eddy, J.M., L. D. Leve, and B. I. Fagot. 2001. "Coercive Family Processes: A Replication and Extension of Patterson's Coercion Model." *Aggressive Behavior* 27, 14-25.

Elder, G. H., Jr. 1998. "The Life Course and Human Development." In R. M. Lerner (ed.), *Handbook of Child Psychology: Theoretical Models of Human Development* (Vol. 1). Fifth Edition. New York: John Wiley and Sons.

Elliott, D. S., D. Huizinga, and S. Menard. 1989. *Multiple Problem Youth: Delinquency, Substance Use, and Mental Health Problems*. New York: Springer.

Farrington, D. P., and J. D. Hawkins. 1991. "Predicting Participation, Early Onset, and Later Persistence in Officially Recorded Offending." *Criminal Behavior and Mental Health 1*-33.

Forgatch, M. S. 1991. "The Clinical Science Vortex: A Developing Theory of Antisocial Behavior." In D. J. Pepler, and K. H. Rubin (eds.), *The Development and Treatment of Childhood Aggression*. Hillsdale, NJ: Erlbaum.

Forgatch, M. S., and D. S. DeGarmo. 1999. "Parenting through Change: An Effective Prevention Program for Single Mothers." *Journal of Consulting and Clinical Psychology 67*, 711-724.

Forgatch, M. S., and C. R. Martinez. 1999. "Parent Management Training: A Program Linking Basic Research and Practical Application." *Tidsskrift For Norsk Psykologforening 36*, 923-937.

Furstenberg, F. F., Jr., and M. E. Hughes. 1995. "Social Capital and Successful Development among At-Risk Youth". *Journal of Marriage and the Family 57*, 580-592

Gottfredson, M. R., and T. Hirschi. 1990. *A General Theory of Crime*. Stanford, CA: Stanford University Press.

Hardy, J.B., N. M. Astone, J. Brooks-Gunn, S. Shapiro, and T. L. Miller. 1998. "Like mother, Like Child: Intergenerational Patterns of Age at First Birth and Associations with Childhood and Adolescent Characteristics and Adult Outcomes in the Second Generation." *Developmental Psychology 34*, 1220-1232.

Herrnstein, R. J. 1970. "The Law of Effect." *Journal of the Experimental Analysis of Behavior 13*, 243-266.

Krohn, M. D., J. L. Massey, and W. F. Skinner. 1987. "A Sociological Theory of Crime and Delinquency: Social Learning Theory." In E.K. Morris, and C. J. Braukmann (eds.), *Behavioral Approaches to Crime and Delinquency*. New York: Plenum Press.

Kushman, J. W., and P. Heariold-Kinney. 1996. "Understanding and Preventing School Dropout." In D. Capuzzi, and D. R. Gross (eds.), *Youth at Risk: A Prevention Resource for Counselors, Teachers, and Parents*. Alexandria, VA: American Counseling Association.

Lerner, R. M., A. M. Freund, I. De Stefanis, and T. Habermas. 2001. "Understanding Developmental Regulation in Adolescence: The Use of the Selection, Optimization, and Compensation Model." *Human Development 44*, 29-50.

Loeber, R. 1996. "Developmental Continuity, Change, and Pathways in Male Juvenile Problem Behaviors and Delinquency." In J.D. Hawkins (ed.), *Delinquency and Crime: Current Theories*. New York: Cambridge University Press.

Loeber, R., and M. LeBlanc. 1990. "Towards a Developmental Criminology." In M. Tonry, and N. Morris (eds.), *Crime and Justice* (Vol. 12). Chicago: University of Chicago Press.

Moffitt, T.E. 1993. "Adolescence-Limited and Life-Course-Persistent Antisocial Behavior: A Developmental Taxonomy." *Psychological Review 100*, 674-701.

Nagin, D. S., D. P. Farrington, and T. E. Moffitt. 1995. "Life-Course Trajectories of Different Types of Offenders." *Criminology 33*, 111-139.

Patterson, G. R. 1982. *A Social Learning Approach: III. Coercive Family Process*. Eugene: Castalia.

Patterson, G. R. 1993. "Orderly Change in a Stable World: The Antisocial Trait as Chimera." *Journal of Consulting and Clinical Psychology 61*, 911-919.

Patterson, G. R. 1996. "Some Characteristics of a Developmental Theory for Early-Onset Delinquency." In M. F. Lenzenweger, and J. J. Haugaard (eds.), *Frontiers of Developmental Psychopathology*. New York: Oxford University Press.

Patterson, G. R., and D. M. Capaldi. 1990. "A Mediational Model for Boys' Depressed Mood." In J. Rolf, A. S. Masten, D. Cicchetti, K. H. Neuchterlein, and S. Weintraub (eds.), *Risk and Protective Factors in the Development of Psychopathology*. Cambridge: Cambridge University Press.

Patterson, G. R., D. Capaldi, and L. Bank. 1991. "An Early Starter Model for Predicting Delinquency." In D. J. Pepler, and K. H. Rubin (eds.), *The Development and Treatment of Childhood Aggression*. Hillsdale, NJ: Lawrence Erlbaum.

Patterson, G. R., B. D. DeBaryshe, and E. Ramsey. 1989. "A Developmental Perspective on Antisocial Behavior." *American Psychologist* 44, 329-335.

Patterson, G. R., T. J. Dishion, and K. Yoerger. 2000. "Adolescent Growth in New Forms of Problem Behavior: Macro- and Micro-Peer Dynamics." *Prevention Science* 1, 3-13.

Patterson, G. R., J. B. Reid, and T. J. Dishion. 1992. *A social interactional approach: Antisocial boys* (Vol. 4. Eugene: Castalia.

Patterson, G. R., M. S. Forgatch, K. L. Yoerger, and M. Stoolmiller. 1998. "Variables That Initiate and Maintain an Early-Onset Trajectory for Juvenile Offending." *Development and Psychopathology* 10, 531-547.

Patterson, G. R., and M. Stoolmiller. 1991. "Replications of a Dual Failure Model for Boys' Depressed Mood." *Journal of Consulting and Clinical Psychology* 59, 491-498.

Patterson, G. R., and K. Yoerger. 1993. "Developmental Models for Delinquent Behavior." In S. Hodgins (ed.), *Mental Disorder and Crime*. Newbury Park: Sage.

_____. 1997. "A Developmental Model for Late-Onset Delinquency." In D. W. Osgood (ed.), *Motivation and Delinquency: Nebraska Symposium on Motivation* (Vol. 44). Lincoln: University of Nebraska Press.

_____. 1999. "Intraindividual Growth in Covert Antisocial Behavior: a Necessary Precursor to Chronic Juvenile and Adult Arrests?" *Criminal Behavior and Mental Health* 9, 24-38.

_____. (in press). "A Developmental Model for Early- and Late-Onset Antisocial Behavior." In J. B. Reid, G. R. Patterson, and J. Snyder (eds.) (in press). *The Oregon Model: Understanding and Altering the Delinquency Trajectory*. Washington, DC: APA.

Reid, J. B., G. R. Patterson, and J. Snyder (eds.). (in press). *The Oregon Model: Understanding and Altering the Delinquency Trajectory*. Washington, DC: APA.

Sampson, R. J., and J. H. Laub. 1990. "Crime and Deviance over the Life Course: The Salience of Adult Social Bonds." *American Sociological Review* 55, 609-627.

Sampson, R. J., and J. H. Laub. 1997. "A Life-Course Theory of Cumulative Disadvantage and the Stability of Delinquency." In T. P. Thornberry (ed.), *Advances in Criminological Theory: Developmental Theories of Crime and Delinquency* (Vol. 7). New Brunswick, NJ: Transaction Publishers.

Scarr, S., and K. McCartney. 1983. "How People Make Their Own Environments: A Theory of Genotype-Environment Effects." *Child Development* 54, 424-435.

Serbin, L. A., J. M. Cooperman, P. L. Peters, P. M. Lehoux, D. M. Stack, and A. E. Schwartzman. 1998. "Intergenerational Transfer of Psychosocial Risk in Women with Childhood Histories of Aggression, Withdrawal, or Aggression and Withdrawal. *Developmental Psychology* 34, 1246-1262.

Shortt, J.W., D. M. Capaldi, T. J. Dishion, L. Bank, and L. D. Owen. 2001. "Adolescent Relationships with Peers, Romantic Partners, and Siblings: Prediction to Young Adult Delinquent Peer Association." Paper presented at the Biennial Meeting of the Society for Research in Child Development, April 19-22, Minneapolis, Minnesota.

Snyder, J. J., and G. R. Patterson. 1995. "Individual Differences in Social Aggression: A Test of a Reinforcement Model of Socialization in the Natural Environment." *Behavior Therapy* 26, 371-391.

Snyder, J., L. West, V. Stockemer, S. Gibbons, and L. Almquist-Parks. 1996. "A Social Learning Model of Peer Choice in the Natural Environment." *Journal of Applied Developmental Psychology* 17, 215-237.

Sroufe, L. A. 1990. "Considering Normal and Abnormal Together: The Essence of Developmental Psychopathology." *Development and Psychopathology* 2, 335-347.

Sroufe, L. A., and J. Fleeson. 1986. "Attachment and Construction of Relationships." In W. W. Hartup, and Z. Rubin (eds.), *Relationships and Development*. Hillsdale, NJ: Lawrence Erlbaum.

Stoolmiller, M. 1994. "Antisocial Behavior, Delinquent Peer Association, and Unsupervised Wandering for Boys: Growth and Change from Childhood to Early Adolescence." *Multivariate Behavioral Research* 29, 263-288.

Warr, M. 1998. "Life-Course Transitions and Desistance from Crime. *Criminology* 36, 183-216.

Wiesner, M., F. W. Vondracek, D. M. Capaldi, and E. Porfeli. 2001. *Career Pathways in Early Adulthood:* "The Impact of Human, Social, and Personal Capital in Childhood and Adolescence on Later Work Life." Unpublished manuscript.

Youth Indicators. 1993. *Trends in the Well-Being of American Youth*. Washington, DC: U.S. Government Printing Office.

Zimmermann, B. J. 1995. "Attaining Reciprocality between Learning and Development through Self-Regulation." *Human Development* 38, 367-372.

# 14

# What Correctional Treatment Can Tell Us about Criminological Theory: Implications for Social Learning Theory

*Francis T. Cullen, John Paul Wright,*
*Paul Gendreau, and D. A. Andrews*

Criminologists, especially those interested in theories of crime, typically know little about correctional rehabilitation programs. This knowledge gap is potentially consequential. Although drawing conclusions is not yet a precise enterprise, research on treatment interventions is a rich source of data on the status of prevailing criminological explanations. The issues involved are complicated, but whether a rehabilitation program succeeds or fails has clear implications for the empirical adequacy of the theory on which this intervention—whether wittingly or unwittingly—is constructed. In particular, rigorous program evaluations and meta-analyses of collections of treatment studies can furnish important evidence on whether factors, targeted for change by treatment programs, are related to criminal involvement in ways predicted by competing criminological theories. Donald Cressey (1958: 764) anticipated this possibility when he suggested that if "correctional work were scientific" (which he did not think to be the case in his day!), "utilization of each correctional technique would be an experiment designed to test the validity of a theory of crime causation" (see also Borowski 2001).

This chapter proposes, then, that correctional treatment has much to tell us about criminological theory. The ability to explain why rehabilitation programs do or do not work is *not* a litmus test for theories; other sources of data, especially those that operationalize key concepts directly and comprehensively, may well deserve more weight in assessing a theory's empirical status. Even so, the results of treatment programs constitute "facts about crime" that warrant explanation. To the extent that theories can or cannot account for these findings, they gain or lose scientific credibility. It is noteworthy that among prevailing sociological perspectives, *social learning theory draws the clearest and most convincing support from extant research on rehabilitation* (see also Andrews 1980).[1] As will be discussed further, consistent with this approach, treatment interventions that target for change antisocial attitudes and antisocial peer associations tend to achieve meaningful reductions in offender recidivism.

We explore the implications of rehabilitation for theories of crime in three stages. First, we focus on the status of correctional treatment research, examining its traditional neglect by criminologists and, more recently, its resurgence as a body of literature that, if only grudgingly and gradually, is prompting more attention. Second, we discuss the potential role of research on treatment interventions for "testing" criminological theories, conveying both what such studies can and cannot tell us about the adequacy of explanatory models. Third, in this context, we assess the extent to which specific theories are supported and challenged by findings from correctional rehabilitation research.

## The Status of Correctional Treatment Research

### The Neglect of Rehabilitation

Although contemporary criminologists are certainly aware that their theories of crime have public policy implications (Lilly, Cullen, and Ball 2002), most contemporary scholars do not explore the implications of their theorizing for correctional rehabilitation (Barlow 1995). Not surprisingly, they cannot take the next step of considering how research on rehabilitation might reflect on the adequacy of their theories. But why do scholars show such little knowledge about correctional programming—beyond, that is, the mere challenge of not being able to master all fields of knowledge? We suggest that, among others, three factors have contributed in influential ways to the neglect of rehabilitation research by criminologists.

*Criminology as Sociology.* First, although the field has become far more interdisciplinary in the past decade, criminology in America was largely institutionalized as a subfield within sociology (Laub and Sampson 1991). In a fascinating account of the "Sutherland-Glueck debate," Laub and Sampson (1991) document Edwin Sutherland's success in challenging Sheldon and Eleanor Glueck's "multiple-factor" approach that linked crime not to a general social process—like differential association—but to a range of variables, with individual differences being prominent among them. Had the Gluecks' perspective prevailed, criminology might well have become more interdisciplinary and, in particular, more psychological in orientation. The neglect of psychology undoubtedly was consequential because this is a discipline in which the link to practice is commonplace, if not fundamental—where knowledge is produced in hopes of treating people's problems.

But this was not to be the case. As Laub and Sampson (1991: 1404) demonstrate, Sutherland perceived the Gluecks' approach as "a threat to the intellectual status of criminology." Hence, Sutherland's attack was aimed largely at extinguishing their interdisciplinary model so that sociology could establish proprietary rights to criminology. Despite accumulating a wealth of empirical data that later proved in many ways to be "essentially correct" (p. 1433), the Gluecks did not prevail against Sutherland's prestige and withering attack. "The power of Sutherland's critique of the Gluecks is hard to overestimate," observe Laub and Sampson. "To this day sociological positivism is dominant and the Gluecks are often seen as relics of a distant past" (p. 1434).

But Sutherland was not anti-treatment (nor were other members of the Chicago school, such as Shaw and McKay). In the third edition of *Principles of Criminology*, for example, Sutherland (1939) devotes an entire chapter to "recidivism and reformation." He notes that the "function of the criminal court cannot be stated in terms of punishment," but rather in terms of "attempting to assist criminals to secure a better adjustment" (p. 323). He favors applying the key elements of the juvenile court—including "definite social investigations, use of summons, reformation as the ideal of treatment, informal procedure, and secret sessions"—to the adult court (pp. 324-325). For Sutherland, the "logic of probation is not the fear of punishment," but the efforts of officers to foster "contacts and assimilation and incorporation of the offender in normal groups that will be most effective in modifying his [her] behavior" (p. 400). And he endorses a core element of the rehabilitative ideal—individual treatment. Thus, he rejects the view of the "classical system" in which the "character of the offender was not included among the pertinent facts of the case" (p. 597). Instead, he favors "individualization":

> Individualization means, first, an intensive study of the individual offender for the purpose of learning the specific conditions, circumstances, processes, and mechanisms involved in the criminality, and second, a policy determined by that knowledge regarding the offender, in connection with knowledge previously secured regarding the methods of dealing with such cases. (p. 597)

Sutherland was not naïve about the challenges of treatment, noting that "knowledge of the techniques of reformation is very scanty" (p. 600). Consistent with his differential association perspective, however, he suggests that it is important to "suppress" the "loyalty of a criminal to his fellow" (p. 600). To understand social situations, it may be useful "if the offender's process of rationalization, by which he justifies and defends himself, is broken" (p. 601). Providing an offender with status for prosocial conduct may be helpful. "Modification of behavior often consists," stated Sutherland, "in giving the offender recognition for something else" (p. 603). Whenever possible, the offender should "be taken early in life" and "every attitude¼directed into socially desirable channels" (p. 604). Most important, the "objective" situation of offenders needs to be changed, "because treatment policies cannot be applied in a vacuum" (p. 600). This means that "larger units must be modified if the individual offender is to be reformed," including "neighborhood organization, group work, local co-ordinating councils, [and] the prison community" (p. 600).

Criminologists such as Sutherland, then, were not enamored with psychological approaches to crime and moved to entrench criminology within sociology.[2] Still, they did not reject rehabilitation but rather saw correctional intervention as the logical extension of their explanations of criminal behavior. Indeed, it is instructive that differential association theory and, more broadly, social learning theory provide a conceptual basis for current treatment interventions, such as cognitive-behavioral approaches (Andrews and Bonta 1998; Patterson, DeBaryshe, and Ramsey 1989). Sociological criminology did not have to be anti-treatment.

Another example of this pro-treatment orientation can be seen in the writings of Donald Cressey, especially a 1955 article titled, "Changing Criminals: The Application of the Theory of Differential Association" (see also, Cressey 1958, 1982). In this essay, Cressey notes that the "now popular policy of 'individualized treatment'" does not require that interventions must be based on psychodynamic models of crime that embrace individual therapy (p. 116). It simply means that a "theory of reformation" must be based on the "proposition that the conditions considered as causing an individual to behavior criminally will be taken into account in an effort to change him" (p. 116). Differential association theory presents a unique focus for correctional workers. "A diagnosis of criminality based on this theory," asserts Cressey, "would be directed at analysis of the criminal's attitudes, motives, and rationalizations regarding criminality and would recognize that those characteristics depend upon the groups to which the criminal belongs" (pp. 117-118). For Cressey, "if criminals are to be changed, either they must become members of anticriminal groups, or their present pro-criminal group relations must be changed" (p. 118).

In Cressey's view, the key challenge for "correctional workers" was to establish "small groups for the specific purpose of reforming criminals" and to induce offenders to join them (p. 118). He rejected the idea that a "group organized for recreational or welfare purposes" will be effective in "influencing criminalistic attitudes and values" (p. 118). Rather, he favored creating "special groups whose major common goal is the reformation of criminals" (p. 118). He noted the promising results of "a group therapy program in the New York Training School for Boys" (p. 118) and in essence was endorsing what later would be called "therapeutic communities." The key point for our purposes is that Cressey clearly embraced rehabilitation and believed that effective programs should be based on the theory of differential association.

A move in a decidedly anti-treatment direction, however, was fostered by three intellectual shifts within criminology during the 1960s and 1970s. First, the structural approach of Mertonian strain theory located the source of crime in the contradiction between open-class ideology (the "American Dream") and restricted economic opportunities. Whereas differential association theory focused on the process of internalizing criminal values—values that could then be changed through treatment—strain theory portrayed offenders as internalizing the dominant culture and being just like everyone else. Crime was located in criminogenic structural *situations*, not people. Solving crime meant not changing people but on transforming opportunity structures. Broader social reform—calling for social justice—thus replaced "treatment" as the favored strategy for intervention.

Second, the rise of labeling or "societal reaction" theory increased criminologists' suspicions toward correctional treatment. Scholars became enamored with the ironic and the unanticipated, participating in what Hagan (1973) called the "sociology of the interesting." Labeling theory's core proposition, of course, is that state intervention into offenders' lives—labeling and treating someone "as a criminal"—sets in motion processes that increase commitment to a life in crime. Ironically, then, correctional treatment would have the unanticipated consequence not of curing the wayward but of ensnaring them in crime—of fostering "secondary deviance." Rather than calling for more and better rehabilitation programs, the preferred strategy was "radical nonintervention"—to "leave the kids alone," as Schur (1973: 155) urged, "wherever possible."

Third, critical (radical or Marxist) criminology pushed strain theory and labeling theory one step further. Merton was now termed a "caution rebel" (Gouldner 1973); he had identified a contradiction in capitalism but had not illuminated the integral role that capitalism played in crime. A class analysis showed that crimes of rich and poor were rooted in class domination. To portray offenders as having deviant personalities or values was to "pathologize" them—to transform a social problem into a personal problem that masked the root causes of crime. Correctional treatment was, at best, a band-aid and, at worst, a practice that only served to prop up an unjust social order. It did nothing to alter the inherent inequality of capitalist America. Solving crime demanded a revolution devoted to equality.

The critique of treatment was even more profound as critical criminologists took the insights of labeling theory and added the dimensions of power and class interest to them. Labeling theorists tended to see purveyors of correctional treatment as well-meaning but misguided. Critical theorists, however, depicted those delivering rehabilitation as exercising bad faith. They were now called "state agents of social control" who were engaged in "state enforced therapy" (Binder and Geis 1984). Rather than being seen as people concerned about the welfare of offenders—as "do-gooders"—they were portrayed as using rehabilitation to "control" offenders and to reinforce their class position. They were trying to regulate the poor, to transform them into a mass of obedient workers with little class-consciousness (Platt 1969). Even worse, treatment was portrayed as using insidious means—technologies of power—to manipulate the minds of offenders (Foucault 1977).

Sociological criminology, in short, had unmasked correctional treatment for what it was: another tool to dominate the poor brought into the prison system. "Whose side are we on?", became a serious question. To provide knowledge that might increase control over impoverished offenders—the victims of inequality—was to give the state a better technology of power. Even today, we are concerned about undertaking "penal science" (Clear 1994) that allows the state to control offenders more effectively (e.g., through selective incapacitation). In fact, as a group, criminologists remain largely committed to delegitimating prisons—to showing that they are inhumane and do not work to reduce crime—and to decreasing state intervention into offenders' lives. Scholars who suggest that prison might serve as a governmental resource to protect the poor are dismissed out of hand as "conservatives" (see Wilson 1975; DiIulio 1994). Criminologists' professional ideology remains ambivalent toward correctional rehabilitation (Cullen and Gendreau 2001). Not surprisingly, few leading criminologists study or write about rehabilitation, and, as a profession, criminologists have contributed little to advancing our knowledge about "what works" in correctional treatment.

*The "Nothing Works" Movement.* Scholars' fears about rehabilitation did not seem farfetched in the late 1960s and 1970s. The rehabilitative ideal was predicated on the assumption that state officials had the expertise and good will to decide who should or should not be incarcerated, who should or should not receive a particular treatment, and who should or should not be paroled (Rothman 1980). Such officials were to act in the best interests of both society and the offender. But why should state officials be trusted to exercise unfettered discretion in a just and efficacious way, to exercise wisdom in balancing the interests of society and offenders? Why not worry that officials would abuse their discretion—sending the poor but not the rich to prison and using the threat of an indeterminate stay behind bars to coerce not inmate reform but obedience to institutional rules?

The key, of course, was whether one trusts or mistrusts the state (Rothman 1980). And, in the sixties and seventies, it was easy to mistrust the government. A series of major events—police-sanctioned violence against Civil Rights protesters, the shootings at Kent State and at the Attica prison uprising, the Vietnam War, and the Watergate scandal—coalesced to prompt a precipitous decline in Americans' confidence in government (Lipset and Schneider 1983). Criminologists were children of this time. They were imbued with a deep suspicion of the state's motives and were inclined to find critical explanations of crime and control appealing. They were also ready to abandon rehabilitation as a benevolent ideology that was corrupted by state officials more interested in controlling than in the social welfare of poor and minority offenders (Cullen and Gilbert 1982; Cullen and Gendreau 1989, 2000, 2001).

It was in this context—one in which criminologists already were deeply suspicious of rehabilitation—that Robert Martinson's (1974a) famous "nothing works" essay appeared. This essay was distilled from a 736-page book that would be published a year later (Lipton, Martinson, and Wilks 1975). The coauthored research project analyzed 231 evaluation studies published between 1945 and 1967. Martinson (1974a: 25) offered the technical conclusion that, "With few and isolated exceptions, the rehabilitative efforts that have been reported so far have had no appreciable effect on recidivism." Provocatively, however, he went on to ask, "Do all these studies lead irrevocably to the conclusion that nothing works, that we haven't the faintest clue about how to rehabilitate offenders and reduce recidivism?" (p. 48). He refrained from asserting that "nothing works," but he clearly meant to convey this message. Shortly thereafter, he admitted that, based on the available evidence, he was persuaded that "rehabilitation is a 'myth'" (1974b: 4).

The Martinson essay (and the Lipton et al. study on which it was based) represented responsible scholarship and did not reach conclusions dissimilar to those of other researchers at the time (see, e.g., Sechrest, White, and Brown 1979). Its main limitation was the decision to categorize studies into 11 types of treatment methods and then to conclude that no one method was a sure-fire way to reduce recidivism. This approach suffered from aggregation bias: it overlooked that across all programs evaluated, about half of the treatments were found to "work"—to reduce recidivism (Palmer 1975). It is also instructive that Martinson's analysis did not include a category for "cognitive-behavioral" programs—a treatment modality shown later to be effective (Andrews and Bonta 1998).

The telling issue is *not* the quality of the Lipton et al. study or Martinson's "nothing works" conclusion. Rather, it is the rapidity with which this view of treatment was accepted as an unquestioned truth. A few scholars aside (Klockars 1975; Palmer 1975), the criminological community showed little of the skepticism it normally accords prominent and provocative studies (Cullen in press; Cullen and Gendreau 2001). Instead, Martinson's "nothing works" doctrine was seen as confirming what criminologists "already knew": that the state could not be trusted to conduct effective interventions. In fact, the rejection of rehabilitation became so complete that positive program findings were dismissed as obviously untrue. In an amusing but poignant exposé of anti-treatment rhetoric, Gottfredson (1979) documented the various "treatment destruction techniques"—impossible methodological standards—that scholars used to delegitimate studies showing rehabilitation's effectiveness (see also, Andrews and Bonta, 1998).

Thus, the "nothing works" movement is a second reason for criminologists' general neglect of correctional rehabilitation. Once it became an established wisdom in criminology that "nothing works" in correctional treatment, a whole generation of scholars were free to ignore research findings on the effectiveness of rehabilitation programs. Further, why would they spend time studying something that "everyone knew" to be a futile enterprise? Not surprisingly, few criminologists devoted their research efforts to investigating how to make correctional interventions more effective.

*The Bifurcation of Criminology and Criminal Justice.* A third factor contributing to the neglect of rehabilitation is the increasing separation between "criminology," which is seen as the study of the nature of criminal behavior, and "criminal justice," which is seen as the study of the legal control of criminal behavior (including corrections). This separation is artificial and would have made no sense to early criminologists, such as Sutherland (1939), who perceived the analysis of crime and control as interrelated and as the subject matter of criminology. In the last two decades, however, the rise of departments of criminal justice—while criminology remained entrenched in sociology departments—created institutional structures for bifurcating the study of crime and the study of control (especially by the criminal justice system). In this context, students in criminal justice could learn little about crime and students in "criminology" could learn little about control. The need to see how criminology and corrections—a core part of social control—are interrelated was not encouraged by this institutional arrangement. Only for a limited number of scholars did this cross-fertilization of ideas take place.

*Reconsidering "Nothing Works"*

Although the rehabilitative ideal was substantially discredited (Allen 1981; Blumstein 1997), a minority of scholars—most from nations other than the United States and from academic disciplines other than criminology—persisted in arguing in favor of correctional treatment. One line of analysis cautioned against the repressive potential in the punitive ideologies that were supplanting rehabilitation and illuminated the humanistic value of the social welfare approach fundamental to rehabilitation (Allen 1981; Cressey 1982; Cullen and Gilbert 1982; Rotman 1990). A second line of analysis confronted the "nothing works" doctrine directly and sought to show *empirically* that Martinson's characterization of treatment effectiveness was incorrect (Andrews and Bonta, 1998; Gendreau and Ross 1979, 1987; Palmer 1975, 1992; see also, Cullen and Applegate 1997). It is this latter response that concerns us here.

As noted, one immediate approach was to dissect Martinson's work and to argue that his interpretation of the findings was excessively pessimistic

(Palmer 1975). The central claim was that about half the studies in his review showed positive findings. Martinson chose to argue that the glass was half empty. From his perspective, the positive findings had a random quality. Sometimes, for example, counseling or job programs "worked," but sometimes they did not. As Martinson (1974a: 49) observed, his study could discern no "sure way of reducing recidivism through rehabilitation." Instances of success were too "isolated" and inconsistent "to indicate the efficacy of any particular method of treatment" (p. 39). However, one could just as easily contend that the glass was half full. For advocates of rehabilitation, the fact that half the programs were successful was a foundation on which to build a science of corrections. Indeed, when one considers that many programs are inadequately implemented and/or based on faulty theories of offending, it was amazing that interventions worked as often as they failed.

A second approach was to conduct extensive "narrative" reviews of the research published following Martinson's study, which assessed studies only until 1967 (for a summary, see Andrews and Bonta 1998: 254-259). In this approach, scholars would compile published and unpublished evaluation studies and then would *describe* what each study or set of studies found (thus the notion of a "narrative" review). Often, they would count how many studies found that treatment programs reduced or did not reduce recidivism. These works—in which tallies of successes and failures were made—were called "ballot box" studies. Regardless, the central message of these reviews was that a host of rehabilitation programs were effective and that programmatic failure occurred largely because interventions lacked "therapeutic integrity." As such, these works sought to provide "bibliotherapy for cynics" (Gendreau and Ross 1979) by presenting empirical evidence that offender behavior not only "could" be changed but also "was" being changed by existing treatment programs.

A third approach—and one by far the most consequential—involved the use of the statistical technique of "meta-analysis" to quantitatively synthesize the results of treatment interventions across tens, if not hundreds, of studies (for a summary, see Andrews and Bonta 1998: 259-273). The generally positive findings derived from this approach furnished a strong challenge to "nothing works" thinking (Cullen and Gendreau 2000, 2001). "It is no exaggeration," notes Lipsey (1999a: 614), "that meta-analysis of research on the effectiveness of rehabilitative programming has reversed the conclusion of the prior generation of reviews on this topic."

For those unfamiliar with this technique, in a meta-analysis, the unit of analysis is the evaluation study. For each study, the relationship between the treatment intervention and recidivism—called the "effect size"—is computed. Then, much like a "batting average" in baseball, the average effect size is calculated across all studies. This effect size can be weighted by sample size.

Furthermore, it is possible to conduct a multivariate analysis in which various methodological and "conditioning" variables are controlled so as to assess whether the effect size varies in certain kinds of studies (e.g., longitudinal, unpublished) and under certain circumstances (e.g., type or dose of treatment) (for a discussion of the technique of meta-analysis and controversies surrounding it, see Hunter and Schmidt 1996; Rosenthal and DiMatteo 2001).

When meta-analyses of treatment programs were conducted, two main findings emerged. First, across all types of interventions, the average effect size was an "r" of about .10 (Lipsey 1992; Losel 1995; McGuire 2001; Redondo, Sanchez-Meca, and Garrido 1999). In practical terms, this means that if the recidivism rate for the control group were 55 percent, the recidivism rate for the treatment group would be 45 percent. Some scholars suggest that this overall effect size is modest and are cautious about its practical policy implications (Gaes, Flanagan, Motiuk, and Stewart 1999; Losel, 1995: 102-103; Whitehead and Lab, 1989). Others would be likely to suggest that a 10 percent reduction in recidivism is meaningful, potentially cost effective, and larger in size than that achieved by many interventions in other social domains, including medicine (Aos, Phipps, Barnoski, and Lieb 2001; Gendreau, Smith, and Goggin 2001; Lipsey 1999b; Losel 2001: 85; more generally, see Welsh, Farrington, and Sherman 2001).

Second and more consequential, the meta-analyses revealed that across types or modalities of treatment, there was considerable *heterogeneity* in effect sizes. Once the extant research was quantitatively synthesized, the data did not show—as Martinson's work suggested—uniformly weak effects across all types of modalities. Instead, the studies showed that for some programs, the effect sizes approached zero or were negative (indicating the programs increased recidivism); for other programs the effects sizes were moderate; and for other programs the effect sizes were substantial, indicating a reduction in recidivism of 20 to 30 percentage points (Andrews, Zinger, Hoge, Bonta, Gendreau, and Cullen 1990; Andrews and Bonta 1998; Lipsey 1992; Lipsey and Wilson 1998). These findings showed the wisdom of developing "principles of effective intervention" that would distinguish effective from ineffective interventions (Andrews 1995; Andrews and Bonta 1998; Andrews et al. 1990; Gendreau 1996). It also supported the conclusion that sufficient scientific data were being accumulated to advance an "evidence-based" corrections in which policy and practice would be guided by empirical information on "what works" (Cullen and Gendreau 2000, 2001; Gendreau, Goggin, Cullen, and Paparozzi in press; Gendreau, Goggin, and Smith 2000; MacKenzie 2000; McGuire 2001).

Most salient for our purposes, the findings from the meta-analyses (and narrative reviews) have implications for the viability of extant criminological theories. It is to this issue that we now turn.

## What Treatment Research Can and Cannot Tell us

*What Treatment Research Can Tell Us*

Our central claim is that research on rehabilitation comprises a data-base that can be invaluable in assessing the adequacy of criminological theories. Because each theory states what causes are offending, it logically suggests that when these causal factors are changed, then there should be a corresponding change in the behavior of offenders. If people are more exposed to these factors, then they should commit more crimes. But, if the causal factors are reduced, then there should be a corresponding reduction in offending. In this context, to the extent that correctional treatment programs seek to change a host of causal factors (e.g., attitudes, job skills, costs of crime), they "test" the underlying logic of numerous theories (more generally, see Hunter and Schmidt 1996; Shadish 1996).

For example, many programs attempt to change offenders' antisocial values. The logic of differential association theory would be that were a program to succeed in having offenders relinquish antisocial values in favor of prosocial values, then offenders should have lower rates of offending than a control group not exposed to this learning experience (Cressey 1955; Sutherland 1939). Now, research showing that treatment programs that target antisocial values for change are effective would, in essence, confirm the theoretical predictions of the differential association model. Further, these findings would be evidence against other perspectives arguing that positive learning of values has no impact on crime and/or that offending is stable across the life course (e.g., Gottfredson and Hirschi 1990). Alternatively, if such programs did not work, then differential association theory would be falsified and have some explaining to do!

The heterogeneity in effect sizes found in the meta-analyses is salient because it suggests that some treatment programs—presumably based on certain theories—are more effective than other treatment programs—presumably based on other theories. The "nothing works" doctrine would have predicted no heterogeneity in effect sizes; every effect size should have been close to zero. If this were in fact true, it would mean that many, if not most, criminological theories were wrong. Instead, heterogeneity in effect sizes, which shows clear patterns of differential effectiveness across treatment modalities, suggests that some theories are more correct than other theories.

Correctional research also provides a different kind of data than are typically used to assess criminological theories: experimental or quasi-experimental data, which, we should add, are longitudinal. Obviously, it is virtually impossible (and unethical) to randomly assign people to a "criminogenic" and "prosocial" condition. But even if in circumscribed ways, treatment programs essentially do this. The treatment condition is assumed to have prosocial effects, while the control condition is assumed to be more criminogenic or, in the least, less prosocial. In any event, experimental data are potentially powerful in isolating the effects of key theoretical variables and of providing strong tests of theoretical propositions.

Such tests may be a welcomed addition to an empirical literature that heretofore has been woefully unable to decide which theories should be falsified and abandoned and which should be retained and built upon (Cole 1975). Some of the problems in assessing theories of crime may be settled by the use of meta-analysis to explore heterogeneity in effect sizes in theoretical predictors (Pratt 2001; Pratt and Cullen 2000; Sellers, Pratt, Winfree, and Cullen 2000). But, for the moment, the discipline primarily relies on narrative reviews to assess the empirical status of theories (see, e.g., Akers 2000; Burton and Cullen 1992; Kempf 1993). Although useful, these works suffer from the same shortcoming that marks all narrative reviews: because the extant literature is not quantitatively synthesized, they are unable to provide a *precise* determination of the relative explanatory power of prevailing theories.[3] One consequence is that it is difficult to conclude definitively whether a theory is viable or should be rejected. For example, in a systematic review of seventy-one studies of Hirschi's social bond perspective, Kempf (1993: 173) concludes that "control theory research comprises a large number of essentially separate studies which have little relation to each other and fail to build on experience. Thus, the research reveals little about the validity of social control as a scientific theory." Meta-analyses of correctional treatment studies will not fully reverse this state of affairs, but they may supply important data (again, based on experimental designs) that add or subtract confidence in prevailing paradigms.

*What Treatment Research Cannot Tell Us*

Using correctional rehabilitation research to draw conclusions about criminological theories has at least five limitations. First, treatment programs largely focus on the prevention of *recidivism* and are limited to samples of offenders (or individuals at-risk for crime). As a result, findings are more applicable to explanations of persistence or desistance from crime than of the onset of misconduct. Second, correctional treatment largely focuses on changing the *proximate* causes of crime—that is, conditions that characterize individuals and/or their immediate micro-environments (e.g., family processes). As a result, the research cannot tell us much about the effects of *distal* structural factors or the *macro-level* causes of crime. Third, because they are not designed to test criminological theories, evaluation studies may allow implications to be drawn in a broad way about a theory or only about certain aspects of the perspective (e.g., role of antisocial attitudes but not of imitation in social learning theory). Fourth, some treatment studies compare interventions from different theoretical perspectives. However, because many interventions are based on a single theory of crime, correctional research usually does not test, in one evaluation study, the merits of one theory versus another. That is, such research does not provide a critical test of competing theories in a single assessment (such as would be done in a self-report study assessing control versus social learning theory; see, e.g., Hirschi 1969).

Fifth, the failure of a correctional intervention to reduce recidivism could, as we have noted, be taken as evidence that a theory underlying the intervention is incorrect; in fact, we make such an assumption, with a measure of caution, in interpreting the results of the treatment evaluation literature. This conclusion may well be warranted. Even so, negative results in an evaluation study might be due to other considerations. For example, the program might have failed not because the theory was faulty, but because the treatment modality was not implemented in an appropriate way (there was not "treatment integrity"); in this case, risk factors central to the theory would not have been targeted appropriately for change. Another possibility is that due to a small sample size, the statistical test used in a study did not have the power to detect a treatment effect that actually existed "in reality."

In short, correctional treatment research should be viewed with appropriate caution. Such studies do not often provide definitive tests of theories. Nonetheless, across numerous evaluations—and as assessed through meta-analyses—this body of research is a potentially rich source of data for examining key aspects of many prominent paradigms. As noted, this research creates facts about crime that require explanation. The ability of various theories to "account for" these findings clearly has implications for the relative viability of these perspectives. In this context, we now consider which criminological theories appear to gain or lose support when scrutinized in light of the extant findings from correctional treatment research.

## Implications for Criminological Theory

A review of existing meta-analyses and narrative reviews of correctional rehabilitation programs leads to three main conclusions. First, the data question the merits of deterrence theory. These data do not pertain as directly to more sophisticated rational choice theories that are multidimensional and incorporate into the model individual propensities or "tastes" for crime. Regardless, the core deterrence proposition that increasing punishment or costs reduces crime is not supported by correctional research. Second, these studies are consistent with theories that link antisocial attitudes and associations to offending. Accordingly, correctional research gives strong support to differential association or social learning theories. Third, a number of other theories receive partial support. Stronger confirmation is not possible either because the effect sizes appear moderate or because research is not specific or extensive enough to allow for a more definitive assessment.

## Problems for Deterrence Theory

There is considerable debate about whether criminal sanction deters offending (compare, e.g., Lynch 1999 and Platt 2001 with Nagin 1998). Scholars commenting on this issue largely cite either macro-level studies associating objective punishment (e.g., arrest rates) with crime rates or individual-level studies associating perceptions of punishment with self-reported crime or intentions to offend (Nagin 1998). Only rarely, however, do they consult the findings from evaluations of correctional interventions (Cullen, Pratt, Miceli, and Moon in press). This omission is unfortunate because evaluations have been made of a number of programs that increase the punishment of or control over offenders. They provide an important opportunity to examine whether increasing the costs of crime reduces re-offending as deterrence theory predicts. In general, the findings are not supportive of this deterrence thesis.

First, a number of reviews of "treatment" programs are not limited to social welfare-type programs oriented toward "fixing" offenders but include interventions aimed at inducing fear of punishment and/or increasing control. In one of the most sophistical meta-analyses conducted, Lipsey and Wilson (1998) examined how various treatment modalities—including "deterrence programs" (e.g., shock incarceration, scared straight)—were related to recidivism by serious and violent juvenile offenders (see also Lipsey 1992, 1999b). The deterrence programs were ranked in a group of unsuccessful interventions labeled "weak or no effects, consistent evidence" (p. 332). In fact, these programs showed signs of *increasing* recidivism (an estimated 53 percent recidivism rate versus 50 percent for a control group). Similar findings were reported in a meta-analysis of programs, conducted by Dowden and Andrews (1999a), that assessed programs based on instilling "fear of official punishment." Again, these programs were found to increase recidivism in youths.

There is also an extensive literature assessing research on "intermediate punishments." Started largely in the 1980s, these were community-based programs that explicitly rejected rehabilitation in favor of interventions that sought to increase control and surveillance over offenders. Underlying these programs was the intention to watch offenders closely enough to make the threat of punishment—usually the promise of a prison sentence—sufficiently certain to deter future criminality. Perhaps the most common intervention was "intensive supervision" for probationers and, less commonly, for parolees. Other sanctions included home incarceration, electronic monitoring, and drug testing.

Narrative reviews of this research have reached the same conclusion: intermediate punishment programs do not reduce recidivism (Cullen, Wright, and

Applegate 1996; Fulton, Latessa, Stichman, and Travis 1997; MacKenzie 2000; Petersilia 1998). A classic experimental evaluation study by Petersilia and Turner (1993) showed that across fourteen sites, intensive supervision programs did not reduce recidivism, even when the level of control over offenders was shown to increase. Furthermore, a meta-analysis of interventions involving "community sanctions" found that these programs did not diminish re-offending (Gendreau, Goggin, Cullen, and Andrews 2000; Gendreau, Goggin, and Fulton 2000). Equally instructive—and again contrary to deterrence theory—the study also revealed that more time spent in prison and the use of prison rather than a community sanction (e.g., probation) were, if anything, associated with higher rates of recidivism (Gendreau, Goggin, Cullen, and Andrews 2000).

The salience of these findings cannot be overstated. Macro-level studies are typically confounded by the inability to separate deterrence from incapacitation effects. Perceptual deterrence studies are usually limited by the use of low-offending populations and the inability to assess how objective increases in control and the threat of punishment affect misconduct. In contrast, the correctional treatment studies include persons who have high base rates of illegal behavior and who are exposed to actual criminal sanctions. The results are consistently incompatible with the predictions of deterrence theory—at least as this perspective is applied to specific deterrence (i.e., when studying offender recidivism, there is no concern with or measurement of general deterrence). In fact, without a major qualification, deterrence theory must be seen as a weak criminological perspective. The onus would now seem to be on advocates of this paradigm to show how the *anomalous* findings cited above can be accounted for.

## *Support for Differential Association/Social Learning Theory*

In decided contrast, research on correctional programs supplies strong and consistent support for theories—such as differential association/social learning theory—that link offending to antisocial associations and to the internalization of antisocial values (see also Andrews 1980; Andrews and Bonta 1998). A consistent finding across meta-analyses, including cross-cultural studies (Redondo et al. 1999), is that "cognitive-behavioral" programs tend to achieve higher reductions in recidivism than other treatment modalities (Andrews and Bonta 1998; Andrews et al. 1990; Gallagher, Wilson, Hirschfield, Coggeshall, and MacKenzie 1999; Hanson, Gordon, Harris, Marques, Murphy, Quinsey, and Seto 2000; Lipsey 1992: 159; McGuire 2001; Pearson, Lipton, Cleland, and Yee 2000; Wilson, Allen, and MacKenzie 2000; Wilson, Gottfredson, and Najaka 2001).[4] In many instances, the reductions are high absolutely (20 to 30 percent) (Andrews and Bonta 1998).

These programs specifically target for change antisocial values and crime-excusing rationalizations, they reward prosocial attitudes and behavior, and they seek to isolate offenders from pro-criminal associations. It is noteworthy that in a meta-analysis that explicitly examined recidivism in programs in which antisocial cognition and associates were targeted for change, the treatment effect size was substantial (Andrews, Dowden, and Gendreau 1999). This finding was replicated for studies on female offenders (Dowden and Andrews 1999b).

Again, these results offer significant support for differential association/social learning theory. Consistent with this perspective, the studies show that when antisocial attitudes, thinking, and associations are targeted and do in fact change, offenders decrease their participation in criminal behavior. These results are found in experimental studies where threats to validity are reduced and in which results contrary to the theory could not be attributed to "other" factors. In short, correctional treatment offers a bold test of social learning theory predictions. By and large, the theory is supported by this research.

### Assessing Alternative Criminological Theories

Although less clear than the research on deterrence and social learning theories, correctional treatment studies provide data that are potentially useful in evaluating other criminological perspectives. First, contrary to theories that emphasis stability in criminal propensity and behavior (Gottfredson and Hirschi 1990), the rehabilitation literature is consistent with theories that emphasize both stability *and* change (e.g., Sampson and Laub 1993). In essence, Martinson's (1974a) "nothing works" finding was consistent with a stability prediction; that is, despite planned interventions aimed at changing offender behavior, there was "no appreciable effect on recidivism" (p. 25). In contrast, the effectiveness of treatment programs supports the view that offenders can change their behavioral trajectories. Theorizing in this area, however, might benefit from examining the process by which change is induced by treatment programs. For example, if cognitive-behavioral programs are effective, it is theoretically plausible that offenders who change their behavior in more "naturalistic" settings are exposed to processes that approximate those in a more formal cognitive-behavioral program

Second, programs that seek to reduce offender impulsiveness and to increase self-control reduce recidivism (see, e.g., Dowden and Andrews 1999b; Wilson et al. 2001). Often, these are cognitive-behavioral programs that also target antisocial attitudes and behaviors. In any event, these findings are consistent with Gottfredson and Hirschi's (1990) general theory. However, this research is inconsistent with the general theory in one regard: it suggests that self-control is not fixed in childhood, can be learned, and can be altered in treatment programs.

Third, correctional research suggests that interventions that increase family supervision and affection achieve reductions in recidivism (Dowden and Andrews 1999b). These findings are consistent with social bond (Hirschi 1969) and social support theories (Cullen 1994; Wright and Cullen 2001). Social learning theory, however, also would predict that appropriate parental supervision and expressions of affection might be conduits through which prosocial values are expressed and prosocial behaviors modeled.

Fourth, the research on correctional education, vocational training, and employment programs is not sufficiently rigorous to rule out the possibility that selection effects might bias findings. Even so, there is beginning evidence that these programs are associated with lower recidivism rates (Adams, Bennett, Flanagan, Marquart, Cuvelier, Fritsch, Gerber, Longmire, and Burton 1994; Bouffard, MacKenzie, and Hickman 2000; Wilson, Gallagher, and MacKenzie 2000). To an extent, these findings lend support to perspectives, such as strain theory, that link crime to material deprivation. Further, to the degree that education and work constitute social bonds, these findings are consistent with control theory, including those that emphasize the ability of adult social bonds to derail a criminal life course (Sampson and Laub 1993). Again, social learning theory also might draw support from these results to the extent that work and education are means through which prosocial values and associations occur.

Fifth, although the results are limited, the effect sizes are modest, and potentially confounding factors are not always disentangled (e.g., treatment services that accompany restorative practices), there is initial evidence that restorative justice programs may be effective in diminishing re-offending (Latimer, Dowden, and Muise 2001; see also, Bonta, Wallace-Capretta, and Rooney 1998). To an extent, therefore, these findings—especially when combined with the dismal results on deterrence programs—provide evidence favorable to theories that argue against excessively coercive controls and in favor of reintegrative, supportive controls (Braithwaite 1989; Colvin 2000; Sherman 1993; Tittle 1995).

## Conclusion

The main premise informing this essay is that research on correctional interventions are an untapped source of data for assessing the merits of criminological theories that seek to explain why some individuals commit more crimes than others. Most treatment programs are not theory "neutral" but theory "informed." Setting aside problems with implementation, this means that the *effectiveness* of interventions has implications for the *correctness* of the theories that underlie—or do not underlie—them. Especially when evaluation studies are based on experimental or rigorous quasi-experimental designs, they may provide salient data on theories: if changes in theoretical variables are followed by changes in criminal behavior—or if they are not—then this should be strong evidence on the theory's viability. At the very least, the results of treatment evaluations are "facts" that competing criminological theories must explain or risk suffering diminished credibility.

The correctional treatment research is clearest in providing evidence supportive of differential association/social learning theory. Because numerous interventions have targeted key components of this paradigm—most notably, antisocial values, antisocial associations, reinforcement of prosocial conduct—the existing studies supply an extensive *de facto* test of the theory. The fact that cognitive-behavioral programs consistently produce reductions in recidivism across a range of studies—conducted in different nations—is persuasive evidence that social learning is integral to an understanding of crime causation.

Correctional rehabilitation studies also reveal that offender *change* is possible, including into adulthood. This insight is noteworthy because it supports life-course theories that incorporate into their models not only continuity but also change. Self-control and family process theories that emphasize parental supervision and affection/support also draw confirmation from the treatment literature. Although less forceful, there is also evidence consistent with strain, adult social bond, and reintegrative shaming theories.

In contrast, core propositions of deterrence theory are, in effect, "falsified" by correctional rehabilitation research. This finding is significant because it runs counter to more positive interpretations of deterrence theory recently drawn from macro-level and perceptual deterrence studies (Nagin 1998). The power of treatment research, however, is that it is based on a range of offenders who have experienced measurable increases in surveillance, control, and/or punishment. The consistent failure of these deterrence interventions to "work" represents a serious problem for advocates of this perspective.

Finally, we urge scholars to become literate about correctional research. The notion that "nothing works" should be consigned to the criminological dustbin (Cullen and Gendreau 2000, 2001). Criminology and corrections are not distinct realms of study but are integrally related. Effective correctional interventions must be based on empirically supported, scientifically credible criminological theories. Similarly, theories of crime that are unmindful of the findings from treatment evaluation studies ignore a potentially rich data source for showing their promise and power.

### Notes

1.  Of course, social learning theory also has its more psychologically oriented versions. See, for example, Andrews and Bonta (1998) and Bandura (1977).
2.  Sutherland was mainly critical of theories that linked crime to traits and psychodynamic processes. In a more contemporary context, Sutherland's views, although applied to the criminal justice setting, would not be out of place in any introductory-

level psychology textbook discussing how the person and the environment interact to generate behavior. In fact, a young psychologist of today reading various of Sutherland's passages might guess that Sutherland was a psychologist—and one, moreover, from the pioneering psychological school of the early 1970s that espoused an interactionist view of personality/traits and situations/environments (see Bowers 1973).

3. This shortcoming is not limited to criminological theory. In the area of rehabilitation, Gendreau and Ross (1987) contributed one of the most comprehensive—and widely cited—narrative reviews of existing treatment evaluation studies. Even so, from this review, it was not possible to discern the overall magnitude of the treatment effect (there was no "effect size" computed) or how the impact of treatment was conditioned by various factors. Further, although persuasive, Gendreau and Ross's review could be dismissed as "biased" reading of the data by scholars who favored rehabilitation. In contrast, meta-analyses are powerful because they offer a more precise estimate of the magnitude of a "treatment effect" and, because they can be replicated, are less open to charges of bias. This is one reason, perhaps, that meta-analyses of treatment studies have furnished evidence against the "nothing works" doctrine that is less open to dispute (Lipsey 1999a, b).

4. For a discussion of what a "cognitive-behavioral" program in a correctional setting might entail, see Andrews and Bonta (1998: 282-290) and Ross and Fabiano (1985). More generally, see Spiegler and Guevremont (1998).

## References

Adams, Kenneth, Katherine J. Bennett, Timothy J. Flanagan, James W. Marquart, Steven J. Cuvelier, Eric Fritsch, Jurg Gerber, Dennis R. Longmire, and Velmer S. Burton, Jr. 1994. "A Large-Scale Multidimensional Test of the Effect of Prison Education Programs on Offenders' Behavior." *The Prison Journal* 74: 433-449.

Akers, Ronald L. 2000. *Criminological Theories: Introduction, Evaluation, and Application*, 3rd ed. Los Angeles: Roxbury Press.

Allen, Francis A. 1981. *The Decline of the Rehabilitative Ideal: Penal Policy and Social Purpose*. New Haven, CT: Yale University Press.

Andrews, D. A. 1980. "Some Experimental Investigations of the Principles of Differential Association Through Deliberate Manipulations of the Structure of Service Systems." *American Sociological Review* 45: 448-462.

_____. 1995. "The Psychology of Criminal Conduct and Effective Treatment." In James McGuire (ed.), *What Works: Reducing Reoffending*. West Sussex, UK: John Wiley.

Andrews, D. A., and James Bonta. 1998. *The Psychology of Criminal Conduct*. Second Edition. Cincinnati, OH: Anderson.

Andrews, D. A., Craig Dowden, and Paul Gendreau. 1999. "Clinically Relevant and Psychologically Informed Approaches to Reduced Re-Offending: A Meta-Analytic Study of Human Service, Risk, Need, Responsivity, and Other Concerns in Justice Contexts." Unpublished manuscript, Carleton University.

Andrews, D. A., Ivan Zinger, Robert D. Hoge, James Bonta, Paul Gendreau, and Francis T. Cullen. 1990. "Does Correctional Treatment Work? A Clinically Relevant and Psychologically Informed Meta-Analysis." *Criminology* 8: 369-404.

Aos, Steve, Polly Phipps, Robert Barnoski, and Roxanne Lieb. 2001. "The Comparative Costs and Benefits of Programs to Reduce Crime: A Review of Research Findings with Implications for Washington State." In Brandon C. Welsh, David P. Farrington, and Lawrence W. Sherman (eds.), *Costs and Benefits of Preventing Crime*. Boulder, CO: Westview.

Bandura, Albert. 1977. *Social Learning Theory.* Englewood Cliffs, NJ: Prentice-Hall.

Barlow, Hugh D. (ed). 1995. *Crime and Public Policy: Putting Theory to Work.* Boulder, CO: Westview.

Binder, Arnold, and Gilbert Geis. 1984. "*Ad Populum* Argumentation in Criminology: Juvenile Diversion as Rhetoric." *Crime and Delinquency* 30: 624-647.

Blumstein, Alfred. 1997. "Interaction of Criminological Research and Public Policy." *Journal of Quantitative Criminology* 12: 349-361.

Bonta, James, Suzanne Wallace-Capretta, and Jennifer Rooney. 1998. *Restorative Justice: An Evaluation of the Restorative Resolutions Project.* Ottawa, Ontario: Solicitor General Canada.

Borowski, Allan. 2001. "The Dangers of Strong Causal Reasoning in Policy and Practice: The Case of Juvenile Crime and Corrections." Paper presented at the Fourth National Outlook Symposium on Crime in Australia, June, Canberra, Australia.

Bouffard, Jeffrey A., Doris Layton MacKenzie, and Laura J. Hickman. 2000. "Effectiveness of Vocational Education and Employment Programs for Adult Offenders: A Methodology-Based Analysis of the Literature." *Journal of Offender Rehabilitation* 31:1-41.

Bowers, Kenneth S. 1973. "Situationalism in Psychology: An Analysis and a Critique." *Psychological Review* 80: 307-336.

Braithwaite, John. 1989. *Crime, Shame and Reintegration.* Cambridge: Cambridge University Press.

Burton, Velmer S., Jr., and Francis T. Cullen. 1992. "The Empirical Status of Strain Theory." *Journal of Criminal Justice* 15 (No. 2): 1-30.

Clear, Todd R. 1994. *Harm in American Penology: Offenders, Victims, and Their Communities.* Albany: State University of New York Press.

Cole, Stephen. 1975. "The Growth of Scientific Knowledge: Theories of Deviance as a Case Study." In Lewis A. Coser (ed.), *The Idea of Social Structure: Papers in Honor of Robert K. Merton.* New York: Harcourt Brace Jovanovich.

Colvin, Mark. 2000. *Crime and Coercion: An Integrated Theory of Chronic Criminality.* New York: St. Martin's Press.

Cressey, Donald R. 1955. "Changing Criminals: The Application of the Theory of Differential Association." *American Journal of Sociology* 61: 116-120.

_____. 1958. "The Nature and Effectiveness of Correctional Techniques." *Law and Contemporary Problems* 23: 754-771.

_____. 1982. "Foreword." In *Reaffirming Rehabilitation,* by Francis T. Cullen and Karen E. Gilbert. Cincinnati, OH: Anderson.

Cullen, Francis T. 1994. "Social Support as an Organizing Concept for Criminology: Presidential Address to the Academy of Criminal Justice Sciences." *Justice Quarterly* 11: 527-559.

_____. "Rehabilitation and Treatment Programs." In James Q. Wilson and Joan Petersilia (eds.), *Crime: Public Policies for Crime Control.* Second Edition. San Francisco, CA: ICS Press.

Cullen, Francis T., and Brandon K. Applegate (eds.). 1997. *Offender Rehabilitation: Effective Correctional Intervention.* Aldershot, UK: Ashgate/Dartmouth.

Cullen, Francis T., and Paul Gendreau. 1989. "The Effectiveness of Correctional Rehabilitation: Reconsidering the 'Nothing Works' Debate." In Lynne Goodstein and Doris MacKenzie (eds.), *American Prisons: Issues in Research and Policy.* New York: Plenum.

_____. 2000. "Assessing Correctional Rehabilitation: Policy, Practice, and Prospects." In *Criminal Justice 2000: Volume 3—Policies, Processes, and Decisions of the Criminal Justice System.* Washington, DC: U.S. Department of Justice, National Institute of Justice.

_____. 2001. "From Nothing Works to What Works: Changing Professional Ideology in the 21st Century." *The Prison Journal* 81: 313-338.

Cullen, Francis T., and Karen E. Gilbert. 1982. *Reaffirming Rehabilitation.* Cincinnati, OH: Anderson.

Cullen, Francis T., Travis C. Pratt, Sharon Levrant Miceli, and Melissa M. Moon. In press. "Dangerous Liaison? Rational Choice Theory as the Basis for Correctional Intervention." In Alex R. Piquero and Stephen G. Tibbetts (eds.), *Rational Choice and Criminal Behavior.* New Brunswick, NJ: Transaction Publishers.

Cullen, Francis T., John Paul Wright, and Brandon K. Applegate. 1996. "Control in the Community: The Limits of Reform?" In Alan T. Harland (ed.), *Choosing Correctional Interventions That Work: Defining the Demand and Evaluating the Supply.* Newbury Park, CA: Sage Publications.

DiIulio, John J., Jr. 1994. "The Question of Black Crime." *The Public Interest* 117 (Fall): 3-32.

Dowden, Craig, and D. A. Andrews. 1999a. "What Works in Young Offender Treatment: A Meta-Analysis." *Forum on Corrections Research* 11 (May): 21-24.

_____. 1999b. "What Works for Female Offenders: A Meta-Analytic Review." *Crime and Delinquency* 45: 438-452.

Foucault, Michel. 1977. *Discipline and Punish: The Birth of the Prison.* New York: Pantheon.

Fulton, Betsy, Edward J. Latessa, Amy Stichman, and Lawrence F. Travis III. 1997. "The State of ISP Research and Policy Implications." *Federal Probation* 61 (December): 65-75.

Gaes, Gerald G., Timothy J. Flanagan, Larry Motiuk, and Lynn Stewart. 1999. "Adult Correctional Treatment." In Michael Tonry (ed.), *Crime and Justice: A Review of Research,* vol. 26. Chicago: University of Chicago Press.

Gallagher, Catherine A., David B. Wilson, Paul Hirschfield, Mark B. Coggeshall, and Doris L. MacKenzie. 1999. "A Quantitative Review of the Effects of Sex Offender Treatment on Sexual Reoffending." *Corrections Management Quarterly* 3 (Fall): 19-29.

Gendreau, Paul. 1996. "The Principles of Effective Intervention with Offenders." In Alan T. Harland (ed.), *Choosing Correctional Interventions That Work: Defining the Demand and Evaluating the Supply.* Newbury Park, CA: Sage Publications.

Gendreau, Paul, Claire Goggin, Francis T. Cullen, and Donald A. Andrews. 2000. "The Effects of Community Sanctions and Incarceration on Recidivism." *Forum on Corrections Research* 12 (May): 10-13.

Gendreau, Paul, Claire Goggin, Francis T. Cullen, and Mario Paparozzi. In press. "The Common Sense Revolution and Correctional Policy." In James McGuire (ed.), *Offender Rehabilitation and Treatment: Effective Programs and Policies to Reduce Re-Offending.* Chichester, UK: John Wiley and Sons.

Gendreau, Paul, Claire Goggin, and Betsy Fulton. 2000. "Intensive Supervision in Probation and Parole Settings." In Clive R. Hollin (ed.), *Handbook of Offender Assessment and Treatment.* Chichester, UK: John Wiley and Sons.

Gendreau, Paul, Claire Goggin, and Paula Smith. 2000. "Generating Rational Correctional Policies: An Introduction to Advances in Cumulating Knowledge." *Corrections Management Quarterly* 4 (No. 2): 52-60.

Gendreau, Paul, and Robert R. Ross. 1979. "Effective Correctional Treatment: Bibliotherapy for Cynics." *Crime and Delinquency* 25: 463-489.

_____. 1987. "Revivification of Rehabilitation: Evidence from the 1980s." *Justice Quarterly* 4: 349-407.

Gendreau, Paul, Paula Smith, and Claire Goggin. 2001. "Treatment Programs in Corrections." In John Winterdyk (ed.), *Corrections in Canada: Social Reaction to Crime.* Toronto, Ontario: Prentice-Hall.

Gerber, Jurg, and Eric J. Fritsch. 1995. "Adult Academic and Vocational Correctional Education Programs: A Review of Recent Research." *Journal of Offender Rehabilitation* 22: 119-142.

Gottfredson, Michael R. 1979. "Treatment Destruction Techniques." *Journal of Research in Crime and Delinquency* 16: 39-54.

Gottfredson, Michael R., and Travis Hirschi. 1990. *A General Theory of Crime*. Stanford, CA: Stanford University Press.

Gouldner, Alvin W. 1973. "Foreword." In *The New Criminology: For a Social Theory of Deviance*, by Ian Taylor, Paul Walton, and Jock Young. London, UK: Routledge and Kegan Paul.

Hagan, John L. 1973. "Labeling and Deviance: A Case Study in the 'Sociology of the Interesting.'" *Social Problems* 20: 447-458.

Hanson, R. Karl, Arthur Gordon, Andrew J. R. Harris, Janice K. Marques, William Murphy, Vernon L. Quinsey, and Michael C. Seto. 2000. "The 2000 ATSA Report on the Effectiveness of Treatment for Sex Offenders." Paper presented at the annual meeting of the ATSA, November, San Diego, CA.

Hirschi, Travis. 1969. *Causes of Delinquency*. Berkeley: University of California Press.

Hirschi, Travis, and Michael J. Hindelang. 1977. "Intelligence and Delinquency: A Revisionist Review." *American Sociological Review* 42: 571-587.

Hunter, John E., and Frank L. Schmidt. 1996. "Cumulative Research Knowledge and Social Policy Formulation: The Critical Role of Meta-Analysis." *Psychology, Public Policy, and Law* 2: 324-347.

Kempf, Kimberly L. 1993. "The Empirical Status of Hirschi's Control Theory." In Freda Adler and William S. Laufer (eds.), *New Directions in Criminological Theory*, Vol. 4,. New Brunswick, NJ: Transaction Publishers.

Klockars, Carl B. 1975. "The Limits of the Effectiveness of Correctional Treatment." *The Prison Journal* 55 (Spring-Summer):53-64.

Latimer, Jeff, Craig Dowden, and Danielle Muise. 2001. *The Effectiveness of Restorative Justice Practices: A Meta-Analysis*. Ottawa, Ontario: Department of Justice Canada.

Laub, John H., and Robert J. Sampson. 1991. "The Sutherland-Glueck Debate: On the Sociology of Criminological Knowledge." *American Journal of Sociology* 96: 1402-1440.

Lilly, J. Robert, Francis T. Cullen, and Richard A. Ball. 2002. *Criminological Theory: Context and Consequences*. Third Edition. Thousand Oaks, CA: Sage Publications.

Lipset, Seymour Martin, and William Schneider. 1983. *The Confidence Gap: Business, Labor, and Government in the Public Mind*. New York: The Free Press.

Lipsey, Mark W. 1992. "Juvenile Delinquency Treatment: A Meta-Analytic Inquiry into the Variability of Effects." In Thomas D. Cook, Harris Cooper, David S. Cordray, Heidi Hartmann, Larry V. Hedges, Richard J. Light, Thomas A. Lewis, and Frederick Mosteller (eds.), *Meta-Analysis for Explanation: A Casebook*. New York: Russell Sage Publications.

_____. 1999a. "Can Rehabilitative Programs Reduce the Recidivism of Juvenile Offenders?" *Virginia Journal of Social Policy and Law* 6: 611-641.

_____. 1999b. "Can Intervention Rehabilitate Serious Delinquents?" *Annals of the American Academy of Political and Social Science* 564: 142-166.

Lipsey, Mark W., and David B. Wilson. 1998. "Effective Interventions for Serious Juvenile Offenders: A Synthesis of Research." In Rolf Loeber and David P. Farrington (eds.), *Serious and Violent Juvenile Offenders: Risk Factors and Successful Interventions*. Thousand Oaks, CA: Sage Publications.

Lipton, Douglas, Robert Martinson, and Judith Wilks. 1975. *The Effectiveness of Correctional Treatment: A Survey of Evaluation Studies*. New York: Praeger.

Losel, Friedrich. 1995. "The Efficacy of Correctional Treatment: A Review and Synthesis of Meta-evaluations." In James McGuire (ed.), *What Works: Reducing Reoffending*. West Sussex, UK: John Wiley.

_____. 2001. "Evaluating the Effectiveness of Correctional Programs: Bridging the Gap Between Research and Practice." In Gary A. Berfeld, David P. Farrington, and Alan W. Leschied (eds.), *Offender Rehabilitation in Practice: Implementing and Evaluating Effective Programs*. Chichester, UK: John Wiley and Sons.

Lynch, Michael J. 1999. "Beating a Dead Horse: Is There Any Basic Empirical Evidence for the Deterrent Effect of Imprisonment?" *Crime, Law and Social Change* 31: 347-362.

MacKenzie, Doris Layton. 2000. "Evidence-Based Corrections: Identifying What Works." *Crime and Delinquency* 46: 457-471.

Martinson, Robert. 1974a. "What Works? Questions and Answers About Prison Reform." *The Public Interest* 35 (Spring): 22-54.

_____. 1974b. "Viewpoint." *Criminal Justice Newsletter* 5 (November 18): 4-5.

McGuire, James. 2001. "What Works in Correctional Intervention? Evidence and Practical Implications." In Gary A. Berfeld, David P. Farrington, and Alan W. Leschied (eds.), *Offender Rehabilitation in Practice: Implementing and Evaluating Effective Programs*. Chichester, UK: John Wiley and Sons.

Nagin, Daniel S. 1998. "Criminal Deterrence Research at the Outset of the Twenty-First Century." In Michael Tonry (ed.), *Crime and Justice: A Review of Research*, vol. 23. Chicago: University of Chicago Press.

Palmer, Ted. 1975. "Martinson Revisited." *Journal of Research in Crime and Delinquency* 12: 133-152.

_____. 1992. *The Re-Emergence of Correctional Intervention*. Newbury Park, CA: Sage Publications.

Patterson, Gerald R., Barbara D. DeBaryshe, and Elizabeth Ramsey. 1989. "A Developmental Perspective on Antisocial Behavior." *American Psychologist* 44: 329-335.

Pearson, Frank, Douglas S. Lipton, Charles M. Cleland, and Dorline S. Yee. 2000. "The Effects of Behavioral/Cognitive Behavioral Programs on Recidivism." Unpublished paper, National Development and Research Institutes, Inc., New York.

Petersilia, Joan. 1998. "A Decade of Experimenting with Intermediate Sanctions: What Have We Learned?" *Federal Probation* 62 (December): 3-9.

Petersilia, Joan, and Susan Turner. 1993. "Intensive Probation and Parole." In Michael Tonry (ed.), *Crime and Justice: An Annual Review of Research*, vol. 17. Chicago: University of Chicago Press.

Platt, Anthony M. 1969. *The Child Savers: The Invention of Delinquency*. Chicago: University of Chicago Press.

Pratt, Travis C. 2001. "Assessing the Relative Effects of Macro-Level Predictors of Crime: A Meta-Analysis." Unpublished Ph.D. dissertation, University of Cincinnati.

Pratt, Travis C., and Francis T. Cullen. 2000. "The Empirical Status of Gottfredson and Hirschi's General Theory of Crime: A Meta-Analysis." *Criminology* 38: 931-964.

Redondo, Santiago, Julio Sanchez-Meca, and Vincente Garrido. 1999. "The Influence of Treatment Programmes on the Recidivism of Juvenile and Adult Offenders: An European Meta-Analytic Review." *Psychology, Crime and Law* 5: 251-278.

Rosenthal, R., and M. R. DiMatteo. 2001. "Meta-Analysis: Recent Developments in Quantitative Methods for Literature Reviews." *Annual Review of Psychology* 52: 59-82.

Ross, Robert R., and Elizabeth A. Fabiano. 1985. *Time to Think: A Cognitive Model of Delinquency Prevention and Offender Rehabilitation*. Johnson City, TN: Institute of Social Sciences and Arts.

Rothman, David J. 1980. *Conscience and Convenience: The Asylum and Its Alternatives in Progressive America*. Boston: Little, Brown.

Rotman, Edgardo. 1990. *Beyond Punishment: A New View of the Rehabilitation of Criminal Offenders*. New York: Greenwood.

Sampson, Robert J., and John H. Laub. 1993. *Crime in the Making: Pathways and Turning Points Through Life*. Cambridge, MA: Harvard University Press.

Schur, Edwin M. 1973. *Radical Nonintervention: Rethinking the Delinquency Problem*. Englewood Cliffs, NJ: Prentice-Hall.

Sechrest, Lee, Susan O. Wright, and Elizabeth D. Brown (eds.). 1979. *The Rehabilitation of Criminal Offenders: Problems and Prospects*. Washington, DC: National Academy of Sciences.

Sellers, Christine W., Travis C. Pratt, L. Thomas Winfree, and Francis T. Cullen. 2000. "The Empirical Status of Social Learning Theory: A Meta-Analysis." Paper presented at the annual meeting of the American Society of Criminology, November, San Francisco.

Shadish, William R. 1996. "Meta-Analysis and the Exploration of Causal Mediating Processes: A Primer of Examples, Methods, and Issues." *Psychological Methods* 1: 47-65.

Sherman, Lawrence W. 1993. "Defiance, Deterrence, and Irrelevance: A Theory of the Criminal Sanction." *Journal of Research on Crime and Delinquency* 30: 445-473.

Spiegler, Michael D., and David C. Guevremont. 1998. *Contemporary Behavior Therapy*. Third Edition. Pacific Grove, CA: Brooks/Cole.

Sutherland, Edwin M. 1939. *Principles of Criminology*. Third Edition. New York: Macmillan.

Tittle, Charles R. 1995. *Control Balance: Toward a General Theory of Deviance*. Boulder, CO: Westview.

Welsh, Brandon C., David P. Farrington, and Lawrence W. Sherman (eds.). 2001. *Costs and Benefits of Preventing Crime*. Boulder, CO: Westview.

Whitehead, John T., and Steven P. Lab. 1989. "A Meta-Analysis of Juvenile Correctional Treatment." *Journal of Research in Crime and Delinquency* 26: 276-295.

Wilson, David B., Leana C. Allen, and Doris L. MacKenzie. 2000. "A Quantitative Review of Structured, Group-Oriented, Cognitive-Behavioral Programs for Offenders." Unpublished paper, University of Maryland.

Wilson, David B., Catherine A. Gallagher, and Doris L. MacKenzie. 2000. "A Meta-Analysis of Corrections-Based Education, Vocation, and Work Programs for Adult Offenders." *Journal of Research in Crime and Delinquency* 37: 347-368.

Wilson, David B., Denise C. Gottfredson, and Stacy S. Najaka. 2001. "School-Based Prevention of Problem Behaviors: A Meta-Analysis." *Journal of Quantitative Criminology* 17: 247-272.

Wilson, James Q. 1975. *Thinking About Crime*. New York: Vintage.

Wright, John Paul, and Francis T. Cullen. 2001. "Parental Efficacy and Delinquent Behavior: Do Control and Support Matter?" *Criminology* 39: 601-629.

# Contributors

*Ronald L. Akers,* professor of criminology and sociology and associate dean for faculty affairs, College of Liberal Arts and Sciences, University of Florida, Gainesville.

*D. A. Andrews,* professor of psychology, Carleton University.

*Candice Batton,* assistant professor of criminal justice, University of Nebraska at Omaha.

*Paul E. Bellair,* associate professor of sociology, Ohio State University.

*Timothy Brezina,* assistant professor in the Department of Sociology, Tulane University.

*Deborah M. Capaldi,* associate director and research scientist, Oregon Social Learning Center, Eugene, Oregon.

*Michael Capece,* associate professor in the Department of Sociology, Anthropology and Criminal Justice, Valdosta State University, Valdosta, Georgia.

*John K. Cochran,* professor and associate chair, Department of Criminology University of South Florida.

*Francis T. Cullen,* Distinguished Research Professor of Criminal Justice and Sociology, University of Cincinnati.

*Stacy De Coster,* assistant professor, Department of Sociology and Anthropology, North Carolina State University.

*Paul Gendreau,* University Research Professor of Psychology and Director of the Centre for Criminal Justice Studies, University of New Brunswick at Saint John.

*Patrick M. Horan,* professor (emeritus) of sociology, University of Georgia, is conducting research through the Institute for Behavioral Research.

*Sunghyun Hwang* is an assistant professor in the Department of Public Administration at Korea Digital University, Department of Public Administration, Seoul, South Korea.

*Gary F. Jensen,* professor and chair of sociology, Vanderbilt University.

*Lonn Lanza-Kaduce,* professor, Center for Studies in Criminology and Law, University of Florida, Gainesville.

*Robbin S. Ogle,* assistant professor of criminal justice, University of Nebraska at Omaha.

*Gerald R. Patterson,* research scientist, Oregon Social Learning Center, Eugene, Oregon.

*Scott Phillips,* assistant professor of sociology, University of Houston.

*Alex R. Piquero,* associate professor, Center for Studies in Criminology and Law, University of Florida.

*Vincent J. Roscigno,* associate professor, Department of Sociology at Ohio State University.

*Christine S. Sellers,* associate professor and director of the Master's Program, Department of Criminology, University of South Florida.

*Darrell Steffensmeier,* professor of sociology and crime, law and justice, Pennsylvania State University, University Park.

*Jeffery Ulmer,* associate professor of crime, law and justice and sociology, Pennsylvania State University, University Park.

*María B. Vélez,* assistant professor, Department of Sociology, University of Iowa.

*Shu-Neu Wang,* associate professor of sociology, Fu-Jen Catholic University, Taipei, Taiwan.

*Margit Wiesner,* research assistant professor, Center for the Advancement of Youth Health, University of Alabama at Birmingham.

*L. Thomas Winfree, Jr.,* professor, Department of Criminal Justice, New Mexico State University, El Paso, Texas.

*John Paul Wright,* assistant professor of criminal justice, University of Cincinnati.

# Subject Index

# Name Index

CPSIA information can be obtained
at www.ICGtesting.com
Printed in the USA
BVHW070328161118
533263BV00001B/18/P

9 781412 806497